THE JOURNAL OF Asian STUDIES

VOLUME 84
NUMBER 2
MAY 2025

Transnational and Comparative

Editorial Foreword

This issue includes five research articles and a forum on race, racialization, and gender in South Korea. The articles and forum essays cover a range of different topics and problems. In nuanced ways that provide insightful theoretical perspectives on the limits of cultural and political regionalism that structure these problems, each article develops an analytical framework that reconceptualizes the particular in terms that reflect general questions concerning the politics of self-representation. The articles bring into focus struggles associated with local self-perception in light of other peoples' preconceptions, real and imagined, about social, political, and gendered hierarchies of power.

In the first article YINGYING HUANG offers a reinterpretation of Kang Youwei's influential role in conceptualizing China's modernity. As a leading reformer and political philosopher who sought to redefine the Confucian utopianism of Great Unity (*datong*) in terms of twentieth-century idealistic pragmatism, Kang Youwei's thought is often interpreted as an articulation of socialism imagined in Sinocentric terms. Huang's interpretation of Kang's writing focuses on the problem of clothing and houses as emblems of modernity and as material things of importance that he thought needed to be modernized to effect greater global unity on the model of *datong*. For Kang, Huang argues, clothing and houses highlight the problem of how a perceived, judgmental, foreign gaze became the reference point for understanding shame as a feeling—theorized in terms of Confucian ethics—that enabled proactive reform rather than a feeling of reactive inhibition that was inherently stigmatizing and oppressively racist. The larger frame that Huang provides for this analysis involves a reinterpretation of Kang's "intellectual journey" to and through other parts of Asia. Kang's understanding of Meiji Japan and the Nationalist Movement in India shaped his understanding of China but, even more, so brings into focus his appreciation for the multiperspectival gaze of those in Asia looking at themselves as they imagined being looked at by others farther afield, in Europe and the United States. Through this kind of displacement of self, we see Kang imagining not only the possibility of Pan-Asianism but a world community beyond the postcolonial limits of that designation.

A general problem in diplomacy, especially when state relations are reestablished after significant political change in the personnel or structure of rule and authority, concerns the performance of ritualized power and hierarchy as a means by which to express unilateral legitimacy and confirm putatively well-established,

DOI: 10.1215/00219118-11591139 © 2025 Association for Asian Studies

bilateral relations. In the second article JOSHUA C. HERR draws on scholarship concerning the politics of ritualized diplomacy to understand how performances of power articulate the power of performative politics, in this case during the seventeenth-century Ming-Qing transition and diplomatic relations with Lê Vietnam in the context of the Kangxi emperor's consolidation of power in China. Specifically, Herr focuses on the 1683 Qing embassy to the Lê court, showing how the staging of spectacles, and the pointedly intentional "scripting" of ritual protocol by the tributary court, reveals the intricate weaving of power into the fabric of ritualized self-perception as a reflection of how you want to be seen by others who are looking at themselves through the eyes of their constituents watching your performance. Herr's analysis of the details of diplomacy provides general insight on the fine art and high drama of statecraft and the important role of mediated, multidimensional performances.

In the third article DAVID GOWEY examines the problems and creative possibilities involved in the translation of epic poetry from the medium of oral recitation to that of codified published print, a process that is not necessarily linear. Gowey's research focuses on the performance of Panay Bukidnon oratory (sugidanon), and specifically on chanting as an expressive medium that changes both dramatically and subtly, depending on how those involved in codification, education, and performance locate themselves along the mutable spectrum of oral recitation based on a pedagogy of preprint memory, at one extreme, and at the other, chanting as memorized recitation based on the internalization of a written-and-read script. Gowey's carefully historicized analysis shows that the "medium is the message becoming the medium" necessarily complicates any simplistic distinction among memorization, remembering, and the articulation of traditional authenticity. His interpretation of how sugidanon is chanted, how it is heard being performed, and how performances are seen and appreciated by audiences in different experiential contexts sheds important light on how to understand epic poetry as a genre within the ambit of Island Southeast Asia, extending from the early colonial to the postcolonial, encompassing imagined communities remembering themselves remembering their traditions using various media.

Agitation and activism for independence from colonial domination and control are most often conceptualized as forms of political nationalism. Movements are supported by the articulation of political philosophies that primarily involve enclaves of special interest framed by localized activism intent on cultural preservation through reform and the ferment of ideas born of situated oppression and incarceration. Recognizing the obvious frame this orientation provides, in the fourth article DARREN WAN critically examines how Malay refugees who fled to Bombay from Singapore during the Japanese occupation engaged with Indian nationalists during the Quit India movement, producing a perspective on British and Japanese imperialism from what might be called the "third eye" of transnational oppression, exiled incarceration, and alienating, militarized occupation. As communities of shared national interest are imagined, it is insightful to note how the subject position of exiled witnesses to a world at war expands the frame, producing genealogies of political thought based on seeing and feeling how others see your oppression in light of their own, and you are a witness, as a refugee, to "world making" as a collective endeavor at the end of empire.

In the fifth article MARCUS YEE provides an analysis of the 1986 antinuclear movement in Hong Kong to show how a "failed" campaign to prevent the construction of a nuclear reactor should be interpreted in terms of the movement's success in building the social, cultural, and political infrastructure to effectively protest against political restrictions, unsustainable development, and projects that damage the environment. In essence, Yee's focus is on the history of mass mobilization in Hong Kong at a critical period leading up to China's increasingly assertive control of the territory following the British handover in 1997. Yee shows us, among other things, how to do critical history on such topics as disasters and mass movements that are "media saturated." As his method and interpretation make clear, it is important to rescue history from the excesses of journalism and from the increasing flood of information on social media. The Daya Bay nuclear reactor project was viewed by many in Hong Kong in light of the Chernobyl disaster in Ukraine, as well as in terms of China's expanding global influence after the dissolution of the USSR. As such, Yee interprets the antinuclear movement in Hong Kong as a case study of popular democracy in action with a granular focus on mobilization, as this brings into sharp relief the political fallout from China's global ambitions.

The forum in this issue engages with the construction of race and the articulation of racialization and racism in the context of contemporary South Korea, and with the globalization of ideas concerning identity, ethnicity, and history. Curated by SOHOON YI and HAN SANG KIM, the six essays locate questions of race, gender, and racialized bodies in contexts of kinship, medical practice, militarization, scientific research, and migration. The underlying problematic in each case is the conception of Korea as racially homogeneous, an erroneous misperception at least in part because of the "commonsense"—but clearly nonsensical—notion that phenotypic similarity in appearance proves the point. Each contributor to the forum untangles the interwoven conceptualization and preconceptions that produce and reproduce cultural practices that stigmatize, alienate, and oppress even as, in some instances, the language of inclusion and government policies draw on a grammar of distinction that it speaks against. The authors collectively provide a powerful critique of how visibility and invisibility, purity and pollution, erasure and inscription factor into contexts in which the racialization of a national imaginary complicates the articulation of cultural critique. It is, in many ways, precisely how race, racialization, and racism manifest in South Korea that provides a valuable Asian studies perspective on this aspect of a pervasive, transnational sociohistorical problem.

—Joseph S. Alter

YINGYING HUANG

Seeing China
Clothes, Houses, and the Foreign Gaze in Kang Youwei's Travels

ABSTRACT This article uses material examples of clothes and houses to show that the gaze of foreigners had a significant power in shaping Kang Youwei's 康有為 (1858–1927) perception of China and was deeply implicated in Kang's national and cosmopolitan aspirations. How China was perceived on the international stage influenced Kang's proposal for a clothing reform and then his objection to it, his assessment of Chinese houses, and his notions about China's material modernity and a world community. Looking back at China from abroad during his travels, Kang employed the gaze to provoke shame, a quality deemed not only crucial for bringing about reforms but also indispensable for maintaining integrity in the future world of great unity.

KEYWORDS Kang Youwei, the gaze, clothes, houses, shame, China's image

Only by leaving home can one truly see one's home, and only by leaving the country can one truly see one's country 離家方能見家, 出國而後見國.

—Jiang Xu 蔣煦, *Xiyou riji* (1903)

Recent endeavors to revitalize discussion on Kang Youwei 康有為 (1858–1927), both in China and abroad, have stressed Kang's importance as a prominent philosopher and reformer, whose Confucian and utopian thinking remains relevant to contemporary times.[1] Kang's role as a globetrotter has received less attention in such discussions, partly because most of his reformist texts were completed or conceived prior to his exile, and partly because his association with foreigners was limited by his inability to speak any foreign language. His international travels are studied for the literati reformer's discovery of foreign countries and a new world order, instead of for foreign observers' influence on his view of China.[2] This article argues, nevertheless, that the gaze of foreigners (mainly Westerners), especially that experienced by Kang during his travels abroad, had a significant shaping power over his perception of China, prompting many radical observations about reforming the nation and building a world community. How China was perceived on the international stage was deeply implicated in Kang's national and universal aspirations, and sentiments provoked by the gaze, shame in particular, joined him with many other concerned Chinese authors of political reports, pamphlets, travelogues, and fiction.

The power of the gaze was felt on many occasions, but given the wide range of subjects, I focus on two material aspects: clothing and housing. Trivial as these matters may seem, they carried Kang's grand dreams of a modern China and a world of *datong* 大同 (great unity or universal community) throughout his overseas travels. Studies of Kang's involvement in the discourse of clothing have focused on his proposal in the late 1890s to cut the queues of Chinese men and Westernize their apparel, which is seen as part of a vestimentary reform that lasted well into the twentieth century (Wang E. 1981: 62–63; Finnane 2008: 69–82; Fan 2020). This classification helps fill out a material history underpinning the cultural vibrations after China's defeat in the Sino-Japanese War (1894–1895), but it leaves out the new developments in Kang's personal history following the ill-fated reform movement of 1898 and overlooks Kang's transformation, during his overseas travels, into an opponent of the clothing reform he had advocated. Houses and other buildings, on the other hand, have been discussed in research of Kang's interest in foreign arts and his patriotic sentiments (Turriziani 2016), but this approach does not address how Kang's experiences of seeing and being seen in an international context influenced his evaluation of China's housing and architecture.

Also note that, despite his passionate push for reforms before his exile, Kang remained an adamant apologist for the Confucian tradition and grew more confident in Chinese culture during his travels abroad. Changes were necessary to achieve modernity and a great unity, but to become one with the world did not primarily mean an amalgamation of cultures or religions for Kang, who had instead a materialistic understanding of modernization and believed that universal unison rested first and foremost on the material well-being of all nations, including the provision of elegant clothing and sumptuous dwellings. He saw the inevitable ideological transition from China as the world to China in the world, which made it imperative to secure the acceptance and respect of other nations. Seeking approval involves looking at the self through the eyes of others, and to present oneself favorably often requires enhancing one's appearance, or *guanzhan* 觀瞻, as Kang often called it, on which he believed hinged the dignity of a nation (Kang [1904b] 2007: 423; [1904e] 2007: 372; [1904f] 2007: 4). How China was viewed by foreigners thus beset Kang's observation about clothing and housing in his travels, stirring up his sense of shame, anxiety about national prestige, and prospects for world unity.

TO CHANGE OR NOT TO CHANGE: CHINESE CLOTHES AND FOREIGN VIEWERS

Late Qing clothing reform did not originate with Kang Youwei. The earliest advocate on record was Chen Qiu 陳虬, who in 1890 recommended adopting Western dressing styles for convenience (Wang E. 1981: 61). Tan Sitong 譚嗣同 (1865–1898), Kang's reformist ally in 1898, also urged removal of the queue and saw Japan's apparel change as the beginning of its transformation into a strong nation (Tan [1897] 1954: 79–80).[3] In the debate that came to agitate the rest of the Qing dynasty, the word for changing clothes, *yifu* 易服, typically referred to the alteration of men's traditional costume, usually in combination with the removal of the queue (*jianbian* 剪辮 or *duanfa* 斷髮).[4] Far from an innocent discussion about fashion, *yifu* occupied the pages of many reformist and revolutionary texts, carrying extensive visual, economic, religious, and political significance (Yoshizawa 1997; Chang 2009; Fan 2010).

Kang's opinion about clothing reform was first articulated around 1898, when he put forth his support for the change in several important treatises. In his most extensive discussion in favor of changing clothes, "Qing duanfa yifu gaiyuan zhe" 請斷髮易服改元摺 ("Memorial to the Throne Requesting Cutting the Queue, Changing Clothes, and Adopting a Year of Origin for the New Era"; henceforth "Clothing Memorial"), Kang gives several reasons for getting rid of the old fashion. In a globalized and industrialized age, he warns, China's peculiar dressing style not only sets it apart from other nations but also holds it back in the very process of modernization—the queue being particularly incompatible with machine operation, besides raising sanitary problems and hurting China's international image (Kang 1911: 62b–63b). Included in his *Wuxu zougao* 戊戌奏稿 (*Draft Memorials of 1898*), first published in 1911, the "Clothing Memorial" has been discredited by modern scholars, who argue that this and some other memorials were never submitted to the throne in 1898 but were written later by Kang to retroactively prove his radical stance.[5] Despite the memorial's apocryphal status, however, as Fan Xue-qing (2020: 98–100) has pointed out, Kang did express his proposition for changing dress on other occasions in 1898. In *Kongzi gaizhi kao* 孔子改制考 (*Confucius as Reformer*) and *Riben bianzheng kao* 日本變政考 (*An Account of Japan's Political Reforms*), for example, Kang views clothing reform as part of a broader reform plan and a means of changing people's mind, notions he repeats in the "Clothing Memorial" (Kang [1897] 2007: 106, 112, 233; [1898] 2007: 124, 125, 143, 144, 159, 166, 186–87; 1911: 62a–63b).

What makes the "Clothing Memorial" particularly interesting is that this ardent petition is followed in the *Draft Memorials of 1898* by a lengthy commentary, written by Kang "fourteen years after the coup of 1898," in opposition to what he has proposed. "How I regret my overtly radical proposition!" exclaims Kang (1911: 65a; henceforth "Commentary"). This is a rare moment in the career of the self-confident Kang, who has been described by many as dogmatically unwilling to admit mistakes (Hsiao 1975: 18–19). In the "Commentary," the former leader of sweeping reforms is relentlessly critical of the shortsightedness of his younger self, calling his previous plan "suicidal" and "exceedingly erroneous," and asking, "Why did I say and do things so recklessly simply to ape foreigners?" (Kang 1911: 73a–73b). If the "Clothing Memorial" was forged years after the reform movement to showcase Kang's foresight, it becomes interesting to examine what Kang is trying to distance himself from in the "Commentary" and what he has carried over into his postreform campaigns.

In the "Commentary," Kang identifies his historical error as *meiwai* 媚外, aping or toadying to foreigners. If we take this disparaging label to include the expressions of shame and inferiority in front of foreigners, then *meiwai* in the "Clothing Memorial" can be seen in Kang's protest against the queue: "In foreign countries, [the queue] is pointed at and laughed at by foreigners and pulled and played with by children. The fact that our country is weak further subjects [the Chinese] to humiliation, [and the queue] is denounced as a pig's tail" (Kang 1911: 63a). The same sense of shame at being gazed at by disapproving Westerners suffuses this remark about the Qing military uniform: in a world that valued militarism, "our military uniform, still featuring a loose fit with flared sleeves, is put on display in the museums of the [foreign] nations, side by side with the armor [of the Western nations]. Doesn't it look all the more ludicrous?" (63b).[6] These are the most conspicuous expressions of unease about being looked down upon by foreigners in the "Clothing Memorial," for which Kang's accusation of *meiwai* may seem a little too harsh.

But perhaps Kang is not only referring to what he has said in the "Clothing Memorial." A persistent anxiety about the gaze of foreigners becomes obvious with a skim through the *Draft Memorials of 1898*, in which foreign observers are almost ubiquitous as Kang attacks the old ways that need reforming. The eight-legged examination essay, for one, is a monstrosity that "foreigners find particularly unreasonable" (Kang 1911: 6b). The primitive canal transportation of grain for another, has also become a corrupt practice "reproved and laughed at by all the nations" (49b, 50b). Besides marveling at China's notorious criminal laws, squalid prisons, and slummy, opium-smoked streets, foreigners even take pictures of Qing's outmoded military exercises, superstitious practices, and foot-binding and circulate those images far and wide, making China a laughing stock on the international stage and, as is apparent in the repeated mention of "shame" (*chi* 恥), deeply hurting Kang's pride (54a, 43a, 27a–27b, 44b, 59a).

Far from merely venting his personal frustration, Kang's memorials could communicate the shame to his implied audience—if not the court, then the intended readers of the published collection—so as to, presumably, shame the readers into action, a strategy shared by reformers and revolutionaries alike. The problem of men's appearance alone was enough cause to shame the Chinese males into changing their outfit, be it a preparation for constitutional reform or a symbol of break with the Manchu regime. Thus Zou Rong 鄒容 (1885–1905), a young revolutionary who had studied in Japan, called on his compatriots to rise against the Manchu government by resorting to their sense of shame: "When a man with a queue and wearing Manchu clothes wanders around London, why do all the passers-by say 'Pig-tail' or 'Savage'? And if he is in Tokyo, why do they all shout 'Chanchanbusu' (meaning pig-tailed slave)?" (Zou [1903] 1957: 346).[7] The cause of this humiliation, Zou averred, was the forced replacement of the dignified dressing styles of the Han and Tang dynasties with the loathsome Manchu hairstyle and garment (Zou [1903] 1957: 346–47).[8] A few years later, Zaitao 載濤 (1887–1970), a reform-minded Manchu prince, pressed for a change of clothes and the abolition of the queue after returning from a world tour, and one reason he gave was that the queue formed a sign of weakness, the removal of which should "show to the world the real desire of the Government to carry out reforms."[9] Although the reasoning was against the queue, in the general understanding the abolition of the queue would inevitably involve a change of the national costume.[10] Similar arguments surrounding the topic of clothing reform proliferated in the final years of the Qing dynasty, epitomizing a far-reaching wrestling with China's image in the eyes of foreigners.

This sense of inferiority, however, becomes the target of Kang's attack in the "Commentary," very likely written during his sojourn in Japan. Following the coup d'état that ended the short-lived reform movement, Kang fled China and spent the next sixteen years abroad, traveling to such places as Hong Kong, Japan, Canada, Europe, and America. By the time the *Draft Memorials of 1898* was published, Kang had completed multiple trips to Europe, the tour of which is considered a major turning point in the development of his worldview (Qian 1990: 330–31). In this sense, he is not unlike his disciple Liang Qichao 梁啟超 (1873–1929), whose harsh criticism of China in an early travel account on America gave way to appreciation of Chinese culture after a tour of post-WWI Europe nearly two decades later (Liang [1904] 2014, [1920] 2014). The "Commentary" presents a well-traveled Kang who, disenchanted by the poverty and chaos he saw in fin-de-siècle Europe, is better positioned to appreciate China's merits, which include the material and cut of traditional clothes. With reclaimed cultural confidence, he is able to rise above the censorious gaze of foreigners on matters regarding clothing and other reforms—or is he?

A closer look at the "Commentary" reveals the persistence of the gaze, the first sign of which becomes obvious in Kang's prompt use of anecdotes from his overseas travels. Kang states his viewpoint early on: "Removing the queue was a necessity, but changing clothes was impractical." Instead of explaining why, he describes a visit by a famous doctor in New York, who says to him: "If you're going to carry out reforms [in China], you may change everything, but by no means shall you change clothes, because Chinese costume is the most suitable for all nations" 他日君變法, 一切皆可變, 惟服制萬不可變, 以中國服裝, 最適於萬國也. The doctor tells him about a big gathering, where a gust of wind made many people catch a cold, but the Chinese envoy alone was unaffected. "That was a living example [of the superiority of Chinese clothing]," says the doctor (Kang 1911: 64b). Kang goes on to name other Westerners—Euro-American ladies, his European servants, a member of parliament, and a doctor he met in Italy—who helped him rediscover the beauty, comfort, convenience, and economic appropriateness of Chinese clothes, on which the livelihood of a large population depends. In the middle of an extended vindication of the advantages of Chinese clothes, he does not forget to reiterate the view of the foreigners:

> When I traveled in the US, the Americans would marvel at the grace of my attire. On the several occasions when I changed into Western clothes, the ladies would say, "You don't look as great [as on other days]." And they would beseech me to wear my national costume and on no account change [into the Western style] in the future.

> 昔吾遊於美, 美之人多羨吾服之美. 吾間易歐服, 其貴婦皆謂, 今日相見不美, 皆謂宜服國服, 他日切不可改也. (70a)

The somewhat bewildering succession of the polysemous *mei* 美, the first two meaning "America" and the last two translating as "beautiful," highlights the significant role of aesthetic sensibility, which for Kang is essential for achieving empathy across cultures and a world community (B. Wang 2022: 19–39). Here to look nice, *mei*, in the eyes of the other (ladies of the "beautiful country" in this case), becomes an indicator of the benefits of Chinese clothes, supported by the testimonies of doctors and servants. Therefore, despite Kang's self-accusation of worshipping foreigners in the "Clothing Memorial," his reference in the "Commentary" to Westerners' opinions does not diminish but, rather, increases. Kang is careful to mark one difference: the negative images captured by foreigners' cameras in his draft memorials are replaced by positive features confirmed by Western medicine and aesthetics in the "Commentary," which is apparently based on an account in his *Falanxi youji* 法蘭西遊記 (*Travel Account on France*; Kang [1904c] 2007: 165). But if *meiwai* suggests the acknowledgment of a mirror image in the foreign gaze, then Kang after his European travels is hardly any less *meiwai* than (he claims) he was fourteen years ago, even with Chinese clothing declared "superior."

A comparison of the "Clothing Memorial" with the "Commentary" also brings to light Kang's persistence in a global unity of clothing. In the "Clothing Memorial," this is his primary reason for a clothing reform: "Today all nations are in communication with each other, and in everything there is a trend towards unison. Yet our country alone stands out with its peculiar dressing style, which makes it difficult to find mutual affection and form diplomatic relations [with other nations]" (Kang 1911: 62b). In the "Commentary," however, he is apologetic about his allegedly previous rush: "I was inexperienced, yet to travel in the foreign countries," and "was advocating unison too radically" 尚同太急 (73a). But is the persona of the widely traveled Kang desiring unison less fervently? The decision not to change dress by no means indicates a turn from unity to diversity, for Kang also suggests that Chinese clothes, being the only option that suited all three climate zones, should be used as the model for a uniform when "the whole world becomes one" 大地合一之時 (67b–68a). Foreigners' approving gaze has obviously emboldened Kang, whose dream of a Great Unity of dress is not abandoned but given a new direction with a longer timeline.

This view is repeatedly expressed in Kang's travel accounts. After traveling to Europe and India, Kang comes to the conclusion that it is no use changing dress without adopting more substantial measures to strengthen the nation (Kang [1904c] 2007: 165). Countries like India and Turkey have been imitating the West in many ways, but they remain weak (165, 166). If China abandons its natural advantage of silk products to follow Western ways, it will be the ruin of the nation's economy. "The strength of a nation depends on its political structure and government [*zhengzhi* 政治], and not its dressing style," Kang asserts. But what follows focuses on something completely different from institutional reforms: "Our nation can easily achieve strength as long as we pay more attention to matters [*wuzhi* 物質] like machines, ships, and cannons" (165). This is an example of Kang's newfound faith in the development of hardware, or what Pablo Ariel Blitstein (2020/21: 46) calls "science of matter," the "knowledge on the 'matterological' aspects of things." The "matters" Kang considers in need of improvement do not include Chinese clothes, at least not its aesthetic aspect, but only the economics of apparel production. His discussion inevitably gravitates to Meiji Japan, whose clothing reform had once been the target of criticism and ridicule by even some of the most "progressive" Chinese scholars but was more and more commended after 1895 for its trailblazing in the Meiji Restoration. Japan's traditional apparel enjoys international adoration now that the nation is fortified by thunderous cannons, Kang remarks, and the path to Chinese clothing's global popularity must also be a matterological one: "As long as our government can be honest and enlightened, our matters [i.e., material products] exquisite and elegant, and our gunships powerfully installed, Chinese silk clothing will naturally be admired and imitated all over the world" (Kang [1904c] 2007: 166). Instead of Westernizing Chinese clothes, Kang is suggesting a Sinofication of clothes of all other nations, maintaining that unison can be achieved the other way around.

LOOKING BACK AT CHINA: HOUSES AND THE PRESTIGE
OF A NATION

Clothing, as mentioned, was only one among the many aspects Kang Youwei suggested changing to improve China's international image. Before his overseas travels, Kang had been witnessing and perhaps reading about how China's customs, policies, cityscapes, and people were viewed by foreigners.[11] The *Draft Memorials of 1898* records how he used to stand beside foreign spectators and photographers in Beijing, "looking from the side" and feeling the sting when he believed Westerners were sneering at the negative image of China (Kang 1911: 10a).[12]

Travel gave him a new mobility and a shiftable viewpoint. In travels, Kang finds himself no longer the stationary object of gaze but the moving subject of looking. After all, travel is not only about being seen; it is also, if not more, about seeing, although for Kang the two are frequently interlocked. According to his travelogues, the objects that catch his eyes most frequently are not clothes or hairstyles but streets, gardens, and buildings, among which museums and houses receive the most detailed treatment. As Kang walks along the walls of an ancient temple or a residential building, inspecting its materials, design, and interior decoration, he adopts an ethnographic perspective and sees in architectural styles a nation's degree of civilization and the proof of social evolution in general (see, e.g., Kang [1904e] 2007: 352, 359; [1908] 2007: 396).

This observation leads Kang to reflect on China's urban constructions. For him, travel is about seeing the foreign countries and looking back at his own for comparison. The act of turning around, *hui* 回, becomes pivotal, and Kang's travelogues use many words to mean looking back, such as *huishi* 回視, *huishou* 回首, *huigu* 回顧, and *huiwang* 回望. Their usages differ. *Huiwang*, for example, with *wang* 望 meaning gazing into the distance, is used by Kang not for cultural comparison but mainly to describe distant scenery (see, e.g., Kang [1901b] 2007: 524; [1904e] 2007: 349). On the other hand, *shi* 視, to look at, observe, or inspect, often signifies for Kang a more critical and comparative view of cultures.[13] Both *huishi* and *huigu* mark the moment of comparing what Kang sees in his travels with things back home, often to the disadvantage of China (see, e.g., Kang [1904a] 2007: 7, 469; [1904f] 2007: 8, 11). This is echoed by Jiang Xu 蔣煦, quoted at the beginning of this article. An entrepreneur who traveled to Europe in 1903, Jiang opens the preface to his travel journal with this illuminating observation, "Only by leaving home can one truly see one's home, and only by leaving the country can one truly see one's country" (Jiang [1903] 2016: 9). He then expounds on the analogy between home and country, arguing that the critical conditions of both can be seen by the otherwise contented homeowner or citizen only when they go out and look back—*huigu*.

China's streets and buildings—palaces, houses, and even prisons—are subject to this returned gaze of Kang as he travels out and looks back. The weaknesses of China's buildings, for Kang, lie in three aspects. First, houses are built of wood, which cannot endure through time. Compared with the stone constructions found in India and some Western cities, China's wooden buildings either have vanished or are destined to perish, consigning its architecture and ancient civilization to oblivion (Kang [1901b] 2007: 529–30; [1904b] 2007: 422; [1904f] 2007: 8). Second, Chinese houses are generally low, with confined spaces. The cramped rooms of a nation can be a sign of the narrow-mindedness of the people (Kang [1904d] 2007: 494), while the lowness of buildings, which Kang repeatedly refers to as *bei* 卑, meaning physically low or lowly in status, carries racial implications. Palaces crawling on the ground become the symbol of a nation's inferiority on the world stage. Third, Chinese buildings usually feature mean finish, poor interior decoration, and abominable sanitary conditions. These weaknesses are believed by Kang to be a chief culprit of foreigners' contempt for China, and his criticism, expressions of shame, and repeated act of looking back betray the anxiety about the foreign gaze, cast over his turned shoulders, at China.

This multilayered gaze plays an important role in a lengthy treatment of Chinese housing in Kang's *Yingguo youji* 英國遊記 (*Travel Account on Britain*). Kang begins this subject by recounting the degrading quality of China's upper society household items in past dynasties and observes that Chinese officials' frugal styles were often mocked by enemy states (Kang [1904f] 2007: 7). Moving on to the contemporary scene, Kang quotes a British civil official, who says to him, "People say Li Hongzhang was a rich man, but I don't believe that, for I have seen his home, which was insufferably shabby" 人謂李鴻章富, 吾不信也, 吾觀其室乃陋不堪 (8). Li Hongzhang 李鴻章 (1823–1901), the most powerful Chinese politician and diplomat of his time, is undoubtedly considered by Kang a token of China's international image. Apparently agreeing with this British official, Kang goes on to praise the luxuriousness of British residential dwellings and public facilities, contrasting each category with the sorry condition of its Chinese counterpart using the verb *huishi* and, in so doing, signifying a motion of looking back and forth (8). After the juxtaposition, he concludes, "No wonder these people, after touring China, become so contemptuous of us!" 宜彼人遊中國而大輕我也! (8). His criticism does not end here but is followed by further comparisons, including one between an American doctor living in a smartly furnished apartment and his Chinese doctor neighbor, who is ridiculed by the former for being gluttonous because, though his apartment is poorly furnished, he insists on having meat on his table (8). By invoking various observers of China—enemy states, the British official, and the American doctor—Kang makes clear that Chinese housing conditions are an international matter and gives the impression that whenever he looks back at China, a foreigner looks with him.

Another notable instance of Kang's anxiety about the gaze occurs during his visit to a prison in Denmark. Prisons had been a popular destination for Chinese travelers since Qing's first mission to Europe in 1866.[14] Impressed by the order, tidiness, and humane management of Western prisons, Qing travelers filled their journal entries with praises, calling the prisons "blessed abodes" (*fudi* 福地) or true heirs of China's ancient "three dynasties" (*san dai* 三代), a synonym for perfection (Zhang [1870] 1981: 74; Wang T. [1887–89] 1985: 149).[15] Kang falls into the group of admirers. "The prison I visited in Denmark was as splendid as paradise" 吾遊丹墨獄, 華嚴若天堂, he writes (Kang [1904a] 2007: 469). Unlike his predecessors, who explicitly or implicitly compared Western prisons with their Chinese counterparts, Kang measures the Danish prison not only against Chinese prisons but also against the homes in China. He makes this contrast more pronounced in verse, segueing from a long appreciative description of the Danish prison into this dismissive appraisal of Chinese dwellings:

Turning around [*huigu*] to look at the people of my country,
[I see their] houses, mean and filthy,
Reeking of all kinds of stenches,
Adding to sickness, sores, and wrenches.
The poor keep their dogs and pigs inside,
Sharing food where filth cannot hide.
The character for "home," *jia*, has a pig sign,
An ancient lesson passed down the line!
Knowing nothing of hygiene, they cannot see,
The paradise of health that ought to be.
Not to mention the prisoners' plight,
For whom death by neglect is a fortunate sight.
When the jailer asked me, if in the Qing,
Prisons were also cool and refreshing,
I blushed scarlet, face aflame,
Unable to hide my burning shame.
Alas! The gap is far and wide
As can heaven and earth divide.
A government lacking mercy and grace,
Keeps my country in a weakened place.

回顧吾國人, 室屋卑污方. 穢惡交騰蒸, 疾病多瘡瘍. 貧者雜犬豚, 矢溺共糟糠.
家文下有豕, 古訓尚未忘. 不知衛生法, 況識安樂鄉. 獄囚更何論, 瘐死幸有喪.
獄吏問我國, 獄室可清涼. 吾顏如渥丹, 忸怩無可藏. 相去何太遠, 天壤乃王郎.
我實政不仁, 宜其國不強. (469)

The act of *huigu* leads Kang through a virtual tour of Chinese houses, especially the homes of the poor, and China's prisons to arrive at the cause of the nation's
weakness. However, Chinese prisoners' (lack of) human rights seem to be less of a
problem, mentioned in only two lines, than the people's poor sanitary conditions
and awareness, as well as his feeling of shame stemming from comparison. The fear
that China looks bad in the eyes of the international community, epitomized in the
figure of the Danish jailer, underlies Kang's criticism of Chinese houses. The same
sentiment is present in the *Draft Memorials of 1898* when Kang observes that China's inhumane criminal laws and sordid prisons shock the foreign community, making it impossible for China to abolish extraterritoriality. "Such national humiliation
[*guochi* 國恥] is unparalleled!" Kang (1911: 54a) writes. No longer standing beside a
jeering visitor to China, Kang has internalized foreigners' critical gaze in his travels
to cast it back on his country, constantly reminding his readers of the shame and
humiliation of being looked down upon by the Other.

Despite his castigation of Chinese houses, however, Kang is not unaware of the
commendable reasons behind China's frugal architectural and living styles. Thrift
had been a virtue advocated and practiced by the wise emperors of the past,[16] and
abstemiousness of the rulers was precisely proof of *ren* 仁 (benevolence), which
Kang accuses China's governance of lacking in the verses quoted above. "[The cultivation of] spiritual virtues," Kang remarks, "requires constriction [*lian* 斂], while

[the development of] materials requires expansion [*zhang* 漲]" ([1904c] 2007: 157). Constriction means being content with a frugal lifestyle and disinclined to upset peace by seeking gain. In contrast, expansion through invention and production greatly facilitates people's enjoyment of material goods, but treachery and deceit also ensue (157).

But constriction could also bring disgrace to China's national prestige and make the people live in destitution (Kang [1904c] 2007: 157). More important for Kang, the promotion of thrift (*shang jian* 尚儉) no longer suits the age of internationalization. "China used to be a world unto itself and had none to compare with," Kang ([1904b] 2007: 422–23) writes, "[but] now in an age of international competition, how can [we] let this country, with a peerless civilization of thousands of years, be subject to contempt merely because its buildings are unattractive?" In another place he pronounces China's humble houses "extremely shameful" in comparison with other nations (Kang [1904a] 2007: 465). In other words, it is because of the presence of the other that what used to be a national merit has now become the cause of shame. Kang sees the transition from China as the world, or an age of self-sufficient unification (*yitong* 一統), to China in the world, as both spatial and temporal. Now that China is thrust into this modern world of multinational states, some obsolete styles should be jettisoned for China to join the universal community and eventually become "one" with it.

This is ultimately because houses, like clothes, inhabit a narrative of progress that fits well into Kang's philosophy of social evolution, which he began to put down in writing in the 1890s. He had taken from the Gongyang 公羊 school's interpretation of Confucius's *Chunqiu* 春秋 (*Spring and Autumn Annals*) the doctrine of the *san shi* 三世 (three ages), according to which human history progressed from the *juluan shi* 據亂世 (age of disorder), through the *shengping shi* 昇平世 (age of approaching peace), to reach the age of *taiping shi* 太平世 (universal peace).[17] This he integrated with the notions of *datong* and *xiaokang* 小康 (minor peace), which he took from *Li ji* 禮記 (*The Book of Rites*).[18] In this way, Kang formed the fundamental principle of his social philosophy, one that designated *datong*, complete unity and harmony for the whole world, as the ultimate stage of social evolution, which he famously illustrated in the *Datong shu* 大同書 (*Book of the Great Unity*).[19]

Just as human history develops through three ages, Kang ([1908] 2007: 396) opines, "houses also fall into three systems [*san tong* 三統). In the past, in the system of the Xia 夏 [dynasty], houses were mean and filthy. Now in the system of the Shang 商, buildings are tall and luxurious. This applies to other matters too." Although he does not say how buildings will look in the next stage, which will be the system of the Zhou 周—for the three systems constitute the Age of Approaching Peace (Kang [1896] 1988: 100)[20]—one can infer from Kang's plan to revamp Chinese houses that, through a mix-up of styles from Middle Eastern and European countries, traditional Chinese styles will be abolished and housing will become universally sumptuous.

Kang is certainly not doing justice to Chinese architecture and is apparently unaware of the Qing's introduction of architecture as a specialization of knowledge from Japan in 1904 during a new series of reforms (Xu 2023: 238), nor can he foresee the nationalist revival of classical Chinese styles alongside the incorporation of

Western architecture in the years to come (Zhou and Ji 2023). By the time Liang Sicheng 梁思成 (1901–1972), son of Liang Qichao, published his *History of Chinese Architecture* (1944), China had witnessed many endeavors to merge foreign and native styles by Western and Chinese architects, Liang Sicheng among them. Kang, however, is no real expert on architecture, and his emphasis here is not on nationalism but on a sumptuary evolution on a global scale. "To live in a low, miserable house," Kang writes, "was a practice befitting only [a ruler] of the Age of Disorder and should be abandoned in a civilized age" (Kang [1902–? b] 2007: 443; Hsiao 1975: 92). The age Kang lived in, though he had to modify his optimistic appraisal at some point, was believed by him to be one of Approaching Peace.[21] While Kang evidently does not have the same confidence in Chinese houses as he does in Chinese clothes, the goal of his reconstruction proposal remains the same: the unification of China with the world in material well-being.

CLOTHES, HOUSES, AND BEYOND: CULTIVATING SHAME IN THE ENCOUNTERS WITH THE GAZE

As shown, Kang's observations about Chinese clothing and housing frequently invoke the sense of shame (*chi*). Shame, of course, was not the only sentiment Kang experienced in his encounters with the gaze—contentment and pride were readily indicated, too—but it was an important one. Scholars have explored the binding force of shame in different cultures, from the Greek society depicted by Homer (Dodds [1951] 2004: 18; 28–63) and traditional Mediterranean communities viewed through the Hebrew Bible (Stiebert 2002), to Japan, controversially labeled a "shame culture" (Benedict 1946: 223–24), and to China in ancient and modern times, when discourses of honor and shame helped guide social conduct (Roetz 1993: 174–84; Lewis 2021; G. C. Huang 2021). Like many other literatures, Chinese classics document persistent teachings about shame. It could be employed by Kang Youwei and his contemporaries as a stimulus to reforms precisely because, more than just a gnawing feeling, it was a crucial quality variously inscribed in Chinese literati's cultural upbringing.

Most relevant, Kang's emphasis on shame evokes the concept of cultivating shame (*yang chi* 養恥), an important practice in Confucian teachings. Here, shame transcends being merely a feeling (*chigan* 恥感) and is embraced as a moral conscience (*chixin* 恥心). Confucius regarded as a gentleman him who "has a sense of shame in the way he conducts himself" 行己有恥 (*Analects* 13.20; Confucius 1979: 121) and advised guiding the people not by edicts but by virtue, so that "they will, besides having a sense of shame, reform themselves" 有恥且格 (*Analects* 2.3; Confucius 1979: 63). Mencius also attached great importance to shame, calling "the mind's feeling of shame and aversion" the "sprout of righteousness" 羞惡之心義之端也 (*Mencius* 3.6; Mencius 2011: 35). "A person must not be without [the sense of] shame" 人不可以無恥, said the Second Sage (*Mencius* 13.6; Mencius 2011: 145). In Kang Youwei's *Menzi wei* 孟子微 (*The Esoteric Meanings of the "Mencius,"* 1901), he expounds on Mencius's discussion of shame and comments, "The reason that a person has some actions that he will not take is because he has the conscience of shame [*chixin*]" (Kang [1901a] 2007: 473). Kang considered it his duty to teach shame to the people and in 1897, he founded the Zhichi Xuehui 知恥學會 (Study Society to Know Shame) with another reformer in Beijing, invoking Confucius's famous line about the courage of knowing shame (*zhi chi jinhu yong* 知恥近乎勇) to arouse popular consciousness about the "shame" of China's defeat by Japan.

Therefore, rather than an undesirable sensation always passively triggered by the gaze, shame is enlisted by Kang as an awareness ready to act, although Kang's formulation often foregrounds the emotional aspect by presupposing the presence of an "other" as the main catalyst. To activate this sense of humiliation in his readers and stir them to action, Kang seems to be seeking out the gaze whenever he can, proffering the extravagant lists of foreigners' opinions discussed above. For that reason, by borrowing and even internalizing the gaze, Kang does not become the mimetic (colonial) subject suggested by Erving Goffman and Michel Foucault in different contexts, who identifies with the values and presumptions of the gaze and mends conduct to conform with the expectations of the agent of surveillance, resulting in what is termed *conversion* by Goffman (1961: 43–64; Foucault 1977). Instead, shame in Kang's encounters with the gaze emerges simultaneously as a painful feeling, a moral quality, and a rhetorical weapon. As the gaze irrepressibly shapes Kang's perception of his country and its people, so he strives just as ardently to reenact that shaping power through his writings. This persistent exercise of shame puts Kang in alliance with many literati and intellectuals of his time: the narration of shame and failure has been shown to be indispensable for the proliferation of Chinese nationalism (Tsu 2005), and foreigners' gaze was diligently reproduced in the portrayal of China in late Qing fiction, not only as a reminder of humiliation but also as a witness to the dreamed conversion of shame into pride (Y. Huang 2018).

In Kang's futurist vision of clothes and houses, shame further acquires a purpose that is independent of the discourse of reform or international rivalry. In the world of *datong*, national and class boundaries will be abolished, races merged, and men and women treated equally. Clothes will not be differentiated by gender (Kang [1902–? a] 2007: 75), and "all will live in public facilities and there will be no need to build [private] houses" (184). All the public facilities, from free shared houses and schools to nursing homes and hospitals, will be perfected to meet the highest standards for human health and development. It is reasonable to assume that housing conditions will be equally perfected for each citizen of this universal community. Yet as Kang tells us, there will still be disparity. Almshouses, for example, will provide crude clothing and clean but "small rooms with low ceilings" with only basic amenities (110). The inmates will be made to feel shame by wearing a uniform, and if they come back after their term of stay, they will have to wear a particular color to further mark their degradation (110). In the nursing homes, similarly, "distinction of grade will remain within the Great Unity" (113). Residents will be divided into hierarchies based on their former social positions and contributions, and their housing, clothing, food provisions, and so on, will vary accordingly (113). This meritorious system, Kang argues, is necessary to "make people know what they should aspire after and what they should be ashamed of and abstain from [*kuijie* 愧戒]" (114). Therefore, although the world of *datong* is said to be without discrimination and sumptuary hierarchies, Kang maintains distinction to preserve the sense of shame, quite contrary to the prison in Denmark, which "did not put [the inmates'] shame on an ostentatious show" (Kang [1904a] 2007: 469).

In doing so, Kang alters the nature of shame that so constantly pricks his conscience during his travels, changing it from the (inter)national to the social. I have used the examples of clothing and housing to show that how China and the Chinese were viewed internationally greatly influenced Kang's notions about China's reforms and the development of a world community. With that community achieved and national boundaries abolished, dishonor of individuals will no longer be magnified as the disgrace of a people, and clothing and housing will cease to be indicators of "national humiliation" on the world stage. The traveler, removed from the predicament of seeing and being seen as a national subject, will be able to look about without the burden of representation or salvation that Kang and his contemporaries must bear during their globetrotting, but the preservation of shame as a noble quality will continue to request the assistance of the gaze.

YINGYING HUANG is a lecturer of Chinese at Lafayette College. Her research interests comprise late Qing literature and culture, travel writings, postcolonial studies, and gender studies. She is working on her book project, "The Alien Eye: Late Qing Representations of China through a Transnational Lens."

ACKNOWLEDGMENTS

I am grateful to Alice Chi-ying Wang for highlighting the distinction between shame as a moral sense and as an emotional feeling, and to Daniel Hsieh for the opportunity to present my research to an enthusiastic audience. I would also like to thank the editors and the two anonymous reviewers of the *Journal of Asian Studies* for their invaluable feedback.

NOTES

1. For a recent discussion of Kang Youwei in English scholarship, see the 2020/21 issue of *Oriens Extremus* (no. 58). For an overview of recent Kang Youwei studies in China, see Lee 2020/21.

2. One exception is Pablo Ariel Blitstein (2016), who examines the influence of life and politics in Mexico on Kang's conception of a Chinese nation outside China. This, however, still differs from my approach to Kang's view of China as shaped by foreign viewers.

3. Tan's *Ren xue* (*A Study of Benevolence*) was written between 1896 and 1897 and was published posthumously by Liang Qichao and others.

4. Reform of women's appearances was most often discussed separately under the topic of foot-binding. See Finnane 2008: 82–92.

5. The first charge of forgery was made by Hwang Chang-chien 黃彰建 (1970: 539–601). Scholars such as Young-Tsu Wong (1992) have refuted Hwang's revisionist argument by proving the authenticity of some of the memorials based on archival evidence, but a possible original of the "Clothing Memorial" has not been found in the First History Archives of China 中國第一歷史檔案館, and it is not included in the list of memorials verified by Kong Xiangji (2008).

6. This remark was very likely written after Kang's travels to France, where he had seen Qing military uniforms on display in a military museum (Kang [1904c] 2007: 8.161).

7. A more literal translation of *chanchanbusu* (チャンチャンブス) is "ugly Chinese."

8. Ironically, this identification of the queue with the Manchu regime became the very cause of Kang's humiliation: he kept his queue, a symbol of his loyalty to the emperor, even when in Japan, and had it cut only after having been repeatedly laughed at by the Japanese, an incident that has been passed down as a joke (Lin 2004: 20–21).

9. "Change of Costume," *North China Herald*, July 1, 1910; "The National Head-Dress," *North China Herald*, September 23, 1910.

10. "The Removal of the Queue," *North China Herald*, September 23, 1910; "The Queue," *North China Herald*, September 30, 1910.

11. According to Kang's ([1899] 2007: 63) autobiography, he began reading "Western books" in 1879.

12. This incident could only have happened before Kang's exile from China in 1898.

13. Comparison is most clearly pronounced with *yishi* 以視, "comparing [it] with." See, e.g., Kang (1907) 2007: 267.

14. Zhang Deyi 張德彝, a student and translator on the trip, wrote about his visit to a prison in London (Zhang [1870] 1981: 74).

15. See also Guo (1876–79) 1984: 33–34, 49, 151–55, 275–76, 305–7, 760–61; and Liu (ca. 1877) 1986: 52–53, 123–25, 178.

16. A famous example is Emperor Wen of the Han dynasty 漢文帝.

17. For the development of the doctrine since the *Chunqiu Gongyang zhuan* 春秋公羊傳 (*Gongyang Commentary on the* Spring and Autumn Annuals), see Chen 2016. Kang's adoption of it can be found, for example, in Kang (1893–97) 2007: 324 and in Kang (1902–? b) 2007: 393.

18. Kung-Chuan Hsiao (1975: 56) notes that it was in the *Chunqiu Dongshi xue* that Kang linked the doctrines of the "Liyun" with the theories of three ages for the first time. See also Kang (1902) 2007: 551–69.

19. The date of the completion of Kang's *Datong shu* is unclear. The most influential opinion is led by Tang Zhijun 湯志鈞 (2016: 12–13, 54–62), who agrees with Liang Qichao 梁啟超 that Kang wrote the book between 1901 and 1902. Tang also believes Kang began to explore the idea of *datong* as early as 1884.

20. This entry is not included in the version in the *Kang Youwei Quanji*.

21. In *Lunyu zhu*, Kang has written with confidence, "Now that all [nations] over the earth are in communication, and Europe and America have gone through a tremendous transformation, [the world] has probably arrived at the Age of Approaching Peace" 今大地既通，歐美大變，蓋進至昇平之世矣 (Kang [1902–? b] 2007: 393). But after touring Italy, his optimism subsides, and he is ready to reassess the West, which "has not fully realized the Age of Approaching Peace" 至今未能盡其昇平之世 (Kang [1904e] 2007: 374). "I used to overestimate Europe and America," he writes, "believing [they] could gradually achieve Universal Peace. [However,] seen from today's situation, [even] Approaching Peace has not yet been achieved" 吾昔者視歐美過高，以為可漸至大同，由今按之，則昇平尚未至也 (374).

REFERENCES

Benedict, Ruth. 1946. *The Chrysanthemum and the Sword*. Boston: Houghton Mifflin.

Blitstein, Pablo Ariel. 2016. "A New China in Mexico: Kang Youwei and His Languages of Cohesion-Making on the Two Sides of the Pacific (1895–1911)." *Oriens Extremus*, no. 55: 209–60.

Blitstein, Pablo Ariel. 2020/21. "A Profitable Side of Things: Kang Youwei's 'On How Matter Can Save the Nation.'" *Oriens Extremus*, no. 58: 27–57.

Chang Shih-ying 張世瑛. 2009. "Qingmo Minchu de jianbian fengchou ji qi suo fanying de shehui xintai" 清末民初的剪辮風潮及其所反映的社會心態 [The pigtail-cutting turmoil and the related social attitudes in early twentieth-century China]. *Journal of Academia Historica* 國史館館刊, no. 22: 1–56.

Chen Hui 陳徽. 2016. "Gongyang san shi shuo de yanjin guocheng ji qi sixiang yiyi" 公羊三世說的演進過程及其思想意義 [The development of the Gongyang doctrine about the three ages and its significance]. *Kongzi yanjiu* 孔子研究 [Confucius studies], no. 2: 110–21.

Confucius. 1979. *The Analects*. Translated by D. C. Lau. London: Penguin.

Dodds, E. R. (1951) 2004. *The Greeks and the Irrational*. Berkeley: University of California Press.

Fan Xue-qing 樊學慶. 2010. "Jianfa yifu yu wan Qing lixian kunju (1909–1910)" 剪髮易服與晚清立憲困局 [Cutting the queue, changing clothes, and the constitutional dilemma of the late Qing]. *Zhongyang yanjiuyuan jindaishi yanjiusuo jikan* 中央研究院近代史研究所集刊 [Journal of the Institute of Modern History, Academia Sinica], no. 69: 41–78.

Fan Xue-qing 樊學慶. 2020. "Kang Youwei wuxu zouqing yifu duanfa gaiyuan kaobian" 康有為戊戌奏請易服斷髮改元考辨 [Textual research on Kang Youwei's memorial of 1898 to change clothes, cut queues, and adopt a new calendar]. *Zhongyang yanjiuyuan jindaishi yanjiusuo jikan* 中央研究院近代史研究所集刊 [Journal of the Institute of Modern History, Academia Sinica], no. 108: 91–131.

Finnane, Antonia. 2008. *Changing Clothes in China: Fashion, History, Nation*. New York: Columbia University Press.

Foucault, Michel. 1977. *Discipline and Punish*. Translated by Alan Sheridan. New York: Vintage Books.

Goffman, Erving. 1961. *Asylums: Essays on the Social Situation of Mental Patients and Other Inmates*. Garden City, NY: Anchor Books.

Guo Songtao 郭嵩燾. (1876–79) 1984. *Lundun yu Bali riji* 倫敦與巴黎日記 [Diary of London and Paris]. Changsha: Yuelu shushe.

Hsiao, Kung-Chuan. 1975. *A Modern China and a New World: K'ang Yu-wei, Reformer and Utopian, 1858–1927*. Seattle: University of Washington Press.

Huang, Grace C. 2021. *Chiang Kai-shek's Politics of Shame: Leadership, Legacy, and National Identity in China*. Cambridge, MA: Harvard University Asia Center.

Huang, Yingying. 2018. "Expo Fantasies: Time, Space, and the Transnational Vision in Three Late Qing Texts." *Modern Chinese Literature and Culture* 30, no. 2: 173–215.

Hwang Chang-chien 黃彰健. 1970. *Wuxu bianfa shi yanjiu* 戊戌變法史研究 [A historical study of the 1898 reform movement]. Taipei: Institute of History and Philology, Academia Sinica.

Jiang Xu 蔣煦. (1903) 2016. *Xiyou riji* 西遊日記 [Journals on a westbound travel]. Changsha: Yuelu shushe.

Kang Youwei 康有為. (1893–97) 2007. *Chunqiu Dongshi xue* 春秋董氏學 [Dong Zhongshu's studies in the "Spring and Autumn Annals"]. In Kang 2007, 2:305–438.

Kang Youwei 康有為. (1896) 1988. *Wanmu caotang koushuo* 萬木草堂口說 [Lectures from the Ten Thousand Trees Thatched Hall]. In *Changxing xueji, guixue dawen, wanmucaotang koushuo* 長興學記, 桂學答問, 萬木草堂口說 [Lectures in Changxingli and two other works], edited by Lou Yulie 樓宇烈, 61–290. Beijing: Zhonghua shuju.

Kang Youwei 康有為. (1897) 2007. *Kongzi gaizhi kao* 孔子改制考 [Confucius as reformer]. In Kang 2007, 3:1–260.

Kang Youwei 康有為. (1898) 2007. *Riben bianzheng kao* 日本變政考 [An account of Japan's political reforms]. In Kang 2007, 4:101–294.

Kang Youwei 康有為. (1899) 2007. *Wo shi* 我史 [My autobiography]. In Kang 2007, 5:58–106.

Kang Youwei 康有為. (1901a) 2007. *Mengzi wei* 孟子微 [The esoteric meanings of the *Mencius*]. In Kang 2007, 5:409–505.

Kang Youwei 康有為. (1901b) 2007. *Yindu youji* 印度遊記 [Travels in India]. In Kang 2007, 5:509–50.

Kang Youwei 康有為. (1902) 2007. *Liyun zhu* 禮運注 [The *Evolution of Rites* annotated]. In Kang 2007, 5:551–69.

Kang Youwei 康有為. (1902–? a) 2007. *Datong shu* 大同書 [Book of the Great Unity]. In Kang 2007, 7:1–188.

Kang Youwei 康有為. (1902–? b) 2007. *Lunyu zhu* 論語注 [The *Analects* annotated]. In Kang 2007, 6:375–540.

Kang Youwei 康有為. (1904a) 2007. *Danmo youji* 丹墨遊記 [Travels in Denmark]. In Kang 2007, 7:461–71.

Kang Youwei 康有為. (1904b) 2007. *Deguo youji* 德國遊記 [Travels in Germany]. In Kang 2007, 7:407–60.

Kang Youwei 康有為. (1904c) 2007. *Falanxi youji* 法蘭西遊記 [Travels in France]. In Kang 2007, 8:143–205.

Kang Youwei 康有為. (1904d) 2007. *Helan youji* 荷蘭遊記 [Travels in the Netherlands]. In Kang 2007, 7:494–502.

Kang Youwei 康有為. (1904e) 2007. *Yidali youji* 意大利遊記 [Travels in Italy]. In Kang 2007, 7:346–406.

Kang Youwei 康有為. (1904f) 2007. *Yingguo youji* 英國遊記 [Travels in Britain]. In Kang 2007, 8:1–26.

Kang Youwei 康有為. (1907) 2007. *Bu Faguo youji* 補法國遊記 [Supplement to the travel account on France]. In Kang 2007, 8:264–69.

Kang Youwei 康有為. (1908) 2007. *Bu Ao youji* 補奧遊記 [Supplement to travel accounts on Austria]. In Kang 2007, 8:384–407.

Kang Youwei 康有為. 1911. *Wuxu Zougao* 戊戌奏稿 [Draft memorials of 1898]. Compiled by Mai Zhonghua 麥仲華. Yokohama.

Kang Youwei 康有為. 2007. *Kang Youwei quanji* 康有為全集 [The complete works of Kang Youwei]. 12 vols. Beijing: Zhongguo renmin daxue chubanshe.

Kong Xiangji 孔祥吉. 2008. *Kang Youwei wuxu bianfa zouzhang Jikao* 康有為戊戌變法奏章輯考 [Compiled and verified memorials by Kang Youwei during the reform movement of 1898]. Beijing: Beijing tushuguan chubanshe.

Lee Ting-mien. 2020/21. "A Preliminary Overview of Kang Youwei Studies in China Today." *Oriens Extremus*, no. 58: 175–90.

Lewis, Mark Edward. 2021. *Honor and Shame in Early China*. New York: Cambridge University Press.

Liang Qichao 梁啟超. (1904) 2014. *Xin dalu youji* 新大陸遊記 [Travels in the new continent]. Beijing: Shangwu yinshuguan.

Liang Qichao 梁啟超. (1920) 2014. *Ouyou xinying lu* 歐遊心影錄 [Impressions from travels in Europe]. Beijing: Shangwu yinshuguan.

Lin Zhu 林洙. 2004. *Liang Sicheng, Lin Huiyin yu wo* 梁思成, 林徽因與我 [Liang Sicheng, Lin Huiyin and I]. Beijing: Qinghua daxue chubanshe.

Liu Xihong 劉錫鴻. (ca. 1877) 1986. "Yingyao siji" 英軺私記 [Private diary of a journey to England]. In *Yingyao siji, Suishi Ying E ji* 英軺私記, 隨使英俄記 [Private diary of a journey to England, and another work], edited by Liu Xihong and Zhang Deyi 張德彝, 1–266. Changsha: Yuelu shushe.

Mencius. 2011. *Mencius*. Translated by Irene Bloom. New York: Columbia University Press.

Qian Mu 錢穆. 1990. "Du Kang Nanhai Ouzhou shiyiguo youji" 讀康南海歐洲十一國遊記 [Reading Kang Youwei's travel accounts on eleven European countries]. In *Zhongguo xueshu sixiangshi lunchong* 中國學術思想史論叢 [Chinese intellectual history series], no. 8, 329–41. Taipei: Dongda tushu.

Roetz, Heiner. 1993. *Confucian Ethics of the Axial Age*. Albany: SUNY Press.

Stiebert, Johanna. 2002. *The Construction of Shame in the Hebrew Bible: The Prophetic Contribution*. London: Sheffield Academic.

Tan Sitong 譚嗣同. (1897) 1954. *Tan Sitong quanji* 譚嗣同全集 [Complete works of Tan Sitong]. Beijing: Sanlian shudian.

Tang Zhijun 湯志鈞. 2016. *Kang Youwei de datong sixiang yu Datong shu* 康有為的大同思想與大同書 [Kang Youwei's Great Unity: The idea and the book]. Shanghai: Shanghai renmin chubanshe.

Tsu, Jing. 2005. *Failure, Nationalism, and Literature: The Making of Modern Chinese Identity, 1895–1937*. Stanford, CA: Stanford University Press.

Turriziani, Martina. 2016. "The Connection between Art and Patriotic Feeling in Kang Youwei's *Yidali Youji*." *International Communication of Chinese Culture* 3, no. 1: 161–74.

Wang, Ban. 2022. *China in the World: Culture, Politics, and World Vision*. Durham, NC: Duke University Press.

Wang Ermin 王爾敏. 1981. "Duanfa yifu gaiyuan—bianfa lun zhi xiangzheng zhiqu" 斷髮易服改元—變法論之象徵旨趣 [Queue-cutting, costume change, and calendar reform: Symbolic indicators of reform]. In *Zhongguo jindaide weixin yundong—bianfa yu lixian taolunhui* 中國近代的維新運動—變法與立憲討論會 [The reform movement in modern China: A conference on reform and constitutionalism], edited by Academia Sinica, 59–73. Taipei: Institute of Modern History, Academia Sinica.

Wang Tao 王韜. (1887–89) 1985. *Manyou Suilu* 漫遊隨錄 [Jottings from my wanderings]. In *Manyou suilu, Huanyou diqiu xinlu, Xiyang zazhi, Ou you zalu* 漫遊隨錄, 環遊地球新錄, 西洋雜誌, 歐遊雜錄 [Jottings from my wanderings and other travel accounts], by Wang Tao, Li Gui 李圭, Li Shuchang 黎庶昌, and Xu Jianyin 徐建寅, 9–166. Changsha: Yuelu shushe.

Wong, Young-Tsu. 1992. "Revisionism Reconsidered: Kang Youwei and the Reform Movement of 1898." *Journal of Asian Studies* 51, no. 3: 513–44.

Xu, Subin. 2023. "Emergence of 'Architecture' in the Reform Years of Late Qing Dynasty." In *Routledge Handbook of Chinese Architecture: Social Production of Buildings and Spaces in History*, edited by Jianfei Zhu, Chen Wei, and Li Hua, 235–50. London: Routledge.

Yoshizawa Seiichiro 吉澤誠一郎. 1997. "Seimatsu senbenron no hito kōsatsu" 淸末剪辮論の一考察 [Study of the late-Qing discourse about cutting the queue]. *Tōyōshi kenkyu* 東洋史研究 [Oriental history studies] 56, no. 2: 307–41.

Zhang Deyi 張德彝. (1870) 1981. *Hanghai Shuqi* 航海述奇 [An account of exotic things from an ocean voyage]. Changsha: Hunan renmin chubanshe.

Zhou, Qi, and Ji Qiu. 2023. "Chinese Classical Revival: Nanjing, Capital of Republican China (1910s–1940s)." In *Routledge Handbook of Chinese Architecture: Social Production of Buildings and Spaces in History*, edited by Jianfei Zhu, Chen Wei, and Li Hua, 288–99. London: Routledge.

Zou Rong 鄒容. (1903) 1957. *Gemingjun* 革命軍 [Revolutionary army]. In *Xinhai Geming Ziliao Congkan* 辛亥革命資料叢刊 [Archives of the 1911 Revolution], 1:331–64. Shanghai: Shanghai renmin chubanshe.

JOSHUA C. HERR

Spectacle, Protocol, Charisma, and the Ming Legacy

Diplomatic Transition in the 1683 Qing Embassy to Lê Vietnam

ABSTRACT Through an examination of a Qing diplomatic mission to Lê Vietnam in 1683, this article proposes that Lê–Qing relations were an integral part of the seventeenth-century Qing consolidation and reflected a regional diplomatic culture. By considering aspects of the 1683 encounter, including public spectacle along the envoy route, debates over ritual protocol, imperial gifts of calligraphy and investiture seal, and articulations of tribute ideology, this article demonstrates how Qing diplomacy in Vietnam was consistent with the Kangxi consolidation. At the same time, these diplomatic interactions were arenas for Lê contestation of Qing hegemony on the basis of the Ming legacy. More broadly, this article argues for the significance of the Ming diplomatic legacy and the aspirations of former Ming tributary states for understanding the changing regional order of the seventeenth century.

KEYWORDS diplomatic culture, Qing, seventeenth-century transition, Southeast Asia, regional order

In 1683 the Qing court sent a diplomatic mission to the Lê court in northern Vietnam. Two years previously, in 1681, the Kangxi emperor had succeeded in putting down the Sanfan (Three Feudatories) Rebellion, arguably one of the greatest threats to Qing rule in China since its inception in 1644 (Spence 1990: 49–53). The diplomatic route between Beijing and Thăng Long (Hanoi), which had been severed during the rebellion's occupation of China's southwestern provinces, was open again, allowing for the first diplomatic mission to the Lê court since 1669. As suzerain in the tributary order inherited from the Ming, the Qing were expected to routinely send representatives to perform ceremonies of sacrifice and investiture at the Lê court. In fulfillment of this obligation, therefore, the 1683 mission was dispatched to invest the current Lê king with the title King of Annan and to sacrifice to the two Lê kings who had died successively during the hiatus in diplomatic relations (Sun 2006: 62–66, 73–76).

Despite its seemingly routine nature, the 1683 Qing embassy to the Lê court was a landmark event in the seventeenth-century transition in East Asia. For the Qing, this represented a reassertion of regional hegemony in the Southwest following the hiatus of the Sanfan Rebellion and a component in the multifaceted Kangxi consolidation of

THE JOURNAL OF ASIAN STUDIES · 84:2 · May 2025
DOI: 10.1215/00219118-11591159 © 2025 Association for Asian Studies

the 1680s (Spence 1990: 49–73). For the Lê, the embassy was an implicit confirmation of their status as sole rulers of northern Vietnam following diplomatic and military victories over their longtime rivals, the Mạc. Moreover, the embassy signaled the renewal and consolidation of the diplomatic relationship between the Qing and the Lê, which would become one of the cornerstones of regional diplomacy long into the eighteenth century (Sun 2006; Kim 2015; Ong 2015). This embassy and the Lê–Qing relationship thus represent a crucial component not only of the Ming-Qing transition but also of the broader regional transition of the seventeenth century.

In the emerging imperial orders of seventeenth-century East Asia, spectacle and public diplomacy were integral to strategies of rule. Kangxi's Southern Tours of 1684 and 1689, which included large-scale public processions, personal interactions with Jiangnan scholars and worthies, and demonstrations of calligraphy and other skills, are a familiar dimension of Kangxi's approach to the consolidation of rule over the heartland of the former Ming empire (Spence 1966: 124–65; Chang 2014). This article demonstrates that these advances toward the former Ming subjects of Jiangnan were paralleled in the 1683 embassy through the public spectacle of the envoy procession in the Lê realm, which included a virtual presence of the emperor in the form of the Dragon Pavilion, charismatic gifts of calligraphy, and promotion of an image of the Manchu ruler as culturally sophisticated and magnanimous. These public diplomacy dimensions of the 1683 embassy not only link it to the Qing consolidation but also suggest parallels with the public spectacle of diplomatic culture elsewhere in East Asia, as seen in what Ronald P. Toby (1986) has described as Tokugawa Japan's "carnivals of the aliens," where the shogunate encouraged and managed a public culture of spectacle around visiting embassies from abroad. Kathlene Baldanza (2016: 141–55, 189–95) has shown how sixteenth-century Ming officials orchestrated political theater around diplomatic reception of Vietnamese rulers and envoys within Ming territory. Here I argue that the Lê court participated in regional cultures of public diplomacy by actively managing the public spectacle of its reception of the Qing embassy for the purposes of demonstrating its legitimacy and power in front of their subjects and the envoys.

While the centrality of protocol, or ritual, in diplomatic interactions is in keeping with the diplomatic tradition in East Asia, the 1683 embassy illustrates the historic specificity of seventeenth-century diplomatic encounters. The Ming *Statutes* and, more broadly, the Ming legacy of regional order and diplomatic tradition stood at the center of discussions and practices of protocol in this embassy but often appear unnamed and contested. On the one hand, the Qing relied on the legal functioning of the Ming *Statutes* and the legitimacy of the Ming for its authority in its dealings with former Ming tributary states such as the Lê. But this claim to the Ming mantle was fraught and also conflicted with a separate Qing strategy of distinguishing itself from the Ming, by asserting Qing superiority to the Ming. On the other hand, while the Lê acknowledged Qing suzerainty and sought to align itself with the emerging hegemonic power in the region, it also sought to carve out a space of negotiation and autonomy through implicit appeals to the Ming *Statutes* and thus the former Ming international order, juxtaposing to Qing universal claims a practice of political relativism.

The 1683 embassy also challenges us to rethink arguments about the formation of global diplomatic cultures. Laura Hostetler and others have rightly drawn attention to the role the Jesuits and other European actors played in mediating between empires in the early modern period, pointing to technologies of cartography and ethnography that formed emerging imperial languages of negotiation in events such as the Treaty of Nerchinsk (Hostetler 2001; Perdue 2010). By paying attention to the historical specificity of the seventeenth century and the distinct actors involved in the 1683 embassy, we can see other ways in which global regions were being connected through distinct diplomatic expertise. For the ascendant Qing state, originating in Northeast Asia, Lê Vietnam represented an unfamiliar world, far to the southwest, an actor for which the Manchus needed intermediaries to deal with. Thus, in envoys such as Zhou Can, drawn from the classically literate former Ming elite, the Qing found another kind of intermediary, often overlooked by historians but just as vital for Qing imperial success and global integration as the better-known Jesuits.

At the same time, the Qing perspective of the 1683 envoy account should not blind us to the limitations of Qing imperial aspirations or the aspirations of the Lê court itself. Through close reading of the Qing envoy account, it is clear that the Lê court contested, implicitly and explicitly, some of the claims of Qing hegemony, including in its insistence on the Ming-associated diplomatic protocols governing rites and seals of investiture. The limited evidence from the Lê perspective also suggests that the Lê court saw the 1683 Qing visit as a diplomatic triumph and cultural achievement for themselves as they sought to establish a "domain of manifest civility" and their place in the regional order (Kelley 2005: 28–36).

CONTEXT, TEXTS, AND INTERPRETATION

The 1683 mission was not the first diplomatic contact between the two courts. In fact, the Lê had normalized tributary relations with the Ming since the 1590s and continued to be in diplomatic contact with the Southern Ming regimes through the 1650s. As the Manchus made gains in southern China against Ming loyalists in the 1660s, the Lê indicated their interest in establishing a diplomatic relationship with the Qing. This led to the first and second Qing embassies to the Lê court, in 1663 and 1667, to perform the tasks of sacrifice and investiture, respectively, for two successive Lê kings.

A special Qing mission in 1669 was occasioned by a dispute between the Lê court and their rivals, the Mạc, over territory. For over a century, the Lê had been in contention with the Mạc to legitimate rule in the Red River Valley. By the later seventeenth century, the Mạc had been driven by the Lê to the northern provinces bordering China, but they continued to hold out and threaten Lê rule. The rival courts had separately established diplomatic relations with the Qing by the 1660s, and as representatives of their suzerain, Qing envoys successfully negotiated a truce between the two courts. However, during the Sanfan Rebellion, the Mạc sided with the leaders of the rebellion, which ultimately cost them Qing diplomatic recognition and protection. This enabled the Lê to obliterate Mạc bases near the northern border and drive the remnants of the Mạc house into Qing territory (Sun 2006: 9–12; Ong 2015: 274–76).

The title of the account of the 1683 mission is *Shi Jiao ji shi* (*Account of the Embassy to Jiao*),[1] and authorship is attributed to the three surviving envoys on the mission, two Manchu bannermen, Wuhei and Mingtu, and the Han official Zhou

Can. (The embassy included a fourth envoy, the Han official Sun Zhuo, who died of illness in Guangxi near the Lê border after the grueling overland trip from Beijing.) The account was presented to the Qing throne following the embassy's return to Beijing. Technically, then, it is a report on the mission and authorship was collective. However, there are good grounds to associate the account primarily with Zhou Can, as the extant edition of the account was published with Zhou Can's collected writings, *Yuanxuetang ji* (preface dated 1685).

There is no comparable account of the 1683 Qing diplomatic mission from the Lê point of view, with the exception of a characteristically brief entry in the Lê court chronicle, the *Dai Viet Su Ky Toan Thu* (*DVSKTT*; see below). My discussion in this article thus relies heavily on the Qing embassy account. However, this unavoidable problem of asymmetry in the sources should not detract from the value of the Qing envoy account, given that it extends our knowledge of the event well beyond the terse and redacted renderings we get through the retrospective nature of court chronicles.

I have attempted to mitigate this asymmetry in two ways. First, I read the Qing envoy account against the grain using several types of sources. These include Samuel Baron's 1685 account of Tonkin and a variety of Ming and Qing sources. As a sometime employee of the Dutch and English East India Companies, Baron did not have a direct stake in the Qing embassy but was well informed of affairs in Tonkin, due to his familial ties (his mother was Vietnamese) and time spent in Lê Vietnam (Dror and Taylor 2006: 74–83). Regarding Ming and Qing sources, I use them to contextualize the 1683 embassy account, revealing the silences and subtexts of its narrative. Second, I have endeavored as much as possible to quote from Lê representatives in the account, in an attempt to listen to and relay the Lê voice in the reported dialogue.

With the above in mind, I quote the *DVSKTT*'s description of the 1683 Qing embassy as a reference point for the discussion that follows:

> In the ninth month, the Qing sent reader-in-waiting Mingtu and compiler Sun Zhuorong to invest the Emperor as King of Annan and to bestow a gift of Qing imperial calligraphy of the words, "preserving the country in loyalty and filial piety"; reader-in-waiting Wuhei and *langzhong* Zhou Can et al. made sacrifice to our two deceased emperors. Mingtu et al. performed the ceremonies at the capital and in addition separately made sacrifice to the deceased Trịnh Lord, Tiên Dương Vương. Upon passing through the border gate, Zhou Can composed and exchanged poetry with the receiving officials such as Hoàng Công Thất and Vũ Duy Khuông and created the *Nanjiao hao yin* collection, which was full of praise for the Southern Kingdom's worthies in the fields of philosophy, belles lettres, and statecraft. Upon his return, he submitted the poetry collection to the Qing emperor. (Chen C. 1984–86, 3:1013)

This brief entry highlights several aspects of the mission from the Lê point of view: a gift of imperial calligraphy, sacrifice to the Trịnh lord, and Zhou Can's poetry exchange with Lê officials, which resulted in a collection presented to the Qing emperor. This establishes that, from the Lê point of view, the 1683 Qing embassy was a celebrated event, a success for the Lê court: honors beyond the routine were shown the Lê court, and the cultural reputation of Dai Viet was extended far beyond its borders. On this buoyant note, I turn to the element of spectacle in the public diplomacy of the 1683 embassy.

PUBLIC SPECTACLE ON THE JOURNEY TO THE LÊ CAPITAL

The seventeenth century in East Asia saw the emergence of public spectacle as integral to imperial cultures of rule. In constructing an early modern Japanese world order, the Tokugawa shoguns cultivated relations with Choson, Ryukyu, and the Dutch East India Company (Vereenigde Oostindische Compagnie), as well as a culture of spectacle surrounding diplomatic processions to Edo. The shogunate carefully managed these visits to show off the country to visitors and to impress its Japanese subjects, but the events also saw widespread spectatorship, participation, and emulation in popular Japanese culture (Toby 1986; 2019: 142–89). Likewise, beginning in the 1680s, the Qing developed a practice of imperial visits to Jiangnan, the Southern Tours, where the Manchu emperors Kangxi and Qianlong participated in carefully orchestrated public appearances and personal interactions with the Han populace of the economic and cultural center of the former Ming empire (Chang 2007).

As I demonstrate below, the 1683 embassy reflected these cultures of spectacle. Lê reception of the Qing embassy was not restricted to the exclusive space of the court. Rather, the public space of procession, involving the gazes of Qing envoys and Lê subjects, was carefully orchestrated as part of the public diplomacy of the 1683 encounter. In this way, the bilateral interactions of the embassy participated in a regional culture of spectacle and diplomatic culture.

It is especially helpful to think about the 1683 Qing embassy as public spectacle in comparison with what Toby (2019: 143) has called the "parade diplomacy" of the Tokugawa shogunate. Foreign relations were a crucial arena in which the new regime of the Tokugawa shogunate established its domestic legitimacy and authority (Toby [1984] 1991: 53–109). Visits from foreign embassies likewise served as propaganda for the shogunate in demonstrating its authority to its Japanese subjects. Toby describes these embassies as "parades" in the sense that they involved not only a procession of foreign dignitaries to the shogun's headquarters but also crowds of curious spectators along the way. The scale of these parades could be great; for example, in 1682, for a Korean embassy that numbered 363 in its full complement, there was a Japanese convoy of approximately 50 samurai, 1,850 additional fighting men, and a large group of porters (Toby 2019: 158). As the embassies made their way to Edo along the Tokugawa road system, spectators numbering in the thousands gathered to see these exotic visitors (142, 165). At the same time, these embassy processions were carefully prepared for and managed, to give the foreign embassies a view of a country well governed and prosperous (143–44).

Qing emperors were no stranger to the use of spectacle either. In 1684 Kangxi went on the first of several Southern Tours, to the prosperous and cultured region of Jiangnan, in part as a means to cultivate the loyalty and goodwill of the Han literati and populace. On this promotional tour, the Kangxi emperor visited cities in the region, made public appearances, interacted with literati, and wrote calligraphy and poetry (Spence 1966: 124–65; Chang 2014). Examples of public spectacle included the emperor entering the city of Suzhou on horseback amid throngs of local spectators, who burned incense in veneration (Chang 2014: 213).

Like the Tokugawa shogunate and the Qing, the Lê also faced issues of legitimacy and authority in the seventeenth century. In addition to a civil war with the Mạc over rightful royal rule over the Red River Valley, the Lê also had the complication of half a century of warfare pitting the two families of the Trịnh and the Nguyễn in Cochinchina, not to mention continuing internal challenges of poor harvests, governance problems, and rivalry between civil officials and military men in government (Nguyễn 1994: 367–80; Taylor 2013: 339–43). For these reasons, the legitimating effect of the spectacle of welcoming an embassy from China would have appealed to the Lê court, both in the eyes of their Qing counterparts and in the eyes of their subjects.

The 1683 Qing mission to the Lê court is a prime example of the regional diplomatic culture of public spectacle. Following a long overland journey from Beijing, the embassy crossed into Lê territory on the twenty-eighth day of the ninth month of the twenty-second year of the Kangxi reign (November 16, 1683). Following standard procedure, the envoys met with Qing local officials at the border gate. The gate was opened to allow Lê officials waiting on the other side to enter the gate area, where they paid their respects to the Dragon Pavilion (*longting*; Zhou 1996: 263–64). A vital part of the public spectacle of the Qing diplomatic procession, the Dragon Pavilion was a canopied carriage that represented the emperor's presence and was used to transport imperial edicts.[2]

In addition to civil officials, the Qing diplomatic party was accompanied by a Lê military escort, consisting of twelve elephants and three thousand soldiers, and began the journey to the Lê capital (Zhou 1996: 5a, 264). The envoys record in their account that they were pleasantly impressed by the elephants and soldiers; in his account on Tonkin, Samuel Baron remarked that that Lê reception during this embassy visit was intentionally ostentatious (Dror and Taylor 2006: 239). At the same time, both parties attempted to manage the public and communication dimensions of the procession. At Lạng Sơn, a settlement near the border, the Qing envoys instructed one of the Lê officials to send advance notice of the embassy so as not to frighten the residents along the route (Zhou 1996: 5a–6b, 264–65). Later in the journey, Lê officials issued warnings to be posted in advance along the route, warning the porters in the convoy and residents along the route against communicating with each other and causing trouble (6b–7b, 265). This recalls similar precautions by the Tokugawa shogunate in dealing with interactions between embassies and the crowds of onlookers: a 1613 English embassy reported being mistook for Koreans and being taunted and harassed as such; in 1682, the shogunate issued orders against this kind of harassment (Toby 1986: 424–25; 2019: 174–78).

On the journey through Lê territory, the envoys also made a point of paying their respects to famous landmarks. The envoys made a sacrifice to the spirit of Ma Yuan at his shrine near a place called the Ghost Door Gate. Ma Yuan was a Han dynasty (206 BCE to 220 CE) general responsible for suppressing a rebellion in Jiao (northern Vietnam) and commonly associated with the border between the realms. At first glance, this gesture of the envoys might seem like a form of symbolic domination. However, as Liam C. Kelley's (2005: 98–107, 192–97) study of Vietnamese envoy poetry suggests, this practice is better understood as part of a Confucian or Sinic culture shared by both Vietnamese and Chinese literati. In fact, as Kelley has documented, Vietnamese envoys also paid homage at this shrine.

The envoys also noted in their account the response of local people to their procession. At a place called Trà Sơn, where the rocky and forested uplands ended, the envoys were treated to a view of lowland paddies spreading ahead of them. From this point on, the envoys passed through villages and towns where they were greeted by cheering crowds of onlookers (Zhou 1996: 8a, 266).

While it is easy to imagine diplomatic encounters between the Qing and Lê in the seventeenth century as affairs of state staged in the exclusive space of the respective courts, the examples above on the envoy route reveal the role of public spectacle in these encounters. The visible symbol of the mobile Qing imperial presence in the form of the Dragon Pavilion, the large entourage of Lê soldiers and elephants, and the crowds of Lê subjects that greeted the procession all point to this event as spectacle and highlight the variety of audiences. While some of the cultural specifics of the journey along the envoy route reflect a transnational Confucian heritage, as Kelley has argued, it also resonates with examples of diplomatic spectacle elsewhere in East Asia, such as how envoy visits from Choson, the Dutch East India Company, and Ryukyu became public events in Edo Japan. At the same time, as Brian Vick (2019) has argued regarding the public and secret aspects of the Congress of Vienna in post-Napoleonic Europe, the public diplomacy of this Lê–Qing encounter is better understood as a regulated and controlled form of publicity, as seen in instructions given by both the Qing and Lê representatives to attempt to direct and limit the interactions between the envoy procession and the Lê subjects along the route.

ARGUING OVER CEREMONY: *WUBAI* VERSUS *SANGUI* AND THE MING LEGACY

Having arrived at the Lê capital, the envoys began discussions with their Lê counterparts on arrangements for conducting the ceremonies of investiture and sacrifice. For several days, the Qing envoys and the Lê officials argued over whether the Qing rite of "three kneelings and nine kowtows" (*sangui jiukou*) or the Lê rite of "five prostrations and three kowtows" (*wubai sankou* or, commonly, just *wubai*) would be used. Eventually, the Lê court relented and the Qing envoys' demand that the *sangui jiukou* be used was respected.[3]

This episode is significant for what it says about Qing attempts to establish its authority as the rulers of China in this transitional moment in the seventeenth century. From the beginning of the Qing conquest of Ming China, the Manchus were working with multiple, sometimes conflicting strategies of authority and legitimacy. On the one hand, during the early Manchu state, in its competition with both the Ming and Choson, the Qing portrayed itself as an alternative Middle Kingdom, in distinction from the Ming (Y. Wang 2018: 21–49). On the other hand, following the 1644 invasion of Ming China, the Qing court also at times presented itself as the inheritor of the Ming mantle, including in its dealings with tributary states, as evidenced in 1647 by Qing edicts directed toward former Ming tributary states, welcoming them to continue the tributary relationship with the new rulers of China (Fu 1966: 5–6).

The debate over ritual in 1683 illustrates the landscape of diplomatic claims in the late seventeenth century and the lingering authority of Ming practice. As Evelyn Rawski (2012: 247–48) has argued, the relative success of the Qing in appropriating and shaping the Chinese tradition of the Mandate of Heaven did not preclude their Northeast Asian neighbors (Choson and Tokugawa) from doing the same and resisting claims by the Qing. Returning to the 1683 embassy, what is left silent in the Qing envoy account is the identification of the Lê rite, the *wubai*, as not only a Lê rite but also the international norm of the Ming diplomatic order. While the Qing sought to establish the universality of their new imperial order, the Lê countered with a strategy of political relativism and pragmatism that implicitly drew on the authority of existing international norms inherited from the Ming.

A few points can be made about the rites of the Ming, the Qing, and the Lê. The rite of *wubai sankou* was originally used as an expression of loyalty and submission to the Ming emperor. Certainly, this rite can be found in the Ming *Statutes*, for example, in the rites used during the bestowal of imperial edicts and seals, and more generally in the literature of the Ming era, such as in the novel *Journey to the West* (Wu 1978: 220; Shen 1989: 362).

At some point the Lê adopted the *wubai sankou* rite for use in their court ceremony. The rite appears ubiquitously in an undated manuscript held by the Institute of Han Nom Studies in Hanoi, which purports to be a copy of the Lê *Statutes* (*Lê triều hội điển*, n.d.). The rite as described here was performed by Lê officials in relation to the Lê king. The seventeenth-century observer Samuel Baron mentions a rite used in relation to the funeral of the Trịnh lord involving five prostrations, which may be a reference to the *wubai sankou* (Dror and Taylor 2006: 270). The *wubai* had become a rite for signifying the greatest honor and reserved for acknowledging the status of the dyarchy of the Lê king and the Trịnh lord, not simply in relation to the Ming court.

Curiously, the Qing envoys of the 1683 mission do not make the connection between the Lê rites and Ming practice in the envoy account. In fact, the Lê *wubai* appeared exotic enough to the envoys to warrant a detailed description of the rite, as it was performed by the Lê king and his officials to pay respect to the deceased Lê kings (Zhou 1996: 18b, 271). Despite the silence in the envoy account, it is unlikely that the Qing envoys would not have recognized the similarity between the Ming and Lê rites. Zhou Can in particular, having been recruited from the gentry families of the former Ming and only one generation from the Manchu conquest, would have existed in a milieu where the ritual forms of the Ming were intimately known. Furthermore, a comparison of the envoy account's description of the ceremonies with the sixteenth-century Ming *Statutes* suggests that the protocol followed in 1683 was based on the Ming *Statutes* (Shen 1989: 362).

The *sangui jiukou*, well known as the "kowtow" (e.g., Hevia 1995), was the Qing rite used in relation to the Qing emperor; its origins are obscure but predate Qing conquest of the Ming.[4] The Manchus did not adopt the Ming *wubai sankou* upon their conquest of China but retained the *sangui jiukou* as the rite used to express loyalty and submission to the Qing emperor. The *sangui jiukou* was likewise demanded of rulers of tributary states such as Choson, Ryukyu, and Annan in their dealings with the Qing. In the Ryukyu case, it seems that the transition from the *wubai sankou* to the *sangui jiukou* was smooth and uneventful, with the Ryukyuans accepting the new rite without dispute. In 1533, the Ming envoy Chen Kan (1995: 180) recorded that the Ryukyuans performed the *wubai sankou* rite during the investiture of their king. By the 1660s and 1680s, during the first two Qing embassies to Ryukyu, the Ryukyuans were performing the *sangui jiukou* without dispute (Wang J. 1997: 336; Zhang 1998: 96). The Lê, however, were less sanguine about this ritual transition.

The 1683 Qing embassy featured a protracted exchange on this issue over five days that revolved around political relativism and the universality of Qing suzerainty. Here we see an attempt, on the part of the Lê, to argue for the use of the *wubai sankou* rite on pragmatic grounds. Lê officials came to see the Qing envoys the day after they arrived at the official embassy hostel on the outskirts of the Lê capital.[5] They submitted two protocols (*yizhu*) for the investiture and sacrifice ceremonies, respectively, and two memorandums, in which the Lê king said the Lê court was not familiar with the Qing rites and requested that the ceremonies be conducted in accordance with the Lê rites. The Qing envoys asserted that Qing rites were followed within the empire and abroad (*hai nei wai*). As the Lê had requested investiture and sacrifice from the Qing, they should follow Qing rites (Zhou 1996: 9a–b, 266).

On the following day, the Lê officials returned with another memorandum from the Lê king, wherein the Lê buttressed their pragmatic argument by a reference to the Confucian classic *Record of Rites* (*Liji*), and by framing the pragmatic argument in terms of not wanting to create an offense against Qing state dignity. The Lê king wrote,

> The Sages "did not change custom but followed custom."[6] The investiture of the current king and sacrifice to two preceding kings are major ceremonies that rarely occur. . . . I fear that if the rites of the Celestial Court are used, the participants will not be able to perform the ceremonies uniformly and may thus cast disrespect on state dignity, which would be a serious offense.

The Qing envoys replied that the Lê officials had themselves performed the Qing rites at the Qing court when they had previously served as tribute envoys and that other Lê officials along the envoy route from the border to capital had also performed the ceremony adequately (Zhou 1996: 9b–10b, 266–67).

The debate finally came to a close on the fourteenth of the tenth month, when two eunuchs and a fresh set of Lê officials were sent to see the envoys. One of the eunuchs apologized for any offense given in the previous discussions and assured the Qing envoys of the Lê's commitment to perform the Qing rites, warning, however, that the Lê court would "rehearse the rites but at short notice like this, it will be hard to avoid some minor mistakes." In reply, the envoys assured the Lê representative that repeating the rites correctly would be sufficient to rectify any mistakes made during the ceremonies and that "we will rely on the Emperor's benevolence and be tolerant of each other's faults" (Zhou 1996: 10b–13a, 267–68).

While this episode, as narrated by the envoys, indicates a diplomatic victory of the Qing over the Lê, it is more helpful as a sketch of the landscape of diplomatic dispute in this intercourt relationship. Given the centrality of the *wubai* for both the Ming and the Lê, clearly in this instance the Lê were insisting on an existing international norm, whereas the Qing were insisting on a new one that signified the acceptance of their hegemony. The silence of the Qing envoys on the Ming connection of the rite suggests a delicacy or sensitivity over the basis for Qing legitimacy in the former Ming tributary relations, namely, the Qing inheritance of Ming institutions. The Lê framing of the debate in pragmatic terms and the Qing framing in terms of benevolence and toleration also suggest that this diplomatic relationship involved contestation over the relativistic claims of the Lê court versus the universalistic claims of the Qing. The Qing image of benevolence and toleration would appear again when issues of tribute came up later in the embassy.

IMPERIAL CALLIGRAPHY: PUBLIC DIPLOMACY AND QING CONSOLIDATION

Although the Qing emissaries arrived at the Lê capital on the ninth day of the tenth month, the investiture and sacrifice ceremonies that were the raison d'être of the 1683 mission did not take place until the fifteenth and sixteenth days, respectively, due to the debates just discussed. With the arrangements in place, however, the ceremonies proceeded smoothly.

Despite the rigid, structured nature of the investiture and sacrifice ceremonies, Qing embassies were also occasions for Qing emperors to cultivate ruler-to-ruler relations with the Lê king. The 1683 embassy was undoubtedly a special occasion, coming upon peace and the restoration of tributary relations between the two courts. In a special gift for the Lê king and in the descriptions by the Qing ambassadors of their sovereign, we can see an attempt by the Qing emperor to establish a ruler-to-ruler relationship of a personal nature. As discussed below, gifts of imperial calligraphy in the early 1680s were becoming an integral part of Kangxi's political practice, and the 1683 embassy was an early example that took place in the diplomatic arena, linking such public diplomacy with broader imperial politics. The 1683 embassy was thus part of the larger pattern of Kangxi's consolidation of Qing imperial rule in the 1680s.

The Kangxi emperor was a prolific calligrapher, and his output has attracted the attention of art historians. In writing about Kangxi's practice of calligraphy and imperial authority, Jonathan Hay (2005) argues that Kangxi's approach was a radical departure. Whereas previous Chinese emperors wrote and gifted calligraphy within a very small circle, Kangxi was noteworthy for his large output and wide distribution of calligraphy to literati, officials, and institutions. Many of these calligraphies were displayed by the recipients in their homes or public places, and there developed a fetishistic appreciation of the calligraphy by these recipients. In some instances, recipients expressed the sentiment that in seeing the calligraphy, it was as if they were seeing the emperor's face. Hay argues that Kangxi used calligraphy as "an art of political authority" through the visibility and publicness of the calligraphy, on the one hand, and the nature of the gift as a way to subject the receiver to imperial authority on the other.

I argue that Kangxi's gift of calligraphy to the Lê monarch during the 1683 embassy was an early instance of Kangxi's emerging practice of calligraphy and imperial authority during the 1678–84 period (Hay 2005: 317). On the fifteenth, the Qing envoys, the Lê king Lê Duy Chân, and the Lê court together successfully performed the rituals of the investiture ceremony and Lê Duy Chân received an edict of investiture and a seal of office. In addition, the Qing envoys presented a special gift from the Qing emperor, a piece of calligraphy of the phrase, "Preserving the country in loyalty and filial piety" (*zhong xiao shou bang*), written in the emperor's own hand. The envoy account describes a scene of surprise and rejoicing, in which Lê Duy Chân and the Lê officials were ecstatic over the gift. One of the translators reported the words of the king to the envoys, "The new King says, 'The imperial calligraphy has spirit and style [*hữu thần hữu pháp*]. Looking at it, it is as if I am beholding the Celestial Visage. This shall be a hereditary state treasure of Annan, to be passed on to ten thousand generations.' This is why he is reluctant to put it down" (Zhou 1996: 13b–14a, 268–69). The following day, the sixteenth, was the day of the sacrifice ceremony and the Qing envoys, Lê Duy Chân, and the Lê court likewise completed the appropriate rituals satisfactorily (Zhou 1996: 18b–19a, 271).

The significance of the calligraphic gift, in the eyes of the Qing envoys, can be seen in the exchange between the Qing envoys and Lê officials the day after the sacrifice ceremony, when Lê officials remarked on the unprecedented and celebrated nature of the gift of imperial calligraphy. The Qing envoys responded:

> Our emperor, when he is not minding the myriad affairs of the world, never ceases to have a book in his hand. He is able to commit to memory anything he lays his eyes on. There is no book, ancient or modern, that he does not peruse; there is no affair under Heaven that he does not comprehend in its fullness. This gift of imperial calligraphy is but a fraction of his erudition. In truth, no emperor or king from antiquity to the present can equal the Sagacious learning of our Emperor. (Zhou 1996: 20a–b, 272)

As the envoy account attests throughout, Qing and Lê representatives were jointly concerned with fulfilling authoritative guidelines for the symbolic orchestration of diplomatic relations. But we should also note that, as seen in the gift of imperial calligraphy, there was a Qing strategy of crafting suzerain-vassal relations through the personal charisma of Kangxi.

Consistent with Qing and previous Ming practice, Kangxi did not personally visit the court of the Lê. But he did visit there by proxy, through his envoys, the Dragon Pavilion, his edicts, and his calligraphy. And, just as the southern tours were an opportunity to impress and acquire the allegiance of the Jiangnan literati through the Manchu emperor's mastery of Chinese arts, the 1683 embassy functioned in part as a promotional campaign for Kangxi and Qing rule in the context of the regional Sinic culture that Lê Vietnam participated in. In fact, Lê Duy Chân's response to the imperial gift, as portrayed in the envoy account, resembles closely the fetishistic response of Qing subjects to Kangxi's calligraphy that Hay documents.

PROMOTING SUZERAINTY AND TRIBUTE

Following the ceremonies, there were a couple of exchanges between the Lê king, Lê officials, and the Qing envoys that illustrate an early Qing ideology of tribute. On the surface these statements appear generic, but when read in the light of other Qing sources, they reveal a conscious attempt to position the Qing in relation to the Ming legacy.

Incidents in the 1660s already reveal that the Qing were in the process of crafting a distinct ideology of tribute in intentional contrast with the Ming. In response to Lê assistance to the Qing, the Qing Ministry of Rites proposed in 1661 to reward the Lê king "according to precedent" (*zhao li*). The Shunzhi emperor was not satisfied with the gifts proposed, chiding the ministry for "making proposals based on the condescending rites [*beishi waiguo zhi li*] of the former Ming" (Yunnan sheng Lishi yanjiusuo 1985, 1:4). Several years later, the Ministry of Rites complained that

Annan's tribute gifts did not accord with the regulations in the (Ming) *Statutes* and requested that the kingdom be ordered to comply in the future. Kangxi responded, "Foreign countries bring tribute because they desire to participate in civilization. Their tribute gifts should simply be accepted. It is not necessary to follow the regulations in the *Statutes*" (1:6). Thus, the early Qing ideology of tribute was more than generic magnanimity. It was a statement that the Qing emperors were capable of filling the suzerain role of the Ming emperors and were superior to them.

This view of the early Qing ideology of tribute allows us to identify the unspoken subtext—comparisons with the Ming—in the exchanges over tribute between the Qing envoys and the Lê king and his representatives. On the sixteenth, following the completion of the ceremony of sacrifice, the Lê king brought up an issue of tributary gifts for the Qing court. According to the envoy account, Lê Duy Chân mentioned with chagrin and gratitude that the Lê's most recent tributary gifts to the Qing court did not meet regulation standards but that the Qing emperor deigned to receive them nonetheless (Zhou 1996: 18b–19a, 271). The envoys reassured the Lê king that the Qing court looked benevolently on the Lê and that he needed only to strive to be more careful to meet regulation standards for tributary gifts in the future (Zhou 1996: 18b–19a, 271).

Central to the early Qing ideology of tribute was the notion of the magnanimity of the Qing emperor. On the seventeenth, the day after the sacrifice ceremony, the envoys received a visit from Lê officials, who again brought up the issue of tribute, remarking on the magnanimity of the Qing emperor and the gratitude of the Lê. In their response, the envoys outlined an early Qing ideology of tribute that involved three elements. First, the Qing emperor did not seek tribute: "China is self-sufficient in all goods. The Emperor has no interest in exotic goods. He only desires that all who draw breath obey the Kingly Law [*wang zhang*), that all who abide under his dispensation content themselves in this peaceful and prosperous age." Rather, it was on the initiative of kingdoms seeking a relationship with him that tribute was presented: "The sending of tribute was not originally demanded by the Celestial Court. It came about as an expression of the sincerity of foreign countries." Second, as a symbolic expression of a tributary ruler's sincerity in seeking a relationship with the Qing emperor, it was necessary for tribute to conform to detailed regulations: "As an expression of sincerity, tribute must conform to regulation standards." Third, the charismatic emperor had the power and magnanimity to waive the regulations as a gesture of favor and goodwill to the tributary state: "In your case, some of your tribute was accepted, some was not. In what was accepted, the Emperor sees your sincerity. In declining a portion of your tribute, he sympathized with the straits you were in. The Emperor is the lord of vassals and subjects of ten thousand domains, yet he deigns to empathize with your country to such an extent." The juxtaposition of the second and third elements was key in that it allowed the envoys to contrast the routine, bureaucratic severity of the Qing Ministry of Rites with the charismatic magnanimity of the Qing emperor: "The offices of the Ministry of Rites scrutinize tribute goods very strictly; you cannot be careless in the least" (Zhou 1996: 20a–b, 272). As my discussion on the seal below indicates, the Lê court could be equally adept at playing the bureaucratic card.

The notions of tribute outlined by the Qing envoys bear a striking similarity to the spirit of Qianlong's famous letter to George III of England in conjunction with the Macartney embassy of 1793 (Hevia 1995: 188). The circumstances of the

Macartney embassy were quite different, but the 1683 embassy suggests that the ideology of the magnanimous Qing emperor had been established early in the Qing assumption of the Ming tributary portfolio. This trope of China's self-sufficiency goes back to the Han dynasty (Yu 1967). This is not to say, however, that the Qing adopted this posture as a matter of course; rather, as evidenced by the 1683 envoy account, it was worked out in the course of diplomatic encounters as the Qing developed relationships with the Ming's former tributary states. In particular, the emerging Qing tribute ideology was an implicit but intentional statement that made claims to the Ming mantle of universal rule and, at the same time, distinguished the Qing as superior to the Ming.

THE SEAL OF INVESTITURE AND BUREAUCRATIC CHANNELS OF REDRESS

Seals were, of course, tokens of office used throughout imperial China's bureaucracy, the Sinic world, and beyond. From the lowliest county magistrate to the most powerful court officials and the emperor himself, all offices in the Chinese empire signified their authority and executive power through the use of unique and carefully guarded seals (Lai 1976: 19–21; McNicholas 2016: 95–96). Similarly, the authority the Chinese emperor delegated to his vassal was signified in a seal. While the approval of the Chinese court was seldom sufficient for either creating or maintaining an otherwise unpopular tributary ruler, the Chinese seal often became an element in the symbols of authority in the courts of tributary states.[7]

One of the tasks of the Qing envoys was to bestow a new seal of office on the invested Lê king and to retrieve the seal previously given to the deceased Lê king. As it turned out, while the Qing envoys understood the seals through the lens of routine, delegated authority, the Lê court attached other meanings and uses to the seals bestowed by the Qing. Moreover, relying on knowledge of existing practice in the Ming *Statutes* and bureaucratic channels of recourse, the Lê court contested and negotiated Qing demands, illustrating the continuing authority of the Ming legacy in the seventeenth-century diplomatic transition in East Asia.

The Qing envoys had asked for the return of the old seal during the investiture ceremony, when the new seal was bestowed on Lê Duy Chân, only to have the Lê king demur and postpone the issue (Zhou 1996: 15b, 269). Later, on the twenty-second, the envoys again inquired after the seal. Lê officials told the envoys that returning the old seal would bring "posthumous ignominy" on the former Lê king and explained that the old seal was considered by the royal family as a "family heirloom to be held in perpetuity," placed in veneration in front of the deceased king's ancestral tablet, and therefore an item the Lê royal family was loath to part with. Attempting to sway the Lê officials, the Qing envoys argued that the new seal was proof enough of the Lê king's invested authority, that the singularity of the seal symbolized the exclusivity of Lê devotion to the Qing, and that the future granting of new seals for each generation of Lê kings precluded any need to hold on to the old seal (Zhou 1996: 22a–23a, 273).

The Qing envoys initially thought they had won over the Lê court on this point, but on the twenty-fourth the envoys received a memorandum from the Lê king regarding the seal, which read:

The preceding king of this country served the Celestial Court in exclusive loyalty and devotion. This is known to the Emperor. It is now demanded that the seal be returned. May it not be that what is given in life is taken away after death. Upon inquiry into the old *Statutes* [*jiu dian*], no regulation could be found that stipulated the return of the old seal upon the bestowal of a new one. It is hoped that the return of the seal be stopped in order to demonstrate the Court's favor and trust.

An accompanying document further elaborated: "A seal is proof during a vassal's lifetime of the responsibility entrusted to him to preserve his border-fief; after death, it becomes a family heirloom to be passed on to future generations in perpetuity. Regarding the old seal, a memorial will be submitted to request an edict on this matter." Ultimately, the Qing envoys left the Lê realm with only a petition from the Lê court on the matter and without the seal itself (Zhou 1996: 24a–25a, 274).

What specific precedents did the Lê court have in mind? The first Qing *Statutes* was the Kangxi *huidian*, a project begun in 1684 and not completed and printed until the 1690s (Wilkinson 2000: 946). At the time of the 1683 embassy, then, the Qing court had not yet produced a version of the *Statutes* and still relied on the Ming *Statutes* in reference to Ming institutions. In fact, the Ming *Statutes* provides for the retention by tributary states of tokens of office bestowed on them. In the sections on protocol for issuing an edict and for issuing seals and other tokens of office in the last edition of the Ming *Statutes*, namely, the Wanli edition, there is an emendation dated to the Zhengde reign (1506–1521) that stipulates: "When envoys go to countries such as Annan to deliver an edict, if the king requests to retain the edict as a state treasure, the envoys shall grant this request" (Shen 1989: 362). Although the emendation does not specifically cover seals, it suggests that there was a precedent—incidentally referencing Annan by name—allowing foreign rulers to retain tokens of office bestowed on them by the Ming.

In this exchange, we see that the Lê position drew on the authority of precedent, specifically existing regulations in the Ming *Statutes*. The idea of keeping a seal as a family heirloom, which at first sight may seem an ad hoc rationalization on the part of the Lê, turns out to have had a long pedigree. Whether as an expression of magnanimity in the Qing ideology of tribute discussed above or as a reflection of the envoys' caution in proceeding on what they realized might be slippery bureaucratic grounds, the Qing envoys ultimately consented to allow the Lê to defer the matter of the seal to the higher authority of the Qing Ministry of Rites. This suggests that, although the Qing held the diplomatic upper hand in hierarchical tributary relations, there were bureaucratic channels of redress that tributary states such as the Lê could deploy, with the support of sources of authority such as the *Statutes*.

CONCLUSION: THE SIGNIFICANCE OF LÊ–QING RELATIONS IN THE SEVENTEENTH-CENTURY TRANSITION

The 1683 Qing embassy to the Lê court offers a window on the regional seventeenth-century transition in East Asia. Despite its routine nature and the scant attention historians have paid it so far, this diplomatic mission reveals new ways in which Lê–Qing diplomatic relations participated in broader regional patterns of change in the seventeenth century. Responding to calls for transnational and global approaches to Vietnamese history, this article has situated the bilateral interactions of the Lê and Qing courts in regional cultures of public diplomacy, emerging imperial orders, and the aspirations of Vietnamese states beyond their borders (Tran and Reid 2006; Hoàng 2011: 247–82).

Through aspects of the 1683 embassy, including the procession to the Lê capital, I have shown how Lê–Qing diplomacy reflected these patterns of public diplomacy in the seventeenth century. Comparison with embassies hosted by the Tokugawa shogunate and the southern tours of the Qing emperors has revealed similar dimensions of spectacle and management in the Lê reception of the Qing mission. Examination of other aspects of the embassy, including a gift of calligraphy and discussions over tribute gifts, has shown that Qing efforts in the diplomatic arena were closely tied to early Qing strategies of imperial consolidation. These strategies included Kangxi's charismatic politics of emperorship and Qing attempts to tack between a dual approach of distinguishing from and identifying with the Ming imperial legacy.

As the Lê and the Qing navigated diplomatic protocol for the investiture and sacrifice ceremonies of the 1683 embassy, their varied stances toward the Ming imperial legacy became the crux of claim making, debates, and contestation. Through close readings of the Qing embassy account, I have shown how the Lê court contested Qing claims regarding the specific rites used in the ceremonies, as well as the status of an imperially bestowed seal, by drawing on Ming diplomatic norms as codified in the Ming *Statutes*. By reading for the agency of Dai Viet actors within the Qing perspective of the account, I have shed light on the Lê court's active role in shaping the diplomatic encounter and its ongoing search for domestic legitimacy and a place in the emerging regional order.

Despite the transitional and tumultuous nature of the decades the led up to the 1683 embassy, this diplomatic event also marks the beginning of roughly a century of state expansion in the Lê–Qing borderlands and close diplomatic collaboration between the two courts. While the Qing story of the southwestern frontier may be more familiar to some readers, other states in the region, such as the Lê, were also active and pursued their own agendas (e.g., Giersch 2006). This emerging vista can be seen in a further *DVSKTT* entry, dated roughly to the beginning of 1684, just months or even weeks after the Qing embassy, which records that native officials (*tusi*) from the Qing side of the border sent emissaries to congratulate the Lê on their triumph over their rivals, the Mạc, with gifts and the words, "Wherever the royal armies reach, homage arrives from the four corners; now that the Mạc villains have been vanquished, chariot tracks and writing have been unified" (Chen C. 1984–86, 3:1013); the last phrase is a quotation from the classic text the "Doctrine of the Mean" ("Zhongyong") chapter from the *Book of Rites* (*Liji*), traditionally an allusion to imperial unification.

This brief but tantalizing entry in the Lê court chronicles suggests that regardless of the strength of the Qing position and the success of the 1683 embassy, the Lê were nonetheless engaged in their own imperial projects in their sphere of influence in the Qing-Lê borderlands. And, despite the sense of finality of this diplomatic settlement and the persistence of Qing and Lê rule into the eighteenth century, this vignette points to the ongoing evolution and tension in the diplomatic relationship that would shape this part of the region.

JOSHUA C. HERR is assistant professor of history and Asian studies at DePauw University. His current book project is *The Transformation of Ming Imperial Legacy: Border, Diplomacy, and Society in Chinese-Vietnamese Relations, ca. 1550–1800.*

ACKNOWLEDGMENTS

I am grateful for the support and feedback I received from Nahyan Fancy, Elizabeth Hines, Christopher Nygren, Abigail Upshaw, and David Gellman in reading and commenting on the manuscript at various stages of its evolution. I am also thankful for the many helpful comments from the two anonymous readers for the *Journal of Asian Studies*, which challenged and encouraged me to refine my arguments and articulate them in a stronger and clearer way.

NOTES

1. *Jiao* was an ancient Chinese name for northern Vietnam.

2. This symbol of imperial presence was not unique to embassies; it was used in all cases where an imperial edict was delivered to an official or vassal of the emperor, within or without the territory of the Qing empire. For an example of a discussion of bureaucratic norms around receiving imperial edicts within Qing territory that mentions the Dragon Pavilion, see Huang Liuhong's late seventeenth-century magistrate's manual *Fuhui quanshu* (Huang 1984: 517).

3. Sun Hongnian (2006: 108) is mistaken when he writes that Qing envoys permitted the Lê court to use the *wubai* to receive the edicts of sacrifice and investiture during the 1683 embassy.

4. The rite appears in the pre-Ming conquest Qing *Veritable Records*, often referred to as a rite for the veneration of Heaven; see *Manzhou shilu* n.d. (e.g., j8, Tianming 11.6.6, for sealing an alliance). See also Yuanchong Wang's (2018: 37–39) discussion of Hong Taiji's declaration of the founding of the Qing imperial dynasty and the reaction to this among Choson envoys present at the ceremony. Possibly the rite existed among the Jurchen tribes prior to Nurhaci's state-building efforts at the beginning of the seventeenth century.

5. The tenth day of the tenth month of the twenty-second year of the Kangxi reign (November 27, 1683)

6. The reference is to the statement in the second part of the "Quli" chapter in the *Record of Rites* (*Liji*): "In performing the rites, the noble person does not seek to change customs" (*junzi xing li bu qiu bian su*)

7. For discussion of Chinese investiture seals in the case of the Ryukyu kingdom, see Akamine 2017: 127–29.

REFERENCES

Akamine, Mamoru. 2017. *The Ryukyu Kingdom: Cornerstone of East Asia.* Edited by Robert N. Huey. Translated by Lina Terrell. Honolulu: University of Hawai'i Press.

Baldanza, Kathlene. 2016. *Ming China and Vietnam: Negotiating Borders in Early Modern Asia.* Cambridge: Cambridge University Press.

Chang, Michael G. 2007. *A Court on Horseback: Imperial Touring and the Construction of Qing Rule, 1680–1785.* Cambridge, MA: Harvard University Asia Center.

Chang, Michael G. 2014. "Historical Narratives of the Kangxi Emperor's Inaugural Visit to Suzhou, 1684." In *The Dynastic Centre and the Provinces: Agents and Interactions*, edited by Jeroen Duindam and Sabine Dabringhaus, 203–24. Leiden: Brill.

Chen Chingho 陳荊和, ed. 1984–86. *Daietsu Shiki Zensho/Dai Viet Su Ky Toan Thu* 大越史記全書 [Complete historical records of Dai Viet]. 3 vols. Tōkyō: Tōkyō Daigaku Tōyō Bunka Kenkyūjo, Fuzoku Tōyōgaku Bunken Sentā.

Chen Kan 陳侃. 1995. *Shi Liuqiu lu* 使琉球錄 [Record of an embassy to Liuqiu]. Annotated by Harada Nobuo 原田禹雄. Ginowan-shi, Okinawa: Yōjusha.

Dror, Olga, and Keith Weller Taylor, eds. 2006. *Views of Seventeenth-Century Vietnam: Christoforo Borri on Cochinchina and Samuel Baron on Tonkin.* Ithaca, NY: Southeast Asia Program Publications, Cornell University.

Fu, Lo-shu. 1966. *A Documentary Chronicle of Sino-Western Relations (1644–1820).* Tucson: University of Arizona Press.

Giersch, C. Patterson. 2006. *Asian Borderlands: The Transformation of Qing China's Yunnan Frontier.* Cambridge, MA: Harvard University Press.

Hay, Jonathan. 2005. "The Kangxi Emperor's Brush-Traces." In *Body and Face in Chinese Visual Culture*, edited by Wu Hung and Katherine R. Tsiang, 311–34. Cambridge, MA: Harvard University Asia Center.

Hevia, James Louis. 1995. *Cherishing Men from Afar: Qing Guest Ritual and the Macartney Embassy of 1793.* Durham, NC: Duke University Press.

Hoàng Anh Tuấn. 2011. "'Quốc tế hóa lịch sử dân tộc'—Toàn cầu hóa cận đại sơ kỳ và lịch sử Việt Nam thế kỷ XVII" [Internationalizing national history: Early modern globalization and Vietnamese history in the seventeenth century]. In *Di Sản Lịch Sử và Những Hướng Tiếp Cận Mới* [Historical heritage and new approaches], edited by Lê Hồng Lý, Lê Thị Liên, and Nguyễn Thị Phương Châm, 247–82. Hanoi: Thế Giới.

Hostetler, Laura. 2001. *Qing Colonial Enterprise: Ethnography and Cartography in Early Modern China.* Chicago: University of Chicago.

Huang, Liuhong. 1984. *A Complete Book Concerning Happiness and Benevolence, "Fu-hui ch'uan-shu": A Manual for Local Magistrates in Seventeenth-Century China.* Translated by Chu Djang. Tucson: University of Arizona Press.

Kelley, Liam C. 2005. *Beyond the Bronze Pillars: Envoy Poetry and the Sino-Vietnamese Relationship.* Honolulu: University of Hawai'i Press.

Kim, Jaymin. 2015. "The Rule of Ritual: Crimes and Justice in Qing-Vietnamese Relations during the Qianlong Period (1736–1796)." In *China's Encounters on the South and Southwest: Reforging the Fiery Frontier over Two Millennia*, edited by James A. Anderson and John K. Whitmore, 288–323. Leiden: Brill.

Lai, T. C. 1976. *Chinese Seals.* Seattle: University of Washington Press.

Lê triều hội điển 黎朝會典 [Statutes of the Lê Dynasty]. n.d. Institute of Han Nom Studies, A.52.

Manzhou shilu 滿洲實錄 [Manzhou veritable records]. n.d. Scripta Sinica. https://hanchi.ihp .sinica.edu.tw/ihp/hanji.htm (accessed August 15, 2014).

McNicholas, Mark. 2016. *Forgery and Impersonation in Imperial China: Popular Deceptions and the High Qing State.* Seattle: University of Washington Press.

Nguyễn Thế Anh. 1994. "State and Civil Society under the Trịnh Lords in Seventeenth-Century Vietnam." In *La société civile face à l'État dans les traditions chinoise, japonaise, coréenne et vietnamienne*, edited by Léon Vandermeersch, 367–80. Paris: École française d'Extrême-Orient.

Ong, Alexander. 2015. "Royal Refuge and Heterodoxy: The Vietnamese Mạc Clan in Great Qing's Southern Frontier, 1677–1730." In *China's Encounters on the South and Southwest: Reforging the Fiery Frontier over Two Millennia*, edited by James A. Anderson and John K. Whitmore, 273–87. Leiden: Brill.

Perdue, Peter C. 2010. "Boundaries and Trade in the Early Modern World: Negotiations at Nerchinsk and Beijing." *Eighteenth-Century Studies* 43, no. 3: 341–56.

Rawski, Evelyn S. 2012. "Sons of Heaven: The Qing Appropriation of the Chinese Model of Universal Empire." In *Universal Empire: A Comparative Approach to Imperial Culture and Representation in Eurasian History*, edited by Peter Fibiger Bang and Dariusz Kolodziejczyk, 233–49. Cambridge: Cambridge University Press.

Shen Shixing 申時行, ed. 1989. *Ming Huidian: Wanli chao chongxiu ben* 明會典萬曆朝重修本 [Ming *Statutes*: Revised edition of the Wanli reign]. Beijing: Zhonghua.

Spence, Jonathan. 1966. *Ts'ao Yin and the K'ang-hsi Emperor, Bondservant and Master.* New Haven, CT: Yale University Press.

Spence, Jonathan. 1990. *The Search for Modern China*. New York: Norton.

Sun Hongnian 孙宏年. 2006. *Qing dai Zhong Yue zongfan guanxi yanjiu* 清代中越宗藩关系研究 [A study of Sino-Vietnamese suzerainty relations]. Harbin: Heilongjiang jiaoyu chubanshe.

Taylor, Keith W. 2013. *A History of the Vietnamese*. Cambridge: Cambridge University Press.

Toby, Ronald P. (1984) 1991. *State and Diplomacy in Early Modern Japan: Asia in the Development of the Tokugawa Bakufu*. Stanford, CA: Stanford University Press.

Toby, Ronald P. 1986. "Carnival of the Aliens. Korean Embassies in Edo-Period Art and Popular Culture." *Monumenta Nipponica* 41, no. 4: 415–56.

Toby, Ronald P. 2019. *Engaging the Other: "Japan" and Its Alter Egos*. Leiden: Brill.

Tran, Nhung Tuyet, and Anthony Reid, eds. 2006. *Việt Nam: Borderless Histories*. Madison: University of Wisconsin Press.

Vick, Brian. 2019. "Negotiating Publics and Power Politics." In *Der Wiener Kongress 1814/1815*, edited by Thomas Olechowki, Brigite Mazohl, Karin Schneider, Reinhard Stauber, and Werner Telesko, 71–78. Vienna: Austrian Academy of Sciences Press.

Wang Ji 汪楫. 1997. *Shi Liuqiu za lu* 使琉球雜錄 [Miscellaneous records of an embassy to Liuqiu]. In *Ō Shū sakuhō Ryūkyū shiroku sanpen* 汪楫冊封琉球史錄三編 (Wang Ji cefeng Liuqiu shi lu san bian) [Three historical documents pertaining to Wang Ji's investiture of the king of Liuqiu]. Ginowan-shi, Okinawa: Yōju Shorin.

Wang, Yuanchong. 2018. *Remaking the Chinese Empire: Manchu-Korean Relations, 1616–1911*. Ithaca, NY: Cornell University Press.

Wilkinson, Endymion. 2000. *Chinese History: A Manual*, rev. ed. Cambridge, MA: Harvard University Asia Center.

Wu, Cheng'en. 1978. *The Journey to the West*. Vol. 2. Translated by Anthony C. Yu. Chicago: University of Chicago Press.

Yu, Yingshi. 1967. *Trade and Expansion in Han China: A Study in the Structure of Sino-Barbarian Economic Relations*. Berkeley: University of California Press.

Yunnan sheng Lishi yanjiusuo 云南省历史研究所, ed. 1985. *Qing shilu Yuenan, Miandian, Taiguo, Laowo shiliao zhai chao* 清实录越南缅甸泰国老挝史料摘抄 [Excerpts from the Qing *Veritable Records* concerning Vietnam, Myanmar, Thailand, and Laos]. 2 vols. Kunming: Yunnan renmin chubanshe.

Zhang, Xueli 張學禮. 1998. *Shi Liuqiu ji* 使琉球紀 [Account of an embassy to Liuqiu]. Annotated by Harada Nobuo. Ginowan-shi, Okinawa: Yōju Shorin.

Zhou, Can 周燦. 1996. *Shi Jiao ji shi* 使交紀事 [Account of an embassy to Jiao]. In *Siku quanshu cunmu congshu*, jibu, vol. 219. Tainan xian, ROC: Zhuangyan wenhua.

DAVID GOWEY

"Let the Story Go Round and Round"
Poetic Devices and Orality in Sugidanon Epics of Panay Island, Philippines

ABSTRACT This article argues that, as Panay Bukidnon chanted epics called *sugidanon* are increasingly transformed from oral into written texts and from community to public performances, scholarly attention paid to markers of oral performance should similarly increase. These markers include variation between performances and performers, semantic parallelism and other forms of repetition, and audience participation. This article proposes a nonhierarchical typology for sugidanon performance contexts to better understand how Panay Bukidnon chanting practices have changed over time from the sixteenth century to the present. An in-depth analysis of semantic parallelisms examines a standard repertoire of poetic speech that appears across all recorded sugidanon epics; the author proposes that these features of semiextemporaneous performance situate the epics alongside other regional poetry forms in Island Southeast Asia.

KEYWORDS orality, epic poetry, sugidanon, Panay Bukidnon, linguistic ideology

Traditions must always be understood as reflecting both past and present in a single breath.

—Jan Vansina, *Oral History as Tradition*

Panay Bukidnon *sugidanon* epics in the Indigenous community of Garangan, Philippines, are undergoing a shift from semi-improvisational individual performances to rote performances by groups of children. These epics relate the military and amorous exploits of elite Panay Bukidnon ancestors in a series of interconnected, multigenerational narratives. While published texts have made sugidanon epics more accessible to outsiders, ethnographic interviews in Garangan have shown that the "archaic" or *binukidnon* (lit. "mountain-style") lexicon used in chanting sugidanon epics can also be a barrier to comprehension for some Panay Bukidnon people themselves. As a result of book publication, group public performances, and memorization-based pedagogy at the Garangan School for Living Tradition, the versions of these epics most often encountered by both Panay Bukidnon people and non-Panay Bukidnon audiences are de/recontextualized into new forms while still retaining markers of their original oral nature. I argue that, in the context of oral performance, literary devices such as ritual formulas, parallelism, and heteroglossia combine to assist both chanters and listeners in following the epics' complex, days-long narratives.

THE JOURNAL OF ASIAN STUDIES • 84:2 • May 2025
DOI: 10.1215/00219118-11591169 © 2025 Association for Asian Studies

Sugidanon chanting is among the many cultural artforms practiced by Indigenous Panay Bukidnon people in Panay Island, Philippines. *Panay Bukidnon*, meaning mountain people of Panay, is a collective term for a number of Kinaray-a–speaking upland groups that has become increasingly used from the 1990s onward. Since then, several significant developments have reified both *Panay Bukidnon* as an ethnolinguistic category and the group's oral literature as a key marker of its ethnic identity. First, beginning in 2001 the School for Living Tradition in the *barangays* of Garangan, Masaroy, and Agcalaga, in the municipality of Calinog, initiated a state-sponsored program of cultural education for Panay Bukidnon people to learn sugidanon epics and other traditional artforms. Second, the creation of the Panay Bukidnon ancestral domain by President Gloria Macapagal-Arroyo in 2005 comprising these same three communities granted them special legal rights over territory, intangible cultural heritage, and customary law under the 1997 Indigenous Peoples' Rights Act. Third, the publication of selected sugidanon epics chanted by the Caballero family of Garangan and Masaroy since 2014 has made these narratives more accessible to both academic and nonacademic audiences. Sugidanon epics have thus been a main focus for scholarly research on Panay Bukidnon culture, highlighting their importance as a source of customary law, pre-Hispanic coastal Visayan lifeways, cosmology, and performance ideologies.

This article explores the following research question: Given the increasing importance of written rather than oral versions of sugidanon epics as the primary means by which non-Panay Bukidnon people learn about them, what can the study of these epics' textural elements and performance contexts add to the study of this cultural artform? I argue that markers of orality such as repetition of ritual formulas, semantic parallelism, invocations, and connections to other Panay Bukidnon performance ideologies such as *sibod* (synchronicity, specifically of musical performers), *palikoliko* (elaboration, lit. to cause something to turn repeatedly), and *pamulak-bulak* (flowery language, as in the addition of descriptive epithets for a person or place) provide additional layers of meaning that can easily be overlooked when working exclusively with written texts. My main sources of data are published sugidanon texts, previous ethnographic studies of Panay Bukidnon people, and ethnographic fieldwork and interviews conducted by two Indigenous teachers and myself in Garangan during summer 2019. I also place these literatures and interview data in dialogue with scholarly work on poetic/ritual speech in eastern Indonesia, specifically case studies by James J. Fox (1988) on various Austronesian-speaking peoples from the islands of Flores, Sumba, Rote, and Sulawesi. First, I frame my discussion of Panay Bukidnon sugidanon epics within the scholarly debate about transformation of oral literature into written texts.

"FIXING THE BUTTERFLY"?

This article's discussion of markers of orality in Panay Bukidnon sugidanon epics speaks to a serious question at the heart of oral literature studies: What is lost or compromised when oral texts become written texts? The question of what is gained may seem fairly straightforward: transferable and preservable sources of cultural knowledge that could otherwise be lost or altered with the passage of time. Yet in the globalized cultural economy that increasingly commodifies Indigenous knowledge and practices for outside consumption, transferability may not be preferable for Indigenous communities without the means to guarantee sufficient protections and accountability (Ragragio and Paluga 2021; Smith 2012: 220). Beyond commodification, there is also the more basic issue of transforming oral traditions—which are variable by their very nature as performed cultural materials—into written texts. Nicole Revel (1996: 126) compares the dilemma thus created to the act of "fixing the butterfly": rendering a once-living thing, meant for insider practice, into a dead object for display to outsiders.

Indigenous and related scholars have shown even greater ambivalence toward this transformation process. Bryan McKinley Jones Brayboy and Emma Maughan (2009), Scott Richard Lyons (2000), and Linda Tuhiwai Smith (2012) situate contemporary Indigenous scholarship within the historical context of compulsory education in boarding schools that intended to destroy family and tribal identities to produce proper—that is, literate, English-speaking, and "modern"—state subjects (Kehoe 1989). Colonial efforts to extirpate Indigenous oral knowledge in favor of Western education have historically gone hand in hand with efforts by both Indigenous and non-Indigenous researchers to preserve these traditions before they can "disappear" as the result of assimilation, neglect, culture change, and the death of local cultural experts. Documentation of oral knowledge in turn raises a number of key questions that Indigenous people worldwide continue to face today: Who should have access to which knowledges (via archives, publication, and translation)? What is lost due to cultural decontextualization? Which local interpretations will be privileged over others? How will storytellers be properly honored for their work? And how will outside researchers demonstrate accountability throughout the research process?

This is not to say that all research into oral traditions is considered by these theorists to be inherently destructive or counter to Indigenous cultural values, regardless of research design. Smith (2012: 232) explicitly argues for research as a means for Indigenous peoples to meet their "own research needs and priorities" in ways that treat cultural protocols as methodological priors rather than obstacles. Wesley Y. Leonard (2023) calls for a reevaluation of language shifts among Native Americans and other speakers of so-called endangered languages that is critical of both the ongoing colonial contexts of these shifts and dominant narratives that highlight potential disappearance over active reclamation efforts from within marginalized communities themselves. Jo-ann Archibald (2008: 92–94) and Nicole Revel (1996) highlight a similar dilemma: that the process of putting oral narratives into writing can give a false impression of comprehensiveness that often excludes additional context, other related stories, and different versions. In the sense that ethnographic research captures subjective snapshots of cultural attitudes and behaviors as they are recorded by a particular observer in a particular time and place, studies of oral literature can assist the transmission of cultural knowledge from one generation to another. By doing so, these studies must acknowledge that tradition is an active process of selection from local cultural repertoires rather than an inert body of knowledge subject only to either rote repetition or inevitable degradation and loss.

All this is not to argue that the transition from oral narrative to written text is always unilinear or that it necessarily replaces oral performance. Examples abound of written texts supporting oral retransmission, such as Quran recitation and Indigenous language revitalization programs that draw from missionary grammars or other colonial sources. Scholars of Island Southeast Asia have highlighted relevant case studies throughout the region. C. C. Macknight (2003) examines how the "lively interaction between orality and writing" catalyzed further reproductions and variations of La Galigo narratives by Bugis people of South Sulawesi (see also Pelras 2016). Thomas Gibson (2013) takes a more comparative approach in his structural analysis of four "hero legends" from the Philippines and Indonesia, connecting Reynaldo Ileto's (1979) foundational work on Tagalog-language *Pasyon* performances with Bugis and Makassarese narratives about historical local rulers. Underlying all these Island Southeast Asian examples is a possible Gujarati origin for regional syllabaries of Sumatra, Sulawesi, and the Philippines, inclusive of Tagalog *baybayin*, as well as the Tagbanwa, Hanunoo, Buhid, and Mangyan scripts (Miller 2016). With this in mind, I also note that, for Panay Bukidnon people in Calinog, printed texts of sugidanon epics act as memorization aids for young people learning from experienced chanters.

Thus the situation this article describes is not one in which the orality of Panay Bukidnon sugidanon epics is being diminished or destroyed by the creation of written texts. The four broad performance contexts I outline below show clearly that sugidanon chanting practices have continued to change over time in relation to larger social contexts and trends. Furthermore, preliminary field research in Garangan suggests that sugidanon chanting practices will continue to change.[1] The present situation of Panay Bukidnon sugidanon chanting is one in which most cultural outsiders have been approaching sugidanon first as a written text—including F. Landa Jocano's and Alicia P. Magos's publications and an online manga project titled *Golden Realms: Inheriting the Panay Sugidanun* that debuted in February 2022—and then as an oral tradition through chanting performances at conferences and festivals.[2] As a result, popular and scholarly analyses of Panay Bukidnon epics (including my own) risk overlooking important considerations about the texts without a sufficient understanding of related vocabulary, cultural associations, aesthetic conventions, performance contexts, and local norms and values surrounding the epics in general and chanting practices specifically.

This situation raises two important cautions. The first is from Victor Turner (1987: 21–22), who suggests that researchers (and general-interest readers) should take cultural performances as being not merely reflective but also reflexive of the social contexts from which they originate. Specifically, the frequent depictions of marriage by capture in many sugidanon epics should not be taken to suggest that all Panay Bukidnon people today—or historically, for that matter—approve of or even prefer abduction as a method of courtship. I suggest instead that these episodes should be understood within the context of audience reactions condemning Labaw Donggon's womanizing (Jocano 1965: 23–24) and ethnographic descriptions of the narratives being performed by *binukot* (elite secluded women) like the captured wives in the epics themselves who learned to chant sugidanon as part of their seclusion.[3] I see this as more than simply a move toward a form of strong cultural relativism that accepts all behavior by characters in the epics as normal or approved. As Barre Toelken and Orville Tacheeni Scott (1981) argued with Navajo coyote tales, audience reactions from cultural insiders within a given performance context can be crucial in discerning whether the characters' actions in oral narratives are viewed as models of proper social behavior or cautionary tales about the consequences of violating traditional norms and values.

The second caution follows Panay Bukidnon chanter and educator Elsie "Lamingan" Caballero-Padernal's (2019) recommendations that additional materials such as glossaries and public school curricula are key to helping all learners, Panay Bukidnon and otherwise, better understand the narratives and their particular cultural context. Echoing Archibald (2008) and Smith (2012), these materials must be created in collaboration with Panay Bukidnon people if they are to center local priorities and meanings rather than impose others' meanings onto the written texts and the living tradition of epic chanting from which they came. The acknowledgment that epic chanting is a living tradition should orient future studies of Panay Bukidnon oral literatures away from essentializing paradigms of Indigenous peoples as being pre-Hispanic, unmodern, or somehow more culturally "pure" than lowland Filipinos. Rather, I argue that sugidanon epics should be understood as products of their respective chanters' skills, knowledge, and circumstances. This is made even more interesting and important because sugidanon is one of the few known oral epics attributed to female performers by contemporary descendant communities.

TEXTURE AND CONTEXT

Writing on the dual masculine ideals exemplified in *sensangan* and *cerito Nosi*, two Gerai oral literature genres from Borneo, Christine Helliwell (2012: 51–52) argues against focusing on "the formal structure of the narrative itself" over creativity and meaning. Similarly, Toelken and Tacheeni Scott (1981: 82) return to the former's previous work on Navajo coyote tales to locate *texture*, consisting of poetic language forms inclusive of "*any* coloration given a traditional item or statement as it is being made." In their study of Pantaron Manobo epic chanting in the Southern Philippines, Myfel D. Paluga and Andrea Malaya M. Ragragio (2021) emphasize the importance of *goynawa* (breath/life) as a polysemic concept, used in one sense of the term by chanters as an embodied practice of breathing to organize sung passages in an aesthetically pleasing fashion. These studies argue that analysis of oral genres is incomplete without also looking to such contingent elements as vocal styles, cultural contexts, innovations, venues, and audience behavior.

With this framing in mind, performance contexts for Panay Bukidnon sugidanon epics have changed significantly over time. I divide these into four roughly chronological types: historical, traditional, ethnographic, and contemporary. This typology does not imply value judgment or preference in terms of authenticity. Rather, I use these categories to show that changes in sugidanon chanting practices have been occurring for as long as Panay epics have been documented. While I divide them into rough arbitrary time frames, these do not suggest clean breaks between one type of context and another. I argue instead that various performance contexts for sugidanon epics have become more or less relevant in relation to broader sociocultural factors that have affected other aspects of Panay Bukidnon lifeways over time (Taton 2019). Attention to the relationships between sugidanon epics' cultural and performance contexts gives greater insight into not only their content and significance but also how Panay Bukidnon people have adapted them to new circumstances.

Historical Contexts

The first written descriptions of oral epics on Panay Island came within the first decades of Spanish settlement in the mid-sixteenth century. This is to say that Panay epics certainly predated European contact but that further information on how they were performed is in the domain of oral rather than written history. Spanish records on colonial-period epics are sparse and focus largely on the sorts of ethnographic details that appealed to colonial officials—cosmologies, political systems, and religious practices—rather than on the narratives themselves. Brandon Reilly (2013: 281) highlights two types of Panay epics mentioned by Spanish chronicler Miguel de Loarca in his 1582 *Relación de las Yslas Filipinas*: one performed during religious and social events, and another used as a rowing song. Later Spanish writers noted the centuries-long efforts by generations of Catholic missionaries in Central Panay to extirpate "worship" of ancestor figures and frequent sugidanon heroes such as Labaw Donggon and Matan-ayon (Fernández 2006; Gowey 2017).

The Spanish colonial period on Panay Island, as in other parts of the archipelago, was marked by movement of local peoples between coastal regions and from lowlands to highlands. Factors influencing this movement include desires to escape taxation, missionization, forced resettlement into *reducciónes* (condensed Spanish-style towns) by colonial authorities, and slave raiding from Mindanao and Sulu to the south (Acabado 2018; Eder and McKenna 2004; Junker 1999; Warren 1985). Contemporary Panay Bukidnon people divide themselves into three broad kin groups, Halawudnon, Pan-ayanon, and Iraynon, referring to the headwaters of the Jalaur and Pan-ay Rivers and upriver (*iraya*) settlements, respectively, though the term *Panay Bukidnon* itself has been adopted by some only in the last few decades (Magos 1996; Taton 2019). More research is needed to situate Panay Bukidnon oral literatures and life histories within this broader context of inland migration throughout the Spanish colonial period.

Traditional Contexts

By *traditional* I mean those observed by researchers or described to them by older generations of Panay Bukidnon people as having been prevalent when they were younger. Eugenio Ealdama (1938: 138) describes only briefly the vocal textures used in a "ballad" performance about Labaw Donggon that he observed: stanzas are sung with a "monotonous" melody punctuated by long pauses and nasal humming. Jocano (1965: 20–21) describes three "chanting patterns" that correlate to different performance contexts: "barked terse phrasing of lines in religious rituals," "more or less uniform, high-pitched intonation on special social occasions such as asking for the hand of a girl in marriage," and "varied intonation pattern when recounting the epic as a piece of oral literature in which the beginning line of each stanza is brought to a rising inflection and the last line to a downward inflection in order to emphasize the drama of the story." Jocano (1965: 21; 2000: 4–5) does not elaborate further on ritual uses except to note that chanters may omit spirit communication rituals from social performances.

Other characteristics noted in traditional contexts include some chanters swaying in a hammock to suggest the motion of a boat on the water (Caballero 2013; Muyco 2016b), nighttime performances (Caballero 2013; Jocano 1965), audience participation (Jocano 1965), and frequent but not exclusive chanting by *nabukot*, or formerly *binukot* women (Caballero 2013; Jocano 1965: 20; Muyco 2016b). Even though *pagbukot* (elite female seclusion) is no longer practiced in upland Panay, *binukot* (secluded) women figure prominently in the epics as wives and occasional rescuers of *datu* (chieftain) characters, and *nabukot* (formerly secluded) women are still viewed as having high degrees of social capital (Muyco 2016a).[4] The end of *pagbukot* in the mid-twentieth century correlates with other social changes in Panay Bukidnon lifeways reported by older generations: the Japanese occupation during World War 2, the introduction of new technologies (namely radios, television, and the internet) and public schooling, and labor migration (Caballero 2013; Magos 1996, 2004; Muyco 2016a). As a result, sugidanon epics have persisted, while chanting practices have changed greatly since the 1930s.

Ethnographic Contexts

These contexts are not necessarily chronologically distinct from traditional contexts. Rather, I use *ethnographic* to signify one-on-one recording sessions conducted by researchers for transcription and publication purposes. As these recording contexts are meant to capture words and melodies clearly, they necessarily omit audience participation and sacrifice metatextual commentary on moral values, cultural significance, and emotional content, unless otherwise noted in the printed text.[5] At present, these written texts consist of an excerpt from a "ballad" about Labaw Donggon published by Ealdama (1938); two epics chanted by Ulang Udig and Hugan-an published by F. Landa Jocano as *Epic of Labaw Donggon* (1965) and *Hinilawod: Adventures of Humadapnon Tarangban I* (2000), respectively; a *Hinilawod* excerpt chanted by Dikoy Dubria and recorded by Gina V. Barte (in Villareal 1997); and fourteen epics chanted by the Caballero family in Calinog recorded by Alicia Magos and Anna Razel Limoso-Ramirez. Other recorded sugidanon epics remain unpublished and unrecorded, so this survey is necessarily incomplete.

The implication in separating traditional from ethnographic contexts is that in the latter, narratives may be truncated, interrupted, and canonized in ways that more extemporaneous performances are not. Specifically, published epics from Hugan-an, Ulang Udig, and the Caballero family are held to be standards to which other tellings of sugidanon narratives are compared, as when they are used in public school and university curriculum materials. At the same time, field recordings can produce cleaner audio that is easier to transcribe and use in teaching learners how to chant. The one-on-one recording setting itself also allows the researcher to ask the chanter clarifying questions about the story and specific elements of poetic speech that may not be feasible in other performance contexts.

Contemporary Contexts

This last category contrasts with traditional while overlapping with ethnographic contexts, as some sugidanon epics have been recorded only in the last few years, and others are not yet recorded. Contemporary contexts are exemplified in two ways: public performances given by Panay Bukidnon chanters at academic conferences, festivals, and other such venues; and chanting instruction in the School for Living Tradition. There are several notable differences between contemporary and traditional performance contexts. First, contemporary performances may feature solo chanters but also frequently include small groups chanting in unison, which necessarily preferences chanters' skill at memorization and imitation over linguistic and stylistic improvisation (see Muyco 2013). Second, audiences at contemporary performances I have observed, at various conferences since 2013 and during a visit to Garangan from Calinog municipal tourism officials in 2019, tend to react in a manner comparable to classical music concerts: listening quietly, occasionally recording the chanter on their cell phones, and applauding politely once the chanting ends.

Sugidanon performances at festivals like the annual Hirinugyaw Suguidanonay in Calinog can also feature additional innovations, such as choreography and musical accompaniment. The purpose of this festival is to celebrate both the Indigenous and Catholic heritage of Calinog through a combination of cultural performances, contests, street dancing, and public veneration of the Santo Niño. Prior to the COVID-19 pandemic, these contests included sugidanon chanting and *binanog* dancing, though the celebration in 2024 was limited to a street dancing performance that incorporated excerpts from the *Tarangban* (Magical Enclosure) episode of the *Humadapnon* epic. The roughly ten-minute show featured several dozen high-school-age dancers and percussionists, though the Panay Bukidnon performers who had taken part in Iloilo City's Kasadyahan sa Kabanwahanan festival the week prior were unable to attend Hirinugyaw Suguidanonay due to unforeseen circumstances. For these two festival performances, dancers marched to various stations along the parade route marked off by grandstands and tarps hung overhead for shade, performing in front of elaborate portable sets with prerecorded background music. Audience members took photos and videos on their cell phones, cheered, and applauded in ways that would be considered inappropriate at an academic conference or other more formal venue. Sugidanon epics are still depicted as a prestigious art form, though one implicitly associated with Calinog—both lowlands and uplands—as well as Catholic faith, despite the fact that many Panay Bukidnon people today are Baptists.

In the Schools for Living Tradition, students learn selected passages from master chanters through a combination of recitation, copying by hand, summaries of the overall narratives, group practices, and vernacular explanation of *binukidnon* vocabulary. I differentiate between this and traditional contexts in recognition of changes in how epics were taught via group instruction and memorization akin to a contemporary public school, rather than *pagbukot* (elite female seclusion). Below I discuss in more depth some possible implications of contemporary sugidanon performance. For now, this overview of various performance contexts for sugidanon epics over time foregrounds the following poetic devices and their cultural significance in Panay Bukidnon epic chanting practices.

POETIC DEVICES AND ORALITY

The following discussion places the work of previous scholars of Panay Bukidnon sugidanon chanting in dialogue with scholarly literature on other oral traditions in Southeast Asia. While a comprehensive comparison is beyond the scope of this article, some apparent thematic, cultural, and linguistic affinities between oral literatures of the Philippines and eastern Indonesia stand out. My main source of regional case studies is the work of Fox (1988) and other authors on the use of semantic parallelism in poetic/ritual speech in a number of eastern Indonesian societies. The list of poetic devices presented here is necessarily incomplete compared to the much wider range that would be recognizable to a Panay Bukidnon master chanter. One shared aspect of many features discussed here is a Panay Bukidnon aesthetic ideology known as *sibod* (synchronicity) (Muyco 2013: 59).

Intonations and Invocations

Regardless of context, performances of sugidanon epics begin with *mangalimog* (intoning), or a sequence of vocables that help center the chanter into a suitable vocal range (Muyco 2013). *Limog* (intonation) is often followed by variations on an invocation noting that the story will continue where it left off, as in this example from *Humadapnon: Tarangban* (*Humadapnon: Magical Enclosure*) (Caballero 1994a: 6):

> *Nadi gani gadulog* (Where we paused)
> *Datu gainmudungan* (There we ended)
> *Iwanon taron lamang?* (What shall we do now?)

In a written form, intonation and invocation may appear to be repetition or a superfluous question that interrupts the steady flow of the written narrative. However, in oral performance this linguistic practice aims to bring chanter and listener into a shared state of awareness within the performance context. Published epics from the Caballero family in Garangan retain these textual markers of sugidanon's oral performance contexts, along with wavy line breaks to indicate the separation of the narrative into different recording sessions.

Limog (intonation) and *sibod* (synchronicity) as aesthetic ideologies are meant to bring chanters into alignment with the story and their audience to achieve an ideal state of *tayuyon* (flow) (Muyco 2013: 60). When *sibod* is not achieved, as in one *binanog* (hawk-eagle dance) performance I attended at an academic conference several years ago in Iloilo City, Panay Bukidnon audience members may grumble and remark aloud, "*Waay gasibod!*" (Out of sync!) as a signal for the musicians to restart the song. Performer-audience repartee to achieve *sibod* extends beyond music and becomes in traditional performance contexts a reflexive process indicative of listeners' attitudes on moral values and style in sugidanon chanting.

Emotions and Audience Interaction

When sugidanon is performed for local people who understand the *binukidnon* Kinaray-a lexicon sufficiently to follow the narratives, audience reactions are crucial indicators of how listeners understand characters' actions in light of local moral values (Toelken and Tacheeni Scott 1981). Jocano (1965: 23–24) noted how audiences and chanters navigated this scenario during performances of *Epic of Labaw Donggon* by the chanter Ulang Udig in the late 1950s:

> Silence during dramatic portions;
> Adults grumbling because of Labaw Donggon's bad behavior;
> Laughter at humorous portions;
> Sighs in sympathy with characters' struggles;
> Chanter's omission of portions he deemed less exciting;

Threats from mothers to sons that Saragnayan (a flesh-eating sorcerer or *aswang*)[6] would come get them for bad behavior;

Condemnation from old women of Labaw Donggon's womanizing to the effect that men never change, which led Ulang Udig to stop chanting temporarily and reply, "That is how it was back then."

Similarly, Caballero-Padernal (2019: 32) points to audience reactions as an indicator of genre shifts within sugidanon, as a single epic narrative may move between "drama, action or comedy" at different points.

This situation is different especially in contemporary contexts, such as academic conferences or festivals, where most audience members are unfamiliar with both the chants and their *binukidnon* Kinaray-a lexicon. As a result, the chanted text becomes flattened into a brief song that listeners may appreciate for its "authentic" or "exotic" melody while missing its emotive dimensions. Moreover, the case for Panay Bukidnon people themselves is increasingly similar, especially younger generations. Many children in Garangan learn sugidanon epics through recitation in a cultural context in which *binukidnon* Kinaray-a is increasingly reserved for oral literature performances rather than colloquial speech.[7] Readers of printed epics must rely on translations and footnotes to interpret characters' actions.

Repetition

Jocano (1965) and Evelyn H. Nunes (1972) mention two types of repetition in sugidanon, clothing rituals and semantic parallelism, which Nunes compares to Hebrew poetry, whereas Fox (1988) suggests it is more likely a cross-cultural feature of poetic language in general. While examples in Fox (1988) largely focus on semantic parallelism as a feature of ritual speech, I also propose several practical applications that lend themselves to the chanted nature of sugidanon epics and other oral narrative forms worldwide.

Sugidanon chanting consists of not only embodied practices of "finding one's voice" in the sense of vocal ranges and tones for chanting but also the performer's choice of style, vocabulary, and scenes in performing for a given audience or situation (Muyco 2013; see also Jocano 1965; Revel 1996). Thus, with the exception of rote recitation in contemporary performance contexts, chanted sugidanon epics are (re)composed in a semiextemporaneous manner (Foley 1988; Lord 2018). Furthermore, vocal melodies in oral literature act as mnemonic devices for performers (Vansina 1985: 16). The acts of singing and remembering are thus selective and generative processes—what Carlo Severi (2015: 261) calls "a craft of thought"—rather than simply mechanical process of sequential and descriptive recall (Archibald 2018).

In that vein, I propose four overlapping purposes for repetition in Panay Bukidnon epics, bearing in mind that portions of text that may appear redundant in writing are significant in oral performance. Repetition in chanted texts should be framed within performance contexts in which the stories are chanted for hours over multiple nights in poetic rather than colloquial speech forms. Thus repetition in sugidanon chanting may help chanters frame extemporaneous chanted passages and follow the epic narratives over a period of days, help audiences follow the stories and summarize parts they may have missed due to absence or falling asleep,[8] mark Panay

Bukidnon cultural associations and aesthetic preferences, and mark ritual speech where portions of the epics model magico-healing practices. Some of these latter two cases are discussed in the following sections.

Traditional Associations and Themes

Previous studies of sugidanon epics have focused largely on their thematic content and narrative content. Magos (1996) argues that the frequency of sea travel episodes and associated sailing terminology in sugidanon epics indicates Panay Bukidnon ancestors were once coastal dwellers who began migrating inland after Spanish colonization of Panay Island in 1569. This hypothesis has met some criticism for privileging a historically reconstructive reading of the epics over upland communities' contemporary political concerns (Talledo 2004). However, it is still worth noting some examples of maritime imagery in sugidanon epics alongside other themes and tropes. The full range of traditional associations known to a master sugidanon chanter cannot be represented here. Rather, I have selected a few examples of poetic language that recur in multiple sugidanon epics.

Clothing Rituals

Clothing in sugidanon epics is an important aesthetic marker of one's social class and supernatural ability. Variations on a recurring phrase like this example from *Epic of Labaw Donggon* (Jocano 1965: 45) appear when one character—often but not always the wife of a *datu* (chieftain)—asks another to fetch a carved wooden chest full of heirloom clothing, for either courtship or combat:[9]

> Open, please, open
> The great wooden chest
> Whose heavy cover
> Is elaborately carved
>
> *Bukada nga bukada*
> *Si Barugbugan Umbaw*
> *Unimbuay takop na*
> *Tinakpay gala-gala*

These repeated lines constitute one of many canonical parallelisms that appear in magical or ritual contexts, blurring the sociolinguistic categories of poetic speech, mnemonic device, and performative utterance. Fox (1988: 13) subsumes all three categories within the frame of ritual language. For now, the apparent cultural connection between poetic speech and magical formulae points to other portions of sugidanon texts with ritual significance.

Invoking Spirits

Individuals in sugidanon epics endowed with magical gifts are known as *dalongdongan* (anointed) and use a *pamlang* (bamboo vial of sacred oils) to communicate with spirits. Spirit communication rituals appear in the Caballero family's epics, particularly in battle scenes, as in this excerpt from *Humadapnon: Pagbihag ni Humadap-*

non kay Paglambuhan (*Humadapnon: Captivity of Humadapnon by Paglambuhan*) (Caballero 1994b: 80–81, translation by the author):[10]

> *I Buyong Humadapnon*
> *Hindun datong gahuypon*
> *Suyon-suyon pay pamlang*
> *Katuod pay dalongdong*
> *Tapat pay pinangalap*
> *Taruhati ko tag-hoy*
> *Kutuyaw kon duhinde*
> *Ko gahuru-wang sa lawas*
> *Gasurog sa tubu-an*
> *Ko gabihagon ko dag-on*
> *Ada gadalumi-on*
> *Si Mamang Paglambuhan*
> *Buyong si Sumagulong*
> *Pag-silabuy lalanhan sura paramiyakan*
> *Lapaw sa alipud-wan*
> *Kuon si Humadapnon*

> Buyong Humadapnon
> Now he blows
> Gently on the *pamlang*
> True *dalongdong*
> Sure amulet
> My spirit messenger[11]
> My spirit companion
> If you support my body
> Help my form
> If I can capture and defeat
> If I can subdue
> Mamang Paglambuhan
> Buyong Sumagulong
> Cause the oil to boil
> Overflow the top
> Says Humadapnon

In the *Pahagunong* epic, Matan-ayon uses her *pamlang* to call on the spirits and take on male form as the powerful Buyong Makalimpong to protect herself from Buyong Pahagunong, who spies her bathing and descends from the skyworld to capture her (Caballero 2016).

Worthy of note in connecting these textual formula to Panay Bukidnon healing practices are the importance of material objects and subjunctive phrasing ("if you support my body") directed toward the *pamlang* holder's spirit companions. Magos (1992: 95–101) describes the process of becoming a *ma-aram* (traditional healer, lit. a wise one) in the mountains of southern Iloilo Province: an individual is first called by the spirits, mentored by an older *ma-aram*, and collects medicinal plants during Holy

Week to create *dalungdong* oil. Beyond semantic parallelisms like *Katuod pay dalong-dong / Tapat pay pinangalap* (True *dalongdong* / Sure amulet) and *Ko gahuru-wang sa lawas / Gasurog sa tubu-an* (If you support my body / Help my form), magical scenes function as ritual speech through repetition and performance outside of epic chanting itself. Portions of sugidanon can also function as ritual texts in *binabaylan* (shamanic) practices.[12]

Bird Calls as Harbingers of Misfortune

Symbolic associations of birds with death, spirits, and the afterlife are common throughout the Philippines (Lasco 2011) and the world (Moreman 2014). This point is important in relation to sugidanon epics not simply for cross-cultural comparison but, rather, to point to the broader social and cosmological context in which Panay Bukidnon epics exist. As they can travel between the middle and upper layers of the Panay Bukidnon cosmos, birds are important messengers who can give warnings of danger (*sawi*) (Ealdama 1938: 488; Gowey 2019). Two examples from the epics illustrate the necessity of paying heed to bird calls before embarking on a voyage or other risky endeavor. Paiburong ignores the call of a bird in *Tikum Kadlum* (*Curly-Tailed Black Dog*) (Caballero and Caballero-Castor 2013) before he cuts down an heirloom bamboo belonging to the monster Makabagting, causing him to give up his two daughters, Matan-ayon and Suranggaon, as recompense. In *Sinagnayan*, Buyong Sinagnayan rejects the counsel of his wife Pinailog sa Pinggan to not fight her brother-in-law Labaw Donggon after hearing a *sawi* and is subsequently killed in battle (Caballero 2017).

Sailing and Coastal Life

Many sugidanon epics depict travel in and around water, either the open ocean or rivers. For instance, the titular character in *Amburukay* uses the mouths of rivers as geographic points of reference while traveling around Panay Island to find the *datu* responsible for stealing her golden pubic hair. Amburukay travels down to the sea coast, squats near the mouth of each of the seven rivers, and slaps her vulva; if it makes a loud popping sound, then the owner of that territory is identified as the thief. A commonly repeated phrase like this example from *Humadapnon: Pagbi-hag ni Humadapnon kay Paglambuhan* (*Humadapnon: Captivity of Humadapnon by Paglambuhan*) invokes the delicate process of navigating through straits, around seacoasts, and on rivers (Caballero 1994b: 1, translation by the author):

> *Liput sa liliputan*
> *Luwang sa luluwangan*
> *Sa napulong likuan*
> *Gatos nga luluwangan*

> Stopping at the stopping place
> Entering at the entrance
> At tens of turning points
> Hundreds of entrances

River mouths mark the respective territories of different *datu* (chieftain) characters—as with Labaw Donggon who is sought unknowingly by Amburukay at the mouths of the seven chief rivers of Panay after he steals her golden pubic hair. Other river mouths throughout the Philippines are also associated with *datu* figures named in the epics, such as Humadapnon with the Pan-ay River on the northern coast of Panay Island (Caballero and Caballero 2014; Caballero-Padernal 2019; Jocano 2000). Once on the open ocean, the geography of the middleworld expands to include such locations as Borneo, the sticky sea that flows as thick as blood, and the rising-place of the sun depicted in *Sinagnayan* that are reached either by boat or by flying on a shield with the help of spirit companions.

In addition to the practice of chanting while swaying in a hammock, I draw a further linguistic connection between sailing, chanting as an embodied musical practice, and *palikoliko* (elaboration) and *pamulak-bulak* (flowery language) as expressions of Panay Bukidnon linguistic ideology.[13] The root word *liko* in the above excerpt refers to the turns of a river but can also reflect an aesthetic preference for elaborate, improvisational speech in chanted sugidanon epics: "*palikoliko-on ang istorya asta mag-sibod*" (let the story go round and round till it reaches a point of synchronicity) (Muyco 2013: 63). Similarly, *pamulak-bulak* serves as a means of self-expression within prescribed contextual limits: too little can render the story overly plain, while too much can cause the narrative itself to get lost (*talang*) in what experienced chanters would consider to be superfluous description. Sugidanon as performed by a Panay Bukidnon cultural master is more than simply a series of plots with their associated characters, symbols, and themes. As an oral tradition, sugidanon is also a process in which chanters select words, lines, and scenes appropriate for constructing narratives appropriate to particular performance contexts. This in turn suggests directions for analyzing sugidanon as representations of Panay Bukidnon aesthetic ideologies through poetic language, especially frequent uses of semantic parallelism.

AESTHETIC SENSITIVITIES AND PREFERENCES

This portion of the article does not present an exhaustive analysis of Panay Bukidnon attitudes toward sugidanon chanting as an artform, due in part to the relative scarcity of published materials on sugidanon and other local oral literature genres. Thus the present discussion of semantic parallelism is intended more as a suggestion for future research that could draw more in-depth comparisons and contrasts between Panay Bukidnon sugidanon epics and oral literatures throughout the Philippines and Southeast Asia. Case studies collected by James Fox and his collaborators in the edited volume *To Speak in Pairs* (1988) look particularly promising in light of longstanding linguistic and economic connections between peoples of Eastern Indonesia and the Philippines.

Further research is needed to understand the broader implications of *palikoliko* (elaboration) and *pamulak-bulak* (flowery language) as expressions of Panay Bukidnon linguistic ideology in light of the increased emphasis on memorization over improvisation used to teach sugidanon chanting to youth in upland Calinog today. Muyco (2013) suggests that *palikoliko* allows for individual innovation that incorporates synonyms with loan words from Sanskrit (via Malay) and Spanish alongside the *binukidnon* Kinaray-a lexicon of Panay Bukidnon oral literatures. *Pamulak-bulak* is similar to *palikoliko* in the sense that it can be used to extend the telling of a sugidanon narrative but expert chanters such as Romulo "Amang Baoy" Caballero do not rely on it in performances. Rather, his performances eschew superfluous elaboration to emphasize the narrative itself, with *pamulak-bulak* being better suited in his opinion for what I would call contemporary contexts, such as academic conferences and festivals where chanters are more likely to show off their skills in chanting rather than only tell the story.

Several observations could be made from the use of semantic parallelism as an aesthetic practice that incorporates new vocabulary and plays an ambivalent role as both ritual and artistic speech. First, an important distinction must be made in sugidanon chanting practice between the particular vocal features used in performances of the epics and the *binukidnon* or archaic Kinaray-a lexicon. Examples of vocal features are the aforementioned *limog* (invocation) tones, what Jose R. Taton (2019) identifies as the *ligbok* accent or style, and the combinations of melody and vocal quality that differentiate individual chanting styles (Muyco 2013).[14] Second, the *binukidnon* Kinaray-a lexicon is sufficiently distinct from contemporary Kinaray-a spoken in Garangan that many community members interviewed in summer 2019 reported difficulty in understanding the epics without explanations from master chanters. Three overlapping potential explanations for this apparently growing mutual unintelligibility stand out:

1. Linguistic shifts over time through interaction with other Kinaray-a speakers, as well as Hiligaynon, Tagalog, Spanish, and English;
2. Historical shifts from lowland/maritime to highland/*kaingin* (shifting rice cultivation) settlement patterns;
3. Cultural shifts due to introduction of transistor radios, TVs, and the internet.

Third, I hypothesize that a combination of these factors contributed to a Panay Bukidnon linguistic ideology which accepted the inclusion of foreign loan words in sugidanon chants.

The presence of Sanskrit (via Malay) and Spanish loan words in sugidanon epics requires further research to understand how they function alongside other aspects of Panay Bukidnon linguistic ideologies. Notably, pairing in sugidanon epics expresses a willingness to incorporate novel or introduced concepts into traditional stories, contradicting popular assumptions that Indigenous peoples are necessarily linguistically conservative (Kroskrity 1992).[15] Barbara Watson Andaya (1997) and O. W. Wolters (1982) have characterized Southeast Asian peoples as being historically receptive of foreign goods, ideas, and merchants, which were granted greater social prestige than their local equivalents due to their associations with elites, foreign and divine powers, and artistic skills (see also Helms 1993). Multilingualism among Philippine ethnolinguistic groups of the early modern and colonial periods has been attributed to interactions between members of different communities through intermarriage, slave raiding, and migration (Buenconsejo 2010; Pallesen 1985). Furthermore, Filomeno V. Aguilar Jr. (1998) argues that appropriation of Roman Catholic symbols—crucifixes, religious garments, Latin and Spanish words, and saints—was an important strategy by which Filipinos turned Spanish colonial power to their own benefit.

Between a historical inclination for valuing foreign symbols and colonial-period interactions with the Spanish that included linguistic borrowing, it is not surprising that Spanish loan words would appear in sugidanon epics. However, what must be explained in terms of Panay Bukidnon linguistic ideologies is how these loan words function in oral literature. One likely explanation is that some, such as *leon* (Sp. *león*, "lion"), *moryon* (Sp. *morion*, "helmet"), and *tore-tore* (Sp. *torre*, "tower"), represented objects introduced during the Spanish colonial period.[16] However, this does not explain the presence of other terms used alongside *binukidnon* synonyms in poetic language. For example, the following pairs match Kinaray-a with Sanskrit (via Malay) and Spanish loans:

> *ka-angay//kapariho* (Sp. *parejo*)
>> equal, a marriageable partner of one's own class
> *away/butalya* (Sp. *batalla*)
>> combat or battle (also *awayan//batalyahan*)
> *midyo/remidyo* (Sp. *medio*, Sp. *remedio*)
>> means or remedy
> *purta/puta-puta* (Sp. *puerta*)
>> doorway or division between rooms
> *derikaryong pada/medalyong bulawan* (Sp. *medallón*)
>> golden medallion
> *bankgo/bayaw-bayaw* (Sp. *banco*)
>> bench/porch or balcony
> *sobra/sulabi* (Sp. *sobra*)
>> much, extremely
> *agila/bakunawa* (Sp. *águila*)
>> eagle/giant serpent that causes a lunar eclipse
> *kabtanga//kahisturaha* (Sp. *historia*)
>> happening, event
> *basula/kastigaha* (Sp. *castigar*)
>> punish, blame
> *yawa//diwata* (Sa. *devata*)
>> spirit/divine being from the skyworld (also *diya/diwata*)[17]

Instances of semantic parallelism that place foreign loans alongside *binukidnon* Kinaray-a terms suggest a Panay Bukidnon linguistic ideology which permits certain degrees of outside influence within culturally appropriate protocols for ritual speech.

Here the discussion returns to *palikoliko* and *pamulak-bulak* as expressions of Panay Bukidnon linguistic ideology that use semantic parallelism in part as an extemporaneous elaboration technique in sugidanon chanting. While the *binukidnon* Kinaray-a lexicon is noted for its archaic vocabulary, the poetic structure of sugidanon epics (and *talda* poetry) also accommodates foreign words in ways that complement rather than replace local terminology in ritual speech. This is not to say that all instances of semantic parallelism in Panay Bukidnon epics use foreign loan words, given pairings such as the following:

> *buntog//binukot*
>> maiden, specifically a secluded elite woman
> *buyong//datu*
>> chieftain

lawdon//layagon
    sea, literally "that which is sailed upon"
iwa//sinaha
    knife or sword
tubu-an//lawas
    body
bulawan//pada
    gold
dinhay//ginhawa
    breath, life, or essence
uripon//iwhay
    slave or servant, literally one left alive or spared after battle
tinubo//binaladbad
    child, literally something sprouted or blossomed
danglas//kalasag
    wooden shield
duyan//ablung
    hammock
gadulog//gainmudungan
    pause, end, come to a stop
banwa//dinun-an
    village, land, world

Instances of semantic parallelism that do place foreign loans alongside *binukidnon* Kinaray-a terms suggest a Panay Bukidnon linguistic ideology that permits certain degrees of outside influence within culturally appropriate protocols for ritual speech. Through the purposeful blending of language, vocal techniques, scenes, and performance contexts, sugidanon epics relate local views on the precolonial past to contemporary circumstances and audiences. The overall effect is not one of linguistic or symbolic domination of Indigenous ingenuity by foreign influence. Instead, Panay Bukidnon master chanters use selective elaboration to weave together diction, melody, and scenes in response to particular performance contexts that are both generalizable into the four broad types described above while also being irreplicable as products of oral performance.

What emerges then from Panay Bukidnon sugidanon epics as an expression of linguistic and musical ideology is also a historiology constructed by a sugidanon chanter for the venue or audience at hand (Vansina 1982: 196). Each performance varies in its particular nuances and emphases but exists within the larger continuity of sugidanon chanting practice. At the same time, the act of recording and transforming an oral performance into written text also changes how it is received by audiences with varying degrees of knowledge about Panay Bukidnon lifeways, artforms, and ontologies.

CONCLUSION

This article has provided a broad typology of four performance contexts for Panay Bukidnon sugidanon epics. I also discussed selected markers of oral performance to argue for increased scholarly and public attention paid to chanting practices themselves. I have attempted to demonstrate how the study of performance contexts, semantic parallelism, intoning, invocation, and traditional associations are important sources of cultural information that may appear superfluous or be missed by unfamiliar readers. Panay Bukidnon people have historically adapted sugidanon chanting practices to their changing circumstances. Future research will be needed to understand how contemporary Panay Bukidnon people—especially youth who attend local Schools of Living Tradition—use sugidanon epics and other cultural artforms to engage with people outside their communities as part of ongoing processes of ethnic identity formation.

DAVID GOWEY is a doctoral candidate in sociocultural anthropology at Arizona State University and adjunct professor at Estrella Mountain Community College. His research focuses on oral literature and Indigenous cultural education among Panay Bukidnon people in the Philippines, specifically how sugidanon epics are taught to young people. Other research interests include ethnohistory, comparative linguistics, and ethnic performance.

ACKNOWLEDGMENTS

An earlier version of the manuscript was presented at the 2022 Association of Asian Studies Annual Meeting in Honolulu, Hawai'i. I also thank the Research Committee at Arizona State University's School of Human Evolution and Social Change for providing funding to conduct the ethnographic fieldwork during summer 2019 that informed this article. Special thanks are also due to Polly Wiessner and Jim Rush for helping see this article through from the original presentation into its current state; Lordjane "Lagdungan" Caballero Dordas and Elsie "Lamingan" Caballero Padernal for their ongoing support and friendship; Rodolfo "Sandigan" and Leopoldo "Paino" Caballero for their time and expertise; Rara Limoso Ramirez, Pow Taton, Rocel "Sinagan" Caballero Casipe, and Romulo "Amang Baoy" Caballero for more information on *pamulak-mulak*; and to the editorial board and reviewers for their welcome suggestions. *Madamo gid nga salamat* to all the members of the Panay Bukidnon community in Calinog, who welcomed me into their homes and shared with me their experiences, desires, and cultural knowledge.

NOTES

1. The sociocultural effects of the COVID-19 pandemic on cultural education in Panay Bukidnon communities have yet to be studied.

2. *Golden Realms: Inheriting the Panay Sugidanun* is a collaboration among Thrive Art Iloilo, the Japan Foundation of Manila, and Panay Bukidnon Elders and sugidanon chanters. For more, visit the project's website at https://goldenrealms.thriveart.org/.

3. A particularly informative episode comes from the epic *Pahagunong* (Caballero 2016) in which Matan-ayon relates the story of her combat against Pahagunong to her ancestor Laonsina from the skyworld, who then remarks that the two women should sit together on a rock by the seashore to watch Labaw Donggon and Pahagunong battle to the death, if that is what the men really want. The narrative ends with Laonsina revealing that Labaw Donggon and Pahagunong are also her descendants, making the two enemies kin, and she arbitrates an end to the conflict.

4. For example, the *binukot* sisters Matan-ayon and Suranggaon marry the *buyong* brothers Labaw Donggon and Paubari, respectively.

5. For both Helliwell (2012) and Toelken and Tacheeni Scott (1981), audience reactions are shown to give ethnographic insights into how the actions of the characters in these stories are received by community members, which in turn connects the stories to norms and values as transmitted from elders to younger generations. Furthermore, Toelken and Tacheeni Scott

(1981: 79–80) also contrast the lengthier, more engaging speaking style used by Yellowman when telling the same coyote story to an audience versus his tendency to summarize when he was accompanied only by a researcher and a tape recorder.

6. Saragnayan in Ulang Udig's *Epic of Labaw Donggon* and Sinagnayan in the Caballero sugidanon epics are equivalent characters in terms of their names (roughly meaning "clear-voiced one") and antagonistic relationship toward the cultural hero Labaw Donggon. Other variations occur between the different sugidanon epics published by Ealdama (1938), Jocano (1965, 2000), Magos (in Caballero 2017), and Barte (in Villareal 1997). While a full analysis of these variations is beyond the scope of this article, it suffices for now to mention them as being the expected result of sugidanon's iterative nature as an oral tradition.

7. This may be in part due to students of the School for Living Tradition in Garangan learning excerpts from the narratives chosen by the organizing committee for the annual Hirinugyaw-Suguidanonay Festival held in Calinog that are then performed in small groups. It also suggests that sugidanon epics are becoming more relevant as a form of ethnic identity than as a form of community entertainment or source of traditional norms and values for young people as they once were.

8. As Panay Bukidnon cultural master Rodolfo "Sandigan" Caballero (author's field notes, August 2, 2019) explained, "*Ang tulog gapamangkot, ang bugtaw kabalo*" (The sleeper asks, the awake one knows), referring to audience members who fall asleep during the chanting performance and must ask in the morning what portions of the story they missed.

9. Jocano (1965: 45–46) explains in a footnote that ideal pieces of clothing are chosen from the middle of the chest rather than the top or bottom, "so that they would not lose any of their supernatural powers." Correspondingly, the human protagonists of sugidanon epics live in the middle layer of the cosmos.

10. With thanks to Lordjane "Lagdunan" Caballero Dordas for corrections to my English translation.

11. *Taghoy* may be translated as a sigh or murmur. Left untranslated, it is the name of a spirit companion who conveys messages across the seven levels of the cosmos, impelling various characters to take (often rash) action, such as pursuing a particular noblewoman as a wife or stealing the golden pubic hair of the witch Amburukay.

12. During my fieldwork in summer 2019, several people in Garangan spoke with us about their desire to expand the curriculum at their School for Living Tradition to include *binabaylan* in the future. Unfortunately, the proposed *binabaylan* instructor, elder and sugidanon chanter Leopoldo "Paino" Caballero, passed away from COVID-19 in August 2021. The School for Living Tradition itself—along with most other schools throughout the Philippines—was closed throughout the pandemic but has since reopened.

13. *Palikoliko* is composed of the causative prefix *pa-* and reduplication of the root *liko* (to turn, curve, or bend as a river or road) and suggesting a serpentine or meandering motion (Kaufmann 1935: 271). *Pamulak-bulak*, literally the act or state of blossoming, is a similar practice in which the intricate verbal *hampang* (play) of *binukidnon* and vernacular Kinaray-a synonyms in extemporaneous couplets is a means by which a master sugidanon chanter can extend an oral narrative (Muyco 2013, 2016b: 120).

14. *Ligbok* is sometimes falsely conflated with the *binukidnon* lexicon or defined as the Panay Bukidnon language distinct from Kinaray-a. However, this term properly refers to particular sounds, such as an "undulating high-pitched syllable at the end of the phrase or sentence" in sugidanon and *talda* (repartee) singing (Taton 2019) and the sound of oars striking water in the Sinagnayan epic (Leopoldo "Paino" Caballero, interview by the author, Calinog, Philippines, August 7, 2019).

15. Kroskrity's (1992: 302) argument is that kiva speech as an expression of Arizona Tewa linguistic ideology reflects "the functioning of ceremonial speech as a local model of linguistic prestige." Thus the so-called linguistic conservatism of kiva speech is to be understood not as merely a sign of Tewa xenophobia or unwillingness to speak other languages but, rather, as a result of the

kiva's significance as a place associated with cosmic power and rule by hereditary elites. Given the documented tendency among early modern Southeast Asian peoples for prowess-based leadership by a *datu* rather than by hereditary rulers and centrally controlled socioreligious institutions, it is reasonable to hypothesize that Panay Bukidnon linguistic borrowings from Sanskrit-derived Malay and Spanish would have developed in this same historical context of decentralized *mandala* polities (Blust 2007; Junker 1999; Paredes 2013; Wolters 1982).

16. The *leon nga bulawan* (golden lion) in which Sinagnayan hides his *ginhawa* (breath or life essence), Labaw Donggon's *moryon* (Sp. *morion*, "helmet"), and the golden *tore-tore* (Sp. *torre*, "tower") where Amburukay keeps the *binukot* sisters Matan-ayon and Suranggaon.

17. In contemporary Kinaray-a the term *yawa* is most often translated as "devil" or "demon," suggesting a particular type or class of being, though described in a decidedly Roman Catholic manner by Alcina (in Lietz 1962: 246–47) as the "lord of the forest" and Aguilar (1998: 161–63) as a singular being "in the image of the devil."

REFERENCES

Acabado, Stephen. 2018. "Zones of Refuge: Resisting Conquest in the Northern Philippine Highlands." *Journal of Anthropological Archaeology* 52: 180–95.

Aguilar, Filomeno V., Jr. 1998. *Clash of Spirits: The History of Power and Sugar Planter Hegemony on a Visayan Island*. Honolulu: University of Hawai'i Press.

Andaya, Barbara Watson. 1997. "Historicising 'Modernity' in Southeast Asia." *Journal of the Economic and Social History of the Orient* 40, no. 4: 391–409.

Archibald, Jo-ann. 2008. *Indigenous Storywork: Educating the Heart, Mind, Body, and Spirit*. Vancouver: UBC Press.

Blust, Robert. 2007. "On Datus, Modern and Ancient." In *Piakandatu ami Dr. Howard P. McKaughan*, edited by Howard McKaughan, Loren Allen Billings, and Nelleke Elisabeth Goudswaard, 36–51. Manila: Linguistic Society of the Philippines and SIL Philippines.

Brayboy, Bryan McKinley Jones, and Emma Maughan. 2009. "Indigenous Knowledges and the Story of the Bean." *Harvard Educational Review* 79, no. 1: 21.

Buenconsejo, José S. 2010. "Inland-Coastal Philippine Hybridity: Heteroglossia in Agusan Manobo Music and Ritual." *Humanities Diliman* 7, no. 1: 140–75.

Caballero, Federico. 1994a. *Humadapnon: Tarangban* [Humadapnon: Magical enclosure]. Translated by Federico Caballero and Maria Fe Espe. Philippine Oral Epics Archive, Ateneo de Manila University, Quezon City.

Caballero, Federico. 1994b. *Humadapnon: Pagbihag ni Humadapnon kay Paglambuhan* [Humadapnon: Captivity of Humadapnon by Paglambuhan]. Translated by Federico Caballero and Maria Fe Espe. Philippine Oral Epics Archive, Ateneo de Manila University, Quezon City.

Caballero, Federico. 2016. *Pahagunong: Sugidanon (Epics) of Panay Book 4*. Translated by Alicia P. Magos. Manila: University of the Philippines Press.

Caballero, Federico. 2017. *Sinagnayan: Sugidanon (Epics) of Panay Book 6*. Translated by Alicia P. Magos. Manila: University of the Philippines Press.

Caballero, Federico, and Leopoldo "Paino" Caballero. 2014. *Amburukay: Sugidanon (Epics) of Panay Book 2*. Translated by Alicia P. Magos. Manila: University of the Philippines Press.

Caballero, Federico, and Teresita "Abyaran" Caballero-Castor. 2013. *Tikum Kadlum: Sugidanon (Epics) of Panay Book 1*. Translated by Alicia P. Magos. Manila: University of the Philippines Press.

Caballero-Padernal, Elsie. 2019. "The Panay Bukidnon *Sugidanon* (Epic) and Prototype Glossaries for Epic Excerpts." *Philippine Journal of Social Sciences and Humanities* 22, nos. 1 and 2: 29–38.

Ealdama, Eugenio. 1938. "The Monteses of Panay." *Philippine Magazine*, March.

Eder, James F., and Thomas M. McKenna. 2004. "Minorities in the Philippines: Ancestral Lands and Autonomy in Theory and Practice." In *Civilizing the Margins: Southeast Asian*

Government Policies for the Development of Minorities, edited by Christopher R. Duncan, 56–85. Ithaca, NY: Cornell University Press.

Fernández, Juan. 2006. *Monografías de los Pueblos de la Isla de Pan-ay* [Monographs of the Towns of the Island of Panay]. Translated by Jose G. Espinoza. Iloilo City: University of San Agustin.

Foley, John Miles. 1988. *The Theory of Oral Composition: History and Methodology*. Bloomington: Indiana University Press.

Fox, James J., ed. 1988. *To Speak in Pairs: Essays on the Ritual Languages of Eastern Indonesia*. Cambridge: Cambridge University Press.

Gibson, Thomas. 2013 "The Hero Legend in Colonial Southeast Asia." *Philippine Studies* 61, no. 4: 437–76.

Gowey, David. 2017. "Depictions of Panayanon Culture Heroes in Indigenous and Spanish Sources." Presentation at the International Conference Marking the Centennial of Philippine Anthropology, University of the Philippines-Diliman, Quezon City, Philippines, December 1–2.

Gowey, David. 2019. "Setting the Stage: A Thematic Analysis of the *Tikum Kadlum* Epic." *Philippine Journal of Social Sciences and Humanities* 22, nos. 1 and 2: 65–75.

Helliwell, Christine. 2012. "Variation in Oral Narrative Performance: A Pacific Example." *Journal of the Polynesian Society* 121, no. 1: 51–73.

Helms, Mary W. 1993. *Craft and the Kingly Ideal: Art, Trade, and Power*. Austin: University of Texas Press.

Ileto, Reynaldo. 1979. *Pasyon and Revolution: Popular Movements in the Philippines, 1840–1910*. Quezon City: Ateneo de Manila University Press.

Jocano, F. Landa. 1965. "The Epic of Labaw Donggon." *Philippine Social Sciences and Humanities Review* 29:1–103.

Jocano, F. Landa. 2000. *Hinilawod: Adventures of Humadapnon Tarangban I*. Quezon City: Punlad Research House.

Junker, Laura Lee. 1999. *Raiding, Trading, and Feasting: The Political Economy of Philippine Chiefdoms*. Honolulu: University of Hawaiʻi Press.

Kaufmann, J. M. H. M. 1935. *Visayan-English Dictionary*. Iloilo: La Editorial.

Kehoe, Alice Beck. 1989. *The Ghost Dance: Ethnohistory and Revitalization*. Fort Worth, TX: Holt, Rinehart and Winston.

Kroskrity, Paul V. 1992. "Arizona Tewa Kiva Speech as a Manifestation of Linguistic Ideology." *Pragmatics* 2, no. 3: 297–309.

Lasco, Lorenz. 2011. "Ang Kosmolohiya at Simbolismo ng mga Sandatang Pilipino: Isang Panimulang Pag-aaral" [The cosmology and symbolism of filipino weapons: A preliminary study]. *Dalumat Ejournal* 2, no. 1: 1–15.

Leonard, Wesley Y. 2023. "Refusing 'Endangered Languages' Narratives." *Daedalus* 152, no. 3: 69–83.

Lietz, Paul S. 1962. *The Muñoz Text of Alcina's History of the Bisayan Islands (1688)*, pt. 1, bk. 3. Chicago: Philippine Studies Program, Department of Anthropology.

Lord, Albert B. 2018. *The Singer of Tales*. 3rd ed. Edited by David F. Elmer. Cambridge, MA: Harvard University Press.

Lyons, Scott Richard. 2000. "Rhetorical Sovereignty: What Do American Indians Want from Writing?" *College Composition and Communication* 51, no. 3: 447–68.

Macknight, C. C. 2003. "La Galigo in Comparative Perspectives." In *La Galigo: Menyelusuri Jejak Warisan Sastra* Dunia, edited by N. Rahman, A. Hukma, and I. Anwar, 1–24. Makassar: Pusat Kegiatan Penelitian Universitas Hasanuddin.

Magos, Alicia P. 1992. *The Enduring Ma-aram Tradition: An Ethnography of a Kinaray-a Village in Antique*. Quezon City: New Day.

Magos, Alicia P. 1996. "The Sugidanon of Central Panay." *Edukasyon: Harnessing Indigenous Knowledge for Education*, edited by Emeteria P. Lee, 117–40. Quezon City: Center for Integrative and Development Studies.

Magos, Alicia P. 2004. "Balay Turun-an: An Experience in Implementing Indigenous Education in Central Panay." *Agham-Tao* 13:95–102.

Miller, Chris. 2016. "A Gujarati Origin for Scripts of Sumatra, Sulawesi and the Philippines." *Berkeley Linguistics Society* 36:276–91. http://dx.doi.org/10.3765/bls.v36i1.3917.

Moreman, Christopher M. 2014. "On the Relationship between Birds and Spirits of the Dead." *Society and Animals* 22, no. 5: 1–22.

Muyco, Maria Christine. 2013. "Mangalimog Ako: Finding One's Voice in Sugidanon (Epic Chanting)." In *Songs of Memory in Islands of Southeast Asia*, edited by Nicole Revel, 59–72. Newcastle upon Tyne: Cambridge Scholars.

Muyco, Maria Christine. 2016a. "Binukot at Nabukot: From Myth to Practice." *Humanities Diliman* 13, no. 2: 49–74.

Muyco, Maria Christine. 2016b. *Síbod: Ideology and Expressivity in Binanog Dance, Music, and Folkways of the Panay Bukidnon*. Manila: Ateneo de Manila University Press.

Nunes, Evelyn H. 1972. "Some Epic Laws of the Donggon: A Study in Structure." *Philippine Studies* 20, no. 4: 563–76.

Pallesen, A. Kemp. 1985. *Culture Contact and Language Convergence*. Manila: Linguistic Society of the Philippines.

Paluga, Myfel D., and Andrea Malaya M. Ragragio. 2021. "Epic Chanting and the Figure of Pantaron Manobo "Breath" (*Goynawa*)." In *Philippine Folklore and Oral Traditions*, vol. 2 of *Reading the Regions*, edited by Luna Sicat-Cleto, 263–90. Manila: National Commission for Culture and the Arts.

Paredes, Oona. 2013. *A Mountain of Difference: The Lumad in Early Colonial Mindanao*. Ithaca, NY: Cornell University Press.

Pelras, Christian. 2016. "Orality and Writing among the Bugis." Translated by C. C. Macknight. In "Orality, Writing and History: The Literature of the Bugis and Makassar of South Sulawesi," edited by S. C. Druce, special issue, *International Journal of Asia Pacific Studies* 12 (suppl. 1): 13–51.

Ragragio, Andrea Malaya M., and Myfel D. Paluga. 2021. "What Netflix Got Wrong about Indigenous Storytelling." *Sapiens*, December 1. https://www.sapiens.org/culture/busaw-trese/.

Reilly, Brandon. 2013. "Epics in the Early Spanish Philippines Revisited." In *Songs of Memory in Islands of Southeast Asia*, edited by Nicole Revel, 279–91. Newcastle upon Tyne: Cambridge Scholars.

Revel, Nicole. 1996. "*Kudaman*: An Oral Epic in the Palawan Highlands." *Oral Traditions* 11, no. 1: 108–32. http://journal.oraltradition.org/files/articles/11i/11_revel.pdf.

Severi, Carlo. 2015. *The Chimera Principle: An Anthropology of Memory and Imagination*. Translated by Janet Lloyd. Chicago: HAU Books.

Smith, Linda Tuhiwai. 2012. *Decolonizing Methodologies: Research and Indigenous Peoples*. 2nd ed. London: Zed Books.

Talledo, Tomasito T. 2004. "Construction of Identity in Central Panay: A Critical Examination of the Ethnographic Subject in the Works of Jocano and Magos." *Asian Studies* 40, no. 1: 111–23.

Taton, Jose R. 2019. "The Panay Bukidnon *Talda*: Expressing Sentiment in Shifting Music Ecologies." *Philippine Journal of Social Sciences and Humanities* 22, nos. 1–2: 47–54.

Toelken, Barre, and Orville Tacheeni Scott. 1981. "Poetic Retranslation and the 'Pretty Languages' of Yellowman." In *Traditional Literatures of the American Indian*, edited by Karl Kroeber, 65–116. Lincoln: University of Nebraska Press.

Turner, Victor. 1987. *The Anthropology of Performance*. New York: PAJ.

Vansina, Jan. 1985. *Oral History as Tradition*. Madison: University of Wisconsin Press.

Villareal, Corazon D. 1997. *Siday: Mga Tulang Bayan ng Panay at Negros* [Siday: Folk Poems of Panay and Negros]. Quezon City: Ateneo de Manila Press.

Warren, James Francis. 1985. *The Sulu Zone 1768–1898: The Dynamics of External Trade, Slavery, and Ethnicity in the Transformation of a Southeast Asian Maritime State*. Quezon City: New Day.

Wolters, O. W. 1982. *History, Culture and Region in Southeast Asian Perspectives*. Singapore: Institute of Southeast Asian Studies.

DARREN WAN

Witnessing Empire's End
Malayan Refugees' Anticolonial Futures in Wartime India, 1942–1946

ABSTRACT This article examines how Malayans seeking refuge in Bombay engaged with anticolonial ideas and practices circulating in soon-to-be independent India. Escaping just days before the Japanese conquest of Singapore in February 1942, refugees drew comparisons between relatively subdued prewar Malayan anticolonialism and the wartime Quit India movement. Treating these narratives of evacuation as evidence for an alternative genealogy of Malayan political thought, this article argues that transcolonial networks across the British Empire complemented processes occurring within Malaya to shape Malayans' imaginations of a new political order. Newspaper articles, correspondence, oral history interviews, and biographies show that witnessing the electrifying lead-up to the transfer of power in India generated varied worldmaking projects that envisioned empire's end in Malaya. Even though some of these projects were suppressed and many transcolonial connections were downplayed after the war, tracking these futures past demonstrates how anticolonial nationalism and internationalism were once mutually constituted.

KEYWORDS transcolonial networks, refugees, worldmaking, World War II, British Empire

In the first two weeks of February 1942, seventeen-year-old Robert Loh Choo Kiat fled his hometown of Singapore for Bombay. Like thousands of other non-European residents of British Malaya, he managed to leave before Singapore fell to the Imperial Japanese Army on February 15. But far from being a safe haven, Bombay was a city in tumult. Apart from the fact that British India was bracing for the arrival of the Japanese in the northeast, there was conflict over Indians' participation in the British war effort and how their participation would affect the colonial government's plan for decolonization. These simmering tensions culminated in the violently suppressed Quit India movement that Gandhi launched in Bombay in August 1942. The world that Loh stepped into, then, was one where the legitimacy of British imperial rule was avidly contested, where the utopic possibility of empire's end was close at hand. In an oral history interview, Loh (2001: reel 4) poignantly noted: "The politicization of myself seemed to coincide with the maturing of India as an independent nation." While Loh ended up seeking refuge in Bombay as a result of contingencies beyond his control, he described Bombay as a central site for his political formation, as the coming of age of the Indian nation aligned with that of the Malayan self. In

THE JOURNAL OF ASIAN STUDIES · 84:2 · May 2025
DOI: 10.1215/00219118-11591179 © 2025 Association for Asian Studies

fact, Loh himself drew a through line between the events he witnessed in Bombay and his political commitments when he returned to Malaya after its reoccupation by the British. "The war," he claimed, "helped to shape us to be ready for what was going to happen to us in the next few years" (reel 3).

The Second World War is widely acknowledged to be crucial to the development of anticolonial thought and action in postwar Malaya. Yet Loh's encounter with anticolonial politics in British India contrasts sharply with the focus in official and academic historiography alike on events that took place within the territorial bounds of Malaya.[1] In these bodies of work, there is consensus that any legitimacy that colonial rule enjoyed was rapidly eroded by the British government's catastrophic failure in defending Malaya (Hack and Blackburn 2004; Bayly and Harper 2005: 106–55; Farrell 2017; Kratoska 2018: 23–54). Resentment at the British for putting Malaya at the mercy of the Japanese military government is further heightened in public memory sanctioned by the Singaporean state. In this narrative, British inaction precipitated the central trauma of Sook Ching, the mass murder over a two-week period of tens of thousands of "undesirables," mostly Chinese men suspected of serving in volunteer armies that fought in Singapore's last stand and of making overseas financial contributions to the Second United Front during the Second Sino-Japanese War (Blackburn 2000; Wong 2000, 2001; Blackburn and Hack 2012). There has also been significant work on resistance during the Japanese occupation, especially on the role of communists in the Malayan Peoples' Anti-Japanese Army (Wan Hashim 1993; Hara 1995; Akashi 1995; Cheah 2003), a point obscured in anticommunist official historiographies that regard that organization not as antifascist freedom fighters but as enemies of the state (Wong 2001: 225–29).

The bulk of this scholarship has limited its scope to how experiences within the territorial bounds of Japanese-occupied Malaya gave a fillip to postwar anticolonialism.[2] In this article, I contend that viewing anticolonialism solely through national frames erroneously reifies the idea that Malayan anticolonialism was distinct from other fields of struggle against imperialism and fascism. By treating narratives of Malayan evacuees in Bombay as evidence for an alternative genealogy of Malayan anticolonialism,[3] I argue that transcolonial networks across the British Empire complemented processes occurring within Malaya to foster Malayans' expectations for a new political order. To make this claim, I draw from historiography that decenters imperial metropoles like London to foreground how transcolonial connections were crucial in forging varieties of anticolonialism (Ghosh and Kennedy 2006; Manjapra 2010; Aiyar 2011; Lewis and Stolte 2019; Harper 2021). None of the subjects discussed in this article explicitly call themselves internationalists, most likely because their experience as refugees that generated transcolonial connections was not a result of premeditation but of unplanned contingency. Their forced displacement inadvertently engendered "their engagement with the world 'out there,' beyond the limits of the nation-state," and thereby resulted in political commitments whose genealogies cannot be presumed to be bound to the national geobody (Leake and Guyot-Réchard 2023: 18). But because these subjects did not set out to establish these transnational connections if war were not waged, all the sources in which they self-narrate their experiences as refugees—in autobiographies, letters, and state-sanctioned oral history interviews—are expressed in normative national frames. Often prepared years after the Second World War, these sources grapple with the transcolonial in only fragmentary form, especially because the nation-state was fast becoming the preeminent form of political organization worldwide. For this reason, I interpolate the transcolonial in these patchy self-narrations by examining contemporaneous government correspondence and newspaper sources. In focusing on these glimmers of evacuees' transcolonial commitments, I heed the recent call to bring transnationality into studies of the eminently global Second World War (Buchanan 2023) and, in so doing, show how the Second World War cannot be assumed to represent a complete break in Southeast Asian history. Despite the fact that the war upended Malayan political and social life, maritime networks of empire continued to enable interactions between colonized people who were collectively fighting for empire's end.

Witnessing the imminent end of empire in India led refugees to imagine plans to remake their Malaya-centered worlds. Because Malaya's and Singapore's transfer of power—effected in 1957 and 1963, respectively—seemed distant in the early 1940s, many Malayan refugees were struck by the concreteness with which decolonization was imagined in India, which gained independence in 1947. By bearing witness to scenes of anticolonial action and engaging with anticolonial thought in circulation, Malayan refugees articulated their visions of anticolonial worldmaking, defined by Adom Getachew (2019: 23) as "the project of overcoming international hierarchy and constituting a postimperial world." Given the many fractures in the anticolonial movement in wartime India, what refugees witnessed in Bombay was anticolonialism in its various and often contradictory forms, leading to their envisioning of Malayan futures that were far from monolithic. Each section of this article examines an array of personal and institutional political engagements that range from radical commitments to more accommodationist and gradualist views toward decolonization.

This wide spectrum of political commitments is further reflected in the divergent postwar trajectories taken by the key figures discussed in this article. Many businessmen became prominent mainstream politicians after the war, including Rajabali Jumabhoy and Mohamed Javad Namazie, members of the Legislative Council of Singapore, and Tan Cheng Lock, founder of the Malayan Chinese Association (MCA), a major political party established in 1949. Others, however, had their political aspirations quashed, including Poh Soo Kai, a prominent socialist politician in postwar Singapore, and Tengku Mahmood Mahyideen, a scion of the deposed sultan of Patani who campaigned for Patani's secession from Siam to join the Malayan Federation. Still others opted to steer away from the turbulence of postwar politics: Robert Loh, whose account opened this article, focused on his career as an ophthalmologist in Singapore.

My analysis of these case studies does not dismiss internal critiques of colonialism that were taking shape within Japanese-occupied Malaya, nor does it assume that anticolonial ideas were simply transplanted wholesale from India to Malaya. Rather, I seek to explain how the understudied experiences of these refugees provided them with an idiom for articulating varied anticolonial futures, thereby setting in motion practices of worldmaking that would be their contribution to the cacophonous political scene of postwar Malaya.[4] This moment of internationalist openness, however, would be foreclosed by the 1960s, as the Malaysian and Singaporean states honed in on the protection of state sovereignty as the main legitimate form of political activity (Amrith 2008).

PEDAGOGIES OF PROTEST

While Malaya in the 1930s was teeming with political activity, most historians have presented this period as significant for the development of forms of nationalism that were not tethered to anticolonialism. Malay elites who were not explicitly anti-British articulated and debated different visions of political community, and by the 1930s these nationalist currents started to be organized against diasporic communities of Indians and Chinese (W. R. Roff 1967; Ariffin 1993; Milner 1995). In response, elite Chinese and Indian expressions of nationalism focused on affirming their sense of being Malayan as compatible with their transnational connections (Ampalavanar 1970; Chua 2012). None of these emergent Malayan nationalisms necessarily translated into anticolonial demands for immediate political independence. In fact, as Siew-Min Sai (2013) and Chua Ai Lin (2008: 26–27) have demonstrated, elite nationalists were often unstinting in their expressions of imperial loyalty.

It was this world where nationalism was pervasive yet anticolonialism was inchoate that was upended with the Japanese invasion. When the Imperial Japanese Army first landed in the Malay State of Kelantan on December 8, 1941, most Malayans did not expect the rapidity with which the Japanese conquered the colony. Many living on the Malayan mainland did not even have the option to leave (Jumabhoy 1981: reel 11), so those who could flee fled from Singapore, the last city to be occupied, located at the southernmost tip of the peninsula. The first ships that left the harbor for Australia or India were filled only with white Europeans, a policy implemented across British Asia but most dramatically in Hong Kong and Penang (Bayly and Harper 2005: 120–21; Kong 2019). Upon realizing this, Rajabali Jumabhoy, president of the Indian Chamber of Commerce in Singapore, cabled Gandhi and Archibald Wavell, then commander-in-chief of India, to send ships for the colony's nonwhite subjects (Jumabhoy 1981: reel 7). Only on February 7, 1942, one day before the start of the Battle of Singapore, did a convoy of four ships carrying approximately five thousand Asian evacuees leave for British India (reel 11).

While it might be expected that only upper-class families with connections to the colonial government could make the cut, the demographics of the evacuees were mixed. Prominent business leaders brought a retinue of servants and workers, who in turn managed to rope in family and friends onto the evacuation rosters. Ruth Shih (1995: reel 3), who like her husband worked as a bookseller, stated explicitly that she managed to acquire passage to India even though "we were not rich leaders of the Overseas Chinese community. But we had worked for them before." Yet in sources like these state-sanctioned oral history interviews, women like Shih were not asked in great detail about their political activities. Despite the variety of Malayan refugees' gender and class positions, the most comprehensive accounts of political activity in Bombay, which form this article's main source base, foreground the perspectives of elite men.

That many of the ships carrying this wide range of evacuees chose Bombay as their landing site was no accident. "The Bay of Bengal was full of Japanese submarines," states Rajabali Jumabhoy (1981: reel 11), so most ships avoided the ports of Calcutta or Madras even if they were much closer to Singapore. Apart from Jumabhoy, who had family and business connections to Bombay (reel 2), all other refugees discussed in this article had no significant prior connection to the city. In this sense, landing in Bombay, the largest port on the western coast of India, was a result of wartime contingencies beyond refugees' control. Estimates of the number of Malayan evacuees range from 4,000 (*Times of India* [*TOI*], October 18, 1945) to "more than 10,000" (*Indian Daily Mail* [*IDM*], March 16, 1946), with the largest concentration in Bombay. Because evacuees lacked connections when they first landed in the city in 1942, a host of volunteer organizations had to support evacuees in finding accommodation, providing food and clothes, and eventually, seeking employment (*TOI*, February 21, 1942; February 23, 1942). So dire was the plight of evacuees in Bombay, "this Mecca of refugees" (*Illustrated Weekly of India*, March 22, 1942, suppl.), that the mayor of Bombay, Yusuf Meherally, appointed an ad hoc Mayor's Indian Evacuees (Overseas) Relief Committee to directly address evacuees' homelessness and destitution (*TOI*, May 30, 1942).

Even though the first few months of Malayan refugees' stay in the city was relatively uneventful, tensions over the failure of the Cripps Mission to guarantee the Indian National Congress's support for the British war effort against the Axis powers culminated in the launching of the Quit India movement in August 1942 (Bhuyan 1975). After the British government rejected Congress's demand for immediate independence, strikes and protests organized by workers and students erupted across the country in what the viceroy labeled "by far the most serious rebellion since that of 1857" (Marquess of Linlithgow 1971). These expressions of anticolonialism were especially prominent in Bombay, where many Congress leaders were arrested in the first days of the campaign. Far from stunting the movement, it "freed [other city inhabitants] from the specific organizational control of Congress" (Masselos 2007: 266), thereby giving the protests a bottom-up character that was generated by the spread of underground literature and by crowd behavior (Greenough 1983; Masselos 2007: 253). While the movement was brutally suppressed within a month, more localized protests persisted for months (Chandavarkar 1998: 232–33, 319–20).

What unites many Malayan evacuees' narratives about their time in Bombay is their account of the electrifying energy of the Quit India movement that shaped daily life during the duration of their stay in the city. In his autobiography, Poh Soo Kai (2016: 75–76) writes of his childhood in Bombay when his family evacuated Singapore:

> I remember the Indian Muslim teacher who spoke critically about British colonialism. I also saw a demonstration by the Indian National Congress party protesting against the British. After the exposure to nationalist manifestations in my primary school years in Bombay, limited though it was, secondary school in Singapore was staid and stuffy as the colonial authorities tried to re-establish its order.

Even though Poh's treatment of Bombay is brief, the juxtaposition of these two phases of his early education emphasizes his imagination of Bombay as a space of political possibility in comparison to life under the British Military Administration

(1945–46) in Malaya. Admittedly, his memories of Bombay are impressionistic, not only because he was a child during the war but also because his narrative's focus on his political engagement within Singapore is a strategic one: these words were published as an autobiography that seeks to revise the state-sanctioned narrative that he was a communist insurgent that threatened Singapore's security. But what these few sentences hint at is the pedagogical function that Bombay served in Poh's subject formation. That Poh clung onto the memory of an Indian teacher's utterance of anticolonial critique in the public space of a classroom demonstrates how these memories reverberated in his future political engagements. This right to dissent that left such an impress on him would ultimately be denied to him in Singapore in the 1960s.

Yet such critical speech stood out in Poh's memories only because it was exceptional. In his experience of wartime Bombay, "among ordinary Indians, the white-sahib-brown-sahib colonial mentality hung thick as the summer heat over them" (Poh 2016: 75). The norm, at least in the middle-class milieu where he found himself, was for the colonized to seek to don the trappings of the colonizer, to have internalized the racialized dynamic of colonial power relations. Having this racial economy laid bare was not just Poh's experience—so many Malayan refugees were acutely aware of racial discrimination in the coordination of evacuation rolls and aboard evacuation ships that the government of India and the Colonial Office were mired in lengthy discussions over these allegations. Within government correspondence, colonial officials admitted that "the reports received from refugees are remarkably consistent regarding the differential treatment accorded to Europeans and Asiatics and that these reports, which have naturally gained not a little publicity, have aroused very bitter comment" (TNA 1942: 39). This fact, however, was publicly denied, with newspapers claiming that there "was absolutely no racial or communal discrimination" in evacuation (*TOI*, February 21, 1942) and that these allegations were based on "generally tainted information" (*Indian Express*, February 24, 1942). Ultimately, these episodes reveal Malayan refugees' attention to racialization that undergirded British colonial rule. While such a racial economy was undoubtedly in operation in prewar Malaya, we might speculate that the chaos of evacuation and the outsiders' perspective from which Malayan refugees viewed Indian society heightened their awareness of racial differentiation.

The irony of stories like Poh's and other relatively elite refugees' is that evacuation to Bombay, which fed into their participation in anticolonial movements in postwar Singapore, was made available to them in 1942 only because of their family's proximity to imperial power. As a grandson of Tan Kah Kee, one of Malaya's most prominent businessmen, Poh and his family had connections that probably guaranteed them passage to Bombay when seats on evacuating ships were highly coveted. The networks of empire, then, contributed to empire's end by facilitating the formation of transcolonial connections through which racism underpinning colonialism was laid bare and by which anticolonial ideas and practices could spread. This seeming paradox brings to mind Engseng Ho's (2004: 212) claim that diaspora and empire are "locked in a tight embrace of intimacy and treachery, a relationship of mutual benefit, attraction, and aversion." The forces that were once responsible for shoring up empire were starting to undo it.

Like Poh's autobiography, Robert Loh's oral history interview emphasizes the pedagogical effect of witnessing unrest on the streets of Bombay that shaped his subsequent engagement with anticolonial politics. An ophthalmologist by the time of the interview in 2001, Loh enrolled in medical school in Bombay. He opened his account of Bombay's political atmosphere by describing his peers: "I would say that the students in India . . . are much more politicized than students in Singapore. They participated in a lot of union activities" (Loh 2001: reel 4). In making this comparison, he appears to be framing his observations in an objective, almost disembodied way. But as he became more comfortable with the topic, he proceeded to thicken his account: "I could see the riots taking place in the streets: the involvement of the police, the crackdown by the police and the British army against rioters, shooting. It was right in front of my eyes" (reel 4). By pivoting to a first-person account of his engagement with the Quit India movement, Loh foregrounded the importance of witnessing acts of anticolonial activism and the colonial government's response to them in allowing him to make common cause with his Indian peers. It is the immediacy of this experience of witnessing—that all this violence was "right in front of my eyes"—that heightens the comparison he made to his relatively quiescent life in prewar Singapore. His time in Bombay, then, was a foundational moment for his postwar anticolonial orientation.

Yet Loh's account goes one step further by emphasizing his politics as a product not simply of witnessing but also of actively participating in the Quit India movement in Bombay. "In fact," Loh (2001: reel 4) recounted, "when I was in college, my first experience with those activities was that I was asked to join them in a strike against the government. So I went and marched with them, and then we came across the police. And the police at that time used these long rattans, you know. I got struck on the back." Unlike Poh Soo Kai, who was a much younger child when he lived in Bombay, Robert Loh was able to engage with anticolonialism in a more embodied way. He emphasizes that protesting British rule in Bombay was simply his "first experience," with many more experiences in anticolonial activism to come in postwar Malaya, thereby suggesting that his participation in anticolonial activism in Malaya was intertwined with his political engagements in Bombay. Anticolonial tactics were shared across different colonies, like elsewhere in the empire, to mount a global challenge to British imperial rule (Silvestri 2000; Grant 2006; O'Malley 2008).

Loh temporally maps his own political self-fashioning onto the ascendancy of the Indian nation. This is not to say, of course, that Malayan anticolonialism would have been impossible without the cross-pollination of anticolonial ideas from India. Loh himself (2001: reel 4) forecloses that interpretation by saying that his hatred of the British "was taking shape inside me already" before he evacuated Singapore for Bombay, but those sentiments "didn't come to the surface." These words suggest that the legitimacy of the colonial government in India had been eroded to such an extent that it quickened and sharpened Malayan refugees' expression of anticolonial sentiments. After all, as discussed above, prewar Malayan critiques of the colonial government were muted compared to those in India. In this way, Loh's account of his own political formation in Bombay generated by witnessing and participating in Quit India protests allowed him to draw strategic connections between two sequential moments of national becoming, as the "attainment of nationhood by one country," India, was "followed later on by my own country" (reel 4). Instead of narrating the independence of Malaya and later Singapore as an internal historical phenomenon, Loh tells a tale of the deep entanglements in the struggle for self-rule at the transcolonial scale.

These entanglements extended beyond connections between Malayans and Indians to also involve refugees from Britain's other colonies. Loh (2001: reel 4) emphasizes his friendship with Burmese evacuees of Indian origin: "There was a natural gravitation towards each other, because we all had a common problem. We were living away from our own country." Loh's words hint at how an intimate understanding of another imminently independent colony further shaped his relationship with anticolonialism. Refugees from Burma were significantly more numerous, with "half a million Indians . . . along with some 50,000 Burmans" having evacuated to India just seven months after the fall of Rangoon (*TOI*, October 22, 1942). It is unsurprising that Loh would have encountered students who were fellow evacuees because, starting with Madras University, many Indian universities changed their matriculation requirements to lower the bar for evacuees to begin or continue their education in India during the war (*Indian Express*, February 21, 1942). While Loh does not elaborate on his encounters with Burmese evacuees, we can understand his "natural gravitation" to other refugees by drawing from work by Manu Goswami, who emphasizes that comparison across different sites has been generative for the development of internationalist anticolonial politics. Establishing "commensurability across worlds conventionally deemed discrete and disparate," Goswami (2012: 1464) argues, has helped produce "a vernacular politics" as colonized people articulated shared futures and translated anticolonial ideas that were deployed against the common imperial enemy at different sites. By suggesting that contingent interactions that evacuation to Bombay made possible gave shape to his politics, Loh's account demonstrates how anticolonialism was negotiated not only in the realm of high politics but also through "personal encounters with fellow anti-imperialists" (Louro 2018: 51; see also Stolte 2023). For this reason, transcolonial politics in this more intimate mode—a politics informed by direct witness and participation—is vital for understanding the forms of anticolonialism that were practiced in postwar Malaya.

VISIONS OF POSTWAR POLITICS

But Malayan refugees did not frame their engagement with anticolonial politics only in this intimate register. Many elite refugees who would become prominent career politicians when they returned to Malaya were engaged with more institutional forms of politics during their time in India. The political activities of Tan Cheng Lock constitute a key instance of Malayan refugees' more conventional practices of worldmaking in India. As a refugee in India, he founded the Overseas Chinese Association (OCA) in 1943. While there were members across most major cities on the subcontinent—many elite refugees opted to live away from Bombay and the political tumult with which it was associated (Ooi 2020: 81)—meetings were held in Bombay, where most Malayan refugees lived (HSL 1943c). The OCA was an organization that could be conceived only under the conditions of wartime evacuation, as its membership included Chinese evacuees not only from Malaya but also from "Burma, China and the other territories" (Tan C. L. 1947: 7). Initially, however, one of Tan's close associates, Lee Hau Shik, objected to the capaciousness of the OCA's membership and found it "unwieldy and impracticable" (HSL 1943a; Tan M. I. 2015a: 108). Lee had envisioned an organization limited to Malayan Chinese, because for him "the Malayan Chinese now in India have nothing in common with their countrymen resident in India except the colour of their skin" (HSL 1943d). Tan, however, responded by standing by the original ambit of the OCA and insisted that organizing with refugees from other British colonies did not have to come at the expense of discussions of Malaya's postwar future conducted among a subset of the association's members (HSL 1943e). Even though in practice the majority of members were Malayans, Chinese evacuees from Burma, for instance, were key sponsors of and avid participants in the OCA (HSL 1943b). The geographical inclusiveness of the OCA's membership demonstrates that refugees' wartime exile was a moment when transcolonial interactions were intensified by the convergence in urban India of wartime refugees from across the empire. Ultimately, Tan articulated a vision of the postwar political order that was predicated upon regarding the fates of different overseas Chinese communities as intertwined by virtue of such transcolonial connections. In this respect, Tan's view parallels the abovementioned narrative of Robert Loh, for whom friendship with Burmese evacuees facilitated the forging of anticolonial solidarity.

The objectives of the OCA as formulated by Tan, however, mark his divergence from the kind of anticolonial politics that Loh espoused. One of the main objectives of the OCA, according to Tan (1947: 5), was to address the "question relating to reparation for war damage and losses sustained in Malaya." Ultimately, the central concern of the OCA, dominated as it was by prominent businessmen, was the postwar well-being of the propertied classes. This point is reinforced by the eligibility criteria for membership in the OCA, which was not restricted to persons but extended also to "partnerships, firms, joint-stock companies, corporations and other business undertakings ... provided that in the case of a firm more than one half of the proprietary interest thereof is held by oversea-Chinese" (HSL n.d.). This notion of corporate personhood reflected in the OCA's constitution reveals that the association acted principally as an advocate for business interests that were severely curtailed by war by working to register information about members' lost assets in Japanese-occupied Malaya and Hong Kong with the government of India (TNA 1943a). Of course, the OCA had other concerns, such as the provision of "relief to the needy Chinese evacuees of British nationality in India" (Tan C. L. 1947: 6).[5] But such problems were regarded as temporary, especially as the tide started to turn against the Japanese in the Pacific theater by 1943 (HSL 1943f). In all his writings published under the auspices of the OCA, Tan's main concern was with the future of Malaya upon British reoccupation (e.g., Tan C. L. 1947: 10–42). Given that the OCA's principal goal was to secure repayment from the British government for wartime property losses, we can conclude that even if Tan was an advocate for political change, he desired the restoration of the economic status quo after the war's end.

That Tan's political project differed from Loh's is marked even more clearly in the speech that Tan delivered at the inaugural meeting of the OCA in Bombay on September 24, 1943. In it, he called for the British reoccupation of Japanese-occupied

Malaya and declaimed that the OCA ought to secure the "recognition and goodwill of the British Government and *incidentally to dispel whatever misgivings that may have arisen in certain quarters in Bombay* and also give a clear indication regarding the future policy and activities of the Association" (Tan C. L. 1947: 3; emphasis added). While Tan campaigned for the eventual decolonization of Malaya, he was at pains to emphasize that the OCA was friendly to the British government, a position that diverged from that of the Quit India movement that galvanized other Malayan refugees into political action. It is precisely to this radical anticolonial position that Tan alluded when he discussed the "misgivings" in "certain quarters in Bombay," a point that suggests his awareness that political unrest in Bombay generated forms of anticolonialism that were more uncompromising than Tan's accommodationist approach. These words underscore not simply that the experience of wartime evacuation produced wide-ranging expressions of Malayan political futures but also that Malayan refugees were well aware of the divergent political visions within their community and avidly debated them. Such contestations that unfolded in Bombay, where Malayans expressed disparate responses to the unfolding of the Quit India movement, would continue when the refugees returned to Malaya after British reoccupation.

An evacuee who articulated a similarly pro-British vision of postwar Malaya was Tengku Mahmood Mahyideen. A son of the last sultan of Patani who was deposed when Siam annexed his kingdom in 1902, Mahmood Mahyideen grew up in the Unfederated Malay State of Kelantan. On the eve of the invasion, he joined the Kelantan Volunteer Force. The unit, however, was disbanded weeks after the Japanese army landed, when the defense of Kelantan was regarded as a lost cause (BWJ 1942: 46). Mahmood Mahyideen then fled to Singapore, where he secured a place on the evacuation roll. En route, he sustained injuries when his ship was bombed. Upon his arrival in Bombay, he was brought by train to Delhi for his convalescence (Wilson 1992; Mohamed Zamberi 1999).

In Delhi, Mahmood Mahyideen was recruited to work for All India Radio, where he designed and disseminated anti-Axis propaganda through Malay language broadcasts. It is during this period of service that his vision of postwar Patani took form. Whereas before the war the frontier between Thailand and Malaya "had the appearance of permanence" resulting from the Anglo-Siamese Treaty of 1909 (Wilson 1992: 44), Thailand's alliance with the Japanese Empire in 1941—along with Thailand's annexation of four Japanese-occupied Malay states in 1943 (TNA 1943h: 19)—provided the conditions for a potential geopolitical reconfiguration (Nik Anuar 1999: 55–56). Mahmood Mahyideen claimed that during his tenure at All India Radio British officials promised that, in exchange for his continued support for the Allied cause in Malaya, the British Malayan government would consider annexing Patani and restoring the sultanate after the war— perhaps with him on the throne—as retribution for Thailand's buttressing of Japanese expansionism (Che Man 1990: 158; Mohamed Zamberi 1999: 73). This promise formed the cornerstone of Mahmood Mahyideen's postwar fight for Patani's secession from Siam (Walker 2013: 221–22). While it is difficult to corroborate his claim, official discussions among British civil servants demonstrate that the postwar annexation of the Kra Isthmus was seriously considered, because this narrow strip of land was perceived to be the "heel of Achilles of the whole British Empire" for having exposed both Burma and Malaya to

Japanese attack (TNA 1943b; see also Tarling 1978: 31–32; Nik Anuar 2008: 24–25). The promise allegedly made to Mahmood Mahyideen, then, was not beyond the realm of possibility. Acting on this symbiotic arrangement, he traveled from India to the Hijaz and Egypt, centers for Patani Malay students and intellectuals (Azra 2013; Hayimasae 2013), to recruit members for Force 136 to conduct covert sabotage operations in Japanese-occupied Malaya (Mohamed Zamberi 1999: 63). With Mahmood Mahyideen's political fate hinging on the promise of Patani's inclusion in postwar British Malaya, it is perhaps unsurprising that where his and Tan's positions converge is their pro-British stance: Mahmood Mahyideen declared himself "a reasoning friend and supporter of the British Empire" (TNA 1943j: 56). This political position was a recurring theme in the Malay-language broadcasts that he wrote and narrated for All India Radio. In one broadcast, he argued that in prewar British Malaya "there was justice and no interference with our religion and culture," whereas the Siamese like the Japanese "favour the extermination of our customs, our race, our religion" (TNA 1943i: 26).

While the stark comparison could be understood simply as propagandistic rhetoric, Mahmood Mahyideen's uncritically pro-British stance might instead be interpreted as an attempt to play off British, Japanese, and Siamese colonial powers against one another in order realize his Patani-centered worldmaking project. More specifically, he appeared to be leveraging his position at the Ministry of Information in Delhi to lobby the British to buy into his vision of Malaya's future. In a memorandum he distributed to various colonial officials who then internally circulated the document to their superiors, he argued that the native Malays "feel themselves being fast submerged by the aliens," especially "the Chinese, who come in hordes into the country." At the same time, however, he felt that a source of cheap labor was necessary for Malaya's economic development and advocated for the curtailment of migration from China and India while promoting the importation of Javanese labor, which in his eyes was "just as good and as cheap as Chinese labour" (TNA 1943j: 63–64). The central thrust of his memorandum, then, was to advocate for a reengineering of the demographic makeup of Malaya while protecting the capitalist interests of the native elite.

Yet even Mahmood Mahyideen recognized that convincing the colonial government to protect what were purportedly "Malay interests" to the detriment of other communities was a hard sell, especially given the fact that rumor was quickly spreading that many Malay sultans and some of their subjects were collaborating with the Japanese military government (e.g., TNA 1943c; 1943d: 172–73; 1943e: 154; 1943f: 97; 1943g: 67–68). For this reason, he made an effort in the same memorandum to explain away any pro-Japanese sentiment among "the Malay upper class" by claiming that it was simply because "they and the Japanese have a common enemy, the Chinese." Put differently, they were not exactly "anti-British and pro-Japanese" but were "first and foremost . . . pro-Malay" (TNA 1943j: 65–66). These assurances that the Malay elite was not collaborationist dovetailed with his insistence that he was in favor of British colonialism, and for this reason he argued that his propaganda work at All India Radio had to focus on convincing "the native inhabitants [to] feel sufficiently interested in the continuation of the British connection" (TNA 1943j: 80). In light of the possibility of Patani's annexation by British Malaya after the war, Mahmood Mahyideen's repeated pledges of allegiance to the British Empire suggest that his objective was to play different colonizing powers against one another to free his father's realm from the Siamese yoke. This move parallels those of earlier elites in the Malay world who appealed to other imperial powers to curb the power of their current overlords, including Acehnese overtures to the United States in the 1870s and the Riau Sultanate's courting of Japan in the 1900s, both intended to stave off Dutch intervention (Andaya 1977; Reid 2005: 261–63). In the wake of these precedents, Mahmood Mahyideen dedicated much of his time in exile to instantiating his vision of Malaya's future, which consisted principally of the territorial reconfiguration of the British Malayan geobody.

Like Mahmood Mahyideen, Tan Cheng Lock participated in discourse about Malaya's postwar future that circulated between Malayan evacuees and British colonial officers. Under the aegis of the OCA, Tan refuted Mahmood Mahyideen's claims about the Chinese as alien to Malaya and staked his position in the debate on the minority question that would mire down the Malayan political sphere in the decades to come. In treatises written during his stay in India, Tan insisted that the Chinese in Malaya deserved political rights equal to the majority Malay community because who constituted a "native" to that land was highly ambiguous. Tan made two historical arguments to shore up this claim in a 1943 paper written in India titled "Memorandum on the Future of Malaya," copies of which he personally mailed to key officeholders in the Colonial Office (TNA 1943k, 1943l, 1943m). First, he demonstrated that "the Malays themselves are . . . comparative newcomers to Malaya, having dispossessed the still earlier aboriginal inhabitants" (Tan C. L. 1947: 11). In effect, this argument that Malays were to some extent foreign to the Malay Peninsula challenged the native/alien binary through which the colonial government understood race and by which political rights were differentially distributed. Second, Tan argued that Chinese migration to Southeast Asia had antecedents that were inaugurated by Faxian's pilgrimage in 399 CE, suggesting that Malayan Chinese ought to be seen as "native" to Malaya (11–12). This claim to the antiquity of Chinese presence in Malaya is coupled with Tan's appeal to stereotypes of the industrious Chinese improving an otherwise poorly cultivated land, making them "one of the greatest colonising powers of the world" (24).[6] Collectively, Tan deploys these twin historical arguments, of Malays being not quite native and Chinese being not quite alien, to make a case for equal citizenship rights. In a different, equally well-circulated memorandum, Tan underscored this point even more unequivocally: "The non-Malay domiciled inhabitants of Malaya feel that they have won as good a title to be regarded as the sons of the soil as have the Malays" (Royal Commonwealth Society 1944). The contrast between Tan's claim to Chinese nativeness and Mahmood Mahyideen's argument that Chinese were aliens in Malaya would be a recurring theme in the political debates of the late 1940s and the 1950s over the precise constitutional arrangements for Malayan independence (Lau 1989; Amoroso 2014: 135–65; Andaya and Andaya 2017: 260–306).

Ultimately, Tan's writings during his time in India reveal that the OCA was conceived as a platform for elite Chinese Malayans to articulate their visions of Malaya's political future. His accommodationist pro-British sentiments, much like Mahmood Mahyideen's, can be understood as an attempt to outmaneuver his political opponents by getting the British on his side in the coming negotiations regarding the precise arrangements for independence. By articulating their plans for Malaya's future through memoranda that found readership among colonial officials from Delhi to London, Tan and Mahmood Mahyideen, despite finding themselves political opponents within the tight-knit Malayan evacuee community in India, both had an eye to remaking the world and Malaya's place in it. In this sense, elite Malayan politicians' experience as refugees in Bombay did not represent a rupture in Malayan politics. Rather, it afforded them opportunities to continue prewar political debates and to jockey for influence with British colonial officials who regarded the Japanese occupation as a "chance to make a fresh beginning" for the seeds of Malaya's eventual decolonization to be sown (TNA 1944: 26).

For these elite evacuees, their time in India during the war left an impress on their postwar political engagements. This point is dramatized most lucidly in the contestations within the Malayan refugee community over their interpretations and responses to the Quit India movement, with Tan advocating for a more gradual form of decolonization than the radical practices of anticolonialism discussed in the previous section. Witnessing the imminent end of empire in Bombay informed the emergence of divergent imaginaries of postcolonial futures, which Tan recognized and sought to address to bolster his political position within the fractious community of Malayan refugees. In this sense, such transcolonial connections forged by the tumult of the Second World War contributed to the plurality of anticolonial ideas and practices that circulated in postwar Malaya.[7]

DREAMS OF PARTITION

Yet Malayan refugees' engagement with politics in India extended beyond such internal contestations within their own community. As varied political ideas circulated across the Indian subcontinent in empire's waning years, Malayan evacuees could not help but engage and experiment with them. While Robert Loh and Poh Soo Kai were especially taken with the Quit India movement's anticolonial claims, elite politicians like Tan Cheng Lock incorporated other political ideas that were hotly debated at the time, demonstrating again that the experience of wartime evacuation was constitutive of certain discourses within the Malayan political sphere.

This point is clearest in Mohamed Javad Namazie's account of his interaction with Tan Cheng Lock. A prominent lawyer of Persian Muslim extraction and a member of the Legislative Council of postwar colonial Singapore, Namazie (1982: reel 6) in his oral history interview fondly remembered the political discussions he had with Tan in Bangalore: "He had ideas of what should happen after the war. In fact we drew up a Constitution which Cheng Lock sent on our behalf—what should happen in Malaysia." While it is unclear to whom Tan Cheng Lock sent this draft constitution, Namazie's account suggests that it was in India that the kernel of the People's Constitutional Proposals for Malaya—which in 1947 the British government rejected as the constitutional basis for independent Malaya—was first formulated,[8] showing that this vision for a postimperial Malayan future had its origins beyond the territorial bounds of the nation.

In this process, Tan, Namazie claimed, was especially drawn to the idea of Partition, which gained popularity during the Second World War through arguments put forth by the All-India Muslim League about the urgent necessity of establishing an autonomous and sovereign state that protected the rights and interests of the Muslim minority. While Muhammad Ali Jinnah was far from the sole representative of Muslims across the subcontinent—a point dramatized by the Muslim League's spectacular electoral losses in 1937—the initially ambiguous demand for a separate Muslim nation had morphed into a more concrete call for the founding of Pakistan by the war's end (Jalal 1985). In particular, more than many other Indian cities located outside of Muslim-majority areas, Bombay's political sphere had a prominent Muslim League presence that would be hard for any politically engaged inhabitant of the city to miss (Khan 2019).

In fact, Tan Cheng Lock (1947: 17) explicitly commented on the League's two-nation theory that undergirded the demand for Pakistan, characterizing British India as a place "where deep, intense and universal racial hatred and distrust seem to be patently prevalent." It is precisely this problem that Tan hoped Malaya could avoid, one evoked in his many treatises on Chinese-Malay race relations discussed in the previous section. Consequently, borrowing from the increasing prevalence of pro-Partition discourse in India, Tan dreamed up the partition of Malaya. Namazie (1982: reel 7) narrated this proposal as follows:

> Tan Cheng Lock had some peculiar views. . . . Cheng Lock's view was that in the south, Johor, probably a part of Pahang and parts of Negeri Sembilan, which were predominantly Chinese, and Singapore—these should become one state. And the rest, give the rest to the Malays. That was his Partition, that was his view. But of course it was not practical. . . . We didn't write the Constitution on that basis. But that was how his mind was working, influenced as he was by what was happening in India.

This plan for a race-based partition of Malaya, which Tan adapted from the impending religion-based partition of India, diverged sharply from any territorial arrangement proposed for postwar Malaya. As tensions between the Malay community and Chinese and Indian minorities flared up during postwar discussions over political arrangements after independence, Tan would never have publicly articulated a plan that would give the Chinese a separate sphere of territorial sovereignty. Yet this plan for Malaya's partition that Tan Cheng Lock formulated in India suggests that even in this earlier period he was concerned with the problem of racial difference and how debates over it would shape postwar Malayan politics. We might also speculate that this partition plan might be pegged to Tan's desire to maintain the economic status quo in postwar Malaya—one of the OCA's goals, as discussed in the previous section—to prevent undue intervention in Chinese capitalist interests by securing a realm of Malayan Chinese sovereignty. After all, contemporary parallels of diasporic businessmen's concerns that geopolitical change on the eve of empire's end would harm their financial interests abounded, as evidenced in Kalyani Ramnath's (2023: 78–101) account of how Chettiar firms in Burma sought to mitigate their tax liabilities that compounded with the India-Burma partition of 1937. In step with other mobile Asian capitalists of the day, Tan considered the Indian plan for partition as one possible solution for defusing the tensions between the Chinese minority and the Malay majority that would bedevil any postwar discussion about Malaya's political and economic future.

In a sense, too, this imagined partition of Malaya foreshadowed the British partition of Singapore from Malaya, as the Colonial Office opted to administer Singapore as a discrete Crown colony, while the rest of the Straits Settlements merged with the Federated and Unfederated Malay States as the Malayan Union in 1946. While the British had intentions other than race-based ones for partitioning British Malaya into Singapore and the Malayan Union, such as the importance of the Singapore's naval base to the empire, this discussion allowed Namazie (1982: reel 6) to mourn the separation of a land whose connections were once unalienable: "The separation of Singapore perhaps was not the right thing to do." These words suggest that, while the result of Namazie's and Tan's debates about the plan for partitioning Malaya was to reject it, they engaged with ideas that were circulating across the Indian subcontinent as a means through which to imagine Malaya anew. After all, plans for partition were circulating across the British Empire as a viable way to manage what were regarded as intractable conflicts between different communities, not only in India but also in Palestine and Ireland (Miller 2010; Dubnov and Robson 2019; Sinanoglou 2019). Partitioning was at this time a transcolonial political experiment.

What emerges in Namazie's and Tan's wartime discussions about the territorial shape of postwar Malaya is that the experience of exile in India did not produce a uniform vision for the Malay Peninsula's future. Malayan refugees encountered a wide range of ideas and practices that they had to sift through to imagine futures that they would strive to realize when they returned to Malaya. Even figures like Namazie and Tan, who are associated with the upper echelons of Malayan political society, had to contend with an array of ideas that represented different political positions. These range from plans for partition based on conservative assumptions about the intractability of racial conflict, to more radical ideas about the value of direct anticolonial action and of forging anticolonial solidarities across overseas Chinese communities in different British colonies. In other words, Indian anticolonial futures were not simply transplanted from the subcontinent to Malaya; rather, Malayan refugees engaged with these ideas and imaginaries in all their contradictions to articulate their vision of a political order free from British sovereign control.

FORKING PATHS

Just as racial discrimination was alleged during the evacuation in 1942, repatriation to Singapore proved contentious after the war's end in 1945. When the British military reoccupied Singapore in September, many Malayans expected immediate repatriation and "sold all they had" in Bombay (*Straits Times*, January 25, 1946), but troop movements were prioritized. In an appeal submitted to Louis Mountbatten, Supreme Allied Commander South East Asia, Rajaboli Jumabhoy and his coauthors alleged that a troopship traveling from Bombay to Singapore was left empty because "it was of rather too good a class to allow mere Malayan evacuees to travel on it at Government expense" (*Straits Times*, January 15, 1946). In March 1946, the debacle continued. The crew of the SS *Largs Bay* initially "refused to carry 50 'coloured' evacuee passengers bound for Singapore" (*IDM*, March 11, 1946; see also *Straits Times*, March 9, 1946) but eventually relented (*IDM*, March 14, 1946). If complaints about racial discrimination during the evacuation from Singapore could be explained away by the chaotic circumstances of the Japanese invasion (*Indian Express*, February 24, 1942), repatriation proceedings that stretched for almost a year must have reignited resentment at the colonial government upon Malaya's reoccupation.

Upon their return to Malaya, many former refugees were quick to take advantage of a political climate that vastly differed from the situation they left behind in 1942. Working with Malayans who had been unable to flee, they set their world-making projects in motion. While those who stayed behind developed their own responses to colonialism and continued struggles initiated during the war (e.g., Cheah 2003), various postwar social movements in Malaya bore the clear impress of evacuees' sojourn in India. Mahmood Mahyideen, for instance, wasted no time galvanizing support for his irredentist cause. After returning to Kelantan—which was reannexed by British Malaya from Thailand through the Anglo-Thai Peace Treaty of 1946—he found ready support because many had tuned in to his broadcasts and "were tortured for listening to me" (BWJ 1946). Apart from building popular consensus among the Malay community, he cultivated outspoken allies such as British journalist Barbara Whittingham-Jones. Three months after the Japanese surrender, he pleaded with Whittingham-Jones to "make some publicity about Pattani" (BWJ 1945). Whittingham-Jones's advocacy and journalism culminated in the publication of an article that portrayed Siamese rule as "systematic oppression" (*Straits Times*, October 30, 1947). Mahmood Mahyideen rode this wave of publicity, and in 1948 he became president of the newly founded Greater Patani Malay Association (Gabongan Melayu Patani Raya) to further the cause of Patani's annexation by the Malayan Federation (Che Man 1990: 66). The popularity of the association, however, was short-lived, and given the violence of the military crackdown in Patani after the 1947 Thai coup d'état (Thanet 2008), Mahmood Mahyideen's focus on "traditional *realpolitik*" led him to be identified as a part of a group of "old school of conservative nationalists" whose methods were deemed not as effective as those of more radical Patani leaders who called for armed struggle against the Thai state (Kobkua 2013: 237–38). While Mahmood Mahyideen's dream for Malaya's annexation of Patani was quickly foreclosed, not least by US refusal to go overboard with punishing Thailand after its surrender (Tarling 1978), it is evident that his time in India made him excessively optimistic that the British would support his plan to curb Siamese colonialism by remaking the Malayan geobody anew.

As for Tan Cheng Lock, the most obvious continuity between his time in India and in postwar Malaya was his founding in 1949 of the MCA, one of the race-based political parties that was a part of the ruling coalition in Malaya/Malaysia from 1955 to 2018. As other scholars have demonstrated, the Bombay-based OCA was the precursor to the MCA (M. Roff 1965; Heng 1988; Tan M. I. 2015a). Yet transcolonial connections go deeper than such institutional continuity. Immediately after the war, Tan led the All-Malaya Council of Joint Action (AMCJA), a broad-based coalition that opposed the Malayan constitutional proposals put forth by the colonial government on various counts, including on citizenship rights, the key issue on which Tan and Mahmood Mahyideen differed as they lobbied colonial officials during their stay in wartime India. The AMCJA called for a series of *hartals*, the Gujarati term used by Gandhi to signify strike action, including an all-Malaya hartal on October 20,

1947 (*Straits Times*, October 17, 1947). The Indian origin of this anticolonial strategy demonstrates the extent to which mainstream Malayan nationalists like Tan drew from the language of politics with which they engaged in the crucible of exile. Ultimately, by tracing these evacuees' political trajectories, I argue that ideas and practices derived from transcolonial networks that were forged during the Second World War were indispensable—just as local responses to colonialism were—in generating visions of Malaya's postimperial future.

Even though relatively few Malayans were able to escape to India before the Japanese conquest, these transcolonial connections were far from trivial. What Ann Stoler (2009: 7) calls "minor histories" furnish "a critical space" that "attends to structures of feeling and force that in 'major' history might be otherwise displaced." In this vein, while it might be impossible to disentangle the domestic and transcolonial scales of anticolonialism and comparatively assess their differential impact, I suggest that these "minor" histories of the articulation of transcolonial solidarities allow us to recognize that the genealogies of postwar nationalist politics in Malaya were multiple. After all, as Adom Getachew (2019: 2–5) has argued, the demand for decolonization was a project not simply of nation making but also of worldmaking. In other words, nationalism and internationalism did not have to be the either/or binary that they might seem to be today, when the nation-state has become the normative spatial unit of politics. What these Malayan refugees articulated was their imagination of a political order that was no longer characterized by British paramountcy and, in Mahmood Mahyideen's case, Thai domination.

Yet, as the contrast between Mahmood Mahyideen's ill fortunes and Tan's prominent role in a mainstream political party suggests, some futures were instantiated while others were foreclosed. In general, visions that made concessions to the reoccupying colonial government were tolerated, especially in the context of the early years of the Cold War. Crackdowns on leftist political activity generated tensions between the Malayan state and the Communist Party of Malaya, which came to a head in 1948 with the outbreak of the "Malayan Emergency," a twelve-year war fought between the Communist Party and British and Commonwealth armed forces. Student movements thrived in Singapore despite harsh crackdowns (Khe 2011), and it was in this age of political ferment that Poh Soo Kai—still a child when he was in Bombay—attended the then Singapore-based University of Malaya, where in 1953 he became a founding member of the University Socialist Club. Along with the other members of the editorial board of the club's publication, he was arrested and charged with sedition. The widely publicized case launched Poh into politics, but on the eve of Singapore's independence from the British in 1963, he was detained without trial for seventeen of the next twenty years (Loh et al. 2012). Evidently, while some visions of Malaya's future that were conceived in wartime India were allowed to flourish, others like Poh's were actively quashed by the blunt instrument of the internal security apparatus. This aspect of the "counterinsurgency repertoire" was keenly deployed by Malayan and Singaporean leaders. In so doing, they proved their anticommunist bona fides, reassuring the imminently departing colonial government that they could hand independence over with little possibility that these dominoes would fall into communist hands (Ngoei 2019: 114–15).

Tracing such "futures past" is not simply an exercise in nostalgia. Rather, by attending to these historical "horizons of expectation," whether they came to pass or were suppressed (Koselleck 2004: 255–75), we can better understand how and why decolonization took the shape it did. In Malaya and Singapore, not all formerly colonized subjects regarded independence as an unmitigated victory, especially because the worldmakers who then became statesmen like Tan Cheng Lock conceived of anticolonialism in gradualist and antirevolutionary terms rather than as the immediate and total severance of links with colonial powers. It becomes clear, too, how political figures ranging from anticommunist nationalists to leftist activists articulated ideas derived not solely from within the territorial bounds of their nation but also from transcolonial connections that inadvertently enabled them to witness how other colonized subjects dreamed of empire's end. That these open-ended futures that all seemed historically possible in the 1940s appear out of focus in ex post facto national narrations reflects the triumph of one strand of anticolonial nationalism over others that have fallen by the wayside.

DARREN WAN is a PhD candidate in the Department of History at Cornell University.

ACKNOWLEDGMENTS
This article began its life as a paper presented at the Bombay and Indian Ocean Urbanisms Workshop hosted at Columbia University in 2020. I am grateful to Sohini Chattopadhyay and Laura Yan, as well as my panel's discussant, Debjani Bhattacharyya. Many thanks to Durba Ghosh, Jingya Guo, Sarah R. Meiners, Arielle Rochelin, Kelsey Jennings Roggensack, Eric Tagliacozzo, Jill J. Tan, Robert Travers, Tsuguta Yamashita, and the anonymous reviewers, all of whom read various versions of this piece and helped me make it stronger. Thank you especially to Faris Joraimi and Aimée Plukker for entertaining my every request for comments on draft upon draft upon draft.

NOTES
1. *Malaya* in the period under study refers to what is today known as Singapore and West Malaysia (or Peninsular Malaysia). In actuality, *Malaya* was not the formal designation for this British colonial possession but a shorthand that referred to a patchwork of polities governed through different administrative arrangements: four Federated Malay States, five Unfederated Malay States, and the Crown colony of the Straits Settlements (which included the cities of Penang and Melaka, as well as the colony's capital in Singapore). Malaya was given coherence as a single polity only under the Malayan Union (1946–48) and the Federation of Malaya (1948–63; independent 1957), but even then only with separation of Singapore, which was administrated discretely as the Colony of Singapore (1946–63). Singapore ceased to be a British colony in 1963 when it merged with Malaya, Sarawak, and North Borneo to form the Federation of Malaysia (1963–present), but Singapore separated from Malaysia in 1965 as an independent, sovereign state. I have opted to use the term *Malayan* to describe these evacuees even though some sources that were published after 1965 describe them as either "Malaysian" or "Singaporean." *Malayan* better encapsulates evacuees' territorial imaginations in the context of the war and the immediate postwar period.
2. The key exception is the historiography on the Japanese-sponsored Indian National Army, which became the armed wing of the Indian Independence League, through which Subhas Chandra Bose founded the Provisional Government of Free India in Singapore in 1943. Given the Indian National Army's international commitments, this historiography is one of the only bodies of scholarship on Malaya during the Second World War that deals with

the transnational articulation of anticolonialism. See Lebra-Chapman 1971; Fay 1993; Bayly and Harper 2005: 321–422; Bose 2011; Hildebrand 2016; and Datta 2021: 125–50.

3. Taking cue from usage in contemporaneous sources, especially government correspondence and newspapers of the time, I use *refugee* and *evacuee* interchangeably. The term *evacuee* was applied with consistency only by the Government of India—because the category constituted the grounds on which Malayans could claim the right to relief and rehabilitation while in India (Ramnath 2023: 41)—as well as in postwar self-narrations by evacuees themselves, most probably because in hindsight they regarded their time in Bombay as a temporary sojourn. Before the definition of *refugee* was standardized under the 1951 Geneva Convention on the Status of Refugees, no attempt was made by international organizations like the League of Nations to agree on a universal definition. Rather, refugee status was accorded on a case-by-case basis and only in the context of Europe after the First World War, as "no one at the time could foresee that [the refugee problem] would become a permanent, global problem" (Cabanes 2014: 184).

4. While Malayan refugees in Bombay are understudied, the work of Tan Miau Ing (2015a, 2015b) represents an important exception. Where this article departs from her articles is that, while she focuses on either an individual refugee or a particular organization for refugees in India, I adopt a broader view of the community as a whole, which allows the wide array of anticolonial politics to come into view.

5. For an account of the challenges that less elite Malayans faced as refugees in Bombay, see, e.g., Shih 1995: reel 3.

6. On the articulation of this trope of the lazy native and the hardworking migrant, see especially Alatas 1997.

7. This point articulates with arguments made in other work on British India as a space of refuge for Asians from Japanese-occupied territories, such as Yin Cao's work on exiles from China. For Cao, the Chinese Nationalist government can be understood to have extended its state-building projects beyond its territorial boundaries to control its subjects in India, suggesting that it was not only in relation to Malayans that the material conditions of the Second World War heightened connections between domestic politics and the politics practiced by exiles abroad. See Cao 2022: 16–21.

8. On the British government's rejection of these constitutional proposals, see "Appendix A: Letter from Edward Gent to H.T. Bourdillon," in PUTERA-AMCJA 2017: 109–16.

REFERENCES

Archival References

BWJ (Papers of Barbara Whittingham-Jones). 1942. "TMM's Escape." PP MS 65/01/16, Special Collections, SOAS Library, University of London.

BWJ (Papers of Barbara Whittingham-Jones). 1945. Letter from Major Mahmood Mahyideen to Barbara Oppenheim, December 5. PP MS 65/01/02, Special Collections, SOAS Library, University of London.

BWJ (Papers of Barbara Whittingham-Jones). 1946. Letter from Major Mahmood Mahyideen to Barbara Oppenheim, January 3. PP MS 65/01/02, Special Collections, SOAS Library, University of London.

HSL (H. S. Lee Private Papers Collection). 1943a. Letter from H. S. Lee to Tan Siew Sin, July 1. Folio 121/003/006. ISEAS Library, ISEAS–Yusof Ishak Institute, Singapore.

HSL (H. S. Lee Private Papers Collection). 1943b. Letter from Tan Siew Sin to H. S. Lee, July 15. Folio 121/003/010. ISEAS Library, ISEAS–Yusof Ishak Institute, Singapore.

HSL (H. S. Lee Private Papers Collection). 1943c. "Oversea-Chinese Association." Circular by Tan Siew Sin, July 16. Folio 121/003/004. ISEAS Library, ISEAS–Yusof Ishak Institute, Singapore.

HSL (H. S. Lee Private Papers Collection). 1943d. Letter from H. S. Lee to Tan Siew Sin, July 16. Folio 121/003/016. ISEAS Library, ISEAS–Yusof Ishak Institute, Singapore.

HSL (H. S. Lee Private Papers Collection). 1943e. Letter from Tan Cheng Lock to H. S. Lee, July 29. Folio 121/003/018-019. ISEAS Library, ISEAS–Yusof Ishak Institute, Singapore.

HSL (H. S. Lee Private Papers Collection). 1943f. Letter from H. S. Lee to Tan Cheng Lock, August 19. Folio 121/003/045. ISEAS Library, ISEAS–Yusof Ishak Institute, Singapore.

HSL (H. S. Lee Private Papers Collection). n.d. "Draft Constitution and Rules of the Oversea-Chinese Association." Folio 121/003/024. ISEAS Library, ISEAS–Yusof Ishak Institute, Singapore.

Jumabhoy, Rajabali. 1981. "Pioneers of Singapore." By Lim How Seng. Oral History Interviews, 37 reels. National Archives of Singapore, Singapore. https://www.nas.gov.sg/archivesonline/oral_history_interviews/interview/000074.

Loh, Robert Choo Kiat. 2001. "Medical Services in Singapore." By Patricia Lee. Oral History Interviews, 11 reels. National Archives of Singapore, Singapore. https://www.nas.gov.sg/archivesonline/oral_history_interviews/interview/002541.

Namazie, Mohd Javad (Haji). 1982. "Pioneers of Singapore." By Helen Choo. Oral History Interviews, 11 reels. National Archives of Singapore, Singapore. https://www.nas.gov.sg/archivesonline/oral_history_interviews/interview/000189.

Royal Commonwealth Society. 1944. "Oversea-Chinese Association, India: Comments on the Association of British Malaya's Memorandum on the Reconstruction of Malaya." GBR/0115/RCS/RCMS 103/1/1/2, Cambridge University Library, Cambridge.

Shih, Ruth Yin Chu. 1995. "Women through the Years: Economic and Family Lives." By Lim Quee Hook. Oral History Interviews, 14 reels. National Archives of Singapore, Singapore. https://www.nas.gov.sg/archivesonline/oral_history_interviews/interview/001655.

TNA (The National Archives of the UK). 1942. Letter from G. S. Bozman, Secretary to the Government of India, to His Majesty's Under Secretary of State for India, Public and Judicial Department, India Office, London, March 16. CO 273/669/6, folios 37–40.

TNA (The National Archives of the UK). 1943a. Letter from Department of Indians Overseas, Government of India, New Delhi, to His Majesty's Under Secretary of State for India, Economic and Overseas Department, India Office, London, February 6. CO 825/38/4, folios 9–10.

TNA (The National Archives of the UK). 1943b. Letter from George Maxwell, March 15. FO 371/35979, folios 16–18.

TNA (The National Archives of the UK). 1943c. Telegram from the British High Commissioner to Australia to the Secretary of State for Dominion Affairs, March 18. CO 825/38/11, folio 15.

TNA (The National Archives of the UK). 1943d. "Attitude of Local Population." Appendix "F" to letter from Far Eastern Department, Colonial Office, to the War Office, May 28. CO 273/669/1, folios 166–75.

TNA (The National Archives of the UK). 1943e. "Malaya under the Japanese up to October 1943." April 30. Appendix "B" to letter from Far Eastern Department, Colonial Office, to the War Office, May 28. CO 273/669/1, folios 153–56.

TNA (The National Archives of the UK). 1943f. "Fortnightly Intelligence Report No. 9." Far Eastern Bureau, British Ministry of Information, New Delhi, July 17. CO 273/669/1, folios 96–109.

TNA (The National Archives of the UK). 1943g. "Fortnightly Intelligence Report No. 11." Far Eastern Bureau, British Ministry of Information, New Delhi, August 14. CO 273/669/1, folios 67–74.

TNA (The National Archives of the UK). 1943h. "Fortnightly Intelligence Report No. 12." Far Eastern Bureau, British Ministry of Information, New Delhi, August 28. CO 825/38/17, folios 19–23.

TNA (The National Archives of the UK). 1943i. "Weekly Talk in Malay No. 62." September 3, British Ministry of Information, New Delhi. CO 825/38/9, folios 26–27.

TNA (The National Archives of the UK). 1943j. Appendix to letter from G. S. Rawlings to N. J. B. Sabine, October 24. CO 825/42/6, folios 56–86.

TNA (The National Archives of the UK). 1943k. Letter from Tan Cheng Lock to G. E. J. Gent, November 1. CO 825/35/15, folios 26–30.

TNA (The National Archives of the UK). 1943l. Letter from Tan Cheng Lock to N. J. B. Sabine, November 1. CO 825/35/15, folios 24–25.

TNA (The National Archives of the UK). 1943m. Letter from Tan Cheng Lock to Rt. Hon. Colonel Oliver Stanley, November 1. CO 825/35/15, folios 36–39.

TNA (The National Archives of the UK). 1944. Enclosure to letter from Theodore Samuel Adams to Edward James Gent, May 31. CO 825/42/6, folios 23–31.

Secondary References

Aiyar, Sana. 2011. "Anticolonial Homelands across the Indian Ocean: The Politics of the Indian Diaspora in Kenya, ca. 1930–1950." *American Historical Review* 116, no. 4: 987–1013.

Akashi, Yoji. 1995. "The Anti-Japanese Movement in Perak during the Japanese Occupation, 1941–45." In *Malaya and Singapore during the Japanese Occupation*, edited by Paul H. Kratoska, 83–120. Singapore: Singapore University Press.

Alatas, Syed Hussein. 1997. *The Myth of the Lazy Native: A Study of the Image of the Malays, Filipinos, and Javanese from the Sixteenth to the Twentieth Century and Its Function in the Ideology of Colonial Capitalism*. London: Frank Cass.

Amoroso, Donna J. 2014. *Traditionalism and the Ascendancy of the Malay Ruling Class in Colonial Malaya*. Petaling Jaya: Strategic Information and Research Development Centre.

Ampalavanar, Rajeswary. 1970. "Tamil Journalism and the Indian Community in Malaya, 1920–1941." *Journal of Tamil Studies* 2, no. 2: 41–58.

Amrith, Sunil S. 2008. "Internationalism and Political Pluralism in Singapore, 1950–1963." In *Paths Not Taken: Political Pluralism in Post-war Singapore*, edited by Michael D. Barr and Carl A. Trocki, 37–56. Singapore: NUS Press.

Andaya, Barbara Watson. 1977. "From Rūm to Tokyo: The Search for Anticolonial Allies by the Rulers of Riau, 1899–1914." *Indonesia* 24: 123–56.

Andaya, Barbara Watson, and Leonard Y. Andaya. 2017. *A History of Malaysia*. 3rd ed. London: Red Globe Press.

Ariffin, Omar. 1993. *Bangsa Melayu: Malay Concepts of Democracy and Community, 1945–1950*. Kuala Lumpur: Oxford University Press.

Azra, Azyumardi. 2013. "The Patani 'Ulamâ': Global and Regional Networks." In *Ghosts of the Past in Southern Thailand*, edited by Patrick Jory, 87–109. Singapore: NUS Press.

Bayly, Christopher, and Tim Harper. 2005. *Forgotten Armies: The Fall of British Asia, 1941–1945*. Cambridge, MA: Belknap Press of Harvard University Press.

Bhuyan, Arun Chandra. 1975. *The Quit India Movement: The Second World War and Indian Nationalism*. New Delhi: Manas.

Blackburn, Kevin. 2000. "The Collective Memory of the Sook Ching Massacre and the Creation of the Civilian War Memorial in Singapore." *Journal of the Malaysian Branch of the Royal Asiatic Society* 73, no. 2: 71–90.

Blackburn, Kevin, and Karl Hack. 2012. *War Memory and the Making of Modern Malaysia and Singapore*. Singapore: NUS Press.

Bose, Sugata. 2011. *His Majesty's Opponent: Subhas Chandra Bose and India's Struggle against Empire*. Cambridge, MA: Belknap Press of Harvard University Press.

Buchanan, Andrew. 2023. "Globalizing the Second World War." *Past and Present* 258, no. 1: 246–81.

Cabanes, Bruno. 2014. *The Great War and the Origins of Humanitarianism, 1918–1924*. Cambridge: Cambridge University Press.

Cao, Yin. 2022. *Chinese Sojourners in Wartime Raj, 1942–1945*. Oxford: Oxford University Press.

Chandavarkar, Rajnarayan. 1998. *Imperial Power and Popular Politics: Class, Resistance and the State in India, c. 1850–1950*. Cambridge: Cambridge University Press.

Che Man, Wan Kadir. 1990. *Muslim Separatism: The Moros of Southern Philippines and the Malays of Southern Thailand*. Singapore: Oxford University Press.

Cheah Boon Kheng. 2003. *Red Star over Malaya: Resistance and Social Conflict during and after the Japanese Occupation of Malaya, 1941–1946*. 3rd ed. Singapore: Singapore University Press.

Chua Ai Lin. 2008. "Imperial Subjects, Straits Citizens: Anglophone Asians and the Struggle for Political Rights in Inter-War Singapore." In *Paths Not Taken: Political Pluralism in Post-war Singapore*, edited by Michael D. Barr and Carl A. Trocki, 16–36. Singapore: NUS Press, 2008.

Chua Ai Lin. 2012. "Nation, Race, and Language: Discussing Transnational Identities in Colonial Singapore, circa 1930." *Modern Asian Studies* 46, no. 2: 283–302.

Datta, Arunima. 2021. *Fleeting Agencies: A Social History of Coolie Women in British Malaya*. Cambridge: Cambridge University Press.

Dubnov, Arie M., and Laura Robson, eds. 2019. *Partitions: A Transnational History of Twentieth-Century Territorial Separatism*. Stanford, CA: Stanford University Press.

Farrell, Brian. 2017. *The Defence and Fall of Singapore*. Singapore: Monsoon Books.

Fay, Peter Ward. 1993. *The Forgotten Army: India's Armed Struggle for Independence, 1942–1945*. Ann Arbor: University of Michigan Press.

Getachew, Adom. 2019. *Worldmaking after Empire: The Rise and Fall of Self-Determination*. Princeton, NJ: Princeton University Press.

Ghosh, Durba, and Dane Kennedy. 2006. Introduction to *Decentring Empire: Britain, India and the Transcolonial World*, edited by Durba Ghosh and Dane Kennedy, 1–15. New Delhi: Orient Longman.

Goswami, Manu. 2012. "Imaginary Futures and Colonial Internationalisms." *American Historical Review* 117, no. 5: 1461–85.

Grant, Kevin. 2006. "The Transcolonial World of Hunger Strikes and Political Fasts, c. 1909–1935." In *Decentring Empire: Britain, India and the Transcolonial World*, edited by Durba Ghosh and Dane Kennedy, 243–69. New Delhi: Orient Longman.

Greenough, Paul R. 1983. "Political Mobilization and the Underground Literature of the Quit India Movement, 1942–44." *Modern Asian Studies* 17, no. 3: 353–86.

Hack, Karl, and Kevin Blackburn. 2004. *Did Singapore Have to Fall? Churchill and the Impregnable Fortress*. London: Routledge.

Hara Fujio. 1995. "The Japanese Occupation of Malaya and the Chinese Community." In *Malaya and Singapore during the Japanese Occupation*, edited by Paul H. Kratoska, 37–81. Singapore: Singapore University Press.

Harper, Tim. 2021. *Underground Asia: Global Revolutionaries and the Assault on Empire*. Cambridge, MA: Harvard University Press.

Hayimasae, Numan. 2013. "The Intellectual Network of Patani and the Haramayn." In *Ghosts of the Past in Southern Thailand*, edited by Patrick Jory, 110–28. Singapore: NUS Press.

Heng Pek Koon. 1988. *Chinese Politics in Malaysia: A History of the Malaysian Chinese Association*. Singapore: Oxford University Press.

Hildebrand, Vera. 2016. *Women at War: Subhas Chandra Bose and the Rani of Jhansi Regiment*. Annapolis: Naval Institute Press.

Ho, Engseng. 2004. "Empire through Diasporic Eyes: A View from the Other Boat." *Comparative Studies in Society and History* 46, no. 2: 210–46.

Jalal, Ayesha. 1985. *The Sole Spokesman: Jinnah, the Muslim League, and the Demand for Pakistan*. Cambridge: Cambridge University Press.

Khan, Danish. 2019. "The Politics of Business: The Congress Ministry and the Muslim League in Bombay, 1937–39." In *Bombay before Mumbai: Essays in Honor of Jim Masselos*, edited by Prashant Kidambi, Manjiri Kamat, and Rachel Dwyer, 285–301. Oxford: Oxford University Press.

Khe Su Lin. 2011. "From the Middle School Students' Union to the Nanyang University Students' Union: Succession and Continuity in the Chinese Schools Student Movement in the 1950s and Early 1960s." In *The May 13 Generation: The Chinese Middle Schools Student Movement and Singapore Politics in the 1950s*, edited by Tan Jing Quee, Tan Kok Chiang, and Hong Lysa, 103–21. Petaling Jaya: Strategic Information and Research Development Centre.

Kobkua Suwannathat-Pian. 2013. "Historical Identity, Nation, and History-Writing: The Malay Muslims of Southern Thailand, 1940s–1980s." In *Ghosts of the Past in Southern Thailand*, edited by Patrick Jory, 228–54. Singapore: NUS Press.

Kong, Vivian. 2019. "'Hong Kong Is My Home': The 1940 Evacuation and Hong Kong-Britons." *Journal of Imperial and Commonwealth History* 47, no. 3: 542–67.

Koselleck, Reinhart. 2004. *Futures Past: On the Semantics of Historical Time*. Translated by Keith Tribe. New York: Columbia University Press.

Kratoska, Paul H. 2018. *The Japanese Occupation of Malaya and Singapore, 1941–45: A Social and Economic History*. 2nd ed. Singapore: NUS Press.

Lau, Albert. 1989. "Malayan Union Citizenship: Constitutional Change and Controversy in Malaya, 1942–48." *Journal of Southeast Asian Studies* 20, no. 2: 216–43.

Leake, Elisabeth, and Bérénice Guyot-Réchard. 2023. "Introduction: South Asia Unbound." In *South Asia Unbound: New International Histories of the Subcontinent*, edited by Bérénice Guyot-Réchard and Elisabeth Leake, 15–35. Leiden: Leiden University Press.

Lebra-Chapman, Joyce. 1971. *Jungle Alliance: Japan and the Indian National Army*. Singapore: Donald Moore for Asian Pacific Press.

Lewis, Su Lin, and Carolien Stolte. 2019. "Other Bandungs: Afro-Asian Internationalisms in the Early Cold War." *Journal of World History* 30, nos. 1–2: 1–19.

Loh, Kah Seng, Edgar Liao, Cheng Tju Lim, and Guo-Quan Seng. 2012. *The University Socialist Club and the Contest for Malaya*. Amsterdam: Amsterdam University Press.

Louro, Michele L. 2018. *Comrades against Imperialism: Nehru, India, and Interwar Internationalism*. Cambridge, MA: Cambridge University Press.

Manjapra, Kris. 2010. "Communist Internationalism and Transcolonial Recognition." In *Cosmopolitan Thought Zones: South Asia and the Global Circulation of Ideas*, edited by Sugata Bose and Kris Manjapra, 159–77. Basingstoke: Palgrave Macmillan.

Marquess of Linlithgow. 1971. "Document no. 662," letter to Winston Churchill (via India Office), mss Eur F125/158, August 31, 1942. In *"Quit India," 30 April–21 September 1942*, edited by P. Nicholas Mansergh, 853–54. Vol. 2 of *The Transfer of Power, 1942–47*. London: Her Majesty's Stationary Office.

Masselos, Jim. 2007. *The City in Action: Bombay Struggles for Power*. New Delhi: Oxford University Press.

Miller, Rory. 2010. "'An Oriental Ireland': Thinking about Palestine in Terms of the Irish Question during the Mandatory Era." In *Britain, Palestine, and Empire: The Mandate Years*, edited by Rory Miller, 157–76. Farnham: Ashgate.

Milner, Anthony. 1995. *The Invention of Politics in Colonial Malaya*. Cambridge: Cambridge University Press.

Mohamed Zamberi A. Malek. 1999. *Harimau Malaya: Biografi Tengku Mahmood Mahyiddeen* [Tiger of Malaya: The biography of Tengku Mahmood Mahyiddeen]. Bangi: Penerbit Universiti Kebangsaan Malaysia.

Ngoei, Wen-Qing. 2019. *Arc of Containment: Britain, the United States, and Anticommunism in Southeast Asia*. Ithaca, NY: Cornell University Press.

Nik Anuar Nik Mahmud. 1999. *Sejarah Perjuangan Melayu Patani, 1785–1954* [The history of the struggle of Patani Malays, 1785–1954]. Bangi: Penerbit Universiti Kebangsaan Malaysia.

Nik Anuar Nik Mahmud. 2008. *The Malays of Patani: The Search for Security and Independence*. Bangi: School of History, Politics and Strategic Studies, National University of Malaysia.

O'Malley, Kate. 2008. *Ireland, India and Empire: Indo-Irish Radical Connections, 1919–64*. Manchester: Manchester University Press.

Ooi Kee Beng. 2020. *As Empires Fell: The Life and Times of Lee Hau-Shik, the First Finance Minister of Malaya*. Singapore: ISEAS–Yusof Ishak Institute.

Poh Soo Kai. 2016. *Living in a Time of Deception*. Edited by Hong Lysa and Wong Souk Yee. Singapore: Function 8 / Petaling Jaya: Pusat Sejarah Rakyat.

PUTERA-AMCJA (Pusat Tenaga Rakyat–All-Malaya Council of Joint Action). 2017. *The People's Constitutional Proposals for Malaya: Seventieth Anniversary Edition*. Petaling Jaya: Strategic Information and Research Development Centre.

Ramnath, Kalyani. 2023. *Boats in a Storm: Law, Migration, and Decolonization in South and Southeast Asia, 1942–1962*. Stanford, CA: Stanford University Press.

Reid, Anthony. 2005. *An Indonesian Frontier: Acehnese and Other Histories of Sumatra*. Singapore: Singapore University Press.

Roff, Margaret. 1965. "The Malayan Chinese Association, 1948–65." *Journal of Southeast Asian History* 6, no. 2: 40–53.

Roff, William R. 1967. *The Origins of Malay Nationalism*. New Haven, CT: Yale University Press.

Sai, Siew-Min. 2013. "Educating Multicultural Citizens: Colonial Nationalism, Imperial Citizenship, and Education in Late Colonial Singapore." *Journal of Southeast Asian Studies* 44, no. 1: 49–73.

Silvestri, Michael. 2000. "'The Sinn Féin of India': Irish Nationalism and the Policing of Revolutionary Terrorism in Bengal." *Journal of British Studies* 39, no. 4: 454–86.

Sinanoglou, Penny. 2019. *Partitioning Palestine: British Policymaking at the End of the Empire*. Chicago: University of Chicago Press.

Stoler, Ann Laura. 2009. *Along the Archival Grain: Epistemic Anxieties and Colonial Common Sense*. Princeton, NJ: Princeton University Press.

Stolte, Carolien. 2023. "Fellow Travelers: Global Decolonization and Gandhian Peace Work." In *South Asia Unbound: New International Histories of the Subcontinent*, edited by Bérénice Guyot-Réchard and Elisabeth Leake, 187–202. Leiden: Leiden University Press.

Tan Cheng Lock. 1947. *Malayan Problems from a Chinese Point of View*. Singapore: Tannsco.

Tan Miau Ing. 2015a. "The Formation of the Malayan Chinese Association (MCA) Revisited." *Journal of the Malaysian Branch of the Royal Asiatic Society* 88, no. 2: 105–24.

Tan Miau Ing. 2015b. "Perjuangan Seorang Pelarian Perang: Lee Hau Shik Semasa Pendudukan Tentera Jepun, 1941–1945" [The struggle of a war refugee: Lee Hau Shik during the Japanese military occupation, 1941–1945]. *Sejarah* 24, no. 2: 31–50.

Tarling, Nicholas. 1978. "Atonement before Absolution: British Policy towards Thailand during World War II." *Journal of the Siam Society* 66, no. 1: 22–65.

Thanet Aphornsuvan. 2008. "Origins of Malay Muslim 'Separatism' in Southern Thailand." In *Thai South and Malay North: Ethnic Interactions on a Plural Peninsula*, edited by Michael J. Montesano and Patrick Jory, 91–123. Singapore: NUS Press.

Walker, Dennis. 2013. "The Formation of the Islamo-Malay Patanian Nation: Ideological Structuring by Nationalist Historians." In *Ghosts of the Past in Southern Thailand*, edited by Patrick Jory, 185–227. Singapore: NUS Press.

Wan Hashim Wan Teh. 1993. *Peranan Gerila Melayu Force 136: Perang Dunia Kedua* [The role of Malay guerrillas in Force 136: The Second World War]. Kuala Lumpur: Dewan Bahasa Dan Pustaka.

Wilson, Hugh. 1992. "Tengku Mahmood Mahyiddeen and the Dilemma of Partisan Duality." *Journal of Southeast Asian Studies* 23, no. 1: 37–59.

Wong, Diana. 2000. "War and Memory in Malaysia and Singapore: An Introduction." In *War and Memory in Malaysia and Singapore*, edited by P. Lim Pui Huen and Diana Wong, 1–8. Singapore: Institute of Southeast Asian Studies.

Wong, Diana. 2001. "Memory Suppression and Memory Production: The Japanese Occupation of Singapore." In *Perilous Memories: The Asia-Pacific War(s)*, edited by T. Fujitani, Geoffrey M. White, and Lisa Yoneyama, 218–38. Durham, NC: Duke University Press.

MARCUS YEE

Mobilizing Hong Kong

Nuclear Anxiety and Mass Protest against the Daya Bay
Nuclear Power Plant (1979–1986)

ABSTRACT The 1986 antinuclear movement in Hong Kong against the construction
of the Daya Bay Nuclear Power Plant was a watershed event. The campaign saw
society-wide mass participation, amassing 1.04 million signatures while becoming a
global protest that confronted the political, developmental, and diplomatic interests
of Chinese, British, and colonial Hong Kong governments. This article traces the origins of the nuclear power project between Guangdong officials and the China Light
and Power Company in 1979 to mass mobilization in Hong Kong in the summer of
1986, after a nuclear reactor meltdown in Chernobyl. Drawing from a range of previously untapped official, corporate, newspaper, and oral history sources, this article
foregrounds nuclear anxiety as a politicizing force that resulted in the emergence
of a collective political consciousness in Hong Kong. Environmental risk and subsequent political disenfranchisement recast the anti–Daya Bay movement's formative
role within Hong Kong's political and environmental histories.

KEYWORDS   antinuclear movement, Chernobyl, democratization, Hong Kong–China relations,
global environmental history

On July 13, 1986, Hong Kong residents were greeted by petition sheets emblazoned
with the words, "No Nuclear Radiation in Hong Kong! Stop the Daya Bay Nuclear
Plant Project Immediately!" (Joint Conference 1986). The campaign was held by the
Joint Conference for the Shelving of Daya Bay Nuclear Power Plant (hereinafter,
Joint Conference), a coalition that swelled to 116 community groups in the summer. Reeling from news of the Chernobyl disaster, the public readily signed in support. That Sunday alone saw 300,000 signatures. In the span of three months, the
campaign would amass 1.04 million signatures. This meant that around one-fifth of
Hong Kong's then population opposed plans for the Daya Bay Nuclear Power Plant
across the border. Until then, a movement of this scale had never been seen before
in Hong Kong.

What was later known as the "million-signature campaign" was unprecedented in 1986, considering that civil society in the former British colony was still
in nascency. This article spotlights Hong Kong's antinuclear movement as testing
grounds for the city's culture of mass mobilization for democracy. Although the
movement had begun in May 1982, public attention peaked after a meltdown at the

THE JOURNAL OF ASIAN STUDIES · 84:2 · May 2025
DOI: 10.1215/00219118-11591189 © 2025 Association for Asian Studies

406

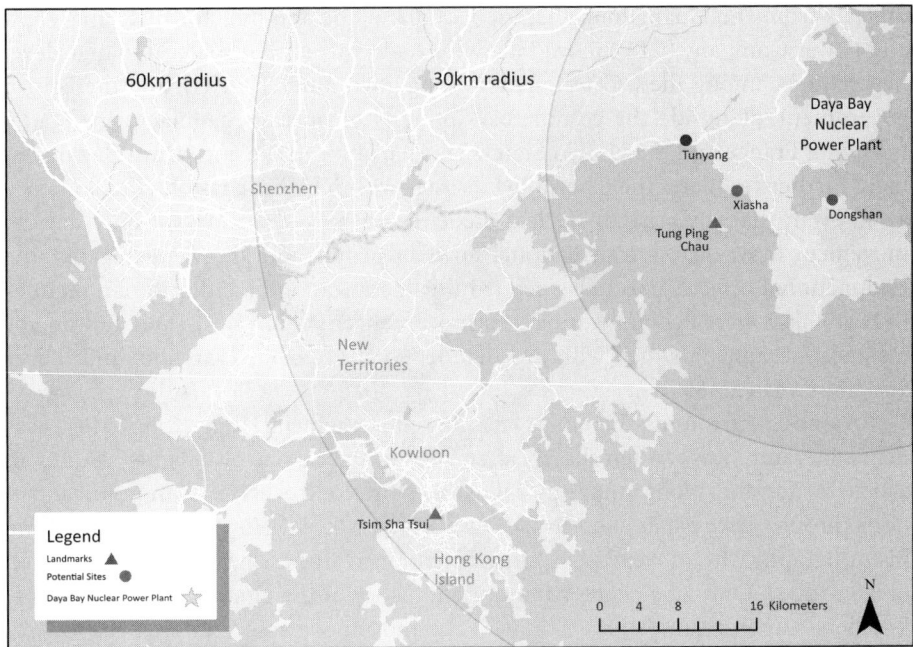

FIGURE 1 Map showing the Daya Bay site and its surrounding radius, alongside other sites considered by the Chinese Communist Party for building a nuclear power plant. Map by author via ArcGIS.

Chernobyl nuclear power plant on April 26, 1986, making nuclear safety an existential anxiety for Hong Kong residents. The bustling city center of Tsim Sha Tsui was 60 km away from the proposed nuclear station, while Tung Ping Chau island was in the middle of its 30-km evacuation zone (fig. 1). Comparatively, Chernobyl's "zone of alienation" formed a 30-km radius around the damaged nuclear reactor, but its disastrous effects traveled far beyond that. Despite mass local resistance, the Chinese Communist Party (CCP) and Hong Kong colonial officials offered only assurances as the planned project got underway.

This article argues that the anti–Daya Bay movement has fomented Hong Kong's democracy movement, establishing a precedence for relations between Hong Kong and Beijing for years to come. This granular account of the movement presents a portrait of late colonial politics in 1980s Hong Kong, as the colonial government's gradualist and decolonial policy of expanding local political autonomy buckled under pressure. Given the movement's apparent failure, few scholars have explored the significance of the anti–Daya Bay movement within Hong Kong and global environmental histories. Yet, this movement was the first that achieved society-wide mass mobilization, and the first where civil society went head-on against their future leaders in Beijing after the signing of the 1984 Sino-British Joint Declaration two years earlier (Lai 2001: 269). Beyond Hong Kong, the nuclear power project was of national and geopolitical consequence. It was the first large-scale commercial nuclear power plant and first overseas joint venture for the People's Republic of China (PRC), propelling paramount leader Deng Xiaoping's Four Modernizations as part of his post-1979 Reform and Opening Up. The project was spearheaded by officials from the Guangdong Electric Company and the director of China Light and Power Company (CLP), Lord Lawrence Kadoorie, evolving later into high-level negotiations among the CCP, the Hong Kong government (HKG), and the British government, alongside the commercial interests of nuclear manufacturing states, including France and the United States. This narrative of the anti–Daya Bay movement further resituates the Chernobyl disaster within global environmental history as an event that gave rise to nuclear anxieties across the world. Not only did the movement draw on the transnational flows of people and knowledge against the multinational project, but it also echoed the liberalization of authoritarian regimes in East Asia, where fledging antinuclear movements in South Korea and Taiwan, for instance, became entwined with pro-democracy movements (Kirchhof and Meyer 2014; M.-S. Ho 2018: 450).

Amnesia surrounds the anti–Daya Bay movement in Hong Kong. Most academic literature was written shortly after the movement; one of the most cited is an article by Yee and Wong (1987) that illustrates the controversy's main political factions through newspaper analysis (see also Ko 1987; K. W. Ho 1988). In Hong Kong historiography, the movement is either mentioned in passing or entirely omitted (Tsang 2004). Only one chapter found in a history of the Hong Kong Professional Teachers' Union features an account of the movement based on archival sources (Luk 2016: 58–87). This research chronicles the anti–Daya Bay movement by drawing on a comprehensive range of government, corporate, and newspaper archives. This article furthermore draws on oral histories with former activists conducted by the author, alongside those conducted by the Hong Kong Heritage Project.[1] Writing about the Chernobyl incident, Kate Brown (2019: 3–6) propounds that archives allow historians to "return to the scene of the crime," without which collective historical understanding of Chernobyl would be "stuck in an eternal video loop" saturated by media portrayals. Similarly, tapping into this broader archival base helps avoid retroactive accounts of the anti–Daya Bay movement.

Most literature on the anti–Daya Bay movement stems from the social sciences, specifically from studies of Hong Kong's social and environmentalist movements. Extensive literature on the city's long history of social movements have highlighted the historical conditions and experiences that made possible the many firsts accomplished through the antinuclear movement (Lui and Chiu 1997; Butenhoff 1999; Chiu and Lui 2000; Bickers and Yep 2009; Dapiran 2017). More pertinent, the anti–Daya Bay movement benefited from the previous "Golden Age" of social movements in the 1970s, led by a postwar generation of residents with an attachment to Hong Kong, unlike their migrant parents, who saw the city as a "borrowed place" on "borrowed time" (Butenhoff 1999; Chiu and Lui 2000). This newly emergent Hong Kong identity sharpened after the 1966–67 social unrest and the colonial government's wide-ranging social campaigns and piecemeal political reforms thereafter (Lui and Chiu 1997; Lou 2022). Much of the antinuclear movement's core leadership derived from this earlier network of activists active across the 1970s.

Scholars of Hong Kong's environmental movement observe the movement's transformation from being led largely by an elite group of foreign expatriates and academics in the 1970s to the entrenchment of "postmaterialist" ideals of "green modernity" led by ethnic Chinese middle-class environmentalists in the 1990s (Man

收工

FIGURE 2 Political cartoon by Zunzi captioned "Knocking Off Work," showing protestors unfairly losing a tug-of-war between colonial Hong Kong and Chinese officials. From Zunzi, Xianggang dazhuan jiaoshi guanzhu Dayawan hedianchang xiaozu, in *Hezifadian: Dayawan jihuamian mianguan* (Hong Kong: Ming Pao, 1987), 64.

1998; Lee and So 1999; Lai 2001; Hung 2012; Lou 2022). The 1986 anti–Daya Bay movement, with its politics of mass mobilization and global scale, does not sit neatly within the trajectory of Hong Kong's environmental movement. Notably, the anti–Daya Bay movement already featured collaborations between both expatriate and Chinese middle-class environmentalists in its early days, and during the movement's escalation after April 1986 environmentalists became a numerical minority as the antinuclear coalition swelled to 116 groups, including student groups, trade unions, and community groups representing a broad range of causes. Many environmentalists, like Simon Chau Siu Cheung and Man Si-Wai, who rose to prominence in the 1990s, participated in the antinuclear movement but did not take on key leadership roles (Man 1998; Greenwoods 2017). Given the anti–Daya Bay movement's mass appeal and broad coalitional politics, Hong Kong's histories of social movements and democratic development speak to the antinuclear movement more than the course of the city's environmental movement.

While scholars have acknowledged the significance of the anti–Daya Bay movement, many frame it as a historical aberration to preconceived notions of Hong Kong politics rather than studying the movement on its own terms. Nicholas Thomas (1999: 172) teleologically frames the assumed failure of the movement as an unspoken "convergence" between the HKG and the PRC leading up to the 1997 handover. Hsin-Huang Michael Hsiao et al. (1999: 264) argue that the movement was "doomed to be a futile exercise from its beginning," given the top-down decision-making structure in the colony, while On Kwok Lai (2001) observes that the "fragile and transient nature" of the movement lies in its opportunity structure, evinced by how quickly activists aborted the movement after the plant's contracts were signed. These scholarly accounts remain insightful, but their conclusions reflect more the authors' cynicism toward Hong Kong politics than the perceptions of historical actors on the conditions of their time (fig. 2).

Grounded in previously untapped archival material, this article offers a detailed account of the anti–Daya Bay movement that highlights contingency, beyond a foreclosed narrative of the movement's failure, and coalitional politics, beyond a historiography of environmentalism as a single-issue social movement. Nuclear anxiety played a crucial role in rallying more than a million Hong Kong residents, resulting in a movement that was perhaps not so much politicized as it was politicizing for the masses. In illustrating the historical process of mobilizing the "masses," namely, ordinary Hong Kong people, this article invokes a multilayered narrative that spans negotiations at the highest echelons of corporate and geopolitical leadership, the movement's centralized organizing, and ad hoc resistance on the city's streets. As the project was sealed by the signing of contracts in September 1986, the movement's so-called failure resulted in mass political disenfranchisement, catalyzing the city's incipient democracy movement. In other words, the anti–Daya Bay movement became a rehearsal for Hong Kong's aspirations toward democratic politics.

WARMING UP TO NUCLEAR: DAYA BAY'S GEOPOLITICAL AND CORPORATE ORIGINS (1979–1983)

"This is but the beginning," Lawrence Kadoorie announced as he inaugurated the Kwai Chung Control Centre on March 31, 1979. Supplying fifty megawatts of electricity from CLP's other power stations to Guangdong, this electricity deal was a first step in Kadoorie's grand strategy for Hong Kong to serve as a "neutral point of contact between the Orient and the Occident," for the prosperous city to render assistance to the PRC's Four Modernizations program (Kadoorie 1980). The next step of this grand strategy came not long after. Guangdong Electric Company management privately proposed to Kadoorie after the ceremony a joint venture to build a nuclear power plant in Guangdong. Before the Daya Bay site was confirmed, the amorphous project was called the Guangdong Nuclear Power Plant. The proposal took flight quickly. Guangdong officials and company management flew to Beijing to seek permission from the central government while meetings between CLP, Guangdong Electric Company, and Guangdong officials were underway (Guo 2008: 3).

Across the border, Kadoorie maneuvered to win political support for the project, targeting the United Kingdom's newly elected Conservative prime minister, Margaret Thatcher. On February 25, 1980, Kadoorie propositioned Thatcher by positioning CLP as "being able to open the door to the UK to provide the PRC with the expertise and advice" (PREM 1980a). On July 30, Thatcher laid out her enthusiasm for the project in a meeting with Kadoorie. The nuclear power project was more than a commercial deal for Thatcher, who perceived its diplomatic stakes in easing Sino-British relations as the expiration of the lease on the New Territories loomed nearer (PREM 1980b). For Thatcher, the future of Hong Kong—which she saw as under continued British colonial rule after 1997—rested on nuclear energy collaboration. She asked, "If ping pong diplomacy could bring about rapprochement between the PRC and the United States, then why cannot a nuclear power station?" (PREM 1980b). The economic aspects of the project were no less attractive: it was "a unique opportunity to reestablish Britain's premier position as a China trader" and crucial for the "creation of employment in British industry" (PREM 1980b). By the tail end of the Cold War, nuclear nonproliferation became a footnote to enthusiasm for nuclear commerce and diplomacy.

For Kadoorie, there were massive profits to be reaped. Under the HKG's 1964 Scheme of Control Agreement, consumers were guaranteed low electricity tariffs by Hong Kong's electricity duopoly. In turn, CLP and Hong Kong Electricity were assured a fixed 13.5 percent return on fixed capital by the government (Hong Kong Government 1982: 7–8). Since the companies' investment portfolio was accounted within the return on fixed capital, the multibillion-dollar project would be a windfall for the CLP. The project was furthermore part of Kadoorie's "intelligent anticipation" for Hong Kong after the 1997 handover: his strategic calculations to preserve the city's future economic success while serving as a "three-legged stool" balancing British, Chinese, and Hong Kong's interests (Kadoorie 1981; Lee 2007: 2; Clifford 2019: 305). Even Kadoorie himself had warmed up to nuclear power gradually. Dismissing it initially in 1960, he later saw in the Guangdong Electric Company's 1979 proposal a business and brokerage opportunity that left governments to absorb the associated costs and risks (CLP 1960). By December 1, 1980, the nuclear power plant's joint feasibility report was completed, after a year of preparation (Kadoorie 1981; Lee 2007: 19–24). Five bound volumes were completed by the US company Nuclear Services International Corporation, co-commissioned by CLP and Guangdong officials, while a joint memo was sent from Guangdong Party Secretary Wang Quanguo and Minister of Electric Power Wang Lin for Beijing's approval (Ko 1987: 32; Xu 2010: 34).

However, Beijing's approval only came two years later (Lee 2007: 24). Within this period of deliberation, Beijing's hesitation was founded on three considerations: ideology, energy alternatives, and location. First, the nuclear power plant was a distrusted object of Deng's Open Door policy, involving foreign direct investments, sovereign borrowing, technology transfer, and foreign expertise, breaking with ideological principles before the PRC's reform (Xu 2010: 35–36). Next, party officials questioned whether nuclear power was necessary in the first place, assuming that the PRC has abundant coal and hydroelectric resources that should be developed first (P. Li 2004: 34). Finally, the project's location became a source of debate. While the feasibility study proposed Tunyang and Dongshan, Chinese officials conducted their own survey and watered down a list of possible sites from forty-eight to four: Tunyang and Xiasha in Mirs Bay, Dakeng and Dongshan in Daya Bay (see fig. 1). Three principles guided their selection: the location should be situated near a water source for reactor cooling, outside a tectonically active zone, and relatively near Hong Kong (Chen 2008: 3–4). Insufficient water supply from Guangdong's inland rivers meant that the surveying process traced along the province's coasts. After eliminating earthquake-prone areas, Mirs Bay was eliminated because "Hong Kong people might have opinions" about its proximity (Chen 2008: 4). Yet, anticipation of Hong Kong public opinion conflicted with the main goal of proximate electricity delivery to earn foreign exchange. Dongshan, the harbor across from Dakeng, was rejected and earmarked by the Central Military Commission as a navy seaplane landing zone (Guo 2008: 17). All things considered, a site between Dakeng and Lingjiaoshi in Daya Bay was ultimately chosen, a location that eventually became the focus of controversy.

The PRC's need for nuclear power was bolstered by several arguments. Exacerbated by the global energy crises of the 1970s, the PRC needed to increase energy production to address shortages. In 1980 Guangdong could meet only 61 percent of its electricity requirements for industry, reportedly resulting in losses of 7.5 billion yuan a year earlier (*Beijing Review* 1980). More pertinent, the nuclear project promulgated Deng's reform program by bringing in much needed foreign currency from Hong Kong, cementing the PRC's new economic geography centering on southern cities as first movers of economic and political experimentation. Despite intense competition from other provinces, such as Jiangsu, to build the country's first commercial nuclear power plant, Guangdong had a powerful backer in the form of CLP, alongside easy access to capital, networks, and technologies across the border. Upon seeing that Daya Bay was not part of the Shenzhen Special Economic Zone, Vice Premier Li Peng redrew the zone's boundaries to include the future nuclear power plant site (Guo 2008: 17–18). Politically, a station in Guangdong would draw Hong Kong further into the PRC's orbit. Echoing Thatcher and Kadoorie, Deng saw the project as tied to Hong Kong's future, having "the effect of linking the economies of Hong Kong and the mainland even more closely," which would eventually contribute "to the prosperity and stability of Hong Kong by boosting the confidence of the people there" (PREM 1985).

On top of economic and energy reasons, the geopolitical insecurity of being a nuclear state without nuclear power loomed across the 1970s. Although Premier Zhou Enlai inaugurated PRC's nuclear energy program in 1970, political tumult and internal scientific rivalries hampered the program's development, at least until the State Council approved the Qinshan Nuclear Power Plant in November 1981 and the Daya Bay Nuclear Power Plant in December 1982. If Daya Bay was a flagbearer for Deng's reforms, Qinshan was a vision of autarkic technological development. Much of this was undoubtedly spurred by Deng, who suddenly announced PRC's decision to purchase two nuclear power stations at a 1978 Sino-Franco economic cooperation summit (Xu 2010: 27). It sent a clear message to the party and the rest of the world that the PRC wanted nuclear energy—the only question remaining was how. The Daya Bay Nuclear Power Plant project began as a web of geopolitical, infrastructural, and corporate interests at a global scale, consequently shaping the conditions for later controversy in Hong Kong.

SCAFFOLDING A MOVEMENT: EARLY ANTINUCLEAR ORGANIZING (1982–1985)

Initial announcements on the nascent nuclear power project caused no more than a ripple, appearing as down-page newspaper reports in early 1980. On May 29, 1982, the Joint Organisation for Concern of Nuclear Energy was formed out of three concern groups: the Asia Monitor Resource Centre, Student Christian Movement, and Conservancy Association, with Asia Monitor Resource Centre representative Trini Leung designated as convener and spokesperson (Anonymous 2021). Around the same time, the Hong Kong chapter of Friends of the Earth was formed by a group of expatriates. These groups laid down the foundation for information collection, network building, and consciousness raising long before mobilization saw mass participation after the 1986 Chernobyl disaster.

In their efforts to disseminate information, these formative antinuclear groups developed a substantial list of concerns, including nuclear waste disposal, a lack of transparency, and radiation safety, among others. They tackled these issues in their quarterly bilingual newsletter *Nuclear News for Hong Kong* (1984–86), which connected local nuclear energy developments with those of the rest of the world. The Joint Organisation for Concern of Nuclear Energy expanded as early as 1983, approaching the Joint Committee for Monitoring of Public Utilities for assistance to frame the Daya Bay issue as an electricity cost issue (Anonymous 2021). Convened by Lau Chin-Shek of the Christian Industrial Committee, the inclusion of the Joint Committee for Monitoring of Public Utilities co-opted trade unionists and industrialists into the antinuclear campaign. Both groups jointly organized their first signature campaign and collected ten thousand signatures, indicating Hong Kong residents' initial lukewarm attitude toward nuclear energy issues.

Public apathy was the result of high-level secrecy. Even though the government had been advised against nuclear power's unfeasibility in Hong Kong by a 1977 commission, it became openly supportive of the Daya Bay project (International Atomic Energy Agency 1977). From an early stage, nuclear safety came after financial interests, seen in the commissioning of a financial viability report from Lazard Brothers first in July 1983, followed by a study on accident probability and contingency planning by British Atomic Energy a year later, also known as the Harwell report. Upon receiving the Lazard Brothers report, the Executive Council permitted CLP to form the Hong Kong Nuclear Investment Company on November 11, 1983. Despite its disinterested posturing, archival reports reveal that the colonial government was covertly concerned about public opinion. According to one activist, it would be unsurprising that the controversial Standing Committee on Pressure Groups, a secret governmental committee established in 1978 to mitigate the influence of pressure groups, was involved in surveilling the early antinuclear campaign (Anonymous 2021). The full extent of state surveillance remains unknown, as the colonial state destroyed records from the Standing Committee after its closure in 1983.

As activists scaffolded their movement, the project accelerated. Formal negotiations in the PRC began in late 1983 alongside site preparation at Daya Bay. After the groundbreaking ceremony on April 1, 1984, the coastline was transformed to accommodate the nuclear power plant. Contractors flattened the bay's hilly topography to create fifty hectares of reclaimed land, followed by an infrastructural network of water and electricity supply, transportation, and communication lines. A photograph in *South China Morning Post* captioned "Daya Bay—just before the engineers moved in" hints at the coastal communities displaced by the plant's construction (Harte 1986).

The year 1985 seemed like the end of the road for Hong Kong's fledging antinuclear movement. On January 3, the Hong Kong Executive Council permitted the Hong Kong Nuclear Investment Company to join with the Guangdong Nuclear Power Company to form the Guangdong Nuclear Power Joint Venture Company (GNPJVC), promising to lend HK$500 million and serve as its financial guarantor of HK$6 million. Two weeks later, Kadoorie and his delegation flew to Beijing to sign the joint venture contracts at the Great Hall of the People. Received by Zhao Ziyang and Deng Xiaoping, this was a shining moment for Kadoorie and his grand strategy. Deng celebrated the nuclear power project "as a model of the open door policy" (PREM 1985). Back in Hong Kong, the Joint Organisation for Concern of Nuclear Energy underwent leadership change. Leung stepped down and was replaced by student activist and Anglican pastor Fung Chi-Wood, representing both the Student Christian Movement and the Conservancy Association. But the perception of the movement's futility would soon prove short-lived.

MOBILIZING HONG KONG AFTER CHERNOBYL (MAY–OCTOBER 1986)

After four days of initial confusion, the Chernobyl disaster of April 26, 1986, reached the headlines of Hong Kong's dailies. In the city, shock waves from Chernobyl reverberated onto the Daya Bay Nuclear Power Plant's fate. An early editorial raised questions about evacuation warnings in the event of a meltdown (*SCMP* 1986). PRC and Hong Kong officials were no less puzzled at first, the former hard-pressed to obtain more information after the Sino-Soviet split. Confusion soon transformed into a barrage of public relations assurances. Daya Bay was "going ahead," an early report from London announced, although construction might take longer than expected (Behrmann 1986). Later codified as the official public relations line, Acting Financial Secretary John Francis Yaxley said that the French-designed pressurized water reactor differed from that at Chernobyl and no delays were needed (*Ming Pao* 1986a). On the Chinese side, Chernobyl's impact was downplayed as the director of the National Nuclear Safety Administration, Jiang Shengjie, affirmed the official Soviet death toll of two, arguing that radioactivity would not cause immediate death and that Western reports of up to two thousand deaths were "groundless," foreshadowing debate over the accounting of long-term radiation within Chernobyl's total death toll (*SCMP* 1986g). The once-faltering antinuclear movement gained ground among the public, who became unconvinced by official assuagement. Fear pervaded public commentary: "Is all we can look forward to the fact that we will all be glowing in the dark of our own volition in the next few years and contracting leukaemia and other cancers?" (Tan 1986).

Riding the wave of nuclear anxiety, the antinuclear movement reconvened as the Joint Conference on May 31, forming a coalition of eighteen different organizations. With his undergraduate training in physics, and perhaps perceived as a political buffer for more seasoned activists, Fung took up the role of Chinese spokesperson, and Friends of the Earth's Linda Siddall became the English spokesperson (Fung 2021). The Joint Conference came up with two central demands: first, the HKG, "concerned about health and safety of its public," should freeze the nuclear power plant proposal; second, HKG should form an independent inquiry committee that included members of the public to reassess the health, environmental, and economic aspects of the project (Joint Conference 1986: 1). The coalition was bolstered with the entrance of the Professional Teachers' Union on June 23, led by charismatic Legislative Councillor Szeto Wah. The union wrote to more than three thousand people with the aim to collect one hundred thousand signatures from teachers, children, and their parents (*SCMP* 1986b). The union became the Joint Conference's unofficial secretariat, providing logistical and administrative support (Luk 2016: 68–69).

在核電恐懼下

FIGURE 3 Scenes from the signature campaign shown next to images of antinuclear protests in Europe. From *Cheng Ming Monthly* 爭鳴 106 (August 1986).

On June 8, a week after the Joint Conference's formation, the antinuclear signature campaign was launched with a goal of five hundred thousand signatures (fig. 3). Around a hundred people marched to the Star Ferry terminal after attending a forum at the Mariner's Club. There, measures to boycott CLP were discussed and Kadoorie was roundly criticized for stating that the nuclear power plant's safety was the PRC's responsibility, not CLP's (*SCMP* 1986m). Activists gathered 10,200 signatures on that Sunday, which increased to 40,000 by the following week. Antinuclear volunteers soon became a regular Sunday spectacle at the Star Ferry terminal, raising banners and encouraging passersby to sign the petition.

By a stroke of luck, sunny skies greeted the Joint Conference's campaign Sunday on July 13—two days after Typhoon Peggy had razed through the city. More than a thousand volunteers set up booths at entrances of all thirty-seven Mass Transit Railway stations and three Kowloon-Canton Railway stations (*SCMP* 1986q). Antinuclear posters adorned the booths, while volunteers handed out stickers with a cartoon sun and slogan, "We Want Sunshine, Not Nuclear Power" (*SCMP* 1986p). After six weeks of campaigning, the Joint Conference expanded to include over a hundred organizations. In early July, it further co-opted the seventeen-thousand-worker-strong Federation of Hong Kong and Kowloon Workers' Union. At its height, the Joint Conference included 116 organizations, comprising grassroots organizations, trade unions, student groups, Christian organizations, and offices of district boards. Under Szeto's influence, membership in the core leadership of the Joint Conference was tightly vetted and organized, fearing infiltration by radical elements across the political spectrum (Chan 2023). One newspaper article captured the diversity of opinions by ordinary Hong Kong people on the antinuclear movement:

> "There's no use in signing, there's no use in protesting. They are already building the nuclear plant, who is going to listen to you?"
> "Sure! I will sign and support all of you!"
> "Daya Bay is really dangerous, but would anything happen to me after signing my name?" (*Ming Pao* 1986d)

That Sunday's campaign received over 300,000 signatures, resulting in an "unprecedented" total of over 700,000 signatures (*SCMP* 1986e). By the following week, almost 1 million people had signed, but these numbers were met with skepticism. Detractors perceived the campaigning of unionized teachers in schools as manipulating schoolchildren for their signatures. One district officer reported that Mass Transit Railway passengers were pressured to sign upon entering and exiting stations, resulting in duplications (PRO 1986l).

In spite of the centralized leadership of the Joint Conference, Hong Kong witnessed an efflorescence of ad hoc and bottom-up initiatives reflecting the grip of nuclear anxiety on broader society. Spin-off antinuclear groups focusing on petitioning and polling local districts, such as the "Joint Committee of Shaukiwan and Chai Wan District on the Shelving of Daya Bay Nuclear Plant," were not uncommon (LCA 1986b). Professional associations like the Hong Kong Journalists Association made demands for transparency, while two lawyer associations signed petitions to the consultative governmental office, the Unofficial Members of the Executive and Legislative Councils (UMELCO) (*SCMP* 1986h; W. Cheung 1986). Academics and staff from the Chinese University of Hong Kong formed one influential front with their eight-hundred-signature petition, the largest drive since the 1970s Chinese language campaigns, and met with legislative councillors to convey their worries (LCA 1986c; Chan 1986a). Christian groups formed another powerful lobby. A published letter by twenty-one Hong Kong Christians appealed to church leaders to "lead local Christians in opposition to the building of the plant" (K.-W. Cheung et al. 1986). Another Christian group sang hymns in an overnight protest, marching to submit their petition the following morning (Chan 1986e).

The Daya Bay controversy raged on through the months of June and July, becoming a "common subject of daily conversation, partly buoyed by intense newspaper coverage" (PRO 1986k). Worst fears were confirmed by sensational reports detailing the skin-peeling effects of radiation (*Ming Pao* 1986j). A flurry of commentaries, petitions, and letters to the editor kept antinuclear sentiments high. Between June and September 1986, local Chinese-language newspaper *Ming Pao* published twenty-three critical essays against the project, averaging one every four days (Luk 2016: 73). Readers were kept abreast with post-Chernobyl developments around the world: Taiwan put a halt to its fourth plant, and the Philippines mothballed the Bataan Nuclear Power Plant. In Europe, photographs of reinvigorated antinuclear movements in West Germany and Ukraine provided visions of possibility for Hong Kong people confronting their own nuclear concerns. The most impactful commentary was *Ming Pao* owner Louis Cha's editorial titled "Fragrant Harbour Would Be Dead Harbour!" Cha argued that in a nuclear meltdown, "it could be that Hong Kong people are spared of death" but the city, along with its status as a tourist haven, an exporter of toys and garments, and a showpiece of the laissez-faire economics and politics, would be decimated. The apocalyptic image of a "dead harbour" became a prime symbol of nuclear anxiety, and Governor Edward Youde sent a translation to the Foreign Colonial Office conveying the fears of Hong Kong residents (PRO 1986e).

During the public debate on nuclear energy, divisive expert opinion caused more heat than light. In July, Friends of the Earth invited to Hong Kong as a "visiting consultant" British nuclear expert Walter Patterson, who characterized the pressurized water reactor's design as the "most dangerous design of reactors." Another group of three nuclear experts, invited by UMELCO members, denounced Patterson's claims as "untrue, unscientific and without basis" (*SCMP* 1986f, 1986n). In August, the University of Hong Kong held a nuclear power seminar after perceiving public ignorance as the root of contention (Tso 1988: 1). At the height of controversy, expert comments degenerated into combative soundbites. Nobel prize–winning physicist Yang Chen-Ning branded antinuclear public opinion as "hysterical fear," while a geography professor mentioned in an interview that naysayers should "jump into the sea and kill themselves, there's nothing in the world that can satisfy everyone" (*Cheng Ming Monthly* 1986: 23). Still, many academics were anxious about the project, as evinced by their multiple open letters and petitions. Rifts in scientific opinion made the controversy ripe for politicization. In early August, the pronuclear Daya Bay—Scientific Approach Group was formed, fashioning themselves as a "counter-force" to the Joint Conference (Chan 1986g). Led by Urban Councillor Kwan Lim-Ho, the group boasted 113 district board members and urban councillors. Through newspaper advertisements, they invited the public to "understand the Daya Bay issue with a scientific attitude" (*Oriental Daily News* 1986). Many, however, doubted the credibility of the lobby because there were no actual experts in the group, despite their calls for scientific rationality (PRO 1986h). Still, the group would later emerge as a serious rival to the Joint Conference.

In the context of Hong Kong's gradual democratization under late colonial governance, the Daya Bay controversy became a staging ground for contentious politics. After the signing of the 1984 Sino-British Joint Declaration, the British government was under pressure to indemnify itself for agreeing to decolonize Hong Kong without granting independence, transferring the colony's sovereignty instead to socialist rule under the PRC (Sing 2004: 74). At the same time, both British and colonial Hong Kong governments were cautious in balancing democratic reform with the colony's stability and were careful to not provoke Beijing, which was perceived to be in opposition to Hong Kong's democratization (Goodstadt 2005: 32). Hence, the HKG took an incremental approach toward political reform, leading to the creation of consultative channels that held little political power. The nuclear controversy tested these newfound institutions. As one commentator cynically pointed out, the government and its consultative channels comprised only "around a 1000 people," yet each of them claimed to "represent or respect the people's desires" (*Ming Pao* 1986c).

One such consultative channel comprised the district boards, where many of its members participated actively in the antinuclear movement. District boards were successors to the city district office scheme, created by the colonial government to bridge a "communication gap" in the wake of the 1966–67 social unrest (Mok 2022: 289–90). Hong Kong's first ever direct elections were the 1982 district board elections. With its proximity to grassroots *kaifong* (街坊) concerns, the district boards became closely involved in the signature campaign and meetings with "unofficials." On some occasions, entire district boards were represented at the Joint Conference. However, its members were careful not to overstep their position due to the government's "terms of reference" that "confined their members to discussing local affairs and matters concerning the well-being of Hong Kong people" (Choi 1986). These terms did not prevent district boards from forming a powerful cross-district lobbying coalition (PRO 1986c). The influence of district board members grew to such an extent that colonial district officers were tasked to submit weekly reports on "matters of unusual and particular general concern" regarding the Daya Bay controversy from the first week of July onward.

Concerns raised by district board members were channeled to members of UMELCO, a body established in 1963 to foster communication between the Legislative and Executive Councils. During the Daya Bay controversy, Maria Tam, convener of the UMELCO Public Utilities Panel, became the face of the committee. Under Tam, the UMELCO was relatively successful in soliciting information from the HKG, CLP, and GNPJVC. As semiofficial representatives, UMELCO members met with a range of stakeholders, positioning themselves as neutral mediators (PRO 1986a). The panel's later fact-finding missions in August had been organized with a similar intention of information gathering, although the group was soon perceived by dissenting public opinion as a "government puppet" (PRO 1986b). Tam and other panel members proposed discussing the nuclear power project as part of the Basic Law Drafting Committee, but it was ultimately decided that the topic was not within the committee's purview (*Ming Pao* 1986g).

The controversy embroiled Hong Kong's Legislative Council. On July 16, the adjournment debate on the Daya Bay controversy lasted four hours, one of the longest in the council's history then. No consensus was reached among the councillors. Tam herself urged that "no contract be signed before our delegations return from trips abroad," noting that "a great number of the people of Hong Kong are not ready to accept it" (PRO 1986a). Harshest criticism came instead from Tam's ally Allen Lee, critiquing the Joint Conference's fanning of a "frenzy of fear" (PRO 1986a). His evidence was a protest poster depicting a devil (labeled "Daya Bay Nuclear Power Plant") sitting atop a radiative cloud and overlooking Hong Kong Island, evidence of the movement's "starkly naked . . . political overtones." Martin Lee and Szeto Wah, key members of the antinuclear faction in the Legislative Council, pushed UMELCO further toward a pronuclear position. Lee and Szeto pressured for the release of classified documents, invoking the controversial Legislative Council (Powers and Privileges) Ordinance, and demanded a special session while the council was on summer recess (Wai 1986). The first cracks in the Legislative Council appeared in early July when Lee contested UMELCO's selection criteria for its fact-finding missions. Not only were requirements deemed unfair, but the names of several members were allegedly preselected in an "in-house meeting" for "consultation" (Wai and Chung 1986). The political split had wider implications for Hong Kong's emergent democratic development, given that Lee and Szeto have been newly elected during the council's first indirect elections in 1985, prior to which the Legislative Council comprised only "state bureaucrats" and "members appointed by the governor drawn from professional and business elites," also known as "unofficials" (Mok 2022: 287). The schism turned into public spectacle in a "bitter" and "emotion-charged" televised debate between Lee and Tam on September 2, where both interrupted each other so often "that viewers had difficulty keeping up with their lines of argument" (*SCMP* 1986i).

Balancing a panoply of interests, the HKG put on a calm facade against widespread antinuclear sentiment, although leaked correspondence and archives reveal otherwise. The government had flatly rejected earlier demands for a referendum but gave in to the request of the release of information, albeit in a piecemeal manner. On top of redacted portions of the feasibility report, parts of the Harwell report and the Lazard Brothers financial feasibility report were released after contracts were signed in September. Although Financial Secretary Piers Jacob prided himself on the fact that the Harwell report was commissioned before the Chernobyl disaster, the consultants were engaged only after the government was guaranteed of the project's financial viability and approved of CLP's participation (Hong Kong Legislative Council 1986a: 1131). Government officials reiterated well-rehearsed lines on the safety of the reactor's design and, at moments of desperation, absolved themselves entirely by emphasizing the project's direction under the CCP.

On the second week of August, leaked government correspondences caused the HKG's impenetrable image to crumble under the public gaze. Newspaper headlines were splashed with a confidential correspondence revealing senior official G. J. Osborne's insecurities over the nuclear power project. Responding to the first phase of the Harwell report, Osborne critiqued that there was "no reference to Chernobyl" and, further, assessed that "we have in the past two weeks made a lot of reassuring statements, [although] nobody in Government has seen in writing the facts upon which these statements were based" (*SCMP* 1986a). Worse still, "Harwell, it seems, are certainly not committing themselves at this stage on verbal statements." Lending more shock was an accident probability of 1 in 166 for the Daya Bay project (*Ming Pao* 1986b). This sentiment reverberated throughout the government. In a confidential telegram to the Foreign Colonial Office, Governor Youde confessed: "The crux of the problem is that there is very little we as a government can do to allay public fear. We have no direct involvement in the project and Daya Bay is not in our territory. Moreover, we have no nuclear expertise and we cannot deal adequately with the questions and worries that are being raised" (PRO 1986f). Like the HKG, the CCP offered many public reassurances through official statements but surveilled antinuclear sentiment in Hong Kong closely. A top Chinese nuclear official assured that a contingency plan was not necessary, while Beijing reportedly knew little about such a plan for Hong Kong (Chan 1986c; *Ming Pao* 1986h). The highest-level spectacle of reassurance came from Vice Premier Li Peng, who visited the Daya Bay site on May 20 and 21 and emphasized in his speech to GNPJVC staff that technological differences did not mean "we should neither relax our vigilance or be complacent" (PRO 1986g). Stronger reassurance came from the PRC's later agreement to sign two pacts with the International Atomic Energy Agency (*SCMP*

1986c). Through oral history records, we know how some nuclear power plant workers felt toward inflammatory sentiment in Hong Kong. One manager recalled that the antinuclear protests served instead to motivate nuclear power plant workers to do their jobs better, after bearing the brunt of questioning by Hong Kong journalists, who asked, "If you could not even manage a toilet, are you able to manage a nuclear power plant?" (Zhou 2008: 31–32). The Beijing line seemed to harden as General Secretary Hu Yaobang explained at a press conference in France that while he understood Hong Kong people's concerns, they should not "blindly protest" (*Ming Pao* 1986i; Wang 1986).

On the ground, the Xinhua News Agency based in Hong Kong began counteroppositional work. A pronuclear pamphlet titled *Should the Daya Bay Nuclear Power Plant Be Built?* was distributed to PRC-affiliated banks and emporiums, persuading readers of the plant's necessity for the PRC's modernization (PRO 1986i). Xinhua organized day trips to the unbuilt Daya Bay site. The colonial government's anxiety over public opinion led them to work together with Xinhua. Secret government correspondence recounts a breakfast meeting between Acting Governor David Akers-Jones and Xinhua Deputy Director Li Chuwen, where Li approved of HKG's "low-key handling of the Daya Bay affair" (PRO 1986d). When Li asked for HKG's support for a pronuclear technology exhibition, Akers-Jones suggested "discreet practical assistance" instead, reasoning that "overt government assistance could be damaging" and cause the exhibition to "become a political problem." Li further added that the PRC had "no quarrel" with Hong Kong's "anti-nuclear lobbyists," such as Fung Chi-Wood, but other figures like Lau Chin-Shek of the Christian Industrial Committee were destabilizing by making "contacts with elements in Taiwan [redacted] and with anti-nuclear activists in the Philippines." Xinhua's covert coordination of counterresponses against antinuclear sentiment could be understood through its role as a "quasi-diplomatic channel for government exchange" between the CCP and the British colonial government, since the former refused to establish a consulate in the territory, while the colony had no independent diplomatic instrument and relied on London to handle its diplomatic relations (Chu 2015). This meeting reveals that through Xinhua, Beijing scrutinized the anti–Daya Bay movement, defining what forms of protest in Hong Kong were permissible while stopping short of explicitly pressuring the HKG into counteraction.

For political stakeholders involved in the nuclear controversy, public opinion was a prime object of concern. One of the biggest independent polls, distributed via a full-page questionnaire in major Chinese and English newspapers, with twenty-eight hundred respondents, asked, "Do you want the Daya Bay Nuclear Power Plant?" (*Ming Pao* 1986f). Over 70 percent of respondents opposed the construction of the station, 16 percent favored a delay of the project, and 10 percent supported the project (*SCMP* 1986j). The most-cited figure was from a *Sunday Morning Post* survey involving 622 telephone interviews, which found 72 percent of respondents against the project. Other polls were carried out on more local levels. Handwritten results from a poll of 616 Southern District residents found that while 66.2 percent rejected the construction of the nuclear power plant in Daya Bay, 49.8 percent agreed to PRC's development of nuclear energy (LCA 1986a). In other words, many residents did not oppose PRC's foray into nuclear energy; rather, they were concerned about its proximity.

As the issue dominated headlines and airwaves, feelings of public cynicism increased alongside the campaign's politicization. One district officer observed that residents felt the controversy to be "a political hobby horse" for aspiring local politicians (PRO 1986j). This opinion was shared by none other than Lawrence Kadoorie, who had been publicly silent after Chernobyl but mentioned in a speech in October that the controversy "created an opportunity for would-be politicians, in their newfound freedom, to raise their voices" (Kadoorie 1986). Conversely, Fung Chi-Wood (2021) estimates that 70 percent of those concerned with the nuclear power project were concerned with safety, while the rest were concerned with politics. Residents protested the project rather than governments. The mainstreaming of antinuclear sentiment was a deliberate choice by the Joint Conference to not overpoliticize the protests (Luk 2016: 70). This was reinforced by the fact that Fung, fresh-faced in the political scene then, was chosen to lead the Joint Conference. Safety, rather than politics, was the main source of anxiety for the masses. Anxiety over safety itself was enough to mobilize a significant proportion of Hong Kong residents, many of whom became participants in mass protest for the first time.

OVERSEAS DELEGATIONS (AUGUST–SEPTEMBER 1986)

The controversy's global orientation is evident in the many overseas delegations from Hong Kong in the months of August and September. UMELCO dispatched one mission to Japan and the United States and another to Europe, while the Joint Conference sent a delegation to Beijing to submit its million-signature petition. Beyond these highly publicized missions, government officials such as Acting Financial Secretary Yaxley, antinuclear Legislative Councillors Lee and Szeto, and the pronuclear Scientific Approach Group made separate attempts at nuclear fact finding and diplomacy overseas. These itineraries reveal the global dimension of the Hong Kong's antinuclear movement, as the city looked outward for solutions to controversy at home.

From its proposal, UMELCO's contentious fact-finding missions were characterized by the public as cosmetic "junket trips" (PRO 1986a). The delegation insisted on their neutrality, emphasizing that their goal was "not to judge" (Chan 1986d). Their mission was also heavily covered by the Hong Kong media as they visited various nuclear power plants overseas. In Vienna, they were met with a team of International Atomic Energy Agency experts promising regular inspections for member countries, including the PRC (*SCMP* 1986k). The outcome, a 213-page report, reiterated that the pressurized water reactor containment building "will be able to contain most of the radioactive products" in the worst of accidents, and the decision to build "lies within the jurisdiction of the Chinese government" (Hong Kong Legislative Council 1986b: 177–80). Fung criticized the report as partial since most of its information was provided by "the industry and relevant Government authorities which were naturally supportive to the issue and would tend to hide the negative aspects of nuclear energy" (*SCMP* 1986l).

As the fact-finding missions took place, the Joint Conference readied to petition Beijing in a trip organized by Xinhua on August 17. With their twelve-person delegation, they were one of Hong Kong's earliest civil society groups to negotiate directly with the CCP government in Beijing (fig. 4). In a time of paper documentation,

FIGURE 4 Joint Conference delegation to Beijing that submitted the million-signature petition. From left to right: Yu Chung-Yin 余仲賢, Chan Kin-Man 陳健民, Ha Man-Ho 夏文浩, Ng Wai-Kei 吳蔚奇, Cheng Bing-Fa 曾炳發, Wong Wai-Hung 黃偉雄, Lau Chin-Shek 劉千石, Fung Chi-Wood 馮智活, Xin Kam-Wei 冼錦維, Hui Qing-Hon 許清漢, Lai Gin-Biu 黎建標, Bruce Liu Sing-lee 廖成利. Photo courtesy of Bruce Liu Sing-lee.

Fung (2021) recalls that signed petitions had to be carted around in some ten cardboard boxes. While the delegation had aimed to state their case to Premier Zhao Ziyang and Head of the Hong Kong and Macau Affairs Office Ji Pengfei, they were instead received by Li Hou, Ji's second-in-command. For the first two days, the delegation demanded Zhao and Ji's audience, threatening to leave without delivering the petition letters. On the third and final day, they relented. Li received the letters and left without saying much to the activists. Official PRC news agencies painted an unflattering picture of the delegation as "impatient" guests with "inappropriate views" that "irked" PRC officials (Chan 1986b). International press gave more airtime to the activists, reporting Fung's disappointment with the Chinese government (Southerland 1986). In retrospect, Fung (2021) remembers every party in the trip to be polite, Xinhua staff even helped load the boxes of signed petitions onto the plane (*Ming Pao* 1986e). Returning to Hong Kong by train via Guangzhou, the delegation was welcomed by supporters. Shortly after returning, the Joint Conference ramped up last-ditch efforts before the contract signing. On September 14, five hundred members marched toward the Government Secretariat; Fung then handed over a blank letter because "what needs to be said has been said"—the HKG had not heeded the demands of the people (C. Li 1986).

After the Joint Conference's trip came the UMELCO Panel's visit to Beijing to submit their fact-finding mission reports. UMELCO representatives were treated to a banquet by Ji and were received by Li Peng—even Youde was said to have only met with Ji (Hong Kong Legislative Council 1986c). Chinese officials praised UMELCO's report, although not every point was agreed upon, such as a guarantee that nuclear energy electricity tariffs would be indefinitely cheaper than from conventional stations (Chan 1986f). However, Li agreed that establishing an independent advisory body would be "productive." More significantly, UMELCO's visit to Beijing was the first time the CCP met with Legislative Council members as political representatives of Hong Kong, rather than under euphemistic titles like "businessmen," making it an ambivalent historical milestone for Hong Kong politics.

At the Great Hall of the People on September 23, seven contracts worth up to HK$28.8 billion were signed between stakeholders, including CLP, GNPJVC, Framatone, and General Electric Company. The moment was celebrated as a victory after eight years of planning, negotiation, and controversy. Hong Kong pundits began to see the Daya Bay Nuclear Power Plant as a fait accompli, writing think-pieces looking back at the seemingly dissipated controversy. The antinuclear movement, clearly enervated, pressed on with their criticism. In early October, the Joint Conference announced "a new battle plan" that would be launched at a rally planned for five thousand people, aiming to show their determination "no matter what the circumstances" (*SCMP* 1986d).

CONCLUSION: BEYOND THE DEAD HARBOR

Protest songs and slogans filled the air at Morse Park on October 6, 1986, in what was to be the last significant protest action of the movement against the Daya Bay Nuclear Power Plant. Initial plans to hold the rally at Victoria Park were scrapped, settling for a humbler setting in Wong Tai Sin. Around 1000 people attended the rally, watching a vaudeville performance (白欖劇) satirizing greedy politicians and collectively singing an antinuclear anthem to the tune of "We Shall Overcome" (Liu Sing-lee 2021; LCA 1986d) (fig. 5). Hong Kong's debilitated antinuclear movement sprung back to life momentarily. For the Joint Conference's Liu Sing-lee (2021), the antinuclear rally was largely ceremonial. The group's plans to protest during Queen Elizabeth's visit on October 12 were aborted.

Even as the Joint Conference had dissipated, concern over nuclear power remained. The anti–Daya Bay movement turned Fung Chi-Wood into a household name. Making headway into the city's democratizing political scene, Fung was elected legislative councillor under the first direct elections into the council in 1991. He joined the Panel on Environmental Affairs and served as a vice-convener of an ad hoc group on Daya Bay affairs. Controversy picked up again in 1987 when steel bars were found missing from the concrete foundation of a reactor's containment shield. Worker injuries, deaths, and engineering faults plagued the project's construction. After much delay, the much-demanded fourteen-member advisory committee was set up by GNPJVC in 1988, although CCP direction made it a largely pronuclear "toothless watchdog" (Lee and Ho 1988; *SCMP* 1988). Hong Kong's environmental groups, such as the Conservancy Association, took up the mantle of the local antinuclear movement as most of the Joint Conference's leadership turned their attention to the prodemocracy movement. In coming years, environmentalists continued to organize antinuclear rallies, conferences, and concerts. For instance, prominent environmentalist Man Si-Wai published a critical volume against the project in 1987 together with other university educators and continued to publicly critique the PRC's nuclear ambitions well after the movement (Xianggang dazhuan jiaoshi guanzhu Dayawan hedianchang xiaozu 1987).

As the first time a social movement pitted Hong Kong local opinion directly against Beijing leaders, what did the Daya Bay controversy mean for residents at that time? For many, the antinuclear movement was a failure, foreshadowing Beijing's intransigence toward society-wide disapproval. This perception of failure was most visible through emigration from Hong Kong. While emigration had an initial uptick

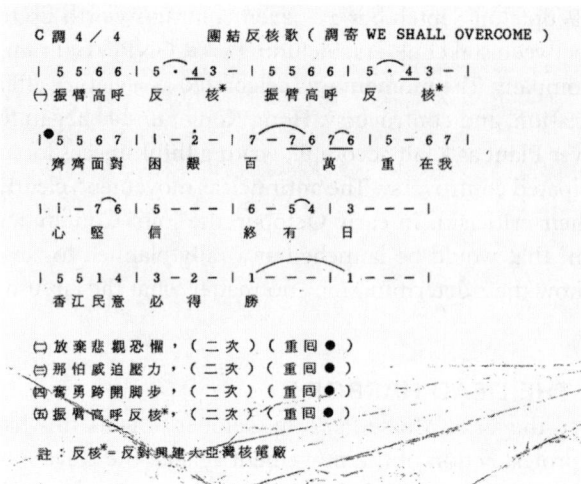

FIGURE 5 Antinuclear anthem composed to the tune of "We Shall Overcome." From "Public Representations on: Daya Bay Nuclear Power Project," Enclosure 94, LAS18/2/8, Legislative Council Archives, Hong Kong.

in 1984, Ronald Skeldon (1990) calls the year 1986 a "watershed," with estimates rising sharply after that year. Perhaps the highest profile emigration was that of Joint Conference spokesperson Linda Siddall, who fulfilled her promise that, "if the Daya Bay comes on stream, I shall leave Hong Kong with my children" (Cawthorne 1986). The Daya Bay controversy confirms historian John Carroll's (2007) characterization of post-1984 Hong Kong as a "jittery city."

However, many activists saw the anti–Daya Bay movement as a blueprint for future civil society movements. For activists such as spokesperson Fung Chi-Wood (2021), the anti–Daya Bay movement was unprecedented in its scale and tactics. Liu Sing-lee (2021) reflects that the movement succeeded on three points: society-wide mobilization, a direct appeal to negotiations with Beijing on Hong Kong affairs, and the development of "peaceful, rational, and nonviolent" (和理非) pressure tactics.[2] Chan Kin-Man (2023), cofounder of the 2014 Occupy Central with Peace and Love movement, observed that the antinuclear movement's highly centralized organizational style and closely vetted leadership lived on in the succeeding prodemocracy movement. Ming Sing (2000) also observes that 1986 was a significant year, with the founding of the Joint Committee on the Promotion of a Democratic Government on October 27 as Hong Kong's first prodemocracy alliance, marking the end of the "formative phase" of the city's prodemocracy movement and the beginning of a "conflicting phase" between influential political factions. This was followed by the Ko Shan meeting on November 2, where prodemocracy groups called for a greater pace of democratic development (Ma 2012: 212). Energies, tactics, and alliances from the anti–Daya Bay movement poured into the prodemocracy movement in the years to come. Many key participants of the Joint Conference became elected politicians and prominent activists. Chan Kin-Man, who was a key organizer in the Joint Conference and part of the twelve-person delegation to Beijing, helped found the 2014 Occupy Central with Peace and Love movement, while vocal legislative councillors Martin Lee and Szeto Wah became charismatic stewards of Hong Kong's democracy movement (So 2015: 451).

The anti–Daya Bay movement was a climactic event for the development of Hong Kong's environmental movement. Environmentalist Simon Chau Siu Cheung notes that the movement was "the first large-scale environmental movement in the city's history," fostering connections between environmental activists (Greenwoods 2017), while Man Si-Wai (1998) sees the movement as an accumulation of decades of environmental resistance. While the antinuclear movement began ostensibly as an environmental one, the mass mobilization after the Chernobyl disaster in 1986 became broadly coalitional and assertive in ways that traced a line of continuity between pressure group organizing in the 1970s and the prodemocracy politics that emerged after 1986. Chau observed that, in the wake of the antinuclear movement, Hong Kong environmentalism moved from social and political organizing toward environmental advocacy that focused on consensual politics and lifestyle changes (Lin 2010). The dissolving of the antinuclear movement's coalitional politics shows, on the one hand, the affective power of nuclear anxiety, which quickly dissipated after contract signing, and on the other hand, the increased specialization of movements into specific issues symptomatic of the decolonial expansion of electoral politics, as more grassroots activists entered high politics (Chiu and Lui 2000). The anti–Daya Bay movement therefore represents an inflection point between mass mobilization and electoral politics in the 1980s, where elected representatives (in district boards and the Legislative Council) organized alongside pressure groups and communities across the city on the ground. This historical conjuncture makes the anti–Daya Bay movement a historical model for building coalitional mass mobilization in Hong Kong.

The eventual opening and continual running of the Daya Bay Nuclear Power Plant has been taken to be a sign of the movement's failure, but a granular historical treatment shows that, more than its teleological end, the controversy was shot through with compromises and disavowals. Archives reveal that popular nuclear anxiety in Hong Kong eclipsed broader political and environmental concerns, despite post hoc scholarly analyses otherwise. This history further shows that, post-Reform, the PRC's ambition for energy modernity and desire for control were inseparable, made evident by official dismissals of other competing forms of modernity expressed by Hong Kong's antinuclear activists, namely, nuclear safety, political transparency, and public participation. The controversy laid bare for Hong Kong residents a sobering awareness of being potentially expendable in the PRC's pursuit of modernization, resulting in the further entrenchment of a Hong Kong political identity that continues to be a source of contention in contemporary Hong Kong–China relations. On top of local and regional dynamics, Hong Kong's antinuclear movement was irrevocably global, whether in the brokerage between major geopolitical powers or the spread of nuclear anxiety as a result of the Chernobyl disaster. These global stakes were well appreciated by activists and politicians at the time, as they traveled across the world hoping to allay fears back home. The intersecting scales of the global, national, and local within the anti–Daya Bay movement resonate with the increasingly complex geographies of climate and geopolitical crisis today.

Rather than a bounded perception of failure, the anti–Daya Bay movement in this article is resituated as a key moment within Hong Kong's history of political development. Activists rode on the antinuclear movement's mass political momentum to launch the prodemocracy movement, later succeeding in their appeals for direct elections into the Legislative Council in 1991, after the Tiananmen Square protests in 1989. A new crop of environmentalists and environmental ideas emerged by the end of the 1980s, advocating for the uptake of everyday environmental practices in Hong Kong. Despite the rapid dissipation of the anti–Daya Bay movement, activists took tactics and networks with them into future movements. Beyond the echelons of civil society leadership, the anti–Daya Bay movement and its aftermath were politicizing forces for the masses. Through the antinuclear movement, many ordinary Hong Kong residents first encountered grassroots organization and protest on a city-wide scale. The ongoing legacy of the antinuclear movement, specifically with its mass mobilization through the million-signature campaign, can be seen in the massive turnouts to Hong Kong's protests in the last decade. Far from an inevitability inscribed into the fate of colonial politics, the anti–Daya Bay movement transformed nuclear anxiety into a collective consciousness of disenfranchisement that cut across Hong Kong society, opening up mass mobilization as one of many possibilities in the fight for the city's future.

MARCUS YEE is a PhD candidate in history at Yale University, researching urban environmental history in South and Southeast Asia. He graduated from the University of Hong Kong with a BA in history and Earth systems science and a minor in Thai. He recently published "Drivers of Urban Heat in Hong Kong over the Past 116 Years" in *Urban Climate* (2022).

ACKNOWLEDGMENTS

I thank my interlocutors, Chan Kin-Man, Fung Chi-Wood, Bruce Liu Sing-lee, and one who chose to remain anonymous, for sharing their memories and reflections on the movement. I am grateful for Frank Dikötter for his guidance on this research while at the University of Hong Kong. Astute comments by Sunil Amrith, Denise Y. Ho, Angela Ki Che Leung, Helen Siu, Odd Arne Westad, and two anonymous reviewers further helped refine the manuscript. I am grateful for research support from Sam Chao, Sallie Lau, and Charlie Lee.

NOTES

1. For newspapers, this article mainly relies on the archives of *South China Morning Post*, the English-language daily with the widest circulation, and *Ming Pao*, a respected Chinese-language daily whose owner was personally invested in the anti–Daya Bay movement. For a comprehensive survey of partisanship in press coverage of the controversy, see Yee and Wong 1987. For oral history interviews, a comprehensive coverage of interviewees was limited by the political situation in the city at the time of the research (2021) under the National Security Law. All interviewees were chosen based on their involvement as core leaders of the anti–Daya Bay movement.

2. Liu Sing-lee's use of the phrase *peaceful, rational, and nonviolent* is anachronistic and meant to reflect the repertoire of nonviolent protest tactics developed during the anti–Daya Bay movement and carried forth into future social movements. The term itself came into popular circulation only during the later 2019–20 protests to describe nonmilitant protest tactics. The term is attributed to Democratic Party lawmaker Emily Lau, who used it to distinguish her party from more radical elements in the pan-democratic camp (Siu, Lai, and Chiu 2022: 352).

REFERENCES

Archival Documents

Chen Heling. 2008. Interview by Edward Kwong, March 31–April 21. Oral history interview transcript, Hong Kong Heritage Project, Hong Kong.
CLP (China Light and Power Company Ltd.). 1960. *Thirty-Eighth Report of Board of Directors Chairman's Review and Statement of Accounts*. Hong Kong Heritage Project, Hong Kong.

Guo Tianjue. 2008. Interview by Edward Kwong, June 23. Oral history interview transcript, Hong Kong Heritage Project, Hong Kong.

Hong Kong Legislative Council. 1986a. *Official Report of Proceedings: Wednesday, 7 May 1986.* Hong Kong Legislative Council Library, Hong Kong.

Hong Kong Legislative Council. 1986b. *Report of LegCo Fact-Finding Delegations on Nuclear Power Generation.* Hong Kong Legislative Council Library, Hong Kong.

Hong Kong Legislative Council. 1986c. *Report of the Visit of the Members of the Legislative Council Delegations on Nuclear Power Generation to Beijing: From 17.9.86 to 21.9.86.* Hong Kong Legislative Council, Hong Kong.

Joint Conference for the Shelving of Daya Bay Nuclear Power Plant. 1986. *Dayawan hedianchang ziliaoce* [Daya Bay Nuclear Power Plant information handbook]. University of Hong Kong Libraries Special Collections, Hong Kong.

Kadoorie, Lawrence. 1980. "Sir Lawrence Kadoorie's Talk on 'Hong Kong's Contribution to the Development of Energy Resources in China.'" December 5. "Lawrence Kadoorie: Speeches, Articles, and Interviews 2," SEK-1A-037. Hong Kong Heritage Project, Hong Kong.

Kadoorie, Lawrence. 1981. "Sir Lawrence Kadoorie's Interview with RTHK, Broadcast on 19/7/81, 'Access Programme.'" July 19. SEK-1A-037. Hong Kong Heritage Project, Hong Kong.

Kadoorie, Lawrence. 1986. "Hong Kong Today." Presentation at the Wells Fargo International Advisory Council—Brazil Meeting, October 5–11 ("A Brief Memorandum by Lord Kadoorie"). SEK-1A-037. Hong Kong Heritage Project, Hong Kong.

LCA (Legislative Council Archives). 1986a. Letter from Hong Kong Caritas Aberdeen Social Service Centre and Southern District Concern for Nuclear Power Plant Action Group. September 9. "Public Representations on: Daya Bay Nuclear Power Project," Enclosure 101, LAS18/2/7. Legislative Council Archives, Hong Kong.

LCA (Legislative Council Archives). 1986b. Letter from Joint Committee of Shaukiwan and Chai Wan District on the Shelving of Daya Bay Nuclear Plant. July 14. "Public Representations on: Daya Bay Nuclear Power Project," Enclosure 44, LAS18/2/7. Legislative Council Archives, Hong Kong.

LCA (Legislative Council Archives). 1986c. Letter from teachers and staff from Chinese University of Hong Kong. July 14. "Public Representations on: Daya Bay Nuclear Power Project," Enclosure 33-4, LAS18/2/7. Legislative Council Archives, Hong Kong.

LCA (Legislative Council Archives). 1986d. Program of Morse Park Rally. October 5. "Public Representations on: Daya Bay Nuclear Power Project," Enclosure 94, LAS18/2/8. Legislative Council Archives, Hong Kong.

Lee, Y. B. 2007. *Dawn of Daya Bay.* Unpublished memoir. Hong Kong Heritage Project, Hong Kong.

PREM (Prime Minister's Office Archives). 1980a. Letter from Lord Kadoorie to Margaret Thatcher. February 5. "Hong Kong. Correspondence with Sir Lawrence Kadoorie Concerning UK Trade with China; Power Projects in Hong Kong Involving UK Companies; Chinese Guandong Nuclear Power Project; Part 1," PREM 19/255. UK National Archives, London.

PREM (Prime Minister's Office Archives). 1980b. Speaking notes of Margaret Thatcher for meeting with Lawrence Kadoorie, July 30. PREM 19/255. UK National Archives, London.

PREM (Prime Minister's Office Archives). 1985. Notes of Meeting between Chairman Deng Xiao Ping and Hong Kong Nuclear Investment Company Delegation Led by Lord Kadoorie. January 19. "Hong Kong. Power Projects in Hong Kong and China Involving UK Companies: Castle Peak Power Station in Hong Kong; Guangdong Nuclear Power Project; Part 3," PREM 19/1532. UK National Archives, London.

PRO (Public Records Office). 1986a. "Adjournment Debate on the HK and Daya Bay Nuclear Power Project." HKRS618-1-613. Public Records Office, Hong Kong.

PRO (Public Records Office). 1986b. "District Officer (K&T)'s Weekly Information Report." HKRS943-13-4. Public Records Office, Hong Kong.

PRO (Public Records Office). 1986c. "North District—Weekly Information Report, Week Ending 19 July 1986." HKRS943-13-4. Public Records Office, Hong Kong.

PRO (Public Records Office). 1986d. Telegram from David Akers-Jones to Foreign Colonial Office. "Nuclear Safety." August. "Guangdong Nuclear Power Station Project at Daya Bay: Safety Concerns in Hong Kong," HKMS189-9-26. Public Records Office, Hong Kong.

PRO (Public Records Office). 1986e. Telegram from Edward Youde to Foreign Colonial Office. June 18. "Guangdong Nuclear Power Station Project at Daya Bay: Safety Concerns in Hong Kong," HKMS189-9-21. Public Records Office, Hong Kong.

PRO (Public Records Office). 1986f. Telegram from Edward Youde to Foreign Colonial Office. June 1986. "Guangdong Nuclear Power Station Project at Daya Bay: Safety Concerns in Hong Kong," HKMS189-9-22. Public Records Office, Hong Kong.

PRO (Public Records Office). 1986g. Translation of Vice-Premier Li Peng's Speech to Guangdong Nuclear Power Joint Venture Company Staff. May 21. HKMS189-9-21. Public Records Office, Hong Kong.

PRO (Public Records Office). 1986h. "Weekly Information Report by District Officer (K & T), August 7, 1986." HKRS943-13-4. Public Records Office, Hong Kong.

PRO (Public Records Office). 1986i. "Weekly Information Report by District Officer (Kowloon City), September 4 1986." HKRS943-13-4. Public Records Office, Hong Kong.

PRO (Public Records Office). 1986j. "Weekly Information Report by District Officer (Tsuen Wan), 31 July 1986." HKRS943-13-4. Public Records Office, Hong Kong.

PRO (Public Records Office). 1986k. "Weekly Information Report on Sha Tin District." HKRS943-13-4. Public Records Office, Hong Kong.

PRO (Public Records Office). 1986l. "WTR from DO(C&W) for the Week Ending 18.7.86." "Extracts from Weekly Information Reports of Daya Bay Nuclear Power Plant," HKRS943-13-4. Public Records Office, Hong Kong.

Zhou Zanling. 2008. Interview by Edward Kwong, March 31. Oral history interview transcript, Hong Kong Heritage Project, Hong Kong.

Interviews and Personal Communications

Anonymous. 2021. Recollection notes from a participant of the Joint Organisation for Concern of Nuclear Energy. Personal communications with author, October 2. Online.

Chan, Kin-Man. 2023. Interview by the author, March 30. Online.

Fung, Chi-Wood. 2021. Interview by the author, September 30. Hong Kong.

Liu Sing-lee, Bruce. 2021. Interview by the author, October 13. Hong Kong.

Secondary Sources

Behrmann, Neil. 1986. "Daya Bay 'Going Ahead.'" *South China Morning Post*, May 2.

Beijing Review. 1980. "Proposal for Nuclear Power Stations." December 8.

Bickers, Robert, and Ray Yep, eds. 2009. *May Days in Hong Kong: Riot and Emergency in 1967*. Hong Kong: Hong Kong University Press.

Brown, Kate. 2019. *Manual for Survival: An Environmental History of the Chernobyl Disaster*. New York: Norton.

Butenhoff, Linda. 1999. *Social Movements and Political Reform in Hong Kong*. Westport, CT: Praeger.

Carroll, John. 2007. *A Concise History of Hong Kong*. Hong Kong: Hong Kong University Press.

Cawthorne, Zelda. 1986. "Putting the Case against N-power. Profile: Environmentalist Linda Siddall." *South China Morning Post*, July 2.

Chan, Albert. 1986a. "Academics Fighting Daya Bay." *South China Morning Post*, July 15.

Chan, Albert. 1986b. "Beijing Accepts Daya Bay Protest." *South China Morning Post*, August 21.

Chan, Albert. 1986c. "Beijing Answers Territory's Daya Bay Critics." *South China Morning Post*, August 9.

Chan, Albert. 1986d. "Daya Bay Group Won't Judge." *South China Morning Post*, August 2.

Chan, Albert. 1986e. "Deadline for Daya Bay Contracts Is Changed." *South China Morning Post*, September 6.

Chan, Albert. 1986f. "No Guarantee of Cheap Electricity." *South China Morning Post*, September 21.

Chan, Albert. 1986g. "Nuclear Plant to Go Ahead, Stresses Beijing." *South China Morning Post*, August 27.

Cheng Ming Monthly 爭鳴. 1986. "Wo keyi he tamen gongkai bianlun—Fangwen Gangda dilixi gaoji jiangshi Xuefengxuan boshi" [I can publicly debate with them—Interview with University of Hong Kong geography professor Victor Sit]. *Cheng Ming Monthly*, August, 23.

Cheung, Kwai-Hung, et al. 1986. "Christians Unite against Daya Bay." *South China Morning Post*, July 10.

Cheung, Walter. 1986. "Angry Lawyers Make Their Case Heard." *South China Morning Post*, September 6.

Chiu, Stephen Wing Kai, and Tai-Lok Lui. 2000. *The Dynamics of Social Movement in Hong Kong*. Hong Kong: Hong Kong University Press.

Choi, Frank. 1986. "District Boards Embroiled in Drive to Halt Daya Bay." *South China Morning Post*, June 20.

Chu, Cindy Yik-Yi. 2015. "Overt and Covert Functions of the Hong Kong Branch of the Xinhua News Agency, 1947–1984." In *Critical Readings on the Modern History of Hong Kong*, edited by John M. Carroll and Chi-kwan Mark, 4:1537–54. Leiden: Brill.

Clifford, Mark Lambert. 2019. "Let There Be Light: China Light and Power and the Making of Modern Hong Kong." PhD diss., University of Hong Kong.

Dapiran, Antony. 2017. *City of Protest: A Recent History of Dissent in Hong Kong*. Sydney: Penguin.

Goodstadt, Leo F. 2005. *Uneasy Partners: The Conflict between Public Interest and Private Profit in Hong Kong*. Hong Kong: Hong Kong University Press.

Greenwoods. 2017. "Lüye boshi tan huanbao he lüshe shenghuo" [Greenwoods professor on environmental conservation and green living]. January 30, 2017. https://www.greenwoodshk .org/post/2017/01/30/%E7%B6%A0%E9%87%8E%E5%8D%9A%E5%A3%AB%E8% AB%87%E7%92%B0%E4%BF%9D%E5%92%8C%E7%B6%A0%E8%89%B2%E7%94%9F% E6%B4%BB.

Harte, Sa Ni. 1986. "Daya Bay: We've to Fend for Ourselves." *South China Morning Post*, October 18.

Ho, Kit Wan. 1988. "The Role of the Legislative Council in the Daya Bay Controversy." Master's thesis, University of Hong Kong.

Ho, Ming-Sho. 2018. "Taiwan's Anti-nuclear Movement: The Making of a Militant Citizen Movement." *Journal of Contemporary Asia* 48, no. 3: 445–64.

Hong Kong Government. 1982. *The Schemes of Control*. Hong Kong: Government Printer.

Hsiao, Hsin-Huang Michael, Hwa-Jen Liu, Su-Hoon Lee, On-Kwok Lai, and Yok-Shiu F. Lee. 1999. "The Making of Anti-nuclear Movements in East Asia: State–Movements Relationships and Policy Outcomes." In *Asia's Environmental Movements: Comparative Perspectives*, edited by Yok-Shiu Lee and Alvin Y. So, 252–68. New York: Sharpe.

Hung, Ho-Fung. 2012. "Cong shehui yundong dao jing ying jie bie wanyi: Xianggang huanjing baohuweiji chutan" [From social movement to elite hobby: A preliminary look at Hong Kong's environmental protection crisis]. *Quasi-blog*, December 18. https://blogqua.wordpress .com/2012/12/18/p1/.

International Atomic Energy Agency. 1977. *Nuclear Power Planning Study for Hong Kong*. Vienna: International Atomic Energy Agency.

Kirchhof, Astrid Mignon, and Jan-Henrik Meyer. 2014. "Global Protest against Nuclear Power: Transfer and Transnational Exchange in the 1970s and 1980s." *Historical Social Research / Historische Sozialforschung* 39, no. 1: 165–90.

Ko, Tin-Ming. 1987. "Pressure Groups and the Daya Bay Controversy." Master's thesis, University of Hong Kong.

Lai, On Kwok. 2001. "Greening of Hong Kong? Forms of Environmental Manifestation of Environmental Movements." In *The Dynamics of Social Movements in Hong Kong*, edited by Stephen Wing Kai Chiu and Tai Lok Lui, 259–95. Hong Kong: Hong Kong University Press.

Lee, Bellette, and Andy Ho. 1988. "Advisory Panel Monitors Safety for Daya Bay." *South China Morning Post*, August 12.

Lee, Yok-shiu, and Alvin Y. So, eds. 1999. *Asia's Environmental Movements: Comparative Perspectives*. New York: Sharpe.

Li, Cinty. 1986. "N-Protestors on the March." *South China Morning Post*, September 15.

Li, Peng. 2004. *Qibu dao fazhan: Li Peng hedian riji (shang)* [From origins to progress: Diary of nuclear energy]. Beijing: Xinhua.

Lin, He An. 2010. "Xianggang lüse shenghuo daren Zhou Zhao Xiang boshi zhuanfang: Cong gao huanbao dao liaoyu 'xixin' jiuzai" [Interview with Hong Kong's doyen of green living Professor Simon Chau Siu Cheung: From environmentalism to self-care]. *Yinyi* 11, no. 12. https://www.cgan.net/science/transaction/10111101.htm.

Lou, Loretta. 2022. "From Hygienic Modernity to Green Modernity: Two Modes of Modern Living in Hong Kong since the 1970s." In *Design and Modernity in Asia: National Identity and Transnational Exchange 1945–1990*, edited by Megha Rajguru and Yunah Lee, 105–20. London: Bloomsbury.

Lui, Tai-Lok, and Stephen Wing Kai Chiu. 1997. "The Structuring of Social Movements in Contemporary Hong Kong." *China Information* 12, nos. 1–2: 97–113.

Luk, Bernard H. K. 2016. *Zuo kan yun qi shi: Yiben Xianggangren de jiaoxieshi juansan* [A people's history of the Hong Kong Professional Teachers' Union, vol. 3]. Hong Kong: City University of Hong Kong Press.

Ma, Ngok. 2012. "80 niandai minzhu yundong dashiji" [Chronology of the 80s democracy movement]. In *Xianggang 80 niandai minzhu yundong koushu lishi* [An oral history of democratic movement of Hong Kong in the 1980s], edited by Ma Ngok, 210–17. Hong Kong: City University of Hong Kong Press.

Man, Si-Wai. 1998. *Xianggang lü se nan chan* [Hong Kong's green dystocia]. Hong Kong: Xianggang Renwen Kexue Chubanshe.

Ming Pao 明報. 1986a. "Dayawan hediancang buhui yanchi xing jian" [Daya Bay nuclear power plant will not be delayed]. May 12.

Ming Pao 明報. 1986b. "Dayawan hedian yiwai fengxian shi yibailiushiliu fen zhiyi" [Daya Bay nuclear power plant's accident probability is 1 in 166]. August 12.

Ming Pao 明報. 1986c. "Fandui hingjian hedianchang de zuijia fangfa" [The best way to oppose the building of the nuclear power plant]. July 1.

Ming Pao 明報. 1986d. "Fanhedian qianming beizhi wuzhi shanghai shimin dui zhengzhi xinxin" [Calling the antinuclear signature campaign ignorant only damages residents' faith in politics]. August 9.

Ming Pao 明報. 1986e. "Fanhe tuanti fangang dui xingcheng anpai biaoshi shiwang" [Antinuclear group returns back to Hong Kong and expresses disappointment with trip]. August 22.

Ming Pao 明報. 1986f. "Gaosuwo: Ni yaobuyao Dayawan hedianchang?" [Tell me: Do you want the Daya Bay nuclear power plant?]. July 19.

Ming Pao 明報. 1986g. "Hedian wenti bulie yicheng sanhuihou zeke ziyou taolun" [Nuclear issue not on the agenda, open discussions allowed only after the meeting]. June 30.

Ming Pao 明報. 1986h. "Hedian yiwai ruhe shusan Beijing Waijiaoju shuo weizhi xiangqing" [Beijing Foreign Office yet to know details on contingency plan for nuclear accidents]. August 2.

Ming Pao 明報. 1986i. "Hedianzhan zuowei xiandaihua zishu Huyaobang shuo buyi mangmu fandui" [Hu Yaobang: As a form of modern technology, nuclear power station should not be blindly opposed]. June 20.

Ming Pao 明報. 1986j. "Yue hedianzhan yidan chu yiwai Gangying siwanglü keneng ruisheng" [Accidents at Guangdong nuclear power station will cause a sharp increase in infant mortality rate]. June 22.

Mok, Florence. 2022. "Town Talk: Enhancing the 'Eyes and Ears' of the Colonial State in British Hong Kong, 1950s–1975." *Historical Research* 95, no. 268: 287–308.

Oriental Daily News 東方日報. 1986. "Yi kexue taidu renshi Dayawan hedianchang de Xingjian" [Approaching the Daya Bay nuclear power plant project with a scientific attitude]. Advertisement, August 4.

Sing, Ming. 2000. "Mobilization for Political Change—The Pro-democracy Movement in Hong Kong (1980s–1994)." In *The Dynamics of Social Movements in Hong Kong*, edited by Stephen Wing Kai Chiu and Tai Lok Lui, 21–54. Hong Kong: Hong Kong University Press.

Sing, Ming. 2004. *Hong Kong's Torturous Democratization: A Comparative Analysis*. Oxfordshire: Routledge.

Siu, Kaxton Y. K., Lai Tsz Chung, and Stephen Wing Kai Chiu. 2022. "Hong Kong as a City of Protest: Social Movement as Motor for Social Change." In *Hong Kong Society: High-Definition Stories beyond the Spectacle of East-Meets-West*, edited by Stephen W. K. Chiu, and Kaxton Y. W. Siu, 329–85. Singapore: Springer Nature Singapore.

Skeldon, Ronald. 1990. "Emigration and the Future of Hong Kong." *Pacific Affairs* 63, no. 4: 500–523.

So, Alvin Y. 2015. "The Tiananmen Incident and the Rebirth of the Democracy Project." In *Critical Readings on the Modern History of Hong Kong*, edited by John M. Carroll, and Chi-kwan Mark, 2:447–76. Leiden and Boston: Brill.

SCMP (*South China Morning Post*). 1986a. "Chernobyl Lessons." August 15.

SCMP (*South China Morning Post*). 1986b. "Children Mobilised in N-Plant Campaign." June 23.

SCMP (*South China Morning Post*). 1986c. "China Acts on N-Safety." September 27.

SCMP (*South China Morning Post*). 1986d. "Daya Bay Lobby on the Offensive." October 3.

SCMP (*South China Morning Post*). 1986e. "Deng Committed to Daya Bay, Says Top Official." July 19.

SCMP (*South China Morning Post*). 1986f. "Experts Scoff at Opinions of Anti-nuclear Scientists." July 25.

SCMP (*South China Morning Post*). 1986g. "Fears Allayed over Daya Bay Nuclear Plant." May 7.

SCMP (*South China Morning Post*). 1986h. "Journalists Call for Information." October 3.

SCMP (*South China Morning Post*). 1986i. "Lee and Tam Fight It Out on Television." September 3.

SCMP (*South China Morning Post*). 1986j. "Mounting Public Opposition." August 9.

SCMP (*South China Morning Post*). 1986k. "Nuclear Experts Will Check Daya Bay Plant." August 9.

SCMP (*South China Morning Post*). 1986l. "Nuclear Safety Report 'Only Highlights Risks.'" September 1.

SCMP (*South China Morning Post*). 1986m. "Protest against China Light." June 9.

SCMP (*South China Morning Post*). 1986n. "Reactor 'Is Most Dangerous Type.'" July 4.

SCMP (*South China Morning Post*). 1986o. "Red Faces over Nuclear Leak." April 30.

SCMP (*South China Morning Post*). 1986p. "Seventy Thousand Sign Anti-Plant Petition." July 14.

SCMP (*South China Morning Post*). 1986q. "Signature Campaign." July 11.

SCMP (*South China Morning Post*). 1988. "Toothless Daya Bay Watchdog." August 2.

Southerland, Daniel. 1986. "Hong Kong Citizens Take a Stand: Chinese Nuclear Power Plant Draws Opposition from Colony." *Washington Post*, August 19.

Tan, Isabella. 1986. "Who Can We Trust to Tell the Facts?" *South China Morning Post*, May 16.

Thomas, Nicholas. 1999. *Democracy Denied: Identity, Civil Society, and Illiberal Democracy in Hong Kong*. Aldershot: Ashgate.

Tsang, Steve. 2004. *A Modern History of Hong Kong.* Hong Kong: Hong Kong University Press.

Tso, M. Y. W. 1988. "Opening Remarks." In *Heneng fadian: Hedian yantaohui lunwen zhuanji* [Nuclear power: Proceedings of the nuclear power seminar], edited by M. Y. W. Tso, 1–2. Hong Kong: Hong Kong University Press.

Wai, S. Y. 1986. "Councilors Step Up Daya Bay Campaign." *South China Morning Post,* August 9.

Wai, S. Y., and Daniel Chung. 1986. "Daya Bay Trips Threaten to Divide Council." *South China Morning Post,* July 15.

Wang, Wei. 1986. "Huyaobang danshu Zhongguo dui hecaijunwenti lichang" [Hu Yaobang on China's position on nuclear disarmament]. *People's Daily* 人民日報, June 21.

Xianggang dazhuan jiaoshi guanzhu Dayawan hedianchang xiaozu. 1987. *Hezifadian: Dayawan jihuamian mianguan* [Nuclear energy: Aspects of the Daya Bay project]. Hong Kong: Ming Pao.

Xu, Yi-Chong. 2010. *The Politics of Nuclear Energy in China.* London: Palgrave Macmillan.

Yee, Herbert S., and Wong Yiu-Chung. 1987. "Hong Kong: The Politics of the Daya Bay Nuclear Plant Debate." *International Affairs (Royal Institute of International Affairs 1944–)* 63, no. 4: 617–30.

SOHOON YI and HAN SANG KIM

Racing the Korean Imaginary

Racialization and Gender in South Korea

ABSTRACT The monoethnic and monocultural fantasy in South Korea has encountered new entanglements in the contemporary era, compelling the need for a reevaluation of the country's ingrained racial hierarchies. This introduction to this forum
on race and racialization in the South Korean context from the perspective of Asian
studies presents a conceptual background and introduces the forum contributions.

KEYWORDS racialization, South Korea, Koreanness, intersectionality, blood lineage

Despite its deep-seated myth of monoethnic nationhood, South Korea has seen challenges to the fantasy of homogeneity in the last two decades. With the increased
influx and efflux of the population in and out of the border in the globalized era,
the monoethnic and monocultural fantasy has encountered new entanglements,
compelling the need for reevaluation of the country's ingrained racial hierarchies.
Nonetheless, South Korea's rhetorical push for "multiculturalism" in policy making, media representation, and education, in response to the country's multiethnic
and multiracial transformation in the twenty-first century, has instead reinforced
the myth of homogeneity by naturalizing the racialized boundaries among people
from different backgrounds.

This forum is a rare endeavor to discuss the topics of race and racialization in
the South Korean context from the perspective of Asian studies. While there has
been ample discussion about race in Korean American and Asian American studies, most of these approaches are rooted in America's local context of race/ethnicity
and migration studies. Meanwhile, similar attempts to conceptualize the sociohistorical meaning of race and the complex racialization process in Korean studies
have been scarce.

The contributions to this forum approach racialization as shifting, plural, mutual,
and simultaneous. As working definitions, this forum conceptualizes race and
racialization as relations of power and domination (Quijano 2000) in a systematic
structure of inferiority and superiority based on an imagination of biological lineage in the unique Asian context. Authors of these articles start from a belief in the
biological essence of race beyond skin color. Doing so, however, does not undermine the importance of appearance or phenotypical differences in racialization or
racism because, as many contributors show, color plays an important role. Instead,

THE JOURNAL OF ASIAN STUDIES · 84:2 · May 2025
DOI: 10.1215/00219118-11591549 © 2025 Association for Asian Studies

this forum puts afore and critically engages with the biological basis *beyond* color to simultaneously investigate "colorless" forms of racialization and its historical and foundational links to its counterpart. For example, Michael Omi and Howard Winant (2014: 13) state that "race is *ocular* in an irreducible way" when explaining a "crucial *corporeal* dimension to the race-concept." We believe that focusing on the irreducible biological appearance may have limited currency beyond white majority societies and does not capture the dynamics of racialization by another racialized group in a nonwhite, decolonizing society.

Moreover, this forum focuses on the interrelational qualities and interactive dynamics in constructing race and processes of racialization in the South Korean context without necessitating the presence of isolatable and visibly distinguishable racial groups. In doing so, the articles in this forum address and challenge existing definitions of race and racialization that involve biological and phenotypical qualities and the reproduction of such. For example, one may describe South Korea as having a strong sense of nationalism in its belief in ethnic homogeneity. One may also say that South Korea does not have a visible minority as a racialized group. However, scholars familiar with the concept of race, such as the contributors to this forum, may recognize those with similar phenotypical appearances, such as Chinese, North Korean, and biracial populations, experiencing acute and severe racialization. How can one experience racism when they "look the same"? More puzzling yet, how can one experience racism when they are of the "same" ethnicity?

Constructing race in the South Korean context has grave ramifications for understanding Koreanness (see also Lim 2009). Given the imagined biological basis of Koreanness (i.e., sharing the same ancestry) and the constructed monoethnicity embedded in its sociopolitical history (Shin 2006), and the unique legacy of Japanese imperialism and its construction of race (Kawai 2015; J. K. Kim 2015), this forum treats Koreanness as a social construct of racial essence.[1]

The scholarship on early modern history in Korea has seen an increasing volume of literature investigating the relationships among intertwining notions of ethnicity and race. Scholars in Japanese studies established that both *jinshu* (人種) and *minjoku* (民族) translate as "race" (Kawai 2015; Robertson 2010). This may surprise some Korean readers because the distinction between *injong* (人種) and *minjok* (民族) is drawn somewhat more clearly as "race" and "ethnicity." Despite such seemingly innocuous distinction drawn by the public, there has been abundant research about the close historical linkages between the two terms. These neologisms were introduced in the late nineteenth and early twentieth centuries during Korea's encounters with Western empires and growing Japanese imperialism. Historians have written on the interchangeable usage of the two concepts at the beginning of the twentieth century (Na 2022; Youn 2022) and the influence of the dominant racial ideologies of social Darwinism and pan-Asianism (Na 2022; Tikhonov 2010; Youn 2022). Na (2022) notes the transition after 1905, the year marked by the Japanese victory in the Russo-Japanese War and the Eulsa treaty, and the intellectual community's preference for the term *minjok* in response to Japanese appropriation of the term *injong*. Thus a distinct notion of Korean ethnicity was inculcated as a counterdiscourse against Japanese colonialist notions of race, eugenics, and hierarchal assimilationism (Na 2022; Youn 2022). As Schmid (2002: 5) observed, ethnic nationalism was an intellectual attempt to position Korea in a new global order, and it was "the first consciously globalizing discourse." As such, race was integral to understanding the international order of the time, and the notion of Koreanness started as an intellectual discourse to define Korea against the global.

Therefore, placing Koreanness at the center of the race question treats Korea not as an exceptional case but as an outcome of the distinct sociohistorical constellation with continuing contemporary relevance, which can be useful to broader Asian studies. Western imperialism and Japanese colonialism, indeed, were not the only global encounters that Korea experienced. Its painful experience of the Korean War, the Cold War, and the glorious emergence as a high-income country during globalization added to the contradictory and convoluted understandings of race and the global order.

This forum's six articles explore diverse social and political issues that stem from the South Korean experience of race through the cross-cutting theme of gender. Scholars have noted the historical linkages among constructions of race, gender, and sexuality, including the Japanese Empire's contradictory policies on intermarriage between citizens of Japan proper and Chosŏn (Yi 2017). During the Cold War, the intersection of sex and militarism in camptowns received much scholarly attention (J.-k. Lee 2010), especially focusing on the gendered motion of morality, women's role in the family, and penalization of women's sexuality outside of wedlock (Doolan 2021; J. Lee 2010), including "hypersexualization" of biracial girls born in camp towns (Doolan 2021). Gender scholarship has paid ample attention to the recent phenomenon of marriage migration in the globalization era, focusing on migrant women's reproductive labor and the South Korean state's involvement in arranging such labor (M. Kim 2013; H. M. Kim 2007; H. Lee 2013).

While women's prostitution in camptowns and biracial children have been examined extensively from the intersectional perspectives of gender and race, the globalization-inspired gendered migration has seen less engagement, comparatively speaking, from the perspective of race. This forum brings perspectives from history, sociology, and women's studies to comprehensively examine this intersection. Inga Kim Diederich documents a history of "scientific" categorization of mixed-blood children in the Cold War context and argues that the idea of Korean race was constructed during this time at the exclusion of mixed-race populations, even when their number was substantial. Sunhye Kim's article, focusing on an assisted reproductive technology clinic in Taiwan that caters to intending parents from South Korea, China, and Japan, analyses the construction of a "Korean baby" by the clinic and the intending parents. Sohoon Yi presents a case study of Ku Sujin, a marriage migrant of Uzbekistani origin, whose experience of discrimination made headlines at the time. Yi focuses on the invisible, colorless, and erasable forms of racialization that took a backseat in Ku's campaign and its portrayal in the media. Ga Young Chung and Hee Jung Choi analyze policies from the Ministry of National Defense on the convoluted treatment of "biracial" soldiers who are conscripted as part of the national military duty that all Korean citizen men undergo. Han Sang Kim examines the so-called roof Koreans memes that were circulated on the web in the recent context of the Black Lives Matter movement and racially driven controversies in South Korea, focusing on how the archival images of the 1992 Los Angeles riots have become a symbol of a racially motivated masculine myth and collective victimhood in South Korea. Yuko Kawai provides a comparative commentary to studying race and racism in South Korea from the perspectives of Japanese and Asian studies.

The problem of appearance and indistinguishability is an issue that the contributors in this forum address in various ways. While H. S. Kim's and Diederich's contributions pivot on otherness engendered by visual differences, Sohoon Yi focuses explicitly on racialization despite invisibility, arguing that certain migrants were selected as marriage partners for their phenotypical similarities (which she calls *erasability*). S. Kim takes a step further to show that Taiwanese in vitro fertilization clinics construct and advertise the "racial ambiguity" of Taiwanese egg donors based on visual similarities between Taiwanese and Koreans. Noting the interplay of gender in the androcentric imagination of the Korean race, she makes a compelling case that the female gametes (which originate from Taiwanese donors) are assumed to be "empty biomaterials" that are malleable to produce a "Korean baby." Her case contrasts sharply with Diederich's documentation of the "scientific" endeavors to exclude and label mixed-race children, making a compelling case of how science and technology have been implicated in the discourse on national reproduction and race over time. Both articles by Sunhye Kim and by Diederich demonstrate the use and appropriation of science and technology to construct and maintain the myth of racial purity and "Korean phenotypes." Such imagination creates moments of friction, as examined by Yi and by Chung and Choi. While the majority of "multicultural" populations (defined legally as people born to one "Korean" and one "foreign" parent) are visibly indistinguishable from Koreans (and not by accident, as Yi reminds us), their phenotypical similarity nonetheless is a testament to racializing and marginalizing treatment experienced by these populations. So-called don't-ask, don't-document policies adopted by the Ministry of National Defense, as Chung and Choi analyze, are precisely an example of such invisiblized racialization. Bifurcating approaches to mixed-race people, according to Kawai, is also observed in Japan, where the government exercised both expulsion (i.e., sending mixed-race orphans to the US after World War II) and assimilation.

This forum recognizes the role of gender as a core force in shaping the racialization process by paying attention to gendered power dynamics, androcentric notions of nationalism, gendered morality, science and reproduction, and masculinity and militarism. While Diederich, S. Kim, and Yi focus on reproduction and gendered power inequality, Chung and Choi and H. S. Kim document militarized masculinity prevalent in South Korean society. Diederich reminds us of the connection made by Jin-kyung Lee (2010) about the close linkages between militarism and sexuality and their implications on race. Given the violent history of the Korean War, the Cold War, and American militarism, the articles by Chung and Choi and by H. S. Kim present a vivid portrayal of the central role of militarism in men's display of their masculinity and androcentric nationalism. As Chung and Choi observe, exempting biracial populations from the mandatory military conscription previously de facto represented the exclusion of biracial—especially male—populations from exercising full citizenship. Subsequent acceptance of them in the military in recent years has been contradictory due to racist imaginations of who "real" Koreans are. H. S.

Kim shows how a masculinist mythical narrative from past memory is invented to respond to both the high demand for the diversification and cosmopolitanization of South Korea and the immediate connectivity to other parts of the world via the internet.

In so doing, the forum seeks to foreground the intersectional nature of hierarchal racialization as a tool to navigate the sociohistorical dimensions. Korea's historical experience of colonialism, the Cold War, and militarism and its contentious gender dynamics at present and in the past are both unique and comparable. Thus, the articles in this forum present compelling case studies with broader significance for studying race in the Asian context.

SOHOON YI is associate professor in the Division of Global Korean Studies at Korea University. Her research interests include migrant subjectivity at the intersection of gender, immigration laws, precarious labor, and the informal market. Her articles have appeared in *American Behavioral Scientist*, *Citizenship Studies*, *Social Politics*, and the *Journal of Ethnic and Migration Studies*.

HAN SANG KIM is associate professor of sociology at Ajou University and vice president of the International Visual Sociology Association. He is the author of *Cine-Mobility: Twentieth-Century Transformations in Korea's Film and Transportation* (2022).

ACKNOWLEDGMENTS

We thank the members of the Race/Racialization Reading Group at the Korean Social History Association, whose comments have significantly improved this article. This work was supported by the Republic of Korea's Ministry of Education and the National Research Foundation of Korea (NRF-2021S1A5C2A02088731).

NOTE

1. We note the limit on the use of the term *Koreanness* to primarily refer to the South Korean context. As we detail in the following text, the invention of the concept in the early twentieth century denotes a common conceptual history between the two Koreas. However, the Korean War, the Cold War and globalization in the next hundred years undoubtedly shaped vastly different experiences in the two countries, and the contributors to this forum are informed primarily by the South Korean examples.

Such blurred boundaries between race and other identity markers, such as ethnicity, are far from unique to the Korean context. For instance, invoking Baber 2004, Balmurli Natrajan (2022: 307) explains that Hindutva "racialization" of Muslims in India does not require a stable set of phenotypical (biological) differences, only the positing of "insurmountable cultural differences." Natrajan's further argument from Baber's point is that "racialization has been shown to be a symbolic attribution of significance to purported 'differences' (be it in phenotype, ancestry, or culture) and the misrecognition of the same as 'natural'" but "the quest to 'bound' Hindu racial identity as different from Muslim does not . . . depend on the demonstration of 'racial purity'" (307–8). This at least theoretically makes room for Muslims to assimilate into the Hindu race, whereas Dalits' fundamental status in the Hindutva caste system does not allow such room. There have been certain attempts to "rebrand" caste in India by labeling each caste as a benign, horizontal "ethnic" group, which Natrajan argues is "*not* a sociological reality as much as an ideological aspiration by Hindutva votaries and caste elites" in the brutally hierarchical environment of Dalits who are ethnicized (309). Natrajan argues that "both 'race' and 'caste' [or 'ethnicity'] are historical and contextual fictions that have acquired the fixity of fact" (308).

REFERENCES

Baber, Zaheer. 2004. "'Race,' Religion, and Riots: The 'Racialization' of Communal Identity and Conflict in India." *Sociology* 38, no. 4: 701–18.

Doolan, Yuri. 2021. "The Camptown Origins of International Adoption and the Hypersexualization of Korean Children." *Journal of Asian American Studies* 24, no. 3: 351–82.

Kawai, Yuko. 2015. "Decentralised Race, Obscured Racism: Japaneseness, Western and Japanese Concepts of Race, and Modalities of Racism." *Japanese Studies* 35, no. 1: 23–47.

Kim, Hyun Mee. 2007. "The State and Migrant Women: Diverging Hopes in the Making of 'Multicultural Families' in Contemporary Korea." *Korea Journal* 47, no. 4: 100–122.

Kim, Jae Kyun. 2015. "Yellow over Black: History of Race in Korea and the New Study of Race and Empire." *Critical Sociology* 41, no. 2: 205–17.

Kim, Minjeong. 2013. "Citizenship Projects for Marriage Migrants in South Korea: Intersecting Motherhood with Ethnicity and Class." *Social Politics* 20, no. 4: 455–81.

Lee, Hyunok. 2013. "Global Householding for Social Reproduction: Vietnamese Women's Marriage Migration to South Korea." In *The Global Political Economy of the Household in Asia*, edited by Juanita Elias and Samanthi J. Gunawardana, 94–109. New York: Palgrave Macmillan.

Lee, Jin-kyung. 2010. *Service Economies: Militarism, Sex Work, and Migrant Labor in South Korea*. Minneapolis: University of Minnesota Press.

Lim, Timothy. 2009. "Who Is Korean? Migration, Immigration, and the Challenge of Multiculturalism in Homogeneous Societies." *Asia-Pacific Journal* 7, no. 30: 1–22.

Na, Inho. 2022. "Injongesŏ Minjok'ŭro: han'gukchŏk injongjuŭiŭi hyŏngsŏnge kwanhan kaenyŏmsajŏk koch'al, 1880–1910" [From "race" to "nation/Volk": A conceptual historical study on the formation of Korean racism, 1880–1910]. *Hankuktongyangchŏchisasangsayŏnku* [Research on Eastern history of politics and thoughts in Korea] 21, no. 1: 77–112.

Natrajan, Balmurli. 2022. "Racialization and Ethnicization: Hindutva Hegemony and Caste." *Ethnic and Racial Studies* 45, no. 2: 298–318.

Omi, Michael, and Howard Winant. 2014. *Racial Formation in the United States*. New York: Routledge.

Quijano, Anibal. 2000. "Coloniality of Power, Eurocentrism and Latin America." *Nepantla: Views from South* 1, no. 3: 533–80.

Robertson, Jennifer. 2010. "Eugenics in Japan: Sanguinous Repair." In *The Oxford Handbook of the History of Eugenics*, edited by Alison Bashford and Philippa Levine, 430–48. New York: Oxford University Press.

Schmid, Andre, 2002. *Korea between Empires, 1895–1919*. New York: Columbia University Press.

Shin, Gi-Wook. 2006. *Ethnic Nationalism in Korea Genealogy, Politics, and Legacy*. Stanford, CA: Stanford University Press.

Tikhonov, Vladimir. 2010. *The Beginnings (1880s–1910s): "Survival" as an Ideology of Korean Modernity*. Vol. 2 of *Social Darwinism and Nationalism in Korea*. Leiden: Brill.

Yi, Jeong-Seon. 2017. *Tonghwawa paeje: ilcheŭi tonghwajŏngch'aekkwa naesŏn'gyŏrhon* [Assimilation and exclusion: Assimilation policy and Korean Japanese marriage of the Japanese empire]. Goyang: Yuksabipyungsa.

Youn, Young-shil. 2022. "Cheguktŭl sait'ŭi shingminji 'minjok'—1900nyŏndae mal chegukchuŭijŏk injong tamnon'gwa han'guk minjok kaenyŏmŭi yŏksajŏk saengsŏng" [Colonial Korea's "minjok" between three empires: Imperial racism and the historical formation of "minjok" as a concept in the late 1900s]. *Hankuhŏntaemunhakyŏnku* [Korean modern literature research] 68: 5–47.

INGA KIM DIEDERICH

Purifying Blood
Scientific Surveys and Medical Definitions of "Mixed-Blood" Koreans

ABSTRACT This article examines the medicoscientific construction of "mixed blood" as a legible racial category in Cold War South Korea to understand how scientists and doctors worked to create a normative "pure-blood" national subject, on the one hand, while marginalizing racially and sexually "impure bloods" on the other. Born from the postwar US military occupation of South Korea, Amerasian "mixed-blood" (honhyŏl) children threatened a postcolonial commitment to ethnic homogeneity that was championed by scientists intent on isolating "Korean blood" by biologically defining, medically pathologizing, and legally disowning "mixed bloods." This article explores the interconnected racial projects of making "Koreans" and "mixed Koreans" during the Cold War decades in which American military personnel and their progeny transformed from a temporary exigency to a permanent fixture on the peninsula. By concentrating on medicoscientific experiments and surveys conducted on Amerasian children at orphanages, segregated "mixed-blood" schools, and criminal detention centers, the author demonstrates how serological, physiognomic, and pathological studies worked in concert with legal rubrics of citizenship and national belonging to define and exclude these proximate racial others from the putatively homogeneous national body. In so doing, the article integrates and expands on scholarship in Korean studies and science, technology, medicine, and society (STMS) studies that have respectively illuminated the rise of ethnonationalism in modern Korean identity and the role of race science in postcolonial nation-building. A mixed-race–centered narrative of South Korea's Cold War pursuit of scientific modernity reveals how pathologizing "mixed bloods" proliferated newly biologized understandings of South Korea as a "pure-blood" nation that continue to resonate in state policies and personal relations today.

KEYWORDS mixed race, eugenics, bionationalism, Amerasian, South Korean nationalism

In 1974, a mixed-race teenager named Sue was interviewed by a foreign journalist writing an article on Korea's community of Amerasians—persons of mixed parentage fathered by American servicemen in Asian postings.[1] Described as a "tall, round-eyed and extremely western looking white-Korean girl," the seventeen-year-old responded to the reporter's questioning by "angrily" protesting the litany of interviews, interrogations, and surveys that she and others like her had been subjected to since childhood. "Why all these questions?" She demanded, recalling a parade of "journalists or social workers or whatever they call them" surveilling

Korean Amerasians like "strange animals" throughout their lives. "Why should we always be victims of all this questioning? We have had enough of that during our childhood." The interviewer, Sue charged, was simply the latest in a long string of "experts" honing their craft on the bodies of exceptionalized mixed-race children. At this point, the journalist regretfully reported, "It was obvious that Sue felt that she was speaking on behalf of her Amerasian sisters and she became very upset and refused to cooperate further" (Moen 1974).

In the decades after Korea's liberation, this regime of routinized examination and intensive surveillance described by Sue expanded in response to the boom of mixed-race births around American military bases in South Korea. The emergence of mixed-race Koreans as a core concern, rather than a peripheral affair, by state agents and institutional accomplices might seem surprising on its face. Ethnic homogeneity, after all, has long been a core pillar of the modern conception of Korean identity, that imaginary distilled into an ever-tighter community in response to waves of foreign invasions and occupations (Pai 2000; Schmid 2002; Shin 2006). Mixed race has little place in the mainstream "story" of Korea, and each generational iteration of mixed race tends to be seen as a novel departure from the purportedly timeless pattern of unadulterated monoracialism in generations past.[2] Meanwhile, the voices of mixed-race Koreans like Sue addressing their own experiences remain exceedingly rare both in the historical record and among researchers authorized to interpret it.[3]

Although mixed-race Koreans have historically been excluded from the national narrative by the homogeneous terms of modern Korean identity, they are by no means absent from the archival corpus of state records, medical journals, and sociological surveys. In contrast to the silencing of mixed-Korean voices (and accompanying denial of subjecthood), mixed-Korean bodies lie littered across the archive in segmented and quantified parts, from the sizes of skulls and teeth measured in one journal to the typology of hair and skin charted in another. Far from erasure, the conjoined Cold War projects of defining "Koreanness" in scientifically objective terms and expunging potential racial pollutants from the desired homogeneous national body demanded the careful identification, categorization, and definition of non-Korean otherness. Imbued with the necessary empirical authority, biological and social scientists rose to the task by producing a barrage of data on mixed-race physiognomy and psychology. In the process, these researchers produced not only a pathologized notion of mixed race but also, by corollary, a newly biologized understanding of normative Koreanness.

Exploring Korean identity formation from the perspective of mixed race underlines the centrality of racial hybridity to the construction of racial purity, on the one hand, while also highlighting the persistence of eugenics in national sciences despite increased globalization in the latter half of the twentieth century, on the other. Korean studies literature has traced the origins of Korean claims to ethnic homogeneity to the colonial period, demonstrating how an anticolonial nationalist discourse of shared bloodline that arose in response to foreign incursion led directly to postcolonial political doctrines that grounded each Korean state's claim to be the rightful unifier of the peninsula (Schmid 2002; Shin 2006). In linking the anti-Japanese context of pre-1945 anticolonial nationalism to the pro-Unification spirit of post-1945 ethnic nationalism, such studies underscore the significance of the unambiguously "them" and despite-division-still "us" to modern Korean identity.

In the decades after liberation, however, the main focus of Korean racial anxiety and the subject of South Korean identity consolidation efforts were not absolute racial others but, rather, racial proximates—that is, those whose inheritance of the "one bloodline" (*hanp'itchul*) was mixed with outside racial stock.[4] In this racial schema, which expanded on the legacy of colonial racial constructions outlined in the editors' introduction to this forum, Korean national identity was articulated as a distinct racial type that cohered across the political division of the peninsula and diaspora beyond the peninsula, on the one hand, while also distinguishing and defending the putative Korean race from external bloodlines (Black, white, or non-Korean Asian) identified as outside races, on the other. So-called mixed bloods (*honhyŏl*) therefore threatened to undermine the premise of the "one people" (*ilmin*) propounded by nation builders like president Syngman Rhee, who asserted a form of Korean identity bound by an unbroken five-thousand-year bloodline dating back to Tan'gun, the mythical progenitor (Oh 2015: 54). Whereas identifying and excluding non-Koreans was relatively simple, dealing with near-Koreans proved a thornier issue. The Korean parentage of "mixed bloods" was undeniable, but acknowledging them threatened to concede the integrity of a core pillar of the Korean nation to the compromises of racial hybridity. Ultimately, the near-but-not nature of mixed race compelled a coalition of politicians, scientists, and educators aligned around a shared nation-building project to create a new category of racial alterity, "mixed blood," thereby catalyzing a new conception of Koreans as "pure bloods" (*sunhyŏl*) in modern, medicoscientific terms.

Meanwhile, attending to the role of scientists in pathologizing mixed-race Koreans foregrounds the persistence of eugenic epistemes in ethnicity-based national identities well into the late twentieth century. The current worldwide wave of reactionary ethnic nationalisms has been viewed with alarm by celebrants of economic globalization who previously assumed that the expansion of multinational corporations, internationalization of supply, production, and distribution chains, and proliferation of cross-border movement and transnational identities would inevitably undercut nationalist focus on local differences, particularly those putatively expressed in physical markers like race (Rose 2001; Stern 2015). But the trajectory of ethnic nationalism in Korea, where scientific development did not undercut but, rather, marshaled ethnocentrism to evolve into "bionationalism," can be read as a demonstrative example of an underappreciated global trend (Gottweis and Kim 2009). That is, the very interconnectivities that enabled the transfer of scientific research and technologies also facilitated the purposing of these methods toward reinforcing national identities set by colonial conditions. The "resurgence" of eugenic epistemologies and ethnic nationalisms, seen from the postcolonial periphery, emerges less as a regression than as the natural progression of the meeting of imperialism, scientism, and technologism in the modern era (DiMoia 2013; Hyun 2015; C. Kim 2017).

Finally, demonstrating that the process of making an exceptionalized other was central to constructing an ideal national self pushes back against the marginalization of mixed-raceness in historiographies of racialization and nation building in favor of accounts that enunciate the constructedness of majority or minority identities within and beyond Korea. To be mixed race is to be always *in* the minority but never *of* the minority. It is that very existential condition of perpetual residence at the edges of socially constructed categories that makes mixed-race persons a threat to social order. Race as a governing hegemony, as noted by this forum's editors, relies on the fiction of biological essentialism—a fiction reproduced and made socially real through reading racial identities onto bodies based on their presentation and performance. As Sandra Mayzaw Lwin explains with regard to intertwined Black-Asian racialization in the United States, social hierarchies built on this "system of racial meaning" (Omi and Winant 1986: 63) hinge on "learning how to read or decode bodies, how to translate a certain shade of skin, shape of lip, or eye or nose. . . . It means knowing how to 'race' a person" (Lwin 2006: 24) and, in so doing, accrete to the racially corporealized subject what Frantz Fanon (1967: 111) describes as "a historico-racial schema . . . woven . . . out of a thousand details, anecdotes, stories." But what happens when bodies do not conform to expected racial categories or do not demonstrate clear racial markers? What happens when what is seen on the outside does not make transparent the putative biological essence contained within? How can a society built on the presumption of timeless racial homogeneity read and respond to bodies without reliable visual referents or the historical meanings that go with them?

Phenotype may be the primary external indicator of race, but racial ideologies are built on assertions of biological essence that lie hidden below the surface. As noted by the editors in the forum introduction, the study of race in Asia contends with the paradoxical possibility that bodies may be phenotypically indistinguishable but racially distinct. Likewise, Lwin (2006: 24) reminds us that mixed race challenges optical racial regimes because "bodily markers are unreliable. The exterior is not always a guarantee of the interior; what we see may not always be what we get." In the South Korean response to such unreliable bodies in the postwar decades, we see the scaffolding of a racial order in a putatively monoracial state that set the template for immigration, citizenship, and Korean identity (Ahn 2018; Choo 2016; J. Lee 2010). Through the case of the postwar generation of mixed-race Koreans, this study therefore broadly asserts that mixed-raceness should be *the* central heuristic, rather than a tangential curiosity, in mainstream scholarly discussions on modern racial orders because it uniquely undercuts the concept of biological race while also highlighting the inescapability of racial constructs in the lived experiences of those whose very existence exposes the falsity of the modern concept of race (Anzaldúa 1987; Joseph-Salisbury 2018; Tate 2019).

THE PROBLEM OF "MIXED BLOOD"

The first generation of so-called Amerasian mixed bloods was seen by South Koreans as a "new" population produced by the post-Liberation development of an unofficial system of regulated prostitution for American military servicemen stationed in Korean camptowns. The perception of Amerasians as a new and anomalous race must be understood in the context of rapid political and social changes on the peninsula in the wake of its liberation from Japanese colonization, division into northern and southern spheres of foreign occupation, and the Korean

War. Against the backdrop of mass displacements of the Korean population and the movement of foreign forces into the peninsula, the camptown institutionalization of intimate contacts between Koreans and foreigners, predicated on an unequal balance of power, provoked anxieties about Korean sovereignty that were grafted onto the bodies of camptown women and Amerasian children (K. Moon 1997; S. Moon and Höhn 2010).

The first generation of Amerasian mixed bloods was consequently seen by South Koreans as a "new" population produced by the postwar development of an unofficial system of regulated prostitution for American military servicemen stationed in Korean camp towns. The sex-work sector catering to foreign soldiers was both politically expedient and economically profitable, but Korean camp-town women were denigrated as a "national shame" (I. Lee 2004; K. Moon 1997). The mixed-race children born to camptown couples were therefore doubly unacceptable—as the children of foreign fathers in a paternalist society, on the one hand, and Korean women considered unfit reproductive subjects, on the other. As a 1969 editorial in the daily newspaper *Maeil kyŏngje* described them, camptown progeny were "fatherless waifs no different than the second-hand GI rags that they are raised in. They have no paternity, no lineage, and as the root of their mothers' misfortune they have no future to look forward to." Together, the sins of the mother and the foreignness of the father undercut the moral and physical potential of the children and marked them as the historically anomalous product of "monstrous intimacies" (Sharpe 2010).

Social approbation, however, bowed to defense imperatives, and as US troops in Korea swelled during the Korean War, so too did the number of mixed-race births, along with frequent instances of abandonment, infanticide, and so-called blonde-baby lynchings in the ever-expanding camp-town environs (A. Kim 2009; Oh 2015). In the decades after the war, interracial unions and their mixed-race by-products became prominent subjects of national concern as policy makers and public intellectuals alike sought to identify the roots of and propose solutions to the "mixed-blood" problem. Such pundits traced the "historical" advent of a mixed-race population in Korea to the moral degradations of the post-Korean War climate, characterizing mixed-race children as regrettable result of "female immorality," "social disorder and gender equality," and "the sinful indulgence of vanity and vice" (*Tonga ilbo* 1947; *Chosŏn ilbo* 1946). Social disapprobation of camp-town sex workers notwithstanding, the perceived political and economic imperatives of the military sex industry guaranteed its survival and the continued growth of a "mixed-blood" population. Consequently, serious efforts to solve the "mixed-blood problem" concentrated not on reforming the system that produced them but, rather, on scientifically defining, quantifying, and regulating mixed Koreans in relation to "true" Koreans.

DEFINING *MIXED BLOOD*

Cold War scientific studies of mixed blood were collaborations between the state and government-funded academic research institutes, with the ultimate goal of producing knowledge in order to enact policy. Beginning in the mid-1950s after the Korean War and continuing in force through the late 1970s with the end of Park Chung Hee's regime, sociological and biological surveys registered biometric data on "mixed-blood" lineages, physiognomy, development, and environments.[5] Such studies were supported indirectly by government funding via state-sponsored research institutes, and their results informed policy making, particularly around the recognition of personhood in medical contexts and defining the legislative terms of national inclusion (Kukka in'gwŏn wiwŏnhoe 2003; Chaewoe tongp'o chaedan 2007). The absence of a clear and legible precedent for identifying the social position of mixed-race persons and the "vacillation" of mixed-Korean bodies between racial categories generated institutional unease because state agents, as Judith Butler has said of bodies that trouble binary gender categories, "[could not] with surety read the body that [they saw]." This failure of "staid and usual cultural perceptions" compelled the state to collaborate with scientific researchers to create a new racial category particular to the Korean context (Butler 1999: xxii–xxiii).

Invariably, studies of "mixed bloods" presented their subjects as both novel and dangerous—a statistically significant divergence from the five-thousand-year unbroken Korean bloodline (Chang 1962). "The rising number of these historical anomalies," cautioned Seoul National University pathologist Yu Yangsŏk (1966) in a typical introduction, "is cause for alarm." This claim was, of course, patently untrue. Amerasians were neither the first mixed-race Koreans in the peninsula's history nor even the first Korean-American mixed-race persons, with marriages between Korean men and missionary women dating back to the early twentieth century (Fujitani 2011; Teng 2013).[6] But in the context of postcolonial racial anxieties and persistent eugenic influences, it became imperative to catalog exactly how these Korean-adjacent bodies could influence the national community as a whole, giving rise to a scientific field of "mixed-blood" study dedicated to observing and defining this new population in relation to a normative Korean racial identity. State-sponsored scientists therefore conducted behavioral, biological, and physiognomic surveys on mixed-race children, registering their lineages, anatomy, development, and environments. Referring to blood as the origin of racial identity and determinant of racial fate, Korean scientists reproduced a eugenic system of blood quantification and colonial order of racial hypodescent. In this way, the threat mixed race existentially posed to reproductive and racial timelines was made manageable by categorizing "mixed blood" as the root of biological difference and pathologizing it as a category of disability.

To this end, researchers developed a methodological formula to seal mixed blood within legible parameters within which they could catalog and identify generalizable characteristics. In this, they reproduced a scientific "fiction of miscegenation" that "posited a finite number of 'pure' races" and "held that racial purity could and should be protected" (Pascoe 2009: 7). Paired with the principle of calculable blood quantum, the principle of racial purity suggested the possibility of a system for classifying amalgamated blood according to contributing types in varying proportions. At Seoul National University and Yonsei University, professors and graduate students in the fields of pathology, physical anthropology, and dermatology created three main categories: "White-Korean," "Black-Korean," and "Yellow-Korean" mixed blood, concentrating particularly on the first two groups (Chang 1961, 1962; Yi 1975; Yu 1966). Reproducing the fiction of finite racial purity, the non-Korean halves of these combinations were presented as homogeneous racial entities. Taken at face value, the facticity of whiteness and Blackness remained uninterrogated. Meanwhile, the Korean half of the formula was subject to intense scrutiny, as researchers asked how a mixed version of Koreanness altered its purer form. "Korean" consistently occupied the control group position, but baseline averages for this group differed from study to study, demonstrating the danger that the normative and putatively constant category of "Korean" was prone to vacillation, vulnerable to change, and ultimately in danger of erosion.[7] To researchers, the Korean constitution was like a pool of water, into which paints of various colors were being poured. As an outside agent, the paint without was left unchanged, but the pool was dyed forever. That is, while whiteness and Blackness were seen as unaffected external additives, Koreanness as a static constant was inherently vulnerable to alteration.

As researchers developed a vocabulary of distinct racial bloods, they confronted the challenge of articulating the effect that the fractionalization of blood had on racial constitutions. Biological and physiognomic studies followed the standard eugenic formula for evaluating mixed-raceness as evolutionary movement up or down the ladder of racial hierarchy, as either hybrid vigor or, more commonly, hybrid degeneration. In the first camp, Yonsei University serologist Yi Samyŏl stood alone in advocating limited forms of racial hybridization to improve the Korean race. Based on his blood-type surveys of blood he drew from white-Korean children and Korean women pregnant by white men, Yi argued that white-Korean reproduction offered a path to racial improvement by moving the nation closer to the racial pinnacle of whiteness (Hyun 2018; Yi 1975). Yi's commitment to a specific form of hybrid vigor, however, was married to his belief that all nonwhite blood mixing resulted in hybrid degeneration—a conviction rooted in a eugenicist approach to racial miscegenation shared by others (Pascoe 2009).

The belief that race mixing was degenerative was bolstered by surveys quantifying blood type, skin pigmentation, anatomy and physiognomy, growth and maturation rate, and such race markers as Mongolian spots and epicanthic eyelid folds. Figure 1 reproduces one example of the detailed measurements of the mixed-blood body that contributed to such studies. There seemed to be no limit to physical characteristics that could be quantified to ascertain the degree of difference between racial populations.

A partial list of the physical features that researchers measured, cataloged, and compared across survey populations of mixed-blood subjects is detailed in table 1. The prolific collection of data by mixed-blood researchers down to the most minute details fell into four primary categories: racial identifiers, color scales, skeletal structures and body measurements, and cranial structures and facial features. In the first category, surveys interrogated the relative durability of racial identity by checking for features associated with Asian racialization, such as the incidence of mono or double eyelids. Ironically, many of the markers examined in this vein, such as the Mongolian spot and Mongolian fold,[8] drew on colonial epistemes deployed to demonstrate the racial atavism of a homogenized "Mongol" Asian racial family (Keevak 2011). Alongside features thought to explicitly identify race, relative degrees of coloring, stature, and facial physiognomy were averaged to determine population-wide characteristics in opposition to a normative Korean racial constitution.[9] Drawing on the notoriously inexact science of measuring skin color, researchers used color slides to determine the skin color spectrum of mixed-blood subjects, focusing on areas

Table 6. The frequency of problem indices according to body parts

		C-G N=285	O-G N=90	H-G N=103	C-G vs O-G x^2 / P	C-G vs H-G x^2 / P	O-G vs H-G x^2 / P
head	몹시큰머리	41(14.4)	43(47.8)	41(39.8)	43,875 P<0.01	29,330 P<0.01	—
	頭髮强調	59(20.7)	45(50.0)	58(56.3)	—	3,831 P<0.05	—
face	輪廓不分明	11(3.9)	10(11.1)	14(13.6)	6,858 P<0.01	61,888 P<0.01	—
	노려보는印象	23(8.1)	8(8.9)	17(16.5)	—	5,821 P<0.02	—
	凶한表情	30(10.5)	14(15.6)	24(23.3)	—	10,306 P<0.01	—
	特히强調	3(1.1)	9(10.0)	12(11.7)	17,682 P<0.01	—	—
eye	强調한눈	107(37.6)	28(31.1)	61(59.2)	—	14,483 P<0.01	15,276 P<0.01
	큰 눈	70(24.6)	29(32.2)	57(55.3)	—	32,552 P<0.01	10,391 P<0.01
	瞳子의省略	93(32.6)	39(43.3)	22(21.4)	—	—	10,735 P<0.01
	瞳子의强調	110(38.6)	36(40.0)	58(56.3)	—	9,670 P<0.01	5,059 P<0.05
	男像에속눈썹	72(25.3)	39(43.3)	20(19.4)	10,728 P<0.01	—	12,941 P<0.01
nose	크게强調	21(7.4)	34(37.8)	24(23.3)	50,542 P<0.01	18,731 P<0.01	4,787 P<0.05
mouth	큰 입	25(8.8)	20(22.2)	30(29.1)	11,718 P<0.01	25,766 P<0.01	—
	입술의强調	30(10.5)	10(11.1)	23(22.3)	—	8,612 P<0.01	4,269 P<0.05
	單純化된입	126(44.2)	54(60.0)	44(42.7)	6,832 P<0.01	—	5,739 P<0.02

FIGURE 1 A data table of anthropometric measurements in the second volume of Chang Chin-yo's study (Chang 1962).

TABLE 1 Categories of data collected through mixed-blood surveys, 1960–1980

Racial identifiers	Coloring	Skeletal structure and body measurements	Cranial structure and facial features
Blood type	Mixture of skin scala	Stature	Head length
Finger prints	Skin basic color of forehead	Trunk length	Head breadth
Mongolian spot	Scala of forehead	Sitting height	Cephalic index
Mongolian fold	Skin basic color of sternal region	Arm length	Head girth and height
Double eyelid	Scala of sternal region	Leg length	Bizygomatic
Darwin's tubercle	Skin basic color of medial	Arm-leg index	Minimal frontal
Hair curl index	aspect of upper arm	Span index	Bigonial
	Scala of medial aspect of	Biacromial index	Total face height
	upper arm	Chest breadth	Upper face height
		Chest depth	Physiognomic facial index
		Thoracic index	Nose height and breadth
		Chest girth	Nasal index
		Pelvic breadth	Ear length and breadth
		Body weight	Mouth breadth
			Thickness of upper lip
			Thickness of lower lip

with less exposure to direct sunlight, such as the medial upper arm, to ascertain "true" base colors (Keevak 2011; C. Pak 2012). Meanwhile, measurements of skeletal and cranial structures fetishized proportion by comparing the degree of torso length to total height or bizygomatic (the measure of facial width between the most lateral points of the zygomatic cheekbone arches) to bigonial (the measure of the diameter between the most lateral points of the gonia, or jawbone) between mixed-blood and pure-blood Koreans to argue that the former exhibited a deterioration from the ideal physical proportions of the latter (Chang 1962; Chŏnghwan Lee 1963; Nam

1966; N. Pak 1969; Yi 1975). The fractionalization of mixed-blood bodies into measurable parts derived from and mirrored the process of naming mixed race on the basis of separable and quantifiable bloodlines, and the conclusions drawn from these data, in turn, facilitated the translation of these surveys from biological research into the establishment of a medical category of disability.

Named *mixed blood*, categorized as a disabled race, and defined as a pressing threat to "pure" Korean racial integrity, mixed-blood Koreans were made subject to processes of political determination. This determination was enacted through a state drive to address the threat of mixed blood in Amerasians through a comprehensive and ongoing project to identify, remove, and erase the threat of this new racial type in a potent program of targeted ethnic cleansing.

POLICING "MIXED BLOODS"

Eugenic studies of mixed blood critically informed a policy agenda towards mixed blood that extended not only throughout the Korean Peninsula but also across the Pacific. The tables of statistical data, physical measurements, and diagnoses of disability authored by researchers of mixed blood were reproduced in South Korean professional journals and popular periodicals but also reappeared in publications aimed at Americans invested in the "mixed-blood problem" (Moen 1974). If we draw back the curtain of scientific objectivity that obscured human networks and connections from eugenic Korean research on mixed blood, it is not surprising that these studies were reproduced and shared outside South Korea. The mixed-blood Koreans surveyed for these studies—reduced to "materials" identified by age, sex, and racial type (most commonly "White-Korean" and "Negro-Korean")—were drawn by researchers from institutions designed to provide medical support and attend to the social well-being of mixed-race children. Far from insulating mixed-blood Koreans from social scrutiny, these social-welfare centers functioned as concentrated sites of disciplinary governance and political oversight and served as the foremost furnishers of bodies for testing and sampling by researchers. Welfare providers, such as hospitals, orphanages and adoption agencies, mixed-blood schools and charities, and juvenile detention centers, granted access to their charges—called "materials" in scientific surveys—with the expectation that the research results would validate and promote their existence.[10] The practices engaged in by researchers to acquire "sample materials" through these mixed-blood concentration centers, the social agendas set forth based on models of racialized pathology, and the investment in these agendas by the South Korean government and American adoption agencies orchestrated a program of disenfranchisement and expulsion from the peninsula.

On the peninsular side, social scientists took up the pathologies propounded by biological researchers to expound policy recommendations aimed at segregating mixed-blood Koreans from the ethnic nation and disenfranchising them from the entitlements of state citizenship. To make broad claims, sociological and psychological studies surveyed broad populations. The reliance of physical surveys on data averaging had already assembled a relatively large pool for social scientists to return to. One study comparing the interdental palette tone of "White-Koreans" and "Black-Koreans" drew its data from "844 Koreans (425 boys, 419 girls), 186 Korean-white mixed-bloods (96 boys, 90 girls) and 119 Korean-black mixed-bloods (60 boys, 59 girls)" between the ages of 7 and 12 who were "registered at Ch'unghyŏn Orphanage, Holt Adoption Agency, Yŏnghwa Elementary School, and It'aewŏn Elementary School." Likewise, a biometric study surveyed "197 Korean-white mixed-bloods (110 boys, 87 girls)" from "Ch'unghyŏn Orphanage, Sŏngyuk Orphanage, Holt Adoption Agency, mixed-bloods enrolled at Yŏnhapsŏngja Academy, and mixed-bloods who visited the dermatology department and Catholic University Hospital" in order to properly map the "mixed-bloods scattered around Seoul" (Chang 1962; Nam 1966). As outlined in the methodology reports of such studies, institutional complicity was crucial to collecting data in such significant numbers. Whether housed in orphanages or adoption agencies, attending school, or seeking medical care, mixed-blood Korean children were constantly subjected to medical and social surveillance.

While biologists and physiognomists examined the degenerative dangers hidden within mixed-race bodies, social scientists considered the threat that degraded mixed-race psychology posed to the Korean nation. Such studies drew a direct line between social conditions and developmental patterns, particularly with regard to psychological stability and sexual deviance. Sociomedical surveys of mixed-race Koreans took the overdetermined association between mixed blood and camptown sex work as their starting point, tracing a causal connection between what one public health adviser declared to be "the relationship between the two problems . . . of pervasive female prostitution and mixed bloods" (Chŏnghwan Lee 1963). Based on this starting assumption, "social medical" surveys set about constructing subject profiles of pathological hypersexuality and juvenile delinquency rooted in genetic predisposition compounded by the neurological effects of poverty, transitory habitation, and low education.

The presumed relationship between sex work and mixed race deeply impacted the methodology, execution, and conclusions reached by sociomedical studies. Researchers assumed a standard pattern of parentage—foreign father and Korean sex-worker mother—and accordingly recorded the father's nationality, education level, and occupation but only noted the mother's level of education in surveys into "typical mixed-blood" living conditions. The emphasis on racial and moral deviance in social science surveys expressed the imbrication of private and public spaces under postwar South Korean recovery and development regimes. Liminal mixed-race Korean children and the transgressive cross-race relations that conceived them upset the ideal order of private domiciles, the public sphere, and a symbiotic relationship cultivated between them under the auspices of what Charles Kim (2017) has conceptualized as a prevailing concern with "wholesome modernization" in Cold War South Korea, with one representative study describing transitory patterns of family cohabitation (23.6 percent of respondents reported that parents cohabitated for 3–6 months, while only 3 percent reported cohabitation lasting over one year) negatively compared to "normal" long-term family living arrangements (Chŏnghwan Lee 1963).

Social psychologists rounded out the "mixed-blood" research program, which began at the anatomical level and extended to the social environment, by returning to the interior realm of the psyche. Neuropsychiatrists like Pak No-t'aek assessed the impact of genetic inheritance and camptown living conditions on "mixed-blood" socialization, arguing that nature and nurture manifested as deviant psychoses. Based on sketches of human bodies that he asked mixed-race children to draw in order to assess physical ideations, Pak (1969) concluded that their "abnormal" environments had induced "premature sexualization and an excessive interest in sexual matters," advising that "measures be taken to account for and curb this truly overwhelming sexual proclivity in a minority population." Such policy recommendations were the norm, rather than the exception, in the concluding remarks of mixed-blood studies regardless of research field.

What measures were taken to limit the threat of blood mixing to the biological integrity and social safety of the nation? It was at this level of policy making that race studies crossed the threshold from research framework to state practice. The first priority of scientists and their state sponsors was to guard against mixed bloods passing as "pure" Koreans. Millions of families had been displaced and separated during decolonization and the Korean War, and the peninsula was consequently awash with children and teenagers unidentifiable by the usual family networks (DiMoia 2013; Oh 2015). The Nationality Law established in tandem with South Korean state formation in 1948 had codified the principle of patrilineal descent by limiting South Korean citizenship to individuals born to Korean men. The dislocations, family separations, and abundance of orphans left in the wake of the Korean War, however, highlighted a loophole in the Nationality Law that entitled children of unknown parentage born on Korean soil to Korean citizenship by law of the land (*jus soli*) rather than the law of blood (*jus sanguinus*).[11] Fearing that abandoned mixed-race Koreans denied citizenship by reason of paternity might take advantage of this loophole to pass themselves off as "normal" Koreans and lay claim to a franchise reserved for "pure" Koreans, researchers repurposed the averages of their data toward identification purposes in defense of ethnic homogeneity. Abandoned and unregistered children of uncertain parentage and ambiguous race were to be identified as Korean or mixed based on such registers as Mongolian spots for infants, measuring racialized hair types according to the "pencil test" for hair curl then employed in apartheid South Africa, and skin tone indexes for older children, teens, and adults (Chang 1962; Ch'oe 1967).

Efforts to guard against the threat of racial passing and citizenship were subsequently expanded into laws to identify, monitor, and expel mixed-blood Koreans from the country altogether. The Ministry of Health practice of labeling mixed-blood orphans slated for adoption as disabled was extended into hospitals and census offices, where mixed-race newborns were documented on medical intake forms and birth certificates as "disabled." Meanwhile, a proposed 1972 law would have required mixed-blood Amerasians to submit to a state identification examination for a racial identification card noting their racial appearance (what the subject in question looked like, or "passed for") and bloodline ancestry (what the subject "actually" was, according to racial blood quantum), which they would be required to carry at all times and submit upon request for verification. This initiative, however, was ironically abandoned because the disenfranchisement of Amerasians by reason of paternity effected by the Nationality Law rendered the population so thoroughly marginal and confined to limited and lawless borderland areas like camptowns that it was nearly impossible to guarantee full identification and compliance with the requirement (H. Kim 2006; Ch'ŏl-u Lee 2003; Sŏk 1997).

The result of peninsular disenfranchisement policies was the near-complete exclusion of mixed-blood Koreans from the privilege of citizenship and such welfare channels as education and medical care reserved for citizens. Already by 1959, based on a survey of mixed bloods in police custody, an estimated 67.6 percent of mixed-race Koreans born and raised in South Korea were stateless persons without citizenship of any kind (*Chosŏn ilbo* 1959). Built on a scientific regime of pathology, state disenfranchisement and its partner program of transnational adoption effectively separated mixed-race Koreans from the social, political, and physical property of the Korean state and ethnic nation.[12] South Korean state policies toward interracial relationships and mixed-race children hinged on the ability to capitalize on and control the transfer of property. On the one hand, as Seungsook Moon (2010) has shown, the state promoted the development of entertainment sectors that furnished sexual services as a means of funneling GI dollars into the struggling South Korean economy in the eras of postwar recovery and rapid development. On the other hand, it also took steps to remove mixed-blood Koreans' competing claims on state properties such as land (through family inheritance) and welfare (through citizenship prerogatives), as well as more abstract national properties, such as Koreanness itself, as a political, cultural, and racial identity/form of communal capital.

LEGACIES AND POSSIBILITIES

South Korean nation builders working at the crossroads of a political mandate for reunification, an educational imperative to define and disseminate a clear sense of South Korean national identity, and a social injunction to maintain sexual purity and middle-class propriety pinpointed "mixed-blood" Koreans in their identity-making project. In seeking to identify, other, and expel "mixed blood" from the Korean national body, this coalition created a new ethnic category while also biologizing all iterations of Korean identity, whether hybrid or whole. This Cold War race-making project has thus had enduring effects on the identities of mixed and "pure" Koreans today.

Mixed-race Koreans far from this "first" generation of Amerasians still know that no degree of cultural competence will ever make up enough for compromised biology to gain entry into the hallowed halls of *uri minjok* (our nation). Neither language fluency nor educational achievements, not even a life spent in Korea is sufficient to overcome the difference marked in the body, as demonstrated in the media othering of model Han Hyun-Min, born and raised in Korea of Nigerian and Korean parentage.[13] A form of Koreanness couched not in citizenship but in the body, which works to cohere a global Korean diaspora and police the dispersed Korean ethnos through racial purity, is the direct legacy of South Korean nation-builders' campaigns to socially engineer a new identity through the bodies of "mixed bloods."

On the other hand, the homogenization of authentic Koreanness into a fragile biological essence that is all too susceptible to dilution has created a form of Korean identity plagued by anxiety about the dangers posed by diaspora, in-migration, and a dropping domestic birthrate. In stark contrast to the concerted state efforts to expel "Amerasians" born in the wake of the Korean War, in the twenty-first century the state pivoted to a conditional embrace of so-called Kosians—mixed-Koreans born to Korean men and South Asian women migrants to South Korean rural provinces. Whereas Amerasians were seen as superfluous and subversive to mainstream Korean identity decades earlier, Kosians have been treated as a necessary corrective to South Korea's precipitously declining birthrate, graying population, and emptied rural labor sector. The multicultural (*tamunhwa*) campaigns of the early 2000s are emblematic of administrative recognition at a local and national level that racial discrimination based on the state-propagated principle of ethnic homogeneity had begun undercutting national goals, and that a multiracial population is increasingly probable and productive in coming decades. The "multicultural movement" notwithstanding, it remains notable that South Korea remains committed to recruiting new bodies to replace its declining population based on ethnic proximity, prioritizing "ethnic compatriots abroad" (*chaeoe tongp'o*) and, in so doing, feeding into hierarchies of biological authenticity that structure Korean diasporas and global identities.

Today, Korea's demographic challenges are forcing reconsiderations of the terms of citizenship and national inclusion, but the biological concept of Koreanness consolidated through the exclusion of mixed bloods endures. Who "counts" as Korean, what constitutes "true" Korean identity, and how mutable authentic "Koreanness" remain cogent terms for a debate derived from terms set by the South Korean scientists discussed in this study. The forms of authentic and adjacent Korean identities established in the medicoscientific surveys of "mixed-blood" Koreans indelibly framed the way Koreans relate to one another, the diaspora, and the world.

INGA KIM DIEDERICH is assistant professor of history at Colby College. She works in the area of modern East Asian history specializing in Korea, the medical humanities, and race and nationalism studies. Her current scholarship explores the historical development of modern Korean ethnonationalism and its medicoscientific dimensions, focusing on the role of blood as both a cultural symbol and a medical material in the formation of modern Korean identity. Her research has been sponsored by the Social Science Research Council, the Fulbright-Hays Program, the Academy of Korean Studies, and the Kyujanggak Institute for Korean Studies at Seoul National University, among others.

NOTES

1. The term *Amerasian* was coined by the author Pearl S. Buck and developed from an informal identification in the international adoption industry into a formal legal category with the 1982 Amerasian Immigration Act codifying American paternal responsibility for children fathered in wars in Asia (Graves 2019; Klein 2003).

2. Just as Cold War Amerasians were regarded as a novel and anomalous deviation from a putatively unbroken tradition of homogeneity—disregarding Korean-Japanese and Korean-Western unions in the colonial period (1910–1945)—the 2000s emergence of a generation of Korean–Southeast Asian parentage has likewise been addressed as an unprecedented departure from the traditional constitution of Korea's population (Lie 2014).

3. At this date, there is no scholarly book in either English or Korean devoted solely to the history of mixed race in Korea, and the majority of research articles that do exist on the subject are authored by monoracial Koreans or non-Koreans—it remains rare for mixed-race Koreans to speak authoritatively on our own experiences and history. The next generation of Korean studies academics, however, ideally can support and amplify the work of mixed-race scholars engaged with the history of mixed race, such as this author, Yuri Doolan (2022), and Laura Ha Reizman (2021).

4. In describing mixed-race Koreans as racially proximate to putatively monoracial Koreans, I invoke both the temporal and locational meaning of *proximate* as defined by Merriam Webster: "(1) immediately preceding or following (as in a chain of events, causes, or effects); (2) a: very near: CLOSE; b: soon forthcoming: IMMINENT" (*Merriam-Webster Online Dictionary*, http://www.merriam-webster.com/dictionary/proximate [accessed Oct. 10, 2023]). The conjoined sense of place and time invoked by analyzing mixed race in terms of relative proximity underscores how mixed-race bodies are conceived of as biologically near to or distant from the constituency of their monoracial counterparts, as well as evolutionary logics of atavistic regression and the so-called fifth or future blended race (Bolton 2023: 46–47). The Latin *prope*, meaning "near," from which *proximate* is derived is also the source of *approach* and *reproach*, drawing attention to the moral implications of the term as well. By recalling these definitions and attendant theorizations, my intention is to highlight South Korean racial formation as a relational process not framed against an absolute other as in the case of Black-white relations in US history but nonetheless employing parallel processes of dualistic opposition and absolute othering such as hypodescent, as outlined in the following sections.

5. The tapering off of biometric surveys of mixed-blood subjects in the late 1970s likely reflects a disruption in government-researcher relationships in tandem with Park's 1979 assassination and the end of his regime (Pae 2003).

6. High-profile examples of pre-1945 mixed marriages include the independence activist Soh Jaipil (Philip Jaisohn), married to Muriel Armstrong—a relative of former U.S. president James Buchanan—in 1894, as well as the first president of South Korea, Syngman Rhee, who famously married the Austrian intellectual Franziska Donner in 1934.

7. For example, Chang's (1962) serological survey stated that the majority of Koreans had an O blood type, while AB blood types were rare, while Yi's (1975) survey concluded that the majority of Koreans were B or AB blood types.

8. Another, more explicitly racial term for a monolid.

9. Pigmentation samples were drawn from the medial forehead, suprasternal notch, medial superior, hair, iris, teeth, and interdentium. Physiognomic measurements were taken for hair type, fingerprints, standing and seated height, length of arms and legs, chest cavity depth, pelvic width, cranial measurements, weight, etc. Other measures included environmental conditions, such as place of residence, parents' education level, mother's age at time of birth, relationship between parents, and living standards, and psychological evaluations, such as mental stability, personality, and sexual maturation.

10. For a broader context on the relationship between South Korean state welfare and authoritarian biogovernance, see Yun 2018.

11. The principles of *jus soli* and *jus sanguinus* as territorial and ethnonational claims to citizenship are intimately imbricated in the logics of the nation-state, as outlined both in theorizations of modern nationalism by Benedict Anderson (1983) and Eugen Weber (1976) and in histories of modern law by Mickaella L. Perina (2006).

12. The origins of the Korean adoption industry in the program to remove mixed-race Koreans from the peninsula have been extensively studied in critical histories including those by Arissa Oh (2015), Soojin Pate (2014), and Crystal Mun-hye Baik (2019).

13. Han has described the discrimination he faced in South Korean society, from the education system to the modeling industry, in several interviews, including one in which he made note that Korean talk show hosts often assume he speaks English rather than Korean, despite the fact he was born and raised in Korea with Korean as his first language (Groom 2017).

REFERENCES

Ahn, Ji-Hyun. 2018. *Mixed-Race Politics and Neoliberal Multiculturalism in South Korean Media*. Cham: Palgrave Macmillan.

Anderson, Benedict. 1983. *Imagined Communities*. New York: Verso.

Anzaldúa, Gloria. 1987. *Borderlands/La Frontera: The New Mestiza*. San Francisco: Aunt Lute Books.

Baik, Crystal Mun-hye. 2019. *Reencounters: On the Korean War and Diasporic Memory Critique*. Philadelphia: Temple University Press.

Bolton, Sony Coráñez. 2023. *Crip Colony: Mestizaje, US Imperialism, and the Queer Politics of Disability in the Philippines*. Durham, NC: Duke University Press.

Butler, Judith. 1999. *Gender Trouble: Feminism and the Subversion of Identity*. New York: Routledge.

Chaewoe tongp'o chaedan 재외동포재단 (Association of Overseas Koreans). 2007. *Miguk kŏju han'gukgye honhyŏl'in silt'ae chosa* 미국거주 한국계 혼혈인 실태조사 [Survey of conditions of Korean Honhyŏl'in living in the United States]. Sŏul-si: Chaewoe tongp'o chaedan.

Chang, Chin-yo 장진요. 1961. "Han'gukin kwa paekin mit hŭkin kwa ŭi hongyŏlin e taehan ch'ejil illyuhakjŏk yŏn'gu" 韓國人과 白人및 黑人과의 混血兒에 對한 體質人類學的研究 [Anthropological studies of Korean-white and Korean-Negro hybrids]. *Sŏulŭidae chapji* 서울의대잡지 2, no. 1: 63–77.

Chang, Chin-yo 장진요. 1962. "Han'gukin kwa paekin mit hŭkin kwa ŭi hongyŏlin e taehan ch'ejil illyuhakjŏk yŏn'gu" 韓國人과 白人및 黑人과의 混血兒에 對한 體質人類學的研究 [Anthropological studies of Korean-white and Korean-Negro hybrids]. *Sŏulŭidae chapji* 서울의대잡지 2, no. 2: 11–34.

Ch'oe, Tongryul 최동률. 1967. "Han-mi honhyŏl adong ŭi kwanhan injong haebuhakjŏk yŏn'gu" 한-미혼혈아동의 관한 인종해부학적 연구 [A study on the racial anatomy of Korean-American mixed-blood children]. *Hyŏndae ŭihak* 현대의학 6, no. 2: 181–85.

Choo, Hae Yeon. 2016. *Decentering Citizenship: Gender, Labor, and Migrant Rights in South Korea*. Stanford, CA: Stanford University Press.

Chosŏn ilbo. 1946. "Hŏyŏng kwa akdŏk ŭi kyŏlkwa, ŏkulhan choe ssŭgo t'aeŏnanŭn honhyŏl'a" 허영과 악덕의 결과, 억을한 죄 쓰고 테어나는 혼혈아 [Mixed-blood offspring of sinful indulgence]. December 1.

Chosŏn ilbo. 1959. "Paekyŏ honhyŏl'a tto tomi" 백여 혼혈아 또 도미 [Another hundred mixed-blood children cross over to America]. March 17.

DiMoia, John P. 2013. *Reconstructing Bodies: Biomedicine, Health, and Nation-Building in South Korea since 1945*. Stanford, CA: Stanford University Press.

Doolan, Yuri. 2022. "The Cold War Construction of the Amerasian, 1950–1982." *Diplomatic History* 46, no. 4: 782–807.

Fanon, Frantz. 1967. *Black Skin, White Masks*. New York: Grove Weidenfeld.

Fujitani, Takashi. 2011. *Race for Empire: Koreans as Japanese and Japanese as Americans during World War II*. Berkeley: University of California Press.

Gottweis, Herbert, and Byoungsoo Kim. 2009. "Bionationalism, Stem Cells, BSE, and Web 2.0 in South Korea: Toward the Reconfiguration of Biopolitics." *New Genetics and Society* 28, no. 3: 223–39.

Graves, Kori A. 2019. "Amerasian Children, Hybrid Superiority, and Pearl S. Buck's Transracial and Transnational Adoption Activism." *Pennsylvania Magazine of History and Biography* 143, no. 2: 177–209.

Groom, Nelson. 2017. "'We Don't Do Dark Skin': What South Korea's First Black Model Was Told by Recruiters as the Teenager Reveals the Racism He Faces Despite Rising through the Fashion World Ranks." *Daily Mail*, July 11. https://www.dailymail.co.uk/news/article4685074/South-Korea-s-black-model-faces-widespread-racism.html.

Hyun, Jaehwan 현재환. 2015. "'Chibangch'a' wa 'korip'han mendel chipdan': Tu 'chungsimbu' kwahak kwa Na Sejin ŭi honjongjŏk ch'ejil illyuhak, 1932–1964" '지방차'와 '고립'한 멘델 집단: 두 '중심부' 과학과 나세진의 혼종적 체질인류학, 1932–1964 [Sejin Rha's hybrid physical anthropology between two "metropolitan" sciences, 1932–1964]. *Han'guk kwahaksahak hoeji* 한국과학사학회지 [Journal of the history of Korean science] 37, no. 1: 345–82.

Joseph-Salisbury, Remi. 2018. *Black Mixed-Race Men: Transatlanticity, Hybridity, and "Postracial" Resilience*. Bingley: Emerald.

Keevak, Michael. 2011. *Becoming Yellow: A Short History of Racial Thinking*. Princeton, NJ: Princeton University Press.

Kim, Aram 김아람. 2009. "1950~1960-nyŏndae chŏnban Han'guk ŭi honhyŏl'in munje 1950~1960" 년대 전반 한국의 혼혈인 문제 [Korea's mixed-blood problem, 1950–1960]. Master's thesis, Ewha Woman's University.

Kim, Charles. 2017. *Youth for Nation: Culture and Protest in Cold War South Korea*. Honolulu: University of Hawai'i Press.

Kim, Hyŏn-sŏn 김현선. 2006. "Kungmin, pankungmin, pikungmin: Han'guk kungmin hyŏnsŏng ŭi wŏlli wa kwajŏng" 국민, 반국민, 비국민: 한국국민 현성의 원리와 과정 [Citizen, half-citizen, noncitizen: The origins and development of Korean citizenship]. *Sahoe yŏn'gu* 사회연구 [Social studies] 12, no. 2: 77–106.

Klein, Christina. 2003. *Cold War Orientalism: Asia in the Middlebrow Imagination, 1945–1961*. Berkeley: University of California Press.

Kukka in'gwŏn wiwŏnhoe 국가인권위원회 (ROK National Human Rights Commission). 2003. "Kijich'on honhyŏl'in in'gwŏn silt'ae chosa" 기지촌 혼혈인 인권 실태 조사 [Survey on the actual human rights conditions of Honhyŏl'in in camptowns]. Sŏul-si: Kukka in'gwŏn wiwŏnhoe.

Lee, Ch'ŏl-u 이철우. 2003. "Kukjŏk kwa chongjoksŏng e ŭihan chipdanjŏk cha'a wa t'aja ŭi Kubyŏl" 국적과 종족성에 의한 집단적 자아와 타자의 구별 [Citizenship, communal identity, and discrimination]. *Sahoe iron* 사회이론 [Social theory] 23: 13–47.

Lee, Chŏnghwan 이정환. 1963. "Honhyŏl'a ŭi sahoe ŭihakjŏk chosa yŏn'gu" 혼혈아의 사회 의학적 조사 연구 [Social-medical survey of mixed-bloods]. PhD diss., Seoul National University.

Lee, Imha 이임하. 2004. "Migun ŭi tongasia chudun kwa seksyuŏllit" 미군의 동아시아 주둔과 섹슈얼리티 [Sexuality and the US military in East Asia]. In *Tongasia wa kŭndae, yŏsŏng ŭi palgyŏn* 동아시아와 근대, 여성의 발견 [East Asia and modernity, women's development], edited by Pak Ŭi-kyŏng, 259–79. Seoul: Ch'ŏngŏram Media.

Lee, Jin-kyung. 2010. *Service Economies: Militarism, Sex Work, and Migrant Labor in South Korea*. Minneapolis: University of Minnesota Press.

Lie, John, ed. 2014. *Multiethnic Korea? Multiculturalism, Migration, and Peoplehood Diversity in Contemporary South Korea*. Berkeley: Institute of East Asian Studies, University of California, Berkeley.

Lwin, Sandra Mayzaw. 2006. "'A Race So Different from Our Own': Segregation, Exclusion, and the Myth of Mobility." In *AfroAsian Encounters: Culture, History, Politics*, edited by Heike Raphael-Hernandez and Shannon Steen, 17–29. New York: New York University Press.

Maeil kyŏngje. 1969. "Wianbudŭl ttŭtkinŭn dallŏeŭi 'kwanyŏk'" 위안부들 뜯기는 달러에의 '과녁' [Appeal of dollars earned by comfort women]. April 24.

Moen, Sveinung. 1974. *The Amerasians: A Study and Research on Interracial Children in Korea*. Chuncheon: Taewon.

Moon, Katharine. 1997. *Sex Among Allies: Military Prostitution in U.S.-Korea Relations*. New York: Columbia University Press.

Moon, Seungsook. 2010. "Regulating Desire, Managing the Empire: U.S. Military Prostitution in South Korea, 1945–1970." In Moon and Höhn 2010: 39–77.

Moon, Seungsook, and Maria Höhn, eds. 2010. *Over There: Living with the U.S. Military Empire from World War Two to the Present*. Durham, NC: Duke University Press.

Nam, Ki-t'aek 남기택. 1966. "Han'guk'in honhyŏl'a e issŏ ch'igan saekjo e kwanhan yŏn'gu" 한국인 혼혈아에 있어 치간 색조에 관한 연구 [A study into the interdental palette tone of Koreans and mixed-bloods]. *Chungang ŭihak* 중앙의학 [Central medicine] 10, no. 6: 723–25.

Oh, Arissa. 2015. *To Save the Children of Korea: The Cold War Origins of International Adoption*. Stanford, CA: Stanford University Press.

Omi, Michael, and Howard Winant. 1986. *Racial Formation in the United States*. New York: Routledge.

Pae, Ŭn-gyŏng 배은경. 2003. "Han'guk sahoe ch'ulsan chojŏl ŭi yŏksajŏk kwajŏng kwa chendŏ: 1970-yŏndae kkaji ŭi kyŏnghŏm ŭl chungsim ŭro" 한국 사회 출산 조절의 역사적 과정과 젠더: 1970연대까지의 경험을 중심으로 [A social history of Korean women's birth control: 1950s–1970s]. PhD diss., Seoul National University.

Pai, Hyun Il. 2000. *Constructing "Korean" Origins: A Critical Review of the Archaeology, Historiography, and Racial Myth in Korean State-Formation Theories*. Cambridge, MA: Harvard University Press.

Pak, Chŏng-hyŏng 박정형. 2012. "Injongjŏk t'aja'rosŏ ŭi honhyŏl'in mandŭlgi: 1950-nyŏndae ~ 1970-nyŏndae Han'guk ŭi ŭihakjisik saengsanmul ŭl chungsim ŭro" 인종적 타자로서의 혼혈인 만들기: 1950년대~1970년대 한국의 의학지식 생산물을 중심으로 [Making racially other mixed-blood people: Focusing on the products of Korean medical knowledge, 1950s–1970s]. MA thesis, Chungang University.

Pak, No-t'aek 박노택. 1969. "Inmulhwa rŭl t'onghan Han'gukkoa mit honhyŏl'a ŭi sinch'esang'e kwanhan yŏn'gu" 인물화를 통한 한국고아 및 혼혈아의 신체상에 관한 연구 [Study of physical ideations of mixed-bloods and orphans in drawings]. PhD diss., Wusŏk University.

Pascoe, Peggy. 2009. *What Comes Naturally: Miscegenation Law and the Making of Race in America*. Oxford: Oxford University Press.

Pate, Soojin. 2014. *From Orphan to Adoptee: U.S. Empire and Genealogies of Korean Adoption*. Minneapolis: University of Minnesota Press.

Perina, Mickaella L. 2006. "Race and the Politics of Citizenship: The Conflict over *Jus Soli* and *Jus Sanguinus*." *International Studies in Philosophy* 38, no. 2: 123–39.

Reizman, Laura Ha. 2021. "Conditions of Containment: Mixed-Race Politics in Cold War South Korea, 1940s–1980s." Ph.D. diss., University of California, Los Angeles.

Rose, Nikolas. 2001. "The Politics of Life Itself." *Theory, Culture, and Society* 18, no. 6: 1–30.

Schmid, Andre. 2002. *Korea between Empires, 1895–1919*. New York: Columbia University Press.

Sharpe, Christina. 2010. *Monstrous Intimacies: Making Post-slavery Subjects*. Durham, NC: Duke University Press.

Shin, Gi-Wook. 2006. *Ethnic Nationalism in Korea: Genealogy, Politics, and Legacy*. Stanford, CA: Stanford University Press.

Sŏk, Tong-hyŏn 석동현. 1997. "Kukjŏkpŏp ŭi kaejŏng panghyang" 국적법의 개정방향 [Revisions in the citizenship law]. *Sŏul kukjebŏp yŏn'gu* 서울국제법연구 [Seoul international law studies] 4, no. 2: 1–26.

Stern, Alexandra. 2015. *Eugenic Nation: Faults and Frontiers of Better Breeding in Modern America*. Berkeley: University of California Press.

Tate, Shirley. 2019. *Decolonizing Sambo: Transculturation, Fungibility, and Mixed Race Futurity*. Leeds: Emerald Group.

Teng, Emma. 2013. *Eurasian: Mixed Identities in the United States, China, and Hong Kong, 1842–1943*. Berkeley: University of California Press.

Tonga ilbo. 1947. "Norang mŏri – kŏmdung'i honhyŏl'a ŭi pŏmnam" 노랑머리-검둥이 混血兒의汎濫 [The deluge of blonde and Black mixed-bloods]. September 1.

Weber, Eugen. 1976. *Peasants into Frenchmen: The Modernization of Rural France, 1970–1914*. Stanford, CA: Stanford University Press.

Yi, Samyŏl 이삼열. 1975. "Caucasian kwaŭi honhyŏl i han'gukin ŭi hyŏlaekhyŏng yŏn'gu e kkich'inŭn munjejŏm Caucasian" 과의 혼혈이 한국인의 혈액형 연구에 끼치는 문제점 [Issues posed to studies of Korean blood-type by Caucasian-Korean hybrids]. *Taehan hyŏlaek hakhoe chapji* 대한혈액학회잡지 [Journal of Korean hematology] 30, no. 1: 33–39.

Yu, Yangsŏk 유양석. 1966. "Han'gukin kwa paekin mit hŭkin kwaŭi honhyŏl'a ch'igung palyuk e kwanhan yŏn'gu" 한국인과 백인 및 흑인과의 혼혈아의 치궁발육에 관한 연구 [Study on the dental arch growth of Koreans as compared to white and Black mixed-bloods]. PhD diss., Seoul National University.

Yun, Hongsik 윤홍식. 2018. "Pak Chŏnghŭi chŏnggwŏn sigi han'guk pokji ch'eje: pangong kaebal kukka, pokji kukka ŭi kinŭngjŏk tŭngkamul" 박정희 정권시기 한국 복시체제: 반공개발국가, 복지국가의 기능적 등가물 [The welfare regime of the Park Chung Hee administration era: The functional equivalence of an anticommunist developmental state and welfare state]. *Han'guk sahoe chŏngch'aek* 한국사회정책 [Korean social policy] 25, no. 1: 195–229.

SUNHYE KIM

Eggs and Sperm from Others
Reproduction and Gendered Racialization
in South Korea

ABSTRACT This article discusses how the concepts of blood ties, paternal lines, and
Koreanness have been challenged, reinforced, and reconstructed through the use of
assisted reproductive technology and, in particular, third-party reproduction practices. This article uses the example of South Korean intended parents entering inter-
Asian gamete markets to explore how donated gametes from Taiwanese egg donors
have become a "pan-East Asian" genetic commodity that both troubles and reveals
the racialized categories and ideologies in South Korea. By examining the marketing
and matching strategies of Asian egg donation agencies in Taiwan, this article discusses the social and cultural justifications for third-party reproduction and examines
its implications for Korean gender and racial politics.

KEYWORDS egg donation, assisted reproductive technology, third-party reproduction,
racial matching, Taiwan, South Korea

In this article, I discuss how the concepts of blood ties, paternal lines, and Koreanness have been challenged, reinforced, and reconstructed through the use of assisted
reproductive technology (ART) and, in particular, third-party reproduction practices.
Third-party reproduction refers to "all cases of human reproduction that involve the
use of gametes, embryos, or gestation from a third party for the purpose of reproduction by the intended parents" (Havelock et al. 2016). After the first Korean in vitro
fertilization (IVF) baby was born in 1985, third-party reproduction in South Korea
has been practiced primarily by infertile couples who need donated eggs or sperm
to conceive a child. In South Korea, third-party reproduction practices are typically
described as stemming from a heterosexual married couple's desperate desire to continue their family's bloodline by having their *own* baby (in contrast to adoption); however, ironically, babies who are born via gamete donation are biologically connected
beyond the heteronormative nuclear family. Furthermore, when Korean intended parents participate in the transnational gamete markets, childbirth, which was once presumed to be the result of the most intimate of relationships, requires the involvement
of foreign strangers. Conversely, for Korean infertile couples, third-party reproduction
via non-Korean gamete donors is not only a way to give birth to a genetically related
baby (when using gametes from at least one of the intended parents) but also a way to
intentionally or unintentionally create a *honhyŏl* (混血, mixed-blood) baby.

THE JOURNAL OF ASIAN STUDIES • 84:2 • May 2025
DOI: 10.1215/00219118-11591569 © 2025 Association for Asian Studies

457

Considering the historical and cultural stigma attached to honhyŏl in South Korea, it is crucial to examine the naturalizing and racializing process of third-party reproduction. As Yi and as Chung and Choi discuss in this forum, *tamunhwa* (multicultural) children born to Korean fathers and immigrant mothers from other Asian countries are racialized as *honhyŏl* despite their seemingly indistinguishable appearance. To extend this discussion, this article focuses on how children born using eggs donated by non-Korean donors are reconfiguring the meaning of *honhyŏl* and the new forms of racialization at work in this process. To this end, this article reviews the marketing and matching strategies of Asian egg donation agencies in Taiwan to explore questions of how third-party reproduction has obtained social and cultural justification in the Korean context, as well as the implications of new reproductive practices for Korea's racial politics.

Taking into account that gamete donors provide genetic traits to donor-conceived babies, it is not surprising that some of the most critical criteria in the donor-recipient matching process are race and ethnicity. For example, in many countries, such as Spain, Norway, and the United States, the racial matching of gamete donors and intended parents has been standard practice; in fact, the UK Human Fertilization and Embryology Authority's official guidance states that IVF clinics are "expected to strive as far as possible to match the physical characteristics and ethnic background of the donor to those of the infertile partner" (Maung 2019: 112). Since ART has developed to *assist* infertile couples who are not able to conceive using their own gametes, it might be important to compensate for the lack of genetic ties between intended parents and donor-conceived babies by matching couples with donors who can support the ideal of family resemblance. In response to these racial matching practices, however, Pande (2021), a feminist ethnographer who studied the surrogacy industry in India, suggested that racial matching for white heterosexual intended parents depoliticizes conversations around race, racialization, and whiteness as privilege by naturalizing the desirability of whiteness as an intimate and innocuous choice. Yet while the desire to have a child is often presumed to be part of human nature or an individual choice, the actual practice of reproduction is deeply embedded in racial politics (Roberts 1997; Speier 2016; Valdez and Deomampo 2019). In the transnational gamete trade, on the one hand, racial matching is practiced to maintain the ideology of racial purity. On the other hand, in some countries the matching of infertile couples to gamete donors of different races is observed to be a "whitening project," allowing couples to conceive babies that might have lighter skin (Nahman 2006; Roberts 2012).

While race, racialization, and racism have been critically examined in feminist critiques about the transnational ART industry, previous studies tend to focus on white intended parents from Western countries who seek white gametes in the transnational gamete markets. Because the studies that center white intended parents often show how they racialize others, such as Asians, as homogenized groups, it is difficult to use these studies to examine racialization and racism by Asians and among Asians in the transnational ART industry—though racism exists in groups that resemble one another (e.g., among Asians or East Asians; Ang, Ho, and Yeoh 2022). Other studies that explore the growing trend of East Asians accessing the transnational gamete industry have focused on how and why Asian American (Deomampo 2019),

Chinese (Weis 2021), and Japanese (Yang 2020) intended parents seek egg donors in countries with liberalized gamete donation laws, such as the United States, India, and Russia. Yet, issues of race, racialization, and racism have not been fully examined within the context of East Asian countries, particularly when Asian intended parents are seeking Asian gametes to conceive their offspring within Asian countries. Thus, to expand discussions of "new racism beyond color and the west" (Raghuram 2022), this article uses the example of South Korean intended parents entering inter-Asian gamete markets to explore how gamete donations from Taiwanese egg donors have become a "pan-East Asian" genetic commodity that both troubles and reveals the racialized categories and ideologies of countries like South Korea.

HISTORICAL AND LEGAL BACKGROUND OF THIRD-PARTY REPRODUCTION IN SOUTH KOREA

To discuss third-party reproduction practices in South Korea, it is important to first examine how the general perception of ARTs has changed from that of a "dangerous technology" to a "hope technology" among Koreans. In 1985, when the first IVF baby was born in South Korea, media coverage focused on moral concerns about artificial medical reproduction, including the possibility of human cloning, the deconstruction of the family, the risk of dehumanization, and the lack of motherhood (Kim 2019). Furthermore, at that time, major social concerns about reproduction tended to focus on family planning, contraception, and abortion, due to governmental policies from the 1960s to the 1980s that emphasized population control. Thus, throughout this time, infertility issues were often neglected and marginalized, even in maternal health policies. However, since the mid-2000s, social perceptions of IVF have changed dramatically as South Korea has transitioned to a low-fertility and aging society. In 2005, South Korea's total fertility rate, 1.09, was the lowest in the world, and it continued dropping to 0.80 in 2021 (Statistics Korea 2022). To promote childbirth, in 2005 the South Korean government enacted the Framework Act on Low Birth Rate in an Aging Society, and in 2006 it initiated the Infertile Couple Support Program. Over the last ten years, governmental supports for infertility treatments have expanded to include an IVF subsidy program and national health care coverage, and as a result, the use of ART in South Korea has increased rapidly: in 2020, the percentage of babies born via IVF in South Korea was more than 12.6 percent of total births, which points to the normalization of using ART as a medical intervention for infertility.

However, while the use of ART with a couple's own eggs, sperm, and womb is now perceived as an effective method to overcome infertility by most Koreans, third-party reproduction remains controversial. Though socially constructed, motherhood is generally understood as a natural or intrinsic characteristic of women in Korean society. Because the concept of motherhood is closely related to nature in Korea, becoming a mother by using artificial technologies can be seen as problematic. For example, according to a 2008 survey conducted in South Korea, 67.9 percent of respondents disagreed with the practice of gestational surrogacy, and 61.5 percent disagreed with the use of sperm donation for single women (Bioethics Policy Research Center 2008). Thus, while ARTs are now recognized as a "hope technology" for infertile couples—and a method for reversing the nation's incredibly low fertility rate—"natural pregnancy" is still deemed the most valuable practice of motherhood. Third-party reproduction is also highly stigmatized because if eggs or sperm are donated from others, the IVF baby is not 100 percent biologically related to the parents, which, for some Koreans, implies that the parent-child relationship is artificial or suspicious.

In this context, the legal regulations and medical guidelines governing the use of ART in South Korea have been developed to protect conventional family norms, such as the value of traditional motherhood, parent-child relationships based on blood ties, and heterosexual normativity (e.g., by Korean law, only heterosexual married couples are allowed access to third-party reproduction). Before enacting the Bioethics and Safety Act in 2005, gamete donation was practiced in IVF clinics following the ethical guidelines of the Korean Society of Obstetrics and Gynecology (KSOG). Interestingly, the guidelines in 1993 stated only that sperm donors should be of *hanminjok hyŏltʻong* (韓民族 血統, Korean bloodline), while there is no mention of the origin, nationality, race, or ethnicity of egg donors. This oversight might reflect "biomedical chauvinism" (Quiroga 2007), in which only sperm is given a pivotal role in determining a baby's bloodline. However, in contrast to the guidelines of KSOG (2021), the Bioethics and Safety Act includes only "the protection of egg donors" (Republic of Korea 2005: Article 27), though the act also prohibits the commercial trade of embryos, eggs, and sperm (Article 23).[1] The exclusion of protections for sperm donors could be based on the fact that the medical procedure for egg extraction is more invasive than that of sperm donation. However, it is questionable that only the frequency and screening procedures for egg donation are defined, while sperm donation is neglected. This might reflect the notion that conception by donated eggs is potentially more acceptable within both the broader culture and the legal discourse—even though, annually, more Korean infertile couples conceive via donated sperm than donated eggs (Korean Ministry of Health and Welfare 2008, 2012, 2016, 2020).

After the Korean government enacted the 2005 Bioethics and Safety Act, egg donation became highly regulated, and since then the Korean government has sanctioned only altruistic egg donation. In addition, a revision of the Bioethics and Safety Act in 2008 specifically noted that egg donors should not donate their eggs more than three times in a lifetime and that egg extractions should be conducted at an interval of at least six months. Following this, local gamete trades shrank as many brokers were arrested on charges of commercial egg trading. According to the governmental report *Embryo Storage and Provision Status Survey* (Korean Ministry of Health and Welfare 2008, 2012, 2016, 2020), the number of IVF cases using donated eggs has been stationary, in the range of three hundred to five hundred annually, from 2008 to 2020. At the same time, the total number of IVF cases in South Korea has increased by four times from the late 2000s to the early 2020s (growing from 30,234 cases in 2008 to 122,633 cases in 2020). As such, many Korean intended parents who want to use donated eggs must go to other countries to do so.

THE TRANSNATIONAL MOVEMENT OF EGGS: A KOREAN PERSPECTIVE

When the transnational gamete trade first emerged as a social issue in the country in the mid-2000s, South Korea was a destination country for Japanese infertile couples seeking Korean egg donors. Because the Japan Society of Obstetrics and Gynecology prohibits the use of donated eggs in IVF procedures (but allows donated sperm), Japanese infertile couples who need egg donation must go to other countries (Yang 2020). The geographical proximity, advanced IVF technology, affordable costs of donated eggs, and lack of regulation made South Korea a popular destination for Japanese intended parents in East Asia in the 2000s.[2] However, as the commercial trade of eggs and gestational surrogacy services for Japanese couples was covered by Korean mass media, the practice of third-party reproduction between South Korea and Japan became labeled as the "colonization of Korean wombs by the Japanese."[3] This rhetoric of the colonization of wombs aroused nationalistic sentiment, and detractors called for an immediate intervention (Paek 2010). With the enactment of the Bioethics and Safety Act in 2005, which prohibits the commercial trade of gametes in South Korea, the brokerage practices between Japan and South Korea shifted, and eventually, many businesses in South Korea involved in the commercial trade of gametes had to close down (Semba et al. 2010).[4]

While young Korean college students were often recruited as egg donors for Japanese couples in the early stages of the transnational gamete market in South Korea, transnational egg donation agencies later reorganized themselves to provide services for Korean intended parents who were seeking third-party reproduction. To evade legal restrictions regarding commercial egg donation, the agencies and brokers continued their businesses by recruiting both Korean intended parents and Korean egg donors and sending them to countries where commercial egg donation was legal (e.g., the United States). Simultaneously, Asian immigrant women living in South Korea (mostly from China and Southeast Asian countries) were targeted as potential egg donors starting in the mid-2000s, even though the commercial egg trade was illegal (Chŏng and Kim 2007). However, while non-Korean Asian women are racially categorized as "Asian egg donors" in the transnational gamete market, in South Korea they were less likely to be preferred egg donors as Korean infertile couples tend to prefer Korean gamete donors. Likewise, in the transnational gamete markets, Koreans have mobilized and played a role both as egg donors and as intended parents in the complicated context of racial and national hierarchies both within and beyond East Asia.

Since the 2000s, demand has increased for third-party reproduction in South Korea, Japan, and China, due to various factors, such as the Chinese government's abolishment of the one-child policy in 2015 (Weis 2021). At the same time, these countries have witnessed increased legal restrictions on commercial egg donation. Under these circumstances, Taiwan has emerged as a new destination country for Korean and other East Asian intended parents entering the inter-Asian gamete markets. Even though the commercial egg trade is de jure illegal in Taiwan, it is the only country to legalize the trade in East Asia in practice. According to Article 8 of Taiwan's Assisted Reproduction Act of 2007, "a recipient couple may commission the assisted reproduction institution to provide a nutrition allowance or nutrition products to the donor" (Government of Taiwan 2007). The nutrition allowance, a euphemism for payment, functions as monetary compensation for egg donors. The legitimizing financial remuneration of egg donors entices East Asian intended parents who have "racial phenotype and common physical traits" that are similar to

Taiwanese individuals (Heng 2007). According to Taiwanese newspapers, fertility clinics in Taipei started recruiting international patients seeking egg donors after 2010, and it became a lucrative business. Amid this new flow of legitimized egg donations in East Asia, many Korean infertile couples have engaged in the Taiwanese gamete market to make "Korean babies."

MAKING A "KOREAN BABY" IN TAIWAN

The XX fertility clinic located in Taipei was launched in 2012.[5] While other transnational ART agencies tend to advertise the diversity of egg donors from different racial/ethnic backgrounds, the XX clinic specializes in egg donation services for East Asian intended parents. While the majority of customers were originally Japanese, in recent years the clinic has successfully expanded to reach Korean and Chinese intended parents. Since 2017, they have implemented aggressive marketing strategies in South Korea to increase their potential customer base. As part of these efforts, they hired two Korean staff members in the clinic who coordinate all supplementary work related to Korean patients, such as translations, paperwork, and counseling, and they held egg donation fairs in Seoul regularly to recruit potential Korean customers.

The major IVF treatment components are (1) induced superovulation, (2) extraction of eggs and sperm, (3) fertilization of the eggs and sperm in vitro, (4) transplantation of the embryos to a woman's womb, and (5) pregnancy and delivery. The only difference in the third-party reproduction process is that it requires two different women to take these steps. In the case of XX clinic, a Taiwanese egg donor typically undergoes steps 1 and 2, and a Korean intended mother carries out steps 4 and 5. Yet, before these steps occur, the most critical part is the matching process. Following Taiwan's Assisted Reproduction Act, the XX clinic has provided intended parents with egg donors' information, including blood type, ethnicity, and skin color, as well as educational level, body type, and appearance.[6] Although they are not able to provide a picture of egg donors, the XX clinic mentions that if the donors are Taiwanese Indigenous people, they will inform intended parents because they believe that the appearance of the Indigenous women is different from non-Indigenous Taiwanese egg donors.[7] The clinic also highlights that conditions for egg donors who are often acceptable include such statements as "a person who looks like a *Korean*, who resembles the *intended father's wife*, and who has *fair skin*."

When I interviewed the director of the clinic in November 2016, he showed me a number of pictures of babies who were born via egg donation in the fertility clinic. He pointed to a baby in the picture and asked whether the baby was Korean, Japanese, or Chinese. Then he said,

> All the babies in the pictures were born via egg donations from Taiwanese women. However, look at this. It is really hard to recognize the (phenotypical) differences among these babies. [Points to a baby on the screen.] This baby was raised in Japan with Japanese parents. The parents visited my clinic when the baby was 3 years old. He learned the Japanese language and lived in Japan as Japanese. [Pointing to another baby.] This baby is Chinese because her (social and legal) parents are Chinese. We—Japanese, Chinese, and Koreans—all look the *same*. So, it doesn't matter if they use donated eggs from Taiwanese women.

He emphasized that Japanese, Chinese, and Korean are interchangeable and that the phenotypical differences are not noticeable—so each set of intended parents from each country could have their own babies. Thus, in the clinic's rhetoric, "making a Korean" is not an issue of biology. The director claimed that a Korean is not born but, rather, becomes a Korean, thus justifying the egg donation trade for Korean intended parents. As discussed earlier, the transnational gamete markets reinforce the biologization of race based on the norm of the single-race family. Because childbirth is understood as a matter of biology, Asian intended parents are assumed to require "Asian eggs" to achieve family resemblance. However, in the process of making a Korean baby in Taiwan, donated eggs as genetic materials become debiologized because they no longer determine a baby's race, as understood in the Korean context. On the one hand, this underscores the sociocultural construction of race and deconstructs the ideology that race is biologically determined. On the other hand, such deconstruction goes only so far: Korean intended parents do not typically seek (and are not usually matched with) *any* donated eggs in transnational gamete markets. Korean intended parents use third-party reproduction primarily because it allows them to create a "normal" family (which, in mainstream culture, consists of a couple and children who look like them). To fulfill such demand, Taiwanese donated eggs thus become rebiologized as "pan-East Asian eggs"—to be used by any East Asian intended parents who want a child that appears to maintain a "pure" bloodline.

In particular, to entice potential Korean customers, the XX clinic highlighted how much Taiwanese egg donors look like Korean women. For example, when the clinic held an egg donation fair in Seoul in 2017, after the director's talk the Korean staff provided detailed information about the general process, price, and profiles of egg donors as a Frequently Asked Questions session. The staff anticipated and addressed major concerns raised by participants, saying, "We understand many of you are concerned about the appearance of the baby. Actually, many Korean people don't know what Taiwanese people look like. Although Korean people think they look like Southeast Asian people, it is not true. They—Taiwanese women—really look like Koreans."

To demonstrate that the appearance of Taiwanese egg donors would not be different from that of Korean women, the staff showed pictures of Tzuyu, Vivian Hsu, and other popular Taiwanese actresses, as well as everyday Taiwanese college students, and the appearances seemed familiar and favorable to many Koreans present. (As expected, in the well-curated and intentionally placed photos of what a typical Taiwanese woman looks like, no Indigenous Taiwanese women were included.) The images of Taiwanese women also indirectly delivered the message that the list of egg donors in Taiwan would be better than potential egg donors in South Korea. The staff emphasized that Taiwanese women are different from Southeast Asian women because they recognize that potential Korean intended parents do not prefer Southeast Asian immigrants in South Korea. Ultimately, by using images of women (the genetic materials) and babies (the final products), the XX clinic persuaded potential Korean intended parents at the information session to have their Korean babies using the donated eggs in Taiwan while also relieving their anxieties about having a baby who does not look like a Korean (i.e., one who is not perceived to be their own child).

GENDERED RACIALIZATION IN THIRD-PARTY REPRODUCTION

Along with the marketing strategies and rationales of the egg donation agencies, the gendered concepts of eggs and sperm also function to naturalize transnational third-party reproduction in South Korea. First, the Taiwanese Assisted Reproduction Act requires that gamete donors be anonymous. When intended parents register at Taiwanese clinics as recipients, the staff reviews the profiles of egg donors and provides specific information regarding potential donors to the recipients. Among two or three candidates, the intended parents select a donor. Information about the ethnicity, height, skin color, and blood type of donors is shared with intended parents. However, although the XX clinic promoted the images of Taiwanese women to help potential Korean intended parents imagine their donors, in the actual process intended parents are not able to see images of their donors. When intended parents cannot access the specific information of an egg donor, such as their occupation, residence, or picture, the donated eggs ironically become separate, independent, and abstract forms of "biomaterial" that are detached from the living humans they came from. In this process, eggs do not have a race, ethnicity, or nationality. At the stage of matching a donor to a recipient, the origin, background, and history of donated eggs would seem important; however, ultimately, it is omitted because the final goal of conception via egg donation is to assist intended parents in having their own baby.

Furthermore, gender norms play a critical role in stabilizing the transnational egg donation market. Although both eggs and sperm are reproductive cells that evenly contribute to the genetic characteristics of offspring, the social and cultural meanings attached to eggs and sperm are strongly associated with the gender roles and stereotypes of a particular society (Martin 1991). Due to gendered perceptions of eggs and sperm, the expectations for egg donors and sperm donors are also different. For example, in the United States, rigorous height/weight ratios are much more important for egg donors than for sperm donors, but college enrollment and degrees attained are more strongly required for sperm donors than for egg donors (Daniels and Heidt-Forsythe 2012). Along with the stereotypical gendered images attached to egg donors and sperm donors, at a fundamental level, eggs and sperm are treated in different ways in Korean society because eggs represent the maternal line while sperm represents the paternal line. As explained earlier, anonymous egg donation can function to facilitate third-party reproduction because eggs can be imagined as empty biomaterial. However, this rationale would be hard to apply to the case of sperm donation in Korea because the paternal line is still assumed to hold the core and essential parts of the Korean family, citizenship, bloodline, and so on. In other words, for Korean intended parents, conception by donated eggs could be more acceptable than via donated sperm because of gendered ideas attached to eggs and sperm.

This emphasis on patrilineage is epitomized by the old Korean phrase, "Man is the seed, and woman is the soil." This means that the sperm is the core, real, and essential part of the genetic traits of a baby and that the role of the womb is to nurture and carry a fetus. This ideology has long played out in Korean customs and laws around parentage and citizenship. For example, before the reform of Korean citizenship laws in 1997, children born between non-Korean men and Korean women could not obtain Korean citizenship due to the patriarchal legal system. In contrast, children who were born between Korean men and non-Korean women could automatically obtain Korean citizenship, and the non-Korean women were expected to play a role as Korean mothers (and Korean wives) even though they could not be recognized as Koreans. However, when a baby is born between a Korean woman and a non-Korean man, the baby is rarely considered Korean because the baby is assumed to belong to the foreign man. As discussed earlier, the guidelines of KSOG, which posit that sperm donors should be "Korean bloodline" (*hanminjok hyŏlt'ong*), also reflect these gendered perceptions regarding reproduction. Because sperm is considered a more critical element in determining whether a baby is Korean or not, eggs can be replaced in the process of conception—as long as the donated eggs do not have the potential to reveal a baby's "otherness."

Moreover, even when Korean intended parents have a baby using donated eggs, the major role of intended mothers is often highlighted in the third-party reproduction process. For example, to reduce the stigma attached to third-party reproduction, the XX clinic emphasizes the role of pregnant women (intended mothers). On its website the clinic announced, "A Korean woman has succeeded in becoming pregnant and will deliver a baby soon. Anyone who hesitates to use donated eggs, please contact us anytime." Along with this advertisement, they provided a striking image of a pregnant woman's body. In the picture, a pregnant woman is holding her belly with her arms, and at the center of the pregnant belly, the clinic put images of the Korean national flag and a *mugunghwa* (rose of Sharon), the national flower of Korea. The image is neither nuanced nor sophisticated, but it directly shows the message that the woman is pregnant with a "Korean baby" regardless of where the donated eggs came from.

CONCLUSION

This article started with questions regarding how and why Korean infertile couples could be potential intended parents in the transnational gamete market when South Korea is considered a single-race/single-ethnicity country. In particular, when Korean intended parents conceive a baby via donated eggs from other countries, one inevitably encounters racialization issues. While Korean and Taiwanese people are considered part of the same racial category in the major transnational gamete markets (i.e., "Asian" or "East Asian"), Taiwanese people, Chinese nationals, Chinese immigrants living in South Korea, and even ethnic Koreans living in China are all differently racialized groups in South Korea.[8] Against this backdrop, babies that are born between Korean men and immigrant women from other Asian countries are racialized as "mixed blood" or a "multicultural family." However, babies born via egg donation from Taiwan are not questioned or problematized in the same ways. Under these circumstances, this article has attempted to explore how the complicated reproductive politics in South Korea are intertwined with the racial politics of the transnational gamete markets.

In the East Asian region, Taiwan has emerged as one of the destination countries for East Asian intended parents who seek egg donors. In the marketing strategies and rhetoric of an egg donation agency in Taiwan, donated eggs from Taiwanese women became "pan-East Asian" multipotent cells, with agency employees emphasizing the phenotypical similarities between Taiwanese people and East Asian intended parents. Through this process of debiologization and rebiologization of eggs in third-party reproduction, Korean intended parents could have their own child using donated eggs from others. The naturalization of egg donor conception is deeply entangled with gendered perceptions about eggs and sperm under the dominant patrilineal ideologies in South Korea. When Korean intended parents have a baby using donated eggs from a Taiwanese donor, racial issues in the transnational third-party reproduction industry have not been conspicuous or controversial, and it might be relevant that the maternal line is not recognized as the same as the paternal line in Korean society.

Transnational third-party reproduction itself has the potential to challenge pure-bloodism or ethnic nationalism in Korea because the practice crosses racial and national lines. Although current third-party reproduction practices (in particular, Taiwanese egg donation markets for Korean intended parents) could expand their business by effectively erasing the otherness of third-party eggs, they might also reveal how much the existing ideas of race could be strategically manipulated, utilized, and reinvented in the transnational ART industry.

SUNHYE KIM is assistant professor in the Department of Women's Studies at Ewha Womans University and a cofounding member of SHARE (Center for Sexual Rights and Reproductive Justice) in South Korea. Her research examines the politics of human (re)production, focusing on technology, gender, and cross-border medical tourism. Specializing in qualitative methods, she explores how race, sexuality, class, and nationality shape reproductive technologies. She is also engaged in Korean reproductive justice movements and transnational feminist dialogues across Asia and beyond.

ACKNOWLEDGMENT

This work was supported by the Ministry of Education of the Republic of Korea and the National Research Foundation of Korea (NRF-2021S1A5C2A02088731)

NOTES

1. Article 23(3) states that "no person shall provide or use an embryo, oocyte, or spermatozoon for money, an interest in property, or any other consideration; solicit another person to provide or use an embryo, oocyte, or spermatozoon for such consideration; or act as a broker for providing or using an embryo, oocyte, or spermatozoon" (Republic of Korea 2005).

2. According to Yŏnggyŏng Paek (2010), DNA-BANK, one of the third-party reproduction agencies established in 2001, had a branch in Tokyo and recruited Korean egg donors for Japanese couples.

3. Chaeŏk Sim (2006) covered the issue of the colonization of Korean wombs. Similar newspapers throughout South Korea subsequently covered the issue (e.g., Sin 2006; Chŏng and Kim 2007).

4. Nevertheless, the IVF clinic doctors and policy makers I interviewed in 2016 were still worried that Korean women's reproductive capacities would be colonized if commercial third-party reproduction were legalized in South Korea.

5. The name of the XX fertility clinic is a pseudonym used to protect the privacy of the research participants

6. According to the Assisted Reproduction Act, Article 13, "medical care institutions shall provide information concerning the donor's ethnicity, skin color, and blood type for the reference of the recipient couple."

7. In Taiwan, the Han Chinese constitute over 95 percent of the population, while Indigenous people account for 2.3 percent; further, sixteen groups of Indigenous peoples in Taiwan are officially recognized, and an additional 10 groups are seeking recognition (Nesterova and Jackson 2018: 58). It was difficult to determine the number of Indigenous egg donors in Taiwan, and according to XX clinic, donated eggs from Taiwanese Indigenous women were rarely matched with Korean intended parents.

8. See the discussion of "colorless racialization" in Sohoon Yi's contribution to this forum, titled "Erasable and Negatable: Invisible Gendered Racialization of 'Foreign Women.'"

REFERENCES

Ang, Sylvia, Elaine Lynn-Ee Ho, and Brenda S. A. Yeoh. 2022. "Migration and New Racism beyond Colour and the 'West': Co-ethnicity, Intersectionality, and Postcoloniality." *Ethnic and Racial Studies* 45, no. 4: 585–94.

Bioethics Policy Research Center. 2008. "Saengmyŏngyulligungmininsikchosa bogosŏ" [Perceptions of Korean citizens on bioethical issues].

Chŏng Ragin, and Kim Chisu. 2007. "'Chagungsingminji' ch'aja kukkyŏngdo nŏmnŭnda" [Crossing national borders to seek "colonized wombs"]. *Sisa Journal*, September 15. http://www.sisapress.com/journal/article/121272.

Daniels, Cynthia R., and Erin Heidt-Forsythe. 2012. "Gendered Eugenics and the Problematic of Free Market Reproductive Technologies: Sperm and Egg Donation in the United States." *Signs: Journal of Women in Culture and Society* 37, no. 3: 719–47.

Deomampo, Daisy. 2019. "Racialized Commodities: Race and Value in Human Egg Donation." *Medical Anthropology* 38, no. 7: 620–33.

Government of Taiwan. 2007. "Assisted Reproduction Act." https://law.moj.gov.tw/ENG/LawClass/LawAll.aspx?pcode=L0070024.

Havelock, Jon, Kimberly Liu, Sherry Levitan, Angel Petropanagos, and Lawrence Kahn. 2016. "Guidelines for Third Party Reproduction." *Canadian Fertility and Andrology Society*, no. 17: 1–31.

Heng, Boon Chin. 2007. "Taiwan (Republic of China) Legitimizes Substantial Financial Remuneration of Egg Donors: Implications for Reproductive Tourism in East Asia." *Expert Review of Obstetrics and Gynecology* 2, no. 5: 545–47.

Kim, Sunhye. 2019. "'Che 3 cha saengsik' kyujerŭl tullŏssan han'gugŭi chaesaengsan chŏngch'inanja· Chŏngjagongyŏwa taerimonŭn wae munjega toeŏnnŭn'ga" [South Korea's reproductive politics surrounding the regulation of third-party reproduction· Why egg and sperm donation and surrogacy have become problematic]. *Yŏsŏnghagyŏn'gu* 29, no. 1: 65–102.

Korean Ministry of Health and Welfare. 2012. *Paeabogwan mit chegonghyŏnhwang chosa* [Embryo storage and provision status survey].

Korean Ministry of Health and Welfare. 2016. *Paeabogwan mit chegonghyŏnhwang chosa* [Embryo storage and provision status survey].

Korean Ministry of Health and Welfare. 2020. *Paeabogwan mit chegonghyŏnhwang chosa* [Embryo storage and provision status survey].

Korean Ministry for Health, Welfare, and Family Affairs. 2008. *Paeabogwan mit chegonghyŏnhwang chosa* [Embryo storage and provision status survey].

KSOG (Korean Society of Obstetrics and Gynecology). 2021. "Taehansanbuin'gwahakhoe pojosaengsiksul yullijich'im" [The ethical guidelines of the Korean Society of Obstetrics and Gynecology]. https://www.ksfs.or.kr/bbs/skin/notice/download.php?code=notice&number=4195.

Martin, Emily. 1991. "The Egg and the Sperm: How Science Has Constructed a Romance Based on Stereotypical Male-Female Roles." *Signs: Journal of Women in Culture and Society* 16, no. 3: 485–501.

Maung, Hane Htut. 2019. "Ethical Problems with Ethnic Matching in Gamete Donation." *Journal of Medical Ethics* 45, no. 2: 112–16.

Nahman, Michal. 2006. "Materializing Israeliness: Difference and Mixture in Transnational Ova Donation." *Science as Culture* 15, no. 3: 199–213.

Nesterova, Yulia, and Liz Jackson. 2018 "Understanding the 'Local' in Indigenous Taiwan." *International Education Journal: Comparative Perspectives* 17, no. 3: 55–66.

Paek Yŏnggyŏng (Paik, Young-Gyung). 2010. "Pojosaengsikkisurŭi minjujŏk chŏngch'iwa 'kyŏmhŏŭi kisul'" [Democratic politics of assisted reproductive technology, citizen participation, and the technologies of humility]. *Kyŏngjewa sahoe*, no. 85: 40–66.

Pande, Amrita. 2021. "Mix or Match? Transnational Fertility Industry and White Desirability." *Medical Anthropology* 40, no. 4: 335–47.

Quiroga, Seline Szkupinski. 2007. "Blood Is Thicker than Water: Policing Donor Insemination and the Reproduction of Whiteness." *Hypatia* 22, no. 2: 143–61.

Raghuram, Parvati. 2022. "New Racism or New Asia: What Exactly Is New and How Does Race Matter?" *Ethnic and Racial Studies* 45, no. 4: 778–88.

Republic of Korea. 2005. "Saengmyŏngyullibŏp" [Bioethics and safety act]. https://www.law .go.kr/영문법령/생명윤리 및 안전에 관한 법률.

Roberts, Dorothy. 1997. *Killing the Black Body: Race, Reproduction, and the Meaning of Liberty.* New York: Random House.

Roberts, Elizabeth F. S. 2012. *God's Laboratory: Assisted Reproduction in the Andes.* Berkeley: University of California Press.

Semba, Yukari, Chiungfang Chang, Hyunsoo Hong, Ayako Kamisato, Minori Kokado, and Kaori Muto. 2010. "Surrogacy: Donor Conception Regulation in Japan." *Bioethics* 24, no. 7: 348–57.

Sim Chaeŏk. 2006. "Il purimbubudŭl wŏnjŏng han'guk taerich'ulssan sŏnghaeng" [The increasing number of Japanese infertile couples using Korean surrogates]. *Seoul sinmun*, October 17. http://www.seoul.co.kr/news/newsView.php?id=20061017001007.

Sin Yŏnhŭi. 2006. "Han'guk myŏngmun yŏdaesaeng ilbon chagungsingminji chŏllak!" [Korean female college students degraded as colonized wombs for Japanese couples!]. *P'ŭllŏsŭ k'oria t'aimjŭ*, October 23. http://www.pluskorea.net/sub_read.html?uid=1152.

Speier, Amy. 2016. *Fertility Holidays: IVF Tourism and the Reproduction of Whiteness.* New York: New York University Press.

Statistics Korea. 2022. "Hapkyech'ulsanyul" [Total fertility rate]. https://www.index.go.kr /unity/potal/main/EachDtlPageDetail.do?idx_cd=1428.

Valdez, Natali, and Daisy Deomampo. 2019. "Centering Race and Racism in Reproduction." *Medical Anthropology* 38, no. 7: 551–59.

Weis, Christina. 2021. "Changing Fertility Landscapes: Exploring the Reproductive Routes and Choices of Fertility Patients from China for Assisted Reproduction in Russia." *Asian Bioethics Review* 13, no. 1: 7–22.

Yang, I-Chieh Michelle. 2020. "A Journey of Hope: An Institutional Perspective of Japanese Outbound Reproductive Tourism." *Current Issues in Tourism* 23, no. 1: 52–67.

SOHOON YI

Erasable and Negatable
Invisible Gendered Racialization of "Foreign Women"

ABSTRACT This article explores invisible and erasable forms of racialization hidden from view in the campaign against racial discrimination surrounding the case of Ku Sujin, a naturalized marriage migrant woman from Uzbekistan. Ku was rejected from entering the public sauna because of her foreign appearance, and her experience made national headlines in 2011. The article considers the racialization(s) of two groups of migrant women that are relevant but made invisible in her case: marriage migrants who are expected to reproduce "indistinguishable" biracial children and migrant entertainment workers in the area where the sauna was located. This article argues that the campaign for Ku's case was a misrepresentation of racism because of the invisibility of these two groups and the historical connections they underscore. By placing gender at the center of analysis, the author investigates the significance of blood lineage in the conceptualization of race and women's bodies by reviewing historical connections to Japanese colonialism and American militarism. The article argues that the imaginations of marriage migrants and migrant entertainment workers are constructed at the intersection of racialization and sexualization. In doing so, it provides an alternative view of racialization that, owing to a complicated history of colonization, goes beyond the politics of color and is interactive, plural, and relational.

KEYWORDS marriage migration, migrant sex workers, biracial children, colorless racialization, blood lineage

On September 25, 2011, Ku Sujin (born Klavdiya Kurbanova), a marriage migrant from Uzbekistan, was stopped from entering a public sauna in South Korea because she was a "foreigner." When this happened, Ku called the police and took out her South Korean ID card in protest, because she had obtained South Korean citizenship through marriage. However, the business owner said she *looked* like a foreigner and pointed to a sign that said "no entry to foreigners." The owner allegedly told the authorities that other Korean customers did not want to share the bathtub with foreigners because they feared they might "catch AIDS" and pleaded that no Korean customers would come if foreigners were allowed. Despite the police intervention, Ku was not able to use the sauna because South Korea has no domestic law prohibiting racial discrimination.

Rightfully indignant, with the help of a local migrant organization, Ku gave a press conference to publicize her upsetting experience of discrimination. She said

THE JOURNAL OF ASIAN STUDIES · 84:2 · May 2025
DOI: 10.1215/00219118-11591579 © 2025 Association for Asian Studies

she was taking action as a mother of a biracial son who would live in South Korea and could be subjected to such discrimination. The media reported her story widely and portrayed her anger as justified and worthy of sympathy, and she also submitted a case to the National Human Rights Commission of Korea. Two months later, the commission advised the business owner not to deny entry to customers based on race and told the local government to monitor the situation better to prevent incidents of racial discrimination (National Human Rights Commission 2011).

This article focuses on two aspects of racialization that demonstrate the invisibility of other migrant women like Ku, beyond her campaign. She appealed to the public immediately and effectively because (a) she was discriminated against due to her appearance and (b) she was a "model migrant" as a mother and wife of Korean citizens. However, this article argues that focus on appearance distorts the underlying dynamics of racialization and racism in the South Korean context. While Michael Omi and Howard Winant (2015: 13) wrote that "race is *ocular* in an irreducible way," I argue that a closer examination of her case suggests the need to study the process *beyond* skin color. My argument neither undermines the importance of color and appearance as the cause of racism nor implies an agreement with postracial society or colorblindness, which I regard as prominently US-centric and not applicable in the South Korean context. I agree with Omi and Winant (2015) that the corporeal dimension is crucial to understanding race and that specific biological knowledge has been shaped, spread, and believed socially and historically to constitute race. However, a belief about irreducible biological differences does not always manifest in an ocular form, and linking it solely with visibility has limited relevance outside of predominantly white societies.

Delinking visibility and racialization is crucial because of the prominence of invisible forms of racialization. Ku stated that her action was motivated by her biracial son, but most "biracial" children (also known as "multicultural" children) in South Korea are physically indistinguishable from Koreans, because most spousal immigrants are from China and Vietnam. As I show below, this is far from coincidence but, rather, a result of purposeful selection.

By examining invisible forms of racialization vis-à-vis visible ones, this article pays particular attention to the politics of visibility and the significance of color and appearance in constructing race in a non-Western context. In doing so, I demonstrate that racialization is a relational, dynamic, and interactive process that is multiple, simultaneously occurring, and problematically agentic. In particular, I pay attention to the centrality of gender and the paradoxes generated historically at the intersection of gender and race. The sauna Ku visited was located in Choryang-dong, Busan City, in an area known as Choryang-dong Texas Streets. "Texas" (*t'eksasŭ*) in Korean means an entertainment district and is often a euphemism for a red-light district. Since the 1950s, this area has hosted American troops; the American presence has declined since the 1980s except for the navy, whose ships occasionally dock at nearby Busan Port. Russian sea crews started coming in the 1990s, and the area has catered to migrant workers from Southeast Asia since the 2000s. The "no foreigner" sign at the sauna targeted migrant entertainment workers from Russia, Central Asia, and Southeast Asia who are widely suspected of having sexually transmitted diseases.

In the next section I discuss the intersectional implication of gender and race from Asian studies perspectives in shaping the politics of visibility. I argue that specific marriage migrants have been selected for their erasability, by which I mean their phenotypical similarity with Koreans and, thus, their biological ability to produce "Korean-looking" children.[1] The following section details the history of Choryang-dong and the plight of migrant entertainment workers from the perspective of race. It explains how the migrant entertainment workers were rendered invisible in Ku's campaign, as it emphasized the gendered morality (Chan 2014; Silvey 2007) of her position as a mother and wife of South Korean citizens.

The article is based on participant observation in Choryang-dong, interviews with persons involved in the campaign for Ku, and a documentary analysis of forty-four media articles about the case. I obtained the media articles from the BIGKinds database by entering the keyword "Ku Sujin" in Korean and setting the time parameter of one month after the press conference.[2]

BIOLOGY OF RACIALIZATION: POLITICS OF VISIBILITY AND ERASABILITY

The activists presented Ku as a model for new citizens and the next generation of mothers and, thus, as someone who did not deserve racism. While this was a deliberate strategy to get the government to formulate a legal deterrent against discrimination, their framing did not stop hate calls from flooding in following the press conference. According to the news reports, Gyeongnam Migrant Center, the nongovernmental organization that assisted Ku's press conference, received many calls from those who identified themselves as "patriots" and questioned her belonging. Callers asked whether she could be "Korean to the bone" (*ppyŏsok'kkaji hangugin*) even if she is a naturalized South Korean.

This section focuses on the imagined biological notion of Koreanness in the historical context and its impact on racialization in contemporary South Korean society. As do Omi and Winant (2015), Anibal Quijano (2000: 533) stresses a perceived biological explanation for inferiority as the basis of race, defining race as "a supposedly different *biological structure* that placed some in a *natural* situation of *inferiority* to the others" and "a mental construction that expresses the basic experience of *colonial domination* and pervades the more important dimensions of *global power*, including its specific rationality: Eurocentrism" (emphasis added).

However, adopting his view in the Korean context brings about several challenges. First, while European empires, colonialism, and the global power structure of the late nineteenth and early twentieth centuries introduced, imposed, and affected the concept of race in the Korean Peninsula, Korea was colonized by the Japanese Empire. Second, the colonial authorities had elaborate ideas on the racial difference between the Japanese and Koreans and racial discourse on Japanese superiority and Korean inferiority. Nonetheless, the discourse did not rely on skin color or physical difference, as the colonizer (Japanese) and the colonized (Koreans) did not have distinguishable appearances—contrary to what the eugenicists of the time claimed. I do not argue that what Quijano called "a supposedly different biological structure" is irrelevant here, but an element beyond skin color or appearance must be explored.

As confirmed by the sauna owner's response, Ku's visible difference resulted in her experience of discrimination despite her legal citizenship. However, her experience reflects only a minority of the discrimination against marriage migrants. Marriage migrants from Uzbekistan comprised merely 1.6 percent of all marriage migrants in 2020, compared to 61.7 percent of Chinese and Vietnamese descent (Ministry of Justice 2021). These statistics demonstrate that marriage migration is not only gendered (81.8 percent were women in 2020) but also a racial phenomenon that overtly prefers and purposefully selects women with phenotypical features similar to Koreans. Do marriage migrants from China and Vietnam experience a different—a "colorless"—kind of racialization than Ku, if they experience it at all? If they share this experience, what is the definitive imagination of biological structure in the South Korean experience, if not skin color or phenotypical appearance?

Third, the basis of Korean racial superiority, as a non-European and nonwhite race, requires even more complex, convoluted, and contradictory logic. The basis of racism is a belief in one's racial superiority over others, so the belief in Korean superiority requires a serious historical, conceptual, and empirical exploration. Last, related to the previous point, in the absence of colonizing history, it is unclear what groups constitute racialized groups in the South Korean context. Ku is Uzbekistani, and Asian migrants constitute most foreign residents in South Korea. While South Korea and the origin countries of these migrants may occupy different positions in the global economic hierarchy, South Korea is also a decolonizing society, like many origin countries.

To this point, I start from a perspective that differentiates racial formation from racialization and focus on the latter process. I partially concur with Adam Hochman's (2019) view of racialization and agree that it is about making racialized *groups*. It differs from race formation (race making), as it is "the process through which a group is *understood to constitute a race*" rather than "*labelled as a race*" (Hochman 2019: 1248).

However, I do not agree with his definition of *racialization* as "the process through which groups come to be understood as major biological entities and human lineages, formed due to reproductive isolation, in which membership is transmitted through biological descent" (Hochman 2019: 1246). Such a view assumes a multicultural (or failed assimilationist) society with sustained reproduction of racialized groups believed to share certain biological traits, akin to white-majority settler-colonial societies. Omi and Winant (2015) point to the *longue durée* of conflicts between white domination and people-of-color resistance. Such a binary view—whites versus people of color—underscores complex, contradictory, and multiple forms of racial conflicts in nonwhite societies.

In South Korea, the force to assimilate has resulted in a minimal number of isolated racialized groups. For example, while being a biracial person may lead to experiences of racialization, biracial populations do not form a distinct *race* and are not a reproducible group, per se, that will continue a biracial lineage. However, biracial people have critically shaped the history of race in South Korea (M. Lee 2008; see also contributions to this forum by Diederich and by Chung and Choi). Furthermore, racialized people can articulate a counterdiscourse of racialization, such as ethnic nationalism (Shin 2010) or "double racialization," where self-aware racialized people actively participate in the racism against and racialization of another group.

Scholars observe that South Korea's ardent ethnic nationalism and belief in ethnic homogeneity create a force of resistance against the multiethnic/cultural society that South Korea has become in the last two decades (Lim 2009; Shin 2010). Ethnic nationalism, according to Shin (2010), was established against the Japanese Empire's attempt to subordinate Koreans as its imperial subjects based on Japan's racial and cultural superiority, which justified its cultural assimilationist policies such as the use of Japanese language in schools and forceful adoption of Japanese names.

While this argument provides convincing evidence of how ideas of race, ethnicity, nation, and nationalism were constructed as part of modernity, it does not explain clear evidence of how Japan's racial discourse influenced that of Korea. While Shin (2010) points out that Koreanness is a conflated articulation of race, nation, and ethnicity, he neglects how similar conflation is observed in Japan. In the Japanese language, *jinshu* 人種 (race) and *minjoku* 民族 (nation) both translate to the concept of race (Kawai 2015; Robertson 2010). Recent historical work in Korean studies reveals this conflation, noting the discursive progression from "Chosŏn race" (*inchong* 人種) to "Korean nation" (*minchok* 民族) in the period between the late nineteenth and early twentieth century (Na 2022). My argument is, of course, not that notions of race in Japan and South Korea are identical but that this colonial history and legacy resulted in a strong influence and moments of convergence between the two countries. As colonial domination over Koreans (in addition to Okinawans, Ainus, and Burakummin) shaped Japan's racial discourse and notions of *jinshu* and *minjoku* (Yoon 2016; Kawai 2015), adopting and resisting Japan's discourse fundamentally affected Korea's understanding of race.

Considering the legacy of Japanese colonization leads us to two salient points about the basis of racialization in the Korean context. First, the perceived biological basis of race is blood lineage, and sanguineous homogeneity and "pure blood" are valued (Yi 2017; see also Kawai 2015; lewallen 2016; Robertson 2010). It is also noteworthy that the Korean term for mixed race is *honhyŏl*, meaning mixed blood. The Japanese Empire conceptualized the Japanese race sanguineously by defining "nationality and citizenship as a matter of blood" (Robertson 2010: 432). Citizens of Japan proper and its colonies (e.g., Korea and Taiwan) were largely indistinguishable in their appearance. Nonetheless, the imperial governance utilized eugenics to "prove" Japanese biological superiority, blood lineage to distinguish citizens of different stature, and bureaucratic documentation technology to regulate and control its populations.[3] Because blood is invisible from the outside, adopting a sanguineous conceptualization of race brings about a complex relationship between appearance and racialization whereby people with similar experiences may be understood to be of different racial composition.

Second, as a nonwhite and decolonizing but high-income country, South Korea exhibits racialization in a multitude of processes that are both active and passive, internal and external, resolute and susceptible. In the case of Japan, Yuko Kawai (2015) observes that the ideas of *jinshu* and *minjoku* were historically formed from Western influence but remained within the specific context of Japan's relationship with the world. Thus, the construction of Japaneseness was built on the intertwining influence of Western and Japanese concepts of race of the late nineteenth and early twentieth centuries, which articulated Japanese superiority in line with the Western notion of white superiority (Kawai 2015). During the same period, Korean intellectuals embraced and engaged with global notions of race to define itself despite a dire backdrop of Western colonial conquests (Na 2022; Shin 2010; Tikhonov 2010). Notions of social Darwinism and white superiority were accepted without a challenge, and intellectuals strived for the survival of the Korean nation by rising in the racial hierarchy and proving that Koreans *also* were part of the superior race category (Tikhonov 2010).

Double racialization consists of two simultaneously interactive processes: one adopts, resists, and reinvents a racialized understanding of oneself; the other makes sense of another racialized group by accepting, interpreting, and evaluating the perceived inferiority of that group vis-à-vis oneself, a process that relies on racializing discourse exported from the outside and is customized to fit the internal social dynamics. In today's South Korean society, racialization is interactive, dynamic, synchronous, and plural.

The idea of racialization through marriage is not new in Korean history. The Japanese Empire practiced eugenics through miscegenation as a means of "improving" the stock of the Asian race through marriage between Japanese and Indigenous populations in Japan proper, Korea, and Taiwan (lewallen 2016; Robertson 2010).[4] ann-elise lewallen (2016) calls the deliberate miscegenation with Indigenous Ainu "bloodless genocide," referring to the legal and institutional measures to assimilate Ainu people through marital unions. Nonetheless, bifurcating tropes of improving the stock and maintaining the purity of the superior race coexisted in colonial Japan. Jeong-Seon Yi (2017) observes that marriages between Japanese from Japan proper and the Chosŏn dynasty (Korea) were part of assimilationist policies by the Japanese Empire, although the practice's success was debatable.

After the Korean War, a substantial number of "Amerasians" were born of American soldiers (both Black and white) and Korean women (often prostitutes in camptowns) in the mid-twentieth century who were excluded and ostracized (Ahn 2014; M. Lee 2008). Inga Kim Diederich's contribution to this forum documents the effort to mobilize science and construct the Korean race as "pure blood" in its nation-building discourse by excluding "mixed-blood" children after the Korean War. Multiracial children were sent overseas for adoption, with active state endorsement (E. Kim 2007; M. Lee 2008). Women who managed to marry their American GI husbands often emigrated with their children away from stigma and discrimination (Ahn 2014).

Thus, it was a surprise to many when South Korea legislated the Multicultural Families Support Act in 2008 and proclaimed itself a "multicultural" society by accepting and supporting the families of Korean citizens and foreign marriage migrants. However, studies on multicultural children from the perspective of race downplayed or did not adequately explain the racialization of children who are physically indistinguishable from Koreans. For example, Claire Seungeun Lee (2017) offers compelling stories of discrimination faced by children born to South Asian and Korean parents with a darker complexion. Although Lee's article contains a story of one "multicultural" child whose "Chinese identity" was found and ridiculed by her peers, it is not clearly explained why this is an experience of racism.[5] Children of Chinese or Vietnamese heritage fearful of being "exposed" are also found in several journalistic accounts.[6]

However, colorless forms of racialization should be at the center of investigation because the invisibility of marriage migrants' racial traits results from purposeful selection. Marriage migrants were selected for their *erasability*. The perceived biological erasability—and a desired "indistinguishability," culturally and physically speaking—forms the basis of a racializing process for marriage migrants.[7]

The men and the commercial matchmakers who assist marriage migration have deliberately selected Chinese and Vietnamese women to comprise the majority of marriage migrants and thus create the next generation of "normal-looking" Koreans. This started as long ago as the 1990s when a population crisis, caused by the severe gender imbalance in rural areas due to rapid urbanization, came to public attention. Local governments and not-for-profit organizations in rural areas offered pilot matchmaking programs between bachelor farmers and "Chosŏnjok [Korean Chinese] maidens" after the normalization of diplomatic ties between South Korea and the People's Republic of China in 1992. The cross-border marriage brokerage industry flourished, facilitated by commercial matchmaking agencies (H. Lee 2014). Described as "pure and innocent" in advertisements, Korean Chinese women were essentialized as a gendered, ethnic ideal and described as a "better version" of Koreans. In contrast, modern South Korean women had left rural men behind to swarm to the cities because they were too "opportunistic and realistic."

The number of cross-border marriages grew, and by the 2000s the marriage migration trend diversified to include Southeast Asians to replace Korean Chinese women. The matchmakers specifically targeted Vietnamese women, citing similar phenotypes, their ability to produce Korean-looking children, and cultural similarities allegedly due to their respect for the Confucian patriarchy. Commercial matchmakers from Taiwan were operating in Vietnam already, and the existing infrastructure facilitated the practical operation of the new players.

I conclude with three interrelated points about colorless racialization in contemporary South Korea. First, like the "patriotic" caller's remark that one must be Korean "to the bone" to exercise one's citizenship adequately, there is a belief in the biological essence of being Korean and "Koreanness" as innate at birth. Eleana Kim (2007) makes a similar observation in her study on global adoptees from Korea (who were born Korean but adopted overseas) and argues the South Korean state's treatment of global adoptees conflates "blood" with "kinship" and "nation" in its ethnonationalist vision of Korea. Unlike Ku, adoptees in Kim's study were surprised and bewildered by the eager willingness of the South Korean government to assume and impose Korean identity on them.

Second, equating Koreanness with blood creates a particular challenge for the study of racialization because blood lineage is not necessarily a visibly noticeable characteristic. Some multiracial people can be cloaked in visual similarity, and this creates incentives and demand for marriage migrants whose phenotypical traits allow them to produce such children. However, people born in South Korea who speak Korean as a mother tongue and have indistinguishable appearances are still identified as *honhyŏl* (mixed blood) or *tamunhwa* (multicultural) simply because of their mixed-blood lineage. Because the term *honhyŏl* has negative connotations, the policy term *tamunhwa* was created as a neologism in 2008 to describe families formed by marriages between Koreans and migrants who were born foreigners. However, there is little evidence that the term addressed negative perceptions and stigma associated with multiracial people.

Third, despite the lack of visible difference, *tamunhwa* families are believed to be inferior, vulnerable, and in need of welfare attention. These socioeconomic characteristics form the basis of racialization. Although the legal definition includes foreigners of any nationality (or former nationality), *tamunhwa* families are popularly imagined to be from less-affluent Asian countries. The Korean husbands are presumed to be low income, low educated, and rural dwelling. The marital union is understood to have been mediated through commercial brokers who operate in inhumane and problematic ways that are shunned by average educated urban dwellers, which further marginalizes multiracial families.

The contemporary cross-border marriage migration has been theorized as transnational industrialization and commercialization of intimacy (Bélanger 2016), a penetration of formerly insulated areas of life by globalized capitalism (Boris and Parreñas 2010; Parreñas, Thai, and Silvey 2016). While acknowledging the historical context of interracial marriages dating from the early and mid-twentieth century, the contemporary context compels the consideration of the forces of globalization that underlie contemporary racialization. The following section turns to another group of migrants located at the intersection of old and new structures of gendered racialization who are made invisible in Ku's campaign.

RACIALIZING WHITES? GENDERED MORALITY AND NEGATED EXISTENCE OF MIGRANT ENTERTAINMENT WORKERS IN CHORYANG-DONG'S TEXAS STREETS

Historically, Choryang-dong's proximity to Busan Port and Busan Train Station has made it an attractive space for foreign visitors. Qing Court's Consulate General opened its doors in 1884, inviting a business district targeting Chinese populations to form, and the area was subsequently named *Chŏng'guan* (meaning "Qing government") Streets. While its history is preserved in today's Chinatown in Choryang-dong, China's tumultuous modern history and defeat in the Sino-Japanese War resulted in the closure of the Qing Consulate General and the decline of Chinese influence in the area. American troops arrived in the 1950s; since then, part of Choryang-dong has been called Texas Streets and once was an exclusive entertainment area of the American forces. The American influence waned with the departure of the nearby military bases, but Russian sea crews (since the 1990s) and Southeast Asian migrant workers (since the 2000s) have replaced the Americans (N.-Y. Kim 2011). Today, Choryang-dong is frequented not only by migrants but also by local Koreans who come for ethnic cuisine and "exotic" adult entertainment. Bars, karaokes, nightclubs, massage parlors, and motels dot the area.

The number of migrant entertainment workers skyrocketed in 1999 when the authorities relaxed immigration restrictions. The influx peaked in 2001, with 8,586 workers coming that year, and until 2003, the majority were from Russia and former Soviet countries in Central Asia (Lee et al. 2014: 1). While the workers received their visas as performers, such as singers and dancers, many worked in adult entertainment shops as bar companions. Human rights violations were common and included breaches of employment contracts, such as wage arrears, confiscation of passports, physical and verbal violence, and forced sex work (Lee et al. 2014). The US State Department (2001: 97) classified South Korea as a Tier 3 country in its *Trafficking in Persons Report 2001.*[8] In response, the South Korean government renewed its immigration rules on migrant entertainment workers, increasing enforcement of entertainment establishments that hire migrants and increasing immigration restrictions to improve antitrafficking measures. Since then, the number of Russian and Central Asian entertainment workers has decreased, and Filipina workers have become more numerous (Lee et al. 2014).

In recent decades, white-looking entertainment workers like Russian women gained considerable popularity. Migrant entertainment workers were deemed necessary, as young local women were not replacing aging Korean sex workers in camptowns near US military bases (Choo 2016). At the same time, there were growing domestic demands for foreign sex workers (Cheng 2000) in globalizing South Korea. According to Jin-kyung Lee (2010: 8), the two clientele of industrialized sex—the American military and the domestic Koreans—are related as part of sexual proletarianization. While seeing gender and sexuality as the site of subject formation, she explores the interconnectedness of domestic prostitution and military prostitution for US troops, in addition to the military labor of Korean men during the Vietnam War. Her approach to understanding South Korea's transformation from a neocolonization to a subempire, as demonstrated in her focus on the Vietnam War and sexualized labor related to the war, is beneficial to understanding Korea's understanding of global hierarchy in the contemporary era.

In explaining the domestic prostitution market and migrant women in sexualized industries, Sea-ling Cheng (2000) claims Korean men's masculinized nationalist sentiments were at odds with the seeming domination of the West from the past to the present. The US participation in the Korean War did more than fortify the "white savior" image; American leadership in the armistice agreement (which excluded South Korea from being a signatory) and the American military's continued presence in the country reified the hegemonic masculinity of white men (N. Y. Kim 2006). South Korea's brutal experience in the Asian financial crisis in the late 1990s reconfirmed South Korea's defeat at the hands of Western hegemony, and Caucasian European (male) International Monetary Fund delegates' visit to sign a bailout agreement in 1997 left imprints on the collective South Korean psyche (Cheng 2000). Cheng (2000) argues the experience of domination has paradoxically contributed to the depiction of white women as exotified sexual "others." Such expressions as *tegeukgireul ggotda* (to raise a South Korean flag pole on a foreign land) or *bekmareul tada* (to ride a white horse) have become sexualized idioms, and encounters with Russian sex workers, in particular, have become popular. According to Cheng, this Korean patriarchal pride in "penetrating" white women stands in stark contrast to the sexual violation of Korean women, commonly portrayed as a national shame. "Comfort women" who were taken as sexually enslaved people by the Japanese Empire during the Second World War and "Western Princesses," Korean entertainment workers serving American GIs in camptowns, are widely regarded as shameful history.

In contrast, as Cheng (2000) documents, Korean men glorify their sexual experience with foreign women, especially Russian sex workers.

In stark contrast to how Korean men fantasize about Western women, migrant entertainment workers in Choryang-dong are imagined as sexually degenerative and immoral. The owner of the sauna said the following to the National Human Rights Commission: "Right in front of the shop is a red-light district, and Koreans pay for prostitution with Russian women there. So, neighbours do not have a good impression of foreign women. Unless such negative perceptions change, I will lose substantial business if I allow them in" (National Human Rights Commission 2011: 2). While the discriminatory sentiments against workers in the sexualized industry are apparent in this statement, is the remark also racist? Can there be racism against those with a "White appearance" or against migrants that look "Western" like Ku?

The idea that whites can be racialized seems contrary to the privilege they enjoy, given their linguistic and cultural capital as Westerners. For example, Western English teachers are perceived as "expatriates" just for using their language capital (Collins 2016), a privilege not afforded to migrant workers from India, Pakistan, and the Philippines who also speak English as their official language.[9]

Nonetheless, the intersection of their white-like appearance, gender, and socio-economic situation creates a unique positionality for Russian women in South Korea. Constructing Russian women as "white" coincides with accepting the presumed inferiority of South Koreans so that Korean men can cathartically overcome their subordination by the measure of masculine conquest. However, demarcating Russian women as white does not signal their superiority. Instead, their ambiguous identity—that they are similar to Westerners in appearance, yet they are "migrant workers" in their position in the global economic hierarchy—creates a unique process of racialized commodification. Men can purchase the feeling of intimacy and "superiority" upon purchasing their sexualized services with "almost-white" women.

In the meantime, their bodies are imagined as defiled by venereal disease and thus unfit to share a bathtub with decent Korean women, who are believed to celebrate sexual modesty. It was an accident that Ku became a target of discrimination against migrant entertainment workers in the area.[10] The media widely reported on the injustice suffered by the naturalized wife of a Korean man and the mother of a biracial child. However, there was a striking silence about the daily discrimination experienced by migrant entertainment workers long before Ku's singular encounter. There was no mention of Texas Streets anywhere in the media, even though sixteen of the forty-four articles I found on the BIGKinds database were from the local press. An activist I interviewed thought the framing of Ku as a deserving citizen was a strategic campaign choice:

> Nationals [*kukmin*] are those who have citizenship, and all citizens should be treated equally. But this person [Ku] had her right to equality violated despite being a citizen because she is of another race. . . . This was the best case to appeal [to the public] and show that racism cannot occur in a civilized society. Because the campaign won sympathy, it became headlines and was published multiple times. If it were a migrant worker, I do not think the media would have made it a big deal when we went to them.[11]

This activist added that the goal was to legislate a deterrent against racial discrimination that would ultimately benefit all migrants, not just marriage migrants. However, the campaign was based on the logic of gendered morality (Choo 2013), with Ku emphasizing her similarity to Korean women's "moral" bodies and implicitly distancing herself from the "immoral" bodies of migrant entertainment workers. Paradoxically, this logic is underscored by the historical discourse on racial purity and the reliance on moral Korean women to maintain racial hygiene for the biological reproduction of the Korean nation (see Diederich's contribution this forum).

Notable is the striking negatability—the deliberate action of forgetting and denying the existence—of discrimination that migrant entertainment workers endured in the campaign, press coverage, and public perception following Ku's experience. One cannot but think of it as mirroring Diederich's discussion of biracial Koreans in this forum, whose existential exclusion was blamed on the imagination of their mothers' sexual conduct. As told in the previous section, those who married the Japanese during the colonial period were also quickly forgotten from history as modern South Korea occupied itself with the construction of ethnonational homogeneity. The denial of women in Choryang-dong, given its history as a camptown, is a history of repetition.

CONCLUSION

This article uses the case study of Ku Sujin, a marriage migrant from Uzbekistan who was barred from entering the public sauna based on her "foreign" appearance, to explore the complex relationships among racialization, gendered morality, and politics of visibility. Although Ku's model migrant status as a naturalized citizen, a mother, and a wife drew substantial attention from the media, it did so at the expense of simplifying the reality of racism. I have focused on two groups of migrant women who were made invisible to demonstrate intersectional aspects of racialization obscured by the campaign for Ku, which I termed *erasability* and *negatability*. While Ku's appearance made her racially distinguishable from Koreans, and this was a reason for her repulsive experience, most marriage migrants have a similar appearance. Without denying the importance of considering appearance-based racism, focusing only on this type presents a myopic understanding of the structures of racism in South Korea. Furthermore, the women who were daily subjected to the discriminatory treatment that Ku suffered, migrant entertainment workers in Choryang-dong, were negated from not only the campaign but also from the press coverage.

Most marriage migrants are of Chinese and Vietnamese descent, and the main reason for the demand is that their genetic traits are erasable and conducive to producing Korean-looking children. Paradoxically, the ability to blend in has not stopped the exclusion of *tamunhwa* people from the racial imagination of "real" Koreanness. The *tamunhwa* family's humble socioeconomic status (as evidenced by such demographic traits as education level, income, and location of residence) and the characteristics of marriage patterns (e.g., matchmaking through commercial brokers and significant age gaps) have shaped an image of an inferior, vulnerable, and welfare-prone group.

This article credits the sanguineous conceptualization of race—blood lineage as the perceived biological basis of race—from the Japanese Empire to explain the politics of colorless racialization in South Korea. In doing so, my intention was not to dissociate from a broader politics of racialization and color that imagines white as superior and darker-colored skin as inferior, or to pretend such logic withstands time and remains constant. Instead, I sought to provide an alternative view of racialization that, owing to a complicated history of colonization, (a) goes beyond the politics of color and (b) is interactive, plural, and relational. Racialization of the other (be it multicultural children, marriage migrants, or other "foreigners") occurs as contingent tropes of Koreanness are shaped.

A second primary focus of the article is the sexual politics of racialization. The sauna's was located adjacent to the red-light district in Choryang-dong, and Ku's appearance was similar to that of the Central Asian and Russian entertainment workers in the area. The sauna's owner stopped Ku because he wanted to exclude migrant entertainment workers from entering the sauna, citing his clients' fear of the sexually transmitted diseases they are understood to carry. Using Jin-kyung Lee's (2010) analysis of sexualized proletarianization and Sea-ling Cheng's (2000) analysis of the exotification of Russian sex workers by South Korean men, I argued that migrant sex workers' service labor is a gendered and racialized commodity. South Korean men found their service appealing because they were migrant workers with the appearance of whites. More precisely, Russian sex workers became a racialized and sexualized commodity in an interactive process whereby South Korean men seek to compensate for their perceived inferiority and desired proximity to whites. This contradiction showcases my understanding of racialization in South Korea as dynamic, relational, and plural.

The striking silence about the migrant entertainment workers is a testament to their negatability, just like the treatment of other women who challenged the ethnonational conception of modern Korea and the sexual virtue of Korean womanhood. Japanese-Korean marriages of the early twentieth century were forgotten in the imagined ethnic homogeneity, and the children of American GIs and Korean women were excluded from the construction of Korean people later in the century. The location of Choryang-dong Texas Streets as a former camptown further attests to the importance of examining race through the historicity of sites and markings of the global power structure that such sites manifest.

SOHOON YI is associate professor in the Division of Global Korean Studies at Korea University. Her research interests include migrant subjectivity at the intersection of gender, immigration laws, precarious labor, and the informal market. Her articles have appeared in *American Behavioral Scientist, Citizenship Studies, Social Politics*, and the *Journal of Ethnic and Migration Studies*.

ACKNOWLEDGMENTS

I thank the members of the Race and Gender Project at the Asian Center for Women's Studies and the Race/Racialization Reading Group at the Korean Social History Association, as well as the two anonymous reviewers whose comments have significantly improved this article. I would also like to express my appreciation to Jieun Kim for her research assistance. This work was supported by the Republic of Korea's Ministry of Education and the National Research Foundation of Korea (NRF-2021S1A5C2A02088731).

NOTES

1. Similarly, scholars researching surrogacy and ova donation have found ova are priced according to genetic traits, including skin color (Deomampo 2016).

2. BIGKinds database accessed via the Korea Press Foundation at https://www.bigkinds .or.kr/ (last accessed January 6, 2025).

3. Historians will find the politics of visibility and conflation of race described here comparable to the Japanese Empire's contradictory practice of eugenics. Japan's belief in its racial superiority, as evidenced by so-called superb physical characteristics (taller and heavier), led to the promotion of its controversial racial-mixing policies through intermarriage to improve stock (Robertson 2010).

4. However, a belief in Japanese racial superiority was highly contradictory, as it sought both to preserve its racial purity and to improve its race by marrying the superior race (i.e., marriage between Japanese men and white women).

5. The child in Lee's (2017) study had a mother who was Korean Chinese (ethnically Korean migrants from China), whose "Chinese identity" was not previously known to her daughter before the name-calling incident. Given that the majority of Chinese citizens living in South Korea are those who are ethnically Korean, such "Really? I'm Chinese?" incidents seem far from few. For instance, a journalist wrote about a reader who had written to him about the fear of her "Chinese" identity being exposed to her children (D. Kim 2019).

6. See, e.g., H. Kim 2021, Park 2021, and Yang 2021. I thank Han Sang Kim for these sources.

7. See the discussion of "empty biomaterial" in Sunhye Kim's contribution to this forum.

8. The *Trafficking in Persons Reports* are published every year and categorize countries into three tiers; Tier 3 countries are places where trafficking is a serious problem.

9. The E-2 (language instructor) visa for English is available only for nationals of seven countries, United States, Canada, Australia, New Zealand, United Kingdom, Ireland, and South Africa, which are countries where white populations speak English, while excluding other countries in Asia, Africa, Bahamas, the Pacific, and the Caribbean that speak English as their official language.

10. I want to point out that Ku, who was born in Uzbekistan, does not have an appearance of a typical white person, especially to someone who is more familiar with white culture, but has facial features that are seen as "Western" (which is sometimes used synonymously with "white" in South Korea). The activist that I interviewed also described her appearance as "Western."

11. Anonymous, interview by the author, August 27, 2013, Changwon City.

REFERENCES

Ahn, Ji-Hyun. 2014. "Rearticulating Black Mixed-Race in the Era of Globalization." *Cultural Studies* 28, no. 3: 391–417.

Bélanger, Danièle. 2016. "Beyond the Brokers: Local Marriage Migration Industries of Rural Vietnam." *positions: asia critique* 24, no. 1: 71–96.

Boris, Eileen, and Rhacel Salazar Parreñas. 2010. *Intimate Labors: Cultures, Technologies, and the Politics of Care.* Stanford, CA: Stanford University Press.

Chan, Carol. 2014. "Gendered Morality and Development Narratives: The Case of Female Labor Migration from Indonesia." *Sustainability* 6, no. 10: 6949–72.

Cheng, Sea-ling. 2000. "Assuming Manhood: Prostitution and Patriotic Passions in Korea." *East Asia* 18, no. 4: 40–78.

Choo, Hae Yeon. 2013. "The Cost of Rights: Migrant Women, Feminist Advocacy, and Gendered Morality in South Korea." *Gender and Society* 27, no. 4: 445–68.

Choo, Hae Yeon. 2016. "Selling Fantasies of Rescue: Intimate Labor, Filipina Migrant Hostesses, and US GIs in a Shifting Global Order." *positions: asia critique* 24, no. 1: 179–203.

Collins, Francis L. 2016. "Labour and Life in the Global Asian City: The Discrepant Mobilities of Migrant Workers and English Teachers in Seoul." *Journal of Ethnic and Migration Studies* 42, no. 14: 2309–27.

Deomampo, Daisy. 2016. "Race, Nation, and the Production of Intimacy: Transnational Ova Donation in India." *positions: asia critique* 24, no. 1: 303–32.

Hochman, Adam. 2019. "Racialisation: A Defense of the Concept." *Ethnic and Racial Studies* 42, no. 8: 1245–62.

Kawai, Yuko. 2015. "Deracialised Race, Obscured Racism: Japaneseness, Western, and Japanese Concepts of Race, and Modalities of Racism." *Japanese Studies* 35, no. 1: 23–47.

Kim, Dongin. 2019. "Ŏnŭ chosŏnjok ŏmmaga ponaen imeil (p'ŭrisŭt'ail)" [An e-mail from a Korean-Chinese mother (freestyle)]. *Sisain*, March 13. https://www.sisain.co.kr/news/articleView.html?idxno=34107.

Kim, Eleana. 2007. "Our Adoptee, Our Alien: Transnational Adoptees as Specters of Foreignness and Family in South Korea." *Anthropological Quarterly* 80, no. 2: 497–531.

Kim, Hyunju. 2021. "Nŏne ŏmma pet'ŭnam saramirago ch'in'gudŭrege somunnaebŏrigetta" [I'll tell my friends that your mom is Vietnamese]. *Segyeilbo*, June 9. https://www.segye.com/newsView/20210608512945.

Kim, Na-Young. 2011. "Pusan ch'ainat'aunŭi karoesŏ nat'ananŭn tamunhwasŏnggwa kukkajuŭi kanŭi kirhang" [Antagonism between the multiculturalism of China Town's streetscape and the nationalism in Busan]. *Yŏksawagyŏnggye* 78: 35–63.

Kim, Nadia Y. 2006. "'Patriarchy Is So Third World': Korean Immigrant Women and 'Migrating' White Western Masculinity." *Social Problems* 53, no. 4: 519–36.

Lee, Byung-Ryul, Yeonju Kim, Jeong-hyeong Park, Myunghi Yun, Hey-Jin Lee, and Sae-Young Hong. 2014. "Yesurhŭnghaengbijasoji ijumin in'gwŏnsanghwang shilt'aejosa" [Survey on the human rights status of migrants with E-6 visas]. National Human Rights Commission. https://www.humanrights.go.kr/storage/synapdocumentviewerhtml/skin/doc.html?fn=in_BB20141223112652256533861.pdf&rs=/storage/synapdocumentviewerhtml/result/202501/.

Lee, Claire Seungeun. 2017. "Narratives of 'Mixed Race' Youth in South Korea: Racial Order and In-Betweenness." *Asian Ethnicity* 18, no. 4: 522–42.

Lee, Hyunok. 2014. "Trafficking in Women? Or Multicultural Family? The Contextual Difference of Commodification of Intimacy." *Gender, Place, and Culture* 21, no. 10: 1249–66.

Lee, Jin-kyung. 2010. *Service Economies: Militarism, Sex Work, and Migrant Labor in South Korea*. Minneapolis: University of Minnesota Press.

Lee, Mary. 2008. "Mixed Race Peoples in the Korean National Imaginary and Family." *Korean Studies* 32: 56–85.

lewallen, ann-elise. 2016. "'Clamoring Blood': The Materiality of Belonging in Modern Ainu Identity." *Critical Asian Studies* 48, no. 1: 50–76.

Lim, Timothy. 2009. "Who Is Korean? Migration, Immigration, and the Challenge of Multiculturalism in Homogeneous Societies." *Asia-Pacific Journal* 7, no. 30: 1–22.

Ministry of Justice. 2021. "2020 ch'uripguk oegugin chŏngch'aek t'onggye yŏnbo" [2020 annual report of immigration and foreigner policy statistics]. July 2. https://www.immigration.go.kr/bbs/immigration/228/549453/artclView.do (accessed October 25, 2022).

Na, Inho. 2022. "From 'Race' To 'Nation/Volk': A Conceptual Historical Study on the Formation of Korean Racism, 1880–1910." *Hankuktongyangchŏngch'isasangsahakhoe* 21, no. 1: 77–112

National Human Rights Commission. 2011. "NHRCK decision 11jinjeong0575700." https://case.humanrights.go.kr/dici/diciList.do.

Omi, Michael, and Howard Winant. 2015. *Racial Formation in the United States*. New York: Routledge.

Park, Sungbin. 2021. "[Tchintta paksŏngbin] Chosŏnjogŭi adŭl" [(Park Sungbin, the loser) The Son of Chosŏnjok]. *At'ŭinsait'ŭ*, August 9. http://www.artinsight.co.kr/news/view.php?no=55287.

Parreñas, Rhacel Salazar, Hung Cam Thai, and Rachel Silvey. 2016. "Guest Editors' Introduction Intimate Industries: Restructuring (Im)Material Labor in Asia." *positions: asia critique* 24, no. 1: 1–15.

Quijano, Anibal. 2000. "Coloniality of Power, Eurocentrism, and Latin America." *Nepantla: Views from South* 1, no. 3: 533–80.

Robertson, Jennifer. 2010. "Eugenics in Japan: Sanguinous Repair." In *The Oxford Handbook of the History of Eugenics*, edited by Alison Bashford and Philippa Levine, 430–48. New York: Oxford University Press.

Shin, Gi-wook. 2010. "Ethnic Pride Source of Prejudice, Discrimination." *Korea Herald*, April 9. https://m.koreaherald.com/view.php?ud=20060803000016.

Silvey, Rachel. 2007. "Mobilizing Piety: Gendered Morality and Indonesian–Saudi Transnational Migration." *Mobilities* 2, no. 2: 219–29.

Tikhonov, Vladimir. 2010. *Social Darwinism and Nationalism in Korea: The Beginnings (1880s–1910s): "Survival" as an Ideology of Korean Modernity*. Leiden: Brill.

US State Department. 2001. "Victims of Trafficking and Violence Protection Act of 2000: Trafficking in Persons Report." https://2009-2017.state.gov/documents/organization/4107.pdf.

Yang, Lily. 2021. "(Naŭi ŏmma iyagi) hwagyo· Changaein . . . ŏmmanŭn nae charang" [(My mom's story) Overseas Chinese and disabled . . . Mom is my pride]. *Yŏsŏngshinmun*, September 3. http://www.womennews.co.kr/news/articleView.html?idxno=215350.

Yi, Jeong-Seon. 2017. *Tonghwawa paeje: Ilcheŭi tonghwajŏngch'aekkwa naesŏn'gyŏrhon* [Assimilation and exclusion: Assimilation policy and Korean Japanese marriage of the Japanese empire]. Goyang: Yuksabipyungsa.

Yoon, Sharon. 2016. "Colorless Racialization: Analyzing the Discrimination of 'Oldcomer' Koreans in Japan and Chinese in Korea from an American Sociological Perspective." *Korean Journal of Sociology* 50, no. 6: 73–99.

GA YOUNG CHUNG and HEE JUNG CHOI

Incomplete or Extraordinary Koreans?
"Multicultural Soldiers" and the Racialized Reconstruction of Authentic Koreanness

ABSTRACT This study explores the South Korean military's ambivalent embrace of "multicultural soldiers," defined as enlistees with one parent born in a foreign country. Drawing on critical analysis of conscription policy and media reports released between 2000 and 2022, the authors identify a mechanism that posits multicultural soldiers in one of two ways, either as "incomplete Koreans" who may lack patriotic spirit and may feel compelled to hide their family backgrounds or as "extraordinary Koreans" who possess a patriotic spirit and multicultural talents that will benefit the military. While this mechanism is shaped and practiced as a duality, the two seemingly contrasting views are in fact based on a common premise that fundamentally associates the multicultural soldiers with a foreignness that others and excludes them from the family of "pure-blooded" Koreans. Unpacking the military policies' convoluted effects, the article demonstrates how a normative authentic Koreanness is reimagined and reconstructed in ways that racialize multicultural soldiers.

KEYWORDS multicultural soldiers, mixed-blood Korean men, racialization, South Korean military, conscription, Koreanness

This article explores how the South Korean military has attempted to grapple with changes in the racial demographics of their new recruits, particularly multicultural soldiers. The South Korean government had actively encouraged international marriages of Korean men and foreign brides as one way to address the country's low marriage and birth rates, thus utilizing the female migrants' reproductive labor for the state's prosperity; it then turned to recruiting the children of these international marriages, seeing them as an alternative source of military labor for the South Korean army. It was not until 2010 that the Military Service Act removed a clause exempting *honhyŏrin*, a Korean term meaning "mixed-blood person," from conscription (Article 65 of the Military Service Act and Article 136 of the Military Service Act Enforcement Decree; H. M. Kim 2012, 2016). Responding to a changing population, the Ministry of National Defense revised the oath of enlistment by striking references to *minjok*, which references people who are ethnically Korean (H. M. Kim 2016), and actively worked to enlist "multicultural soldiers" (*tamunhwa changbyŏng*). According to Article 120 of the Order of Unit Management within the military, the term *multicultural soldiers* refers to members of multicultural families

THE JOURNAL OF ASIAN STUDIES • 84:2 • May 2025
DOI: 10.1215/00219118-11591589 © 2025 Association for Asian Studies

as defined by the 2008 Multicultural Families Support Act of South Korea. Whereas *multicultural soldier* was sometimes used as an umbrella term inclusive of transnational Koreans, such as early study-abroad students and Koreans with permanent residency, discussions of multicultural soldiers in government policy centered on enlistees with one parent born in a foreign country. More specifically, the Ministry of National Defense defined *multicultural soldiers* as those with at least one parent who has, or once had, foreign citizenship.

For decades, the Military Service Act stipulated that *honhyŏrin* whose skin color was not generally recognized as Korean could not serve in the South Korean military; this racist policy was abolished when the South Korean military began to encounter a decline in the available pool of enlistees and an increase in the number of so-called multicultural children. In part a result of the country's low birth rate, the Ministry of National Defense estimated that the population of young male adults eligible for military service will decrease from 240,900 in 2020 to 149,300 in 2050, a reduction of approximately 40 percent (S. Y. Kim 2014). The government observed that the number of children from "multicultural" families had steadily increased since the 1990s and that by 2014 five of every one hundred births were children with a multicultural family background (Lim 2014). The Ministry of National Defense projected that, on average, 8,657 multicultural soldiers could be examined for potential conscription each year between 2028 and 2032 (Cho 2016). Given that serving in the army has been a significant means by which men may secure full citizenship in South Korea, the enlistment of multicultural children became an important task for social integration of this increasing population.

Drawing on critical analysis of policy and media reports released between 2000 and 2022, this study examines how the South Korean military has answered questions related to ethnoracial differences among the newly enlisted. Materials we reviewed include policy reports released by the Ministry of National Defense, the Military Manpower Administration, and the Headquarters of the Army and 110 news articles that address policies and narratives surrounding multicultural recruits. We give particular attention to how ethnoracial ideologies about multicultural soldiers are (re)produced in ideological state apparatuses such as the military and the media (Althusser 1971). In doing so, we identify a mechanism that posits multicultural soldiers in one of two ways, either as "incomplete Koreans" who may lack patriotic spirit and may feel compelled to hide their family backgrounds or as "extraordinary Koreans" who possess a patriot spirit and multicultural talents that will benefit the military. Focusing on how the duality of this mechanism is shaped and practiced, we argue that the two seemingly contrasting views are in fact based on a common premise that fundamentally associates the multicultural soldiers with a foreignness that others and excludes them from the family of "pure-blooded" Koreans. Unpacking the military policies' convoluted effects, we demonstrate how a normative authentic Koreanness is reimagined and reconstructed in ways that racialize multicultural soldiers.

Echoing the editors' introduction to this special forum, we use ethnoracial Koreanness "as a social construct of racial essence," recognizing the difficulty in clearly distinguishing "Korean ethnicity" from "Korean race." Noting that race and ethnicity are not an accumulation of individual phenotypical traits but, rather, a product of social interaction (Lewis 2003), we situate the discussions and policies regarding multicultural soldiers as sites of "doing race or the production of race in interaction," an instance of producing differences rather than expressing natural differences (Lewis 2004: 629). The categorization of heterogeneous people as multicultural soldiers—and as multicultural children more broadly—is not solely based on a single factor, such as skin color, the ideology of pure-bloodism, or the hierarchy of countries (where their foreign parent came from); rather, we hold that skin color, the ideology of one blood, and the hierarchy of countries are entangled in complicated ways that affect how multicultural soldiers are defined in and beyond the military.

MULTICULTURAL SOLDIERS AND SOUTH KOREA'S MILITARIZED CITIZENSHIP

In the face of military tensions with North Korea, South Korea has practiced male-only conscription for more than half a century. As of 2022, every able-bodied man between nineteen and thirty-five years of age is required to serve eighteen to twenty-one months of active military duty, or up to thirty-six months if they choose an alternative form of service (Military Manpower Administration, n.d.). To further legitimize male-only conscription, the state made sustained efforts to establish the symbolic and tangible significance of military service. Over time, completing one's military service increasingly has been represented as a sacred patriotic duty of all male citizens, one whose value has been (re)produced and strengthened through formal education and an androcentric nationalist historiography (Moon 1998). Through narratives portraying Korean history as continually threatened by foreign invasion, a threat that requires patriotic struggle by male warriors, military service also became the legitimate underpinning of full citizenship (Jager 2002; Moon 1998). The rhetorical "universality" of conscription framed and legitimized the practice as central to a culture where the notion of citizenship based on homogeneous normative masculinity is reproduced through shared military experiences (H. Y. Kim 2001; Kwon 2001; Lie 1998; Moon 2005a, 2005b). The fact that South Korea is pervaded by a widespread and primordial sense of ethnic homogeneity based on shared blood (Grinker 1998; Shin 2006) only strengthens this mechanism. In keeping with this understanding, failure to complete one's military service stigmatizes and casts doubt on one's ability to perform normative masculinity and earn full citizenship.[1] The symbolic construction and legitimation of the triangular relationship among military service, (homogeneous) Korean manhood, and citizenship in South Korea have been reinforced by establishing military service as both precondition and preparation for employment, another core aspect of hegemonic masculinity (Moon 2002b). In addition, military service has been associated with tangible rewards, such as a point system that granted former conscripts advantages on lower-level public employment tests. Though the formal point system was abolished by a Constitutional Court ruling in 1999, it is still customary to honor and recognize military service in employment (Choi 2022; Moon 2002a).

Given the symbolic and tangible rewards of military service, the exclusion and exemption of *honhyŏrin* from conscription denied them the ability to attain full membership in Korean society. Yet the increasing numbers of multicultural children eventually led to a reconsideration of the exclusionary clauses. Until 2005, a person "of mixed-blood who may be plainly distinguished in appearances" from ethnic Koreans was excluded from conscription by Article 65 of the Military Service Act and Article 136 of the Military Service Act Enforcement Decree, with no option to join the military and receive physical examination. With the 2005 revision of the Enforcement Decree, that exclusion changed to an exemption. The revision newly added that mixed-blood men with distinguishable appearances can apply to serve, depending on their draft physical. Thus, after 2005 it was possible for mixed-blood men to voluntarily serve. As there were increased discussions around the need to enlist the growing number of multicultural children, the Military Service Act was amended in 2007 to add a nondiscrimination clause stating that all persons "shall be protected against discrimination on the grounds of race, skin color, and so on" (Article 3). With this revision, which went into effect on January 1, 2009, most multicultural children with Asian backgrounds became legally eligible for enlistment. However, the act also added a new clause under Article 65 that preserved the exemption of mixed-blood men whose "skin color clearly identified them as non-Korean," despite the addition of the nondiscrimination principles in Article 3.[2] Not until 2010 did the Military Service Act and its Enforcement Decree remove the clause exempting mixed-blood men of a recognizably non-Korean ethnicity from conscription, which went into effect January 1, 2011. Since that time, all men of South Korean nationality are subject to conscription, regardless of their ethnic and racial background. The comprehensive inclusion of mixed-blood men has been justified based on the equal rights guaranteed in Article 1 of the Constitutional Law in South Korea (National Assembly of the Republic of Korea 2007: 14–15). However, the particular timing of the revisions should be understood in the context of then-prevailing modes of multicultural discourse, as well as the increasing number of multicultural families and children and the need for their social integration (National Assembly of the Republic of Korea 2007: 14–15; 2009: 15).

In the following sections, we discuss how the South Korean military has tried to manage the new recruits by making accommodations for the new multicultural soldiers. In particular, we examine polices and media representations associated with military camps for multicultural children, the "don't investigate, don't document" policy, and the celebration of multicultural soldiers as exceptional Koreans.

THE DUAL MECHANISM: HOW MULTICULTURAL SOLDIERS HAVE BEEN IMAGINED AS EITHER INCOMPLETE OR EXTRAORDINARY KOREANS

The Military Camp Program for Multicultural Children: Advancing Chinguneŭisik

On May 18, 2017, KBS News, one of the major South Korean television broadcasters, released a video clip titled "Multicultural Youth Experienced Army Lives at a Military Training Camp . . . 'I'm a Proud Korean, Too'" (J. Y. Lee 2017). In the video, a group of elementary and middle-school-aged children from multicultural families sat on the ground at an armory, trying on military uniforms. Surrounded by adult drill instructors, they raised their eyes to watch a peer about to rappel from a hovering helicopter. The youth in question carefully began his descent after shouting his name in response to an order from the instructor. The next scene showed children around ten years old learning how to fire guns. An instructor was paired with each child to help aim toward the target. Some instructors helped hold the barrel or trigger of the gun when the weapons were too heavy for the small children to manage. "We prepared this military camp program for the multicultural children to give them a sense of pride as citizens of South Korea and help them enhance their confidence, believing 'I can do it,'" a lieutenant colonel named Young-Gyu Jeong mentioned in the clip. The reporter narrated that the program, named "Military Camp for the Love of Our Country" ("Nara sarang sagwan k'aemp'ŭ"), had since 2012 been run by the Korea Military Academy in collaboration with the local government of North Kyŏngsang Province. By 2017 approximately seven thousand multicultural children had attended the camp.

Spearheaded by the Ministry of National Defense, this type of military camp program for multicultural children has been held in various provinces since the early 2010s, including Kyŏngsang, Kyŏnggi, Ch'ungch'ŏng, and Kangwŏn. The camps were intended to enhance *chingunŭisik*, a term meaning "a consciousness of familiarity with the military" (Bahn 2011; D. I. Kim 2010). *Chingunŭisik* has become a key term used by the South Korean military when discussing ethnically and racially diverse enlistees. For instance, the Ministry of National Defense's policy report titled *Advanced Elite Military* (*Chŏngyehwadoen Sŏnjin'gang-gun*) (Ministry of National Defense 2013a) picked "improving *chingunŭisik*" as one of its primary policy objectives as it worked to promote a multicultural military. Followed by the subheading "Advancing Multicultural Families' Awareness of National Security and Expanding Familiarity with the Military," the report proposed two approaches: providing multicultural families with lectures on national security, field trips to military zones, and open-house events at military camps; and actively supporting nonprofit organizations working with multicultural families to help them experience the South Korean military firsthand through such activities as short-term military training camps. The specific action plans included inviting multicultural children to military camps on National Children's Day and to the Armed Forces Day festival. These policy projects to promote *chingunŭisik* resulted in many children from multicultural families attending short-term military training camps such as the one described above.

The *chingunŭisik* framework is built on the assumption that multicultural family members are subjects who may need supplementary education to fully appreciate the need for national security and cultivate a patriotic spirit, qualities assumed to be inherent in ethnic Koreans. Given that most multicultural soldiers were born and raised in South Korea, received the same K-12 education as their Korean peers, and spoke Korean as their native language (Abelmann et al. 2015), this disparate treatment suggests the state's discriminatory classification system that considers only those born to two ethnic South Korean parents to be fully Koreans. This assumption others multicultural children by presuming their ethnoracial backgrounds automatically keep them from being authentically Korean. As these programs for multicultural children implicitly cast them as lacking in patriotic spirit, the Ministry of National Defense's program (re)produces a binary framework that perpetuates a discriminatory ethnoracial hierarchy.

The "Don't Investigate, Don't Document" Policy

When it began to conscript multicultural soldiers, the Ministry of National Defense treated their identification information as official records. The Military Manpower

Administration asked them to indicate their parents' nationalities when undergoing their mandatory physical examinations—the first step for any conscript—and then required them to provide their parents' countries of origin upon their admission to boot camp (Ministry of National Defense 2013a). According to the 2013 *Comprehensive Preparation for a Multicultural Military* policy report, this initial approach aimed to provide the support necessary to ensure multicultural soldiers' smooth adjustment to military life (Ministry of National Defense 2013b). However, there are hints of coming changes in the same document. It states that the military administration would keep the soldiers' personal information confidential and would not single them out for educational activities, as the disparate treatment could make them uncomfortable. Referencing policy suggestions from the Seoul Multicultural Family Support Center and the Multicultural Family Research Center at Seoul National University, the report indicated that the Ministry of National Defense intended to refrain from making any policies directly targeting multicultural soldiers.

Indeed, in 2015, for example, the Order of Unit Management added a section on multicultural soldiers that reads: "Multicultural soldiers are not the object of separate management as citizens [*gukkungmin*] of the Republic of Korea" (Article 121(1)); and "conducting surveys or gathering data in order to identify multicultural soldiers is prohibited" (Article 122). Upon implementation of this new "don't investigate, don't document" policy, it was no longer possible to calculate the total size of the multicultural soldier population. As a result, while the number of multicultural soldiers enlisted was recorded as 51 in 2010, 223 in 2012, 400 in 2014, and 776 in 2016, by 2019 there was no official entry in the demographic data for multicultural soldiers (S. H. Lee 2019). When asked about this, an officer at the Ministry of National Defense explained that "we do not investigate the demographic data of multicultural soldiers these days" because "it is a *discriminatory action* to identify the multicultural soldiers and gather data about them" (S. H. Lee 2019). The new policy and its rationale held that the equal treatment of multicultural soldiers in the barracks could in part be achieved by not documenting their backgrounds.

In spite of the benign intentions of the don't investigate, don't document policy and its goal of nondiscrimination, implicit in the policy are limitations that often appear in colorblind racial ideology. Colorblind racial ideology starts from a belief that one's racial or ethnic background should not affect how they are treated in society and assumes that "if people do not notice race, then race will no longer matter" (Apfelbaum, Norton, and Sommers 2012: 207). This assumption has resulted in policy making and social systems that fail to account for the racial and ethnic dimensions of individuals, even to the extent of refusing to document information related to race or ethnicity. Many scholars in racial studies have expressed concerns with this approach because colorblindness "makes it more difficult to challenge biases, and thus increases the likelihood of discrimination"; it not only discourages recognition and discussion of racial matters but also operates on the belief that "the best practice is to ignore the realities of racism" (Wise 2010: 15). Taking the form of "covert and highly institutionalized" racism (Wise 2010: 219), racial colorblindness can legitimize ignorance of systemic racism (Mueller 2017).

There is another wrinkle that merits discussion: the don't investigate, don't document policy essentially presumes that many multicultural soldiers are actually indistinguishable from ethnic Koreans, because the majority of marriage migrants come from Asian countries. The military believes that categorizing the multicultural soldiers as a distinctive group could be disadvantageous. Considering that some multicultural soldiers may not exhibit the physical appearance, skin color, or full name that many associate with being "authentically" Korean, the don't investigate, don't document policy runs the risk of ignoring issues by declining to look at them.³ Further, while the military changed its initial prejudicial view that multicultural soldiers need special support in order to adjust to military life, the don't investigate, don't document policy operates within, while declining to challenge, the ethnoracial hierarchies endemic to South Korean society. By not documenting the backgrounds of multicultural soldiers in an attempt to ensure equal treatment in the military, the policy in actuality conceals the marginalization of multicultural soldiers within the social hierarchy. The colorblind approach is further problematic as its normative language functions to "direct attention away from the larger patterns of racial inequality in society" and fosters a damaging myth that puts the responsibility for life outcomes solely on racially marginalized people (DiTomaso, Parks-Yancy, and Post 2013: 193). In doing so, it espouses equal opportunity and individual achievement in policy discussions about ethnoracial relations. While their multicultural family background was not to be investigated or documented under the don't investigate, don't document policy, some multicultural soldiers were still celebrated as exceptional Koreans, as we detail below.

Celebrating Exceptional Koreans

In its policy report, the Ministry of National Defense declared that the military should establish an environment where multicultural soldiers and their backgrounds would be welcomed and respected (Cha 2020: 296–97). The report suggested that the military actively publicized the multicultural soldiers' personal stories and examples of their successful incorporation into the conscription system as a way to raise awareness. Indicating that any interviews or media coverage of the multicultural soldiers should be preapproved by the Ministry of National Defense, the report confirmed that the promotion of the groups' stories would be managed by the military. A 2014 news article in *Chungang* titled "Private First Class Jisu Oh Reveals That He's a 'Multicultural' Child—'I'm Proud to Complete My Military Service" well reflects this approach. It features the stories of multicultural soldiers and their families who were invited by the Ministry of National Defense to Armed Forces Day celebrations marking the sixty-sixth anniversary of the founding of the South Korean military. In the interviews, the soldiers explained,

> I've always thought of myself as Korean but I am not sure whether other Koreans would have considered me in the same way. Now I strongly feel that I am a real Korean after going through all the processes [mandatory military service] that are the responsibilities of Koreans, though. (Sergeant Yeongu Jeong, born to a Dominican mother and a Korean father, twenty-three years old)

> My multicultural family background is an asset that helps give me a more competitive edge, and I am proud to fulfill my military duty as a Korean national [*kungmin*]. (Private First Class Jisu Oh, born to a Filipina mother and a Korean father, twenty years old)

We can be exempted from military service if we renounce our South Korean citizenship, but we don't want to avoid the military duty. Because it is the best opportunity for us to grow as Koreans. (Prospective enlistees Changhoon Song, twenty-one years old, and Heejun Lim, eighteen years old, born to Japanese mothers and Korean fathers) (H. Kim 2014)

In the media coverage, these soldiers were celebrated as exceptional Koreans who successfully served the Korean military with pride, despite their "exotic" features. Quotes such as these, in which soldiers share that they gladly chose to serve in the military even though they could have avoided conscription by renouncing their Korean citizenship, highlight the young men's patriotic spirit. Serving the army was portrayed as a way to become a "real Korean," and their multicultural upbringing was presented as an advantage that made them more competitive as young adults. Similar stories continue to appear in major news and other outlets, including *Kukpang Ilbo*, published by the Defense Media Agency under the Ministry of National Defense.

As institutions praise multiculturalism as a means to eliminate ongoing racism, they often generate "happy talk," a practice of "telling a happy story of the institution that is at once a story of the institution as happy" (Ahmed 2012: 10). This practice helps institutions celebrate their successful management of the racially marginalized without engaging in uncomfortable dialogues on systemic oppression or racial hierarchy. In the South Korean military, this approach involved promoting the stories of particular multicultural soldiers that portray a certain image, what we call *happy patriots*. The Ministry of National Defense approved media coverage of these happy patriots in order to publicize an image of an inclusive multicultural military, yet its basic stance is not to investigate and document multicultural family backgrounds. While the two policies—not investigating or documenting yet publicizing multicultural soldiers and their family backgrounds—seem contradictory, we claim that they are based on the shared assumption that multicultural soldiers are always somewhat incomplete, fundamentally different Koreans who embody both foreignness and Koreanness.

CONCLUSION

This article traces the changes in South Korean military policies addressing multicultural soldiers. Our analysis of these military policies reveals two seemingly contrasting views about multicultural soldiers. We suggest that the military camp programs and the "don't investigate, don't document" policy treat multicultural soldiers as "incomplete Koreans," yet they are also celebrated as extraordinary Koreans who are willing to serve their country with patriotism and multicultural talents. We argue that this dual mechanism that simultaneously casts multicultural soldiers as not fully Korean, on one hand, and extraordinary on the other is based on a shared assumption associating multicultural soldiers with foreignness and ethnoracial backgrounds that mark them as not "authentic" Koreans.

The use of the term *multicultural soldiers* and the particular military policies addressing them did not emerge in a vacuum but arose from the particular context of contemporary South Korea's multicultural project. Narrowly focused on female marriage migrants and their families, the South Korean multicultural policies have focused on the cultural assimilation of the group, fearing a threat to

Korea's monoethnic and monocultural identity and hierarchical understanding of culture (H. M. Kim 2007; J. K. Kim 2011; N. H.-J. Kim 2012). Within Korea's multicultural policies, female marriage migrants came to be seen as vulnerable and in need of special care and support, given their role as future mothers who must learn how to raise "Korean" children (M. Kim 2013, 2018). Paralleling this image of marriage migrants, their children, who came to be seen as prospective recruits, were thought to be soldiers who need special attention. Our analysis of the transformations in military policy addressing multicultural soldiers reveals an assumption underpinning these policies, one that associates multicultural soldiers with foreignness and defines normal/authentic Koreanness primarily on the basis of a racial Korean background. In spite of the Ministry of National Defense's intention to provide equal and humane treatment to multicultural soldiers, our analysis of military policies indicates that the racialized imagination of Koreanness is constantly (re)produced and reinforced within the military's policies.

Within the racialized imagination of Koreanness, unmarked "authentic," "real," or "full" Koreanness is still rooted in the myth of a shared biological lineage within a "pure" Korean bloodline. Our analysis of the racialization of multicultural soldiers, many of whom are visibly indistinguishable from Koreans, exposes a "colorless" form of racialization. While we recognize that color certainly matters to the racialized boundaries of Koreanness, our research shows that people with similar phenotypical appearances can also be racialized. Our emphasis on the persistence of a racialized imagination of Koreanness notwithstanding, we do not view it as fixed or unchangeable. Rather, we have traced the dynamic processes of racialized boundary making and Koreanness. Responding to a particular sociohistorical context—one in which Korea has become a high-income, low-birth-rate country faced with immigrants from different backgrounds—the racialized line of Koreanness has transformed from obvious to subtle, from codified exclusion and the exemption of *honhyŏrin* to the recruitment of multicultural soldiers who are yet viewed as incomplete or extraordinary Koreans. In addition, multicultural soldiers include those whose parents are ethnic Koreans, such as Korean Chinese who immigrated to South Korea. This implies that even immigrants of the same ethnicity can be racialized depending on where one (or one's parent) comes from, given the South Korean racial ideology that posits "pure-blood" Koreans as superior.

The Korean military has declared it intends to transform itself into a multicultural military. In this article we have pointed out that discussions of multicultural military narrowly defined as incorporating "multicultural soldiers" are based on and reproduce the myth of a homogeneous "authentic" Koreanness. While the discourse on multicultural soldiers otherizes them and casts them as either incomplete Koreans or exceptional Koreans, it also obscures the need to recognize all recruits who have nonhomogeneous backgrounds with regard to race, ethnicity, gender, sexuality, religion, dietary restrictions, and so on. To meaningfully transform itself into a multicultural institution, the military needs a different approach, one that provides for a more nuanced understanding of people's differences and how inequities associated with those differences have been generated. Policies must come to embrace a more expansive definition of multicultural military than that embodied in the category of "multicultural" soldiers.

GA YOUNG CHUNG is assistant professor in the Department of Asian American Studies and an affiliated faculty member at the Cultural Studies, Human Rights Studies, and East Asian Studies programs at the University of California, Davis.

HEE JUNG CHOI (corresponding author) is research professor at the Social Science Research Institute of Jeonbuk National University.

ACKNOWLEDGMENTS

First and foremost, we would like to express our appreciation to Minjeong Kim for her comments on the earlier version of the manuscript. We would also like to recognize the anonymous reviewers, whose comments have significantly improved this article. This work was supported by the Republic of Korea's Ministry of Education and the National Research Foundation of Korea (NRF-2021S1A5C2A02088731).

NOTES

1. These nationalist constructions equating (homogeneous) Korean manhood, military service, and citizenship are more complicated than they might appear. While the "universality" and "equality" of conscription regardless of socioeconomic background have been used to legitimize conscription, many studies show that socioeconomic backgrounds matter when it comes to recruitment, assignments, military experiences, and the meanings/values of military service after discharge (Choi 2022; Choi and Chung 2018; Choi and Kim 2017; Moon 2005a).

2. The newly added clause Article 65(4) of the Military Service Act preserving the exemption of mixed-blood men with distinguishable appearances was justified by concerns over the potential it would hinder their adaptation to the military. The clause stipulates that "in spite of Article 3(3)" (the non-discrimination clause), "persons whose military service would be seriously affected due to their race or skin color" may be exempted from military service.

3. Indeed, commanding officers who have worked with multicultural soldiers note that the difficulties multicultural soldiers can experience in the military frequently stem from their appearance not being recognized as ethnically Korean in South Korean society (Youn 2021: 227).

REFERENCES

Abelmann, Nancy, Ga Young Chung, Sejung Ham, Jiyeon Kang, and Q-Ho Lee. 2015. "Makeshift Multiculturalism: The Transformation of Elementary School Teacher Training." In *Multiethnic Korea? Multiculturalism, Migration, and Peoplehood Diversity in Contemporary South Korea*, edited by John Lie, 95–115. Berkeley: Institute of East Asian Studies, University of California, Berkeley.

Ahmed, Sara. 2012. *On Being Included: Racism and Diversity in Institutional Life*. Durham, NC: Duke University Press.

Althusser, Louis. 1971. *Lenin and Philosophy, and Other Essays*. London: New Left Review.

Apfelbaum, Evan P., Michael I. Norton, and Samuel R. Sommers. 2012. "Racial Color Blindness: Emergence, Practice, and Implications." *Current Directions in Psychological Science* 21, no. 3: 205–9.

Bahn, Jeong Mo. 2011. "Pyŏngyŏngch'ehŏmhamyŏ Hogukchŏngshin Paewŏyo" [We learn a patriotic spirit through the military camp]. *Jangseong News*, June 6. http://www.jsinews.com/news/articleView.html?idxno=1903.

Cha, Yonghwan. 2020. "Tamunhwa gundae daebi gugbangjeongchaeg baljeon bangan(1): sahoetonghab iloneul jungjeomeulo" [A study on the policy development plan for the multicultural military of South Korean army in accordance with the social integration theory]. *Hangukgunsahangnonjip* [Journal of Korean military science] 76, no. 3: 285–314.

Cho, Ah Mee. 2016. "Tamunhwa kajŏng ch'abyŏl? Yennal yaegi hanmaŭmŭro choguk chik'ijyo" [Discrimination against the "multicultural" family? It does not exist anymore. Our hearts guard our nation]. *Kukpangilbo*, September 12.

Choi, Hee Jung. 2022. "From Enviable Other to One of Us? Class, Militarized Masculinity and Citizenship among Korean Study Abroad Men." *Korea Journal* 62, no. 3: 234–61.

Choi, Hee Jung, and Ga Young Chung. 2018. "Divergent Paths toward Militarized Citizenship." *Korea Journal* 58, no. 3: 76–101.

Choi, Hee Jung, and Nora Hui-Jung Kim. 2017. "Of Soldiers and Citizens: Shallow Marketisation, Military Service, and Citizenship in Neo-liberal South Korea." *Journal of Contemporary Asia* 47, no. 4: 515–34.

DiTomaso, Nancy, Rochelle Parks-Yancy, and Corinne Post. 2013. "White Views of Civil Rights: Color Blindness and Equal Opportunity." In *White Out: The Continuing Significance of Racism*, edited by Ashley W. Doane and Eduardo Bonilla-Silva, 190–99. New York: Routledge.

Grinker, Roy Richard. 1998. *Korea and Its Futures: Unification and the Unfinished War*. New York: St. Martin's.

Jager, Sheila Miyoshi. 2002. "Monumental Histories: Manliness, the Military, and the War Memorial." *Public Culture* 14, no. 2: 387–409.

Kim, Doo Il. 2010. "Tamunhwa Chanyŏ Wihan K'aemp'ŭ, 13~15Il Yangp'yŏngsŏ" [Camp for the multicultural children will be held in yangpyung from thirteenth to fifteenth]. *Financial News*, August 9. https://www.fnnews.com/news/201008091032323471?t=y.

Kim, Haemee. 2014. "Tamunhwa 2se tangdanghi palk'in ojisu ilbyŏng 'pyŏngyŏgŭimu ppudŭt'" [Private First Class Jisu Oh reveals that he's a "multicultural" child—"I'm proud to complete my military service"]. *JoongAng*, October 2. https://www.joongang.co.kr/article/15992119#home.

Kim, Hyun Mee. 2007. "The State and Migrant Women: Diverging Hopes in the Making of 'Multicultural Families' in Contemporary Korea." *Korea Journal* 47, no. 4: 100–122.

Kim, Hyun Mee. 2012. "The Emergence of the 'Multicultural Family' and Genderized Citizenship in South Korea." In *Contested Citizenship in East Asia: Developmental Politics, National Unity, and Globalization*, edited by Kyung-Sup Chang and Bryan S. Turner, 211–25. New York: Routledge.

Kim, Hyun Mee. 2016. "Can 'Multicultural Soldiers' Serve the Nation? The Social Debate about the Military Service Management of Mixed-Race Draftees in South Korea." In *Multiculturalism in East Asia: A Transnational Exploration of Japan, South Korea, and Taiwan*, edited by Koichi Iwabuchi, Hyun Mee Kim, and Hsiao-Chuan Hsia, 127–40. London: Rowman and Littlefield.

Kim, Hyun Young. 2001. "Byeongyeoguimuwa geundaejeok gungminjeongcheseongui Seongbyeoljeongchihak" [Compulsory military service and the gender politics of Korean national identity]. Master's thesis, Ewha Woman's University.

Kim, Joon K. 2011. "The Politics of Culture in Multicultural Korea." *Journal of Ethnic and Migration Studies* 37, no. 10: 1583–1604.

Kim, Minjeong. 2013. "Citizenship Projects for Marriage Migrants in South Korea: Intersecting Motherhood with Ethnicity and Class." *Social Politics* 20, no. 4: 455–81.

Kim, Minjeong. 2018. *Elusive Belonging: Marriage Immigrants and "Multiculturalism" in Rural South Korea*. Honolulu: University of Hawai'i Press.

Kim, Nora Hui-Jung. 2012. "Multiculturalism and the Politics of Belonging: The Puzzle of Multiculturalism in South Korea." *Citizenship Studies* 16, no. 1: 103–17.

Kim, Seon Young. 2014. "Nŭrŏnanŭn tamunhwa changbyŏng, han'gukkun pyŏnhwa shigŭp'ada" [An urgent need to transform the Korean military: The rise of the "multicultural" soldiers]. *Segyeilbo*, December 23. https://www.segye.com/newsView/20141223003878?OutUrl=naver.

Kwon, Insook. 2001. "A Feminist Exploration of Military Conscription: The Gendering of the Connections between Nationalism, Militarism, and Citizenship in South Korea." *International Feminist Journal of Politics* 3, no. 1: 26–54.

Lee, Jong Young. 2017. "Tamunhwa chŏngsonyŏn pyŏngyŏng ch'ehŏm . . . nado tangdanghan han'gugin" ["Multicultural" youth's military camp experience . . . "I feel myself as a proud Korean"]. *KBS News*, May 18. https://news.kbs.co.kr/news/view.do?ncd=3483017&ref=A.

Lee, Sang Heon. 2019. "3000myŏng pongmu chung, tamunhwa 2se iptae pon'gyŏk'wadoenŭndet't kich'o chosado ŏpta" [There are three thousand "multicultural" soldiers in service . . . we don't even have any primary data about them]. *Kungminilbo*, April 22. http://news.kmib.co.kr/article/view.asp?arcid=0924074041&code=11131100&sid1=all.

Lewis, Amanda E. 2003. "Everyday Race-Making: Navigating Racial Boundaries in Schools." *American Behavioral Scientist* 47, no. 3: 283–305.

Lewis, Amanda E. 2004. "'What Group?' Studying Whites and Whiteness in the Era of 'Color-Blindness.'" *Sociological Theory* 22, no. 4: 623–46.

Lie, John. 1998. *Han Unbound: The Political Economy of South Korea*. Redwood City, CA: Stanford University Press.

Lim, Mi Na. 2014. "Tamunhwa changbyŏng 1ch'ŏnmyŏng shidae(sang)" [The era of "multicultural" national defense and the one thousand "multicultural" soldiers (Part 1)]. *Yŏnhamnyusŭ*, November 24. https://www.yna.co.kr/view/AKR20141120154800372.

Military Manpower Administration. n.d. "Byeongyeogihaengannae Gaeyo" [Outline of military service information]. https://www.mma.go.kr/contents.do?mc=usr0000041. Accessed November 30, 2021.

Ministry of National Defense. 2013a. *Chŏngyehwadoen Sŏnjin'gang-gun* [Advanced elite military]. Seoul: Gukguninswaechang.

Ministry of National Defense. 2013b. *Damunhwa Gundae Daebi Jonghapdaechaek* [Comprehensive preparation for a multicultural military]. Seoul: Gukguninswaechang.

Moon, Seungsook. 1998. "Begetting the Nation: The Androcentric Discourse of National History and Tradition in South Korea." In *Dangerous Women: Gender and Korean Nationalism*, edited by Elaine Kim and Chungmoo Choi, 33–66. Abingdon: Routledge.

Moon, Seungsook. 2002a. "Imagining a Nation through Differences: Reading the Controversy Concerning the Military Service Extra Points System in South Korea." *Review of Korean Studies* 5, no. 2: 73–109.

Moon, Seungsook. 2002b. "The Production and Subversion of Hegemonic Masculinity: Reconfiguring Gender Hierarchy in Contemporary South Korea." In *Under Construction: The Gendering of Modernity, Class, and Consumption in the Republic of Korea*, edited by Laurel Kendall, 79–114. Honolulu: University of Hawai'i Press.

Moon, Seungsook. 2005a. *Militarized Modernity and Gendered Citizenship in South Korea*. Durham, NC: Duke University Press.

Moon, Seungsook. 2005b. "Trouble with Conscription, Entertaining Soldiers: Popular Culture and the Politics of Militarized Masculinity in South Korea." *Men and Masculinities* 8, no. 1: 64–92.

Mueller, Jennifer C. 2017. "Producing Colorblindness: Everyday Mechanisms of White Ignorance." *Social Problems* 64, no. 2: 219–38.

National Assembly of the Republic of Korea. 2007. *Che 269 hoe kukpang che 7 cha hoeŭirok* [Seventh National Defense Committee of the 269th National Assembly meeting minutes]. November 15. Republic of Korea National Assembly database. https://likms.assembly.go.kr/record/.

National Assembly of the Republic of Korea. 2009. *Che 284 hoe kukpang che 11cha hoeŭirok* [Eleventh National Defense Committee of the 284th National Assembly meeting minutes). November 24. Republic of Korea National Assembly database. https://likms.assembly.go.kr/record/.

Shin, Gi-Wook. 2006. *Ethnic Nationalism in Korea: Genealogy, Politics and Legacy*. Stanford, CA: Stanford University Press.

Wise, Tim. 2010. *Colorblind: The Rise of Post-racial Politics and the Retreat from Racial Equity*. San Francisco: City Lights Books.

Youn, Won Kyu. 2021. "Tamunhwa gajeong janyeoui gukbang injeokjawoneuroui hwaryong-siltae gwallyeon yeongu? Haegun, haebyeongbudae gun bongmusiltae mit jedogaeseon jungsimeuro" [A study on the utilization of children of multicultural families as defense human resources—Focusing on the status of military service and improvement of the system of the Navy and Marine Corps]. *Munhwagyoryuwa damunhwagyoyuk* [Cultural exchange and multicultural education] 10, no. 2: 211–37.

HAN SANG KIM

The "Roof Koreans" Meme

The Collective Memory of Los Angeles 1992 in South Korea

ABSTRACT When a protest to support the Black Lives Matter (BLM) movement was organized in Seoul in the summer of 2020, not a few commentators in South Korea's online communities expressed their cynicism about the movement. While some referred to the recent hate crimes conducted against Asians after the coronavirus outbreak, many others summoned the memory of the 1992 Los Angeles riots. The fact that many Korean American–owned stores had been looted and damaged during the riots was brought to notice by these commentators as an evidential basis for the uselessness of Koreans' solidarity with the BLM movement. This article attempts to narrativize how the racial tensions between Black and Korean Americans in Los Angeles in 1992 have been collectively remembered in South Korea to examine the role of the collective memory of the event in the South Korean public's current attitude toward race issues. The images of the so-called roof Koreans, Korean American shopkeepers who kept watching with rifles in hand on the rooftops of their buildings during the 1992 riot, were resummoned during the BLM movement and used in internet memes as a symbol of ideal citizens who could protect their neighborhood with their military training experience back in their home country, South Korea. This collective memorization of roof Koreans as military veterans of the ROK Army raised masculine self-esteem of South Korean males compared to their male counterparts in the United States, in their imagined racial hierarchy, when the hierarchy was questioned and challenged.

KEYWORDS 1992 Los Angeles civil unrest, Black Lives Matter (BLM) movement, collective memory, masculinity, internet meme

This article attempts to narrativize how the racial tensions between Black and Korean Americans in Los Angeles in 1992 have been collectively remembered in South Korea. I investigate the news reports in the South Korean media right at the time of the riots to trace the discursive construction of those self-defensive, armed Korean American store owners, or "roof Koreans," at the early stage of the discourse. Then I analyze more recently circulated visual and textual materials processed from the archival images of those Korean Americans who appeared on American television—the "roof Korean" memes—and related discourses in both Korean and English. In so doing, the article examines the role of the collective memory of LA 1992 in the South Korean public's current attitude toward race issues.

THE JOURNAL OF ASIAN STUDIES • 84:2 • May 2025
DOI: 10.1215/00219118-11591599 © 2025 Association for Asian Studies

The year 2020 saw a burgeoning discourse about race or racism in both South Korea's traditional and social media. For a long time, multiracial and/or multiethnic social changes in South Korea have been discussed in the context of the Korean government's multicultural policies that connote the basic object as the relationship between South Korean–born, ethnic South Koreans as the majority and immigrants from other parts of the world and their families as the minority. However, the circumstances of the year 2020 both at home and abroad paved the way for a more racially contextualized understanding of what South Koreans encountered, which the familiar rhetoric of (anti)multiculturalism failed to explain. The global outbreak of COVID-19 and the subsequent increase in racist attacks against Asians generated racial consciousness from South Koreans to a degree. The Black Lives Matter (BLM) movement that summer sparked heated discussions about race and racism among South Koreans, even though most of them saw the issue as foreign-born and unrelated to their own society. When a protest to support the BLM movement was organized in Seoul, more than a few commentators on South Korea's online communities expressed their cynicism about the movement, pointing to what they believed as "age-old mistrust and discord" between Black and Asian American communities.[1] While some referred to the recent hate crimes conducted against Asians after the coronavirus outbreak, many others summoned the memory of the 1992 LA riots. The fact that many Korean American–owned stores had been looted and damaged during the riots was brought to notice by these commentators as an evidential basis for the uselessness of Koreans' solidarity with the BLM movement. This cynicism was then developed in August of the same year and linked to a more aggressive reaction to the controversy over a high school yearbook photograph with blackface makeup, which made South Koreans begin to recognize the issues of race and racism as domestic ones. Through this dispute over whether those blackfaced high schoolers offended people of color or not (discussed in further detail later in this article), people in South Korea started discussing race and racial differences in relation to the matters of victimization, which also summoned memories of the year 1992.

The key issue of this article, in these circumstances, is an internet meme. When several documentaries came out in 2017 commemorating the LA riots twenty-five years after the event, including *L.A. Burning: The Riots Twenty-Five Years Later*, *LA 92* (see Lindsay and Martin 2017), and *Let It Fall: Los Angeles 1982–1992*, one of the unexpected consequences was the burgeoning of the so-called roof Korean memes. Usually comprising captured images of news footage depicting Korean American shopkeepers holding rifles on rooftops, these casual digital creations on the internet have humorously circulated certain ideas that these Korean men were brave, orderly, and righteous. These memes, first circulated on American English-based social media networks and then imported to Korean-based internet communities and social media, have demonstrated the diverse and disparate symbolic meanings of these archival images in global and transnational contexts, especially depending on how racial relations in the specific historical event are differently remembered and sometimes reinvented.

In doing so, this article specifically aims to foreground how the media memory of a diasporic group is summoned, invented, and transplanted in the diaspora's homeland to form a transnational collective identity in response to a heightened global sensitivity to racial injustice. The meme's military nature, in particular, has created an environment for the Korean-based internet sphere to connect the race relations inscribed in the meme to a masculine mythology that appeals to a specific gender group's interest in South Korea's domestic discursive space.

COLLECTIVE VICTIMHOOD: HOW TO DEFINE SYMPATHY, OR HOW TO LOCATE ONESELF IN THE WORLD

South Korean media's initial reaction to the civil unrest in 1992 was definitely more related to how Korean Americans suffered material and psychological damage from the violent event in LA than what caused the incident. The event was broadcast on national television as a serious affair that sent all domestic news to the rear. The sense of immediacy and connectivity through the voices and images delivered from correspondents, US broadcasters, and local Korean American informants in LA might have aroused the viewer's attention and excitement. It is undeniable that the event itself had lots of eye-catching elements for South Korean viewers, including exotic cityscapes, violence and disorder, and objects of pity with whom South Koreans could easily identify. While the first news report on LA Mayor Tom Bradley's declaration of a state of emergency for the city at LA time 20:30 on April 29 (12:30 on April 30 in Seoul time), printed on the front page of *Tonga ilbo*'s evening edition on April 30, focused on the early development of the event as a whole and drily mentioned an arson attack and gunfights at a couple of swap-meet buildings run by Korean Americans, nightly television news programs on that day had already started discussing the incident from the perspective of the country sending Korean immigrants to the United States. The *MBC News Desk* episode that night consisted of several news reports related to potential damage and possible measures for that. South Korea's other major broadcaster, SBS, invited Ho Min Kim, former president of the Korean American Chamber of Commerce of Southern California, to a telephone interview for its *SBS 8 News* program, reporting that about a hundred Korean stores were being looted or damaged. These nightly news reports drew viewers' attention to the demographic characteristics of South Central LA as an ethnic enclave accommodating Korean immigrants and seriously discussed possible measures from the Korean Ministry of Foreign Affairs. In this way, less than half a day after its first news coverage, the civil unrest in LA became the main news of South Korean media, framed as a disastrous incident for Koreans who had ties to their home country.

The following day, May 1, saw enormous media coverage of the damage to Korean people in LA during the second day of the unrest. Some notable headlines in major newspapers included "Blaze . . . Gunfire . . . Lawless Black LA" (*Chosŏn ilbo*), "'Mobs Are Surging' . . . Dreadful Koreatown" (*Tonga ilbo*), "Black Time Bombs Everywhere" (*Kyŏnghyang sinmun*), "Lamenting Koreans at Stores Burned to Ashes" (*Chosŏn ilbo*), "Sustained Looting by Black People, a Deadly Night for Six Hundred Thousand Compatriots" (*Han'gyŏre*), "Boiling, Furious Melting Pot" (*Kyŏnghyang sinmun*), and "Swamped with International Calls to LA" (*Tonga ilbo*). These news reports detailed the extent of the damage, including both numerical scales of physical damage and testimonies and interviews describing the psychological damage Koreans suffered. As seen in the expressions used in the headlines above, the barbarous and uncontrolled aspect of the incident was emphasized and, sometimes, linked to the skin color of the rioters, giving a negative impression of the color black ("Black LA" and "Black Time Bombs").[2] On that day, *MBC News Desk* started with a compilation of the now-notorious news footage clips from US broadcaster NBC, depicting looted Korean stores and armed Korean shopkeepers with guns in their hands, with the background sound of sirens and anxious music, which was followed by the first report of the news episode about a gunfight at a Korean-owned store. Then followed a correspondent report on the delayed commitment of the National Guard to Koreatown and a Radio Korea correspondent's phone interview about the "abruptly implicated" Black-Korean conflict. In this way, the event was introduced as a media spectacle in the age of color television and satellite communication, stimulating the South Korean viewer's sense of curiosity through provocative headlines and graphic images. The images of looted stores owned by Korean Americans, armed Korean American shopkeepers confronting an uncontrollable mob, and burning store buildings with Korean signs became a proto-landscape of LA in the South Korean media.

Returning to the time of the incident, however, it did not take long for the South Korean media to define their standpoint and direct their viewers where to see and how to sympathize with their fellow compatriots. According to social psychologists Masi Noor and colleagues, collective victimhood is "the psychological experience and consequences" of "harm by one group toward another," and it is not uncommon that "it also extends to group members who did not experience the harm-doing directly but identify with the targeted group" (Noor et al. 2017: 121–22). The South Korean media indeed extended the sense of victimhood to South Koreans who did not directly experience the conflict, by sharing the beliefs that the victim group, in this case Korean Americans, was suffering more than the adversarial group, in this case Afro-Americans, and that their suffering was "decidedly more unjust than that of the other group" (123–24). By sympathizing with Korean Americans with this sense of competitive victimhood, South Koreans could locate themselves in the imagined racial hierarchy of the cosmopolitan world.

As of May 2 (May 1 in LA time), the acute situation in LA had wound down and the South Korean media's editorial direction seemed to focus on investigating the deep-rooted cause of the victimization of Korean Americans. One of the frequently assumed causes was African American people's sense of inferiority and the resultant venting of their anger on Korean Americans. *Manmulssang* ("General Store"), an editorial comment feature on the front page of *Chosŏn ilbo*, on May 2 put the situation of Korean Americans in a nutshell: "a shrimp's back," quoting a Korean proverb, "The back of a shrimp bursts amid a fight between whales," which means the weak subject would suffer a side blow in a fight between the strong two. The anonymous author of this comment presented an analysis that, while Black people's empowerment had been deadlocked because white people did not treat them equally, Korean Americans' challenging spirit and self-esteem might have been the target of Black people's inferiority complex and victim mentality. The comment wrapped up by pointing to the suspicion that white supremacy was driving this issue to a conflict between ethnic minorities. Another comment section by a named editorialist, "Yi Kyu-t'ae's Corner," on the same day used an analogy that the rioting and rage of Black people against Koreatown was like a daughter-in-law kicking a puppy's belly when she could not fight her mother-in-law. Yi also raised doubt on the intentional passivity of the LA Police Department (LAPD) in repressing the riot in Koreatown to divert the Black-white conflict into a Black-Korean one, saying, "Our fellow countrymen are so underserved."

The US government authorities' intentional neglect in performing protective measures for the Korean American community was the other frequently assumed cause that South Korean media spotted. *Han'gyŏre* presented the headline "The US Police Turns Away from Rescuing Koreans," with the subhead, "Suspicious of Intended Focus Change onto the Black-Korean Conflict," for a correspondent report on May 2. The report conveyed Korean Americans' complaints that LA fire engines responded to Koreans' requests for rescue too slowly while they responded immediately to requests from white areas. *Tonga ilbo* covered the South Korean public's response to the event in its evening edition on the same day, with the headline "Why Do Only Korean Americans Suffer? Citizens' Rage."

Another cause South Korean media often pointed at was the US media's scapegoating of Korean shopkeepers who were filmed while shooting against looters. *Chosŏn ilbo*'s May 2 morning edition reported that South Korea's consulate general in LA made a call to NBC News on April 30 to urge the broadcaster to refrain from continuously airing the gunfight scene between Korean American shopkeepers and Black looters, since the repetitive exposure to that scene could lead viewers to misunderstand the nature of the incident. The same edition had a third-page headline, "A Wrong Target, Korean Americans . . . LA in a Frenzy," and the report delivered complaints from Korean Americans that US television broadcasters were showing the gunfight scene repeatedly to give the impression that the riot was due to a Black-Korean conflict. *Kyŏnghyang sinmun*, the next day (May 3), carried an analysis report about the US media, pointing out that Korean was the most frequently mentioned ethnicity in the US media's coverage of the LA civil unrest; that America's top three national television broadcasters, ABC, CBS, and NBC, along with the cable news network CNN, so vividly and continuously showed the damage suffered by Koreans that there was a negative effect on the Korean community; and that some TV networks, including NBC, made a hasty diagnosis that the Soon Ja Du case was the reason that Koreans became the target during the riot.

These assumed causes might be valid in some respects and invalid or, perhaps, too subjective in some other respects. However, regardless of what history has concluded as the causes of the historical event, it looks like the directions provided in South Korea's media coverage of the LA civil unrest contributed to South Koreans forming a sense of collective victimhood. According to these assumed causes, Korean Americans were multiply the victims of the Black-white conflicts, of white supremacy, of Black people's inferiority complex, of the US media, and of the institutional racism against the in-between minority in the racial hierarchy. The victims' cultural and physical proximity to the viewer, with regard to their appearance, language, and customs, allowed room for South Korean viewers to identify with Korean Americans, which led to a sense of victimhood among South Koreans.

Korean American storeowners' arming themselves and firing their weapons were therefore understood as self-rescue measures and were portrayed that way in South Korean popular media. MBC's TV series *Ŏksae param* (*Wind in the Silver*

Grass, 1992–93) was quick enough to dramatize the LA riots in November that same year, revolving around the lives of two Korean American families based in Chicago and LA, respectively. The show's climax is the looting of the Mun family's convenience store in LA during the riots, in parallel with an armed robbery at the Yi family's dry cleaner shop in Chicago. While Yi gets shot by the African American robber after wrestling with him, Mun's daughter bravely takes a gun and fires it at the looters. Although her armed defense comes out to be unequal to the rushing crowd, the shooting scene is cathartic enough to legitimize the use of a gun toward the mob without firearms.

THE ROOF KOREANS: THE IMAGE OF ARMED KOREAN AMERICANS IN THE AMERICAN CONTEXT

What was the meaning of the armed Korean Americans to Americans, then? Nancy Abelmann and John Lie's (1995) ethnographic monograph on the 1992 LA riots starts with this statement: "The focused destruction of Korean American businesses and the dramatic image of armed Korean Americans on Los Angeles rooftops during the LA riots piqued public attention" (1). This dramatic image of self-guarding Korean store owners and their family members strikingly synthesizes the contrasting representations of retail spaces and war veterans. The media representation of this historic event served as an epic for Korean Americans to overcome the gap between their confined representation in retail spaces and their self-representation as brave, free people. These Korean Americans depicted in the TV news footage have become the source of a certain stereotype of self-defensive Koreans, who have been well trained in their military service while in South Korea and/or Vietnam. South Korea's universal conscription system (*kungmingaebyŏngje*), which was introduced into legislation in 1949 and began implementation in 1957, made the "mass military mobilization" of young Korean men possible, and its "intense and repetitive physical discipline and indoctrination" generated "a collective ethos that justifies the sacrifice of individuals for the sake of a larger goal" (Moon 2005: 45–49). While the "frightening" images of the armed Koreans on the supermarket rooftop during the chaos "with no police coming to help" them became the "iconic" pictures of the event (David Jackson, quoted in Lindsay and Martin 2017), it is not inappropriate to infer that their devoted but sacrificial attitude in a well-organized manner was related to the collective identity of South Korean male under the universal conscription system. Those among them who were veterans of the Vietnam War even played a "central role" in the "informal militia" during the event (Abelmann and Lie 1995: 65).

Aside from these immigrants' military background context from their origin, those images of "vigilante Koreans" had an emblematic signification in an American context, namely, a "signifier" of the "'justice' of Reaganomics as much as the racism of the judicial system" (Palumbo-Liu 1999: 183, 189). As the model minority that stood in a "liminal position" in the "Black/white dichotomy," Asian Americans (including Korean Americans) served as "emblems of the inherent logic of laissez-faire capitalism" and "*self*-affirmative action" whose protective action, therefore, justified American capitalism, as well as its "neutrality" (185–86, 190). The "absence of whites" (183) in those roof Korean memes effectively hides white supremacy in the logic of American capitalism behind the Confucian values of diligence, self-help, and family centeredness, while the actual absence of the white authorities at the time of upheaval led to the "triple scapegoating" of Korean-owned stores, Koreatown, and the Korean community as a whole in the media (Cho 1993: 197).

It is noteworthy, at this point, that the LAPD did not come to help those Koreans and even "cut off traffic out of Koreatown" as a measure of "containment" (Lah 2017): "They found themselves defending the Korean American community as it was abandoned by the public organs of the United States" (Abelmann and Lie 1995: 65). While their heroic roles as the neighborhood patrol somehow expanded the sociospatial scope of those retail storeowners, it was only a limited exertion of their physical ability within the boundary the actual authorities had planned and drawn. This limitation is definitely related to the surrogate aspect of the Black-Korean tension.[3] While the civil unrest started as a direct response to the broadcasting of a video depicting white LAPD officers beating an African American civilian, the tension between Black American protesters and Korean American grocers was escalated through the framing of the Soon Ja Du case and its media coverage in the context of the Rodney King verdict. The Korean American storeowner Du's killing of Latasha Harlins at the suspicion of the African American teen's attempted theft and the Superior Court's decision to sentence Du to probation stirred anger among the African American community, and Korean Americans continuously complained that the media illustrated the major cause of the LA civil unrest as the tension between Blacks and Koreans, rather than that between Blacks and whites (Abelmann and Lie 1995: 151–52; Park 1996: 492). Of course, there was tension between African Americans and Korean Americans. Korean Americans were highly influenced by the negative stereotypes of African Americans in US media, and "the high crime rate inherent in businesses such as liquor or convenience stores" reinforced such prejudice; African Americans, conversely, saw Korean Americans as "callous" and "greedy" and assumed that Koreans "got easy bank loans" (Cho 1993: 200). But, in such antagonistic tension, there was no "inquiry into the structure of an economic system that historically has placed Asians against blacks and Latinos" (Palumbo-Liu 1999: 186). David Palumbo-Liu argues that in this situation Korean Americans were the "white surrogate in the battle of capitalism against chaos" since they were "represented as the frontline forces of the white bourgeoise" (Palumbo-Liu 1994: 369–71). Therefore, those Korean American patrollers' brave acts on the rooftops were represented as supplementing governmental power in exchange for relatively higher status than the protesters guaranteed. I argue that, even though their direct military service as surrogate labor ended when the Vietnam War was over (Lee 2010: 45–46), Koreans have still been serving to maintain the racialized capitalist order inside and outside of American society by conducting (sometimes symbolic) surrogate service, such as voluntary citizen patrol activities and being an orderly model minority.

The LA Koreatown, a neighborhood for a retailer collective, was now displayed in the media as a fortress of the surrogate warfare of Korean Americans protecting the white middle-class American ideal from the angry Black protestors who had been misguided to challenge the system. The fortress, or "buffer zone" (Palumbo-Liu 1994: 371), seems to have carried weight with some Korean American Vietnam veterans by giving them a sense of "rebirth" or a "new vision of the Korean diaspora" in their pursuit to protect their neighborhood "by [their] own power" (Abelmann and Lie 1995: 30). The surrogate military labor in Vietnam and the surrogate semimilitary police labor in Korean America intersect at the point where Koreans are "not afraid to arm themselves against" the minor while being "*in between* the dominant and minor" (Palumbo-Liu 1994: 371). In that sense, when Michael Douglas vandalizes the store of a rude Korean American grocer in the 1993 film *Falling Down*, it must have come to Korean Americans as a reverse-surrogate war of a white middle-class American man standing in for the Black and Latino minorities and hijacking the in-between position from Korean Americans. Those "rude" Korean American store owners in reality had learned and internalized negative stereotypes of African Americans through "U.S. films, television shows, and other popular forms of cultural production" (Cho 1993: 199) predominantly governed by white Hollywood producers, while the same mainstream media industry was now disseminating negative depictions of Korean Americans, targeting the other people of color.

THE ROOF KOREANS REVISITED: THE MASCULINE MYTHOLOGY THAT DEFINES THE CURRENT AGGRESSIVITY TOWARD OTHERS

Twenty-five years after the event, the archival images of those armed Korean Americans, especially those who were depicted in NBC's gunfight scene, have been given a new lease of life by the aforementioned commemorative documentaries. The "roof Koreans" meme has obtained colorful moving image sources and became well known not only in the American domestic context but also in a transnational flow of Korean digital communities and networks. Now that we have examined the historical contexts of LA civil unrest and Korean American vigilantes in both South Korea and the United States, we can return to the initial discussion of the recent internet phenomenon and trace how this meme has been introduced, translated, and localized from an American context into a South Korean one.

The original contexts of the roof Koreans meme are deeply rooted in old typical imageries of the LA riots in the American mainstream media and the uniqueness of these excavated images in terms of the current racial dynamics in the United States. For instance, white nationalist journalist Steve Sailer (2017) posted a picture of self-guarding LA Korean American store owners in 1992, using the hashtag #RoofKoreans, and tweeted that the *Atlantic*'s article "Where Have All the Black-Owned Businesses Gone?" did not "redline" those roof Koreans on their twenty-fifth anniversary, using the specific event of Black-Korean conflict in 1992 as a basis for counterargument to a hardly related, generic analysis of the American society (see fig. 1). An anonymous X (formerly Twitter) user named Captain Kahuna posted the image of the "Roof Korean" Morale Patch sold online,[4] mentioning Reginald Denny, whom a group of Black men had attacked during the 1992 LA riots (Kahuna 2018). Another anonymous X user named Daniel (2019), who claimed to be a Korean American teaching assistant and politically center-right, posted a picture of rooftop Koreans holding rifles and tweeted, "'Self-defense with a gun isn't a real thing.' It is very much a real thing. . . . The rioters stopped burning down Koreatown once the Koreans pulled out their weapons in self-defense," demonstrating the surrogate service of another Korean American model minority. This seemingly pro-gun rights tweet was liked by 1,188 users and retweeted eighty-five times as of February 6, 2023.

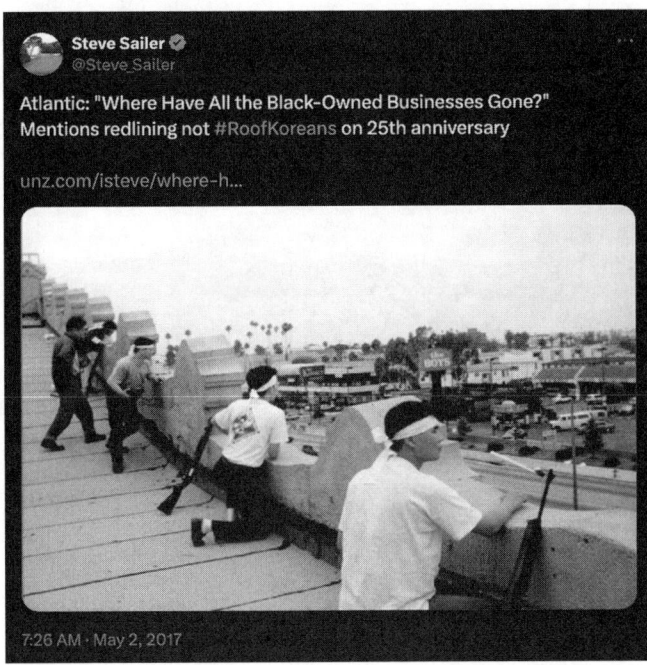

FIGURE 1 Steve Sailer's post on X regarding the *Atlantic*'s article, hashtagging #RoofKoreans.

Several other X users who were liked or retweeted more than a few times usually related these roof Koreans memes with certain libertarian topics, such as gun ownership, self-defense with arms, and, especially during the COVID-19 outbreak, cynicism toward government control (Being Libertarian 2019; A Devoted Yogi 2019; Ken Willey 2020; Rosie's Mylar Turkey Shoot 2020).

Of course, such digital creations easily cross borders and, especially, rapidly appeal to the population that believes they share the same ethnic identity as the referred group. Therefore, recently, even before the BLM movement, it has not been uncommon to find the roof Koreans memes quoted in South Korea's social media content in a positive manner. In a YouTube video published November 12, 2019, viewed 597,407 times as of February 7, 2023, titled "Our Skillful Reserve Forces Dudes in LA Who Established a 'Unit' in Only Four Hours" (KLAB 2019), the story of Korean American shopkeepers who were armed with shotguns and rifles is narrated with interviews and images quoted from various documentaries, becoming a tale of heroism by those who had been trained in South Korea's mandatory military service. This recognition of South Korean veterans' good skill to use guns and well-disciplined bodies to line up for battle seems to serve for self-esteemed masculinity over the average American men who have not been trained in the military, as well as identification of the Korean as the responsible minority who could protect the community against the adversarial group.

This popular mythology of the roof Koreans defines the current aggressivity among some South Koreans. When the BLM movement was taking place in the United States and being reported in South Korean media in 2020, the memory of the roof Koreans was resummoned into South Korea's social media platforms in a

FIGURE 2 "Roof Koreans and Road Koreans" posted on Clien.net, June 3, 2020.

similar manner, placing Korean Americans in the opposite side of the BLM activists and giving the impression that the 1992 situation could be repeated. MBC's YouTube channel published a video on June 4, 2020, titled "Korean Americans Who Went up to the Rooftop during the 1992 LA riots: Why Is It Uncomfortable to Bring Back 'Roof Koreans' at This Time?," questioning the reason why there were many hashtags and memes quoting "roof Koreans" in American English–based social media. While the video is critical about rematching Korean Americans with Black Americans at the time of BLM, its own view of roof Koreans is also problematic. The video's thumbnail image has a headline that translates into "LA reserve forces dudes who fought against Black rioters," showing how even a mainstream South Korean media outlet uses the rhetoric of the brave reserve forces in relating the past event to the current BLM movement and demonizing the African American protesters.

An important point to note is that this aggressivity is rooted in militarism that affirms the military service as the source of South Korean masculinity and, more important, that posits Koreans in a war against the angry mob who are mostly understood as Black. It is suggestive that there are localized roof Korean memes on South Korea's social media platforms and internet communities, which show the masculinized and militarized way of understanding democracy, protest, and safety (see fig. 2). Images like this that recognized roof Koreans were a popular phenomenon in South Korea's internet communities like Clien, regardless of whether the community was liberal or conservative in terms of South Korean domestic politics.[5] Similar images of roof Koreans popularly circulated again in August of the same year when an African-born Black celebrity, Samuel Okyere, publicly criticized a blackface high school yearbook photograph, which shows how the American war between the roof Koreans and Black rioters has been naturalized in South Korea. When Okyere criticized the high school students' mimicking of Ghana's Coffin Dance in blackface by directly quoting those students' yearbook photograph on his Instagram, without anonymizing their faces, many South Korean internet users started regarding his act as an intentional leak of the personal information of those minors. Some of them even tracked back old postings and comments on Okyere's Instagram and found he once had not responded appropriately to a "sexual joke considered racist" (Lee 2020).[6] These two negative issues immediately stained his reputation, and the latter especially helped mobilize Korean male internet users to aggressively damage Okyere's name. The roof Koreans memes appeared again in this context (Oesŏni 2020). By quoting the roof Koreans memes, these South Korean internet users created a virtual war front between ethnic Koreans and Black people in general and stimulated the sense of competitive victimhood by accusing Okyere of being a Black male who has a sense of sexual superiority over Korean men.

When discussing South Korea's collective victimhood, especially "victimhood nationalism," it is frequently related to the nation's colonial past and certain atrocities that happened in such colonial and postcolonial contexts (Im 2021: 23–28). The collective memory of the LA riots in 1992 in South Korea, however, is transnationally summoned to construct a new proto-landscape of victimization to legitimize and justify the racial hierarchy and racialized misogynist system in a globalized, or cosmopolitan South Korea, that is, "victimhood racism" (Kim 2023: 130).[7]

HAN SANG KIM is associate professor of sociology at Ajou University and vice president of the International Visual Sociology Association. He is the author of *Cine-Mobility: Twentieth-Century Transformations in Korea's Film and Transportation* (2022).

NOTES

1. In a previous study on the discourses of BLM in South Korea, Kim (2023: 110–14) observed that online commentators on a Korean-language-based internet community summoned the memory of the LA riots and used phrases that naturalized the mistrust and antagonism between Korean Americans and African Americans.

2. The tone of press comments slightly differed between mainstream newspapers, such as *Chosŏn ilbo* and *Tonga ilbo*, and a then relatively minor but newly rising liberal mouthpiece, *Han'gyŏre*. While both of them seem to have tried to deliver detailed contexts, such as how racial minorities had been marginalized (*Chosŏn ilbo*, May 1, 1992; *Han'gyŏre*, May 1, 1992; *Tonga ilbo*, May 1, 1992); why African Americans had been discontented with Korean American shop owners, especially since the release of Soon Ja Du (*Chosŏn ilbo*, May 1, 1992; *Han'gyŏre*, May 1, 19924; *Tonga ilbo*, May 1, 1992); and how people, including the LA mayor and influential African American leaders, had negatively reacted to the Rodney King verdict until the riot arose (*Chosŏn ilbo*, May 1, 1992; *Han'gyŏre*, May 1, 1992; *Tonga ilbo*, May 1, 1992), the headlines of the mainstream newspapers were more provocative and prejudice oriented than those of *Han'gyŏre*. However, as of 1992, *Han'gyŏre* was still very minor in the market, so its influence on the public might have been small.

3. Invoking Jin-kyung Lee's notion of surrogate labor in South Korea's military engagement in the Vietnam War would be relevant here in understanding such tension. In her book *Service Economies* Lee (2010: 39) argues: "South Korean military labor in the Vietnam War functioned as intranational class surrogate labor for South Korea and as transnational

racialized surrogate labor for the United States, while the South Korean state simultaneously reconstituted such military proletarian labor as a supra-class, ethnonationalist, and masculinist service." The dispatched Korean troops were engaged in surrogate labor in such a double-layer structure of exploitation. The roles and practices those Korean troops conducted in the war defined their own relationship with the ruling class in their home country, as well as that with the ruling race in the global hierarchy.

4. The seller of this item describes this as "the 'Foreign' National Guard.... Nobody messed with these dudes during the 1992 LA Riots. The Roof Korean Morale Patch is a reminder that nobody will screw [you] if you have the higher ground and superior firepower" (https://www.amazon.com/Violent-Little-Machine-Shop-Korean/dp/B075DJ193M).

5. These creators and distributors of South Korean–version roof Koreans memes are presumed to be primarily male users. According to Kim (2023: 128–29), those internet users who were antagonistic against BLM or Sam Okyere's criticism of blackface also showed hostile attitudes toward feminists and people who supported political correctness. Figure 2 demonstrates how those who endorsed this meme hated the disorder and chaotic situations caused by the BLM protests, which also provides supporting evidence for their antagonism against "violent" or "unauthorized" demonstrations by labor unions or human rights activists.

6. According to the news reports, an anonymous follower commented about a South Korean actress in a photo with Okyere, "Cute, once you go black you never go back. Lol," and Okyere responded by writing, "Preach," on his Instagram posting from March 2019 (Lee 2020).

7. According to Kim (2023: 130), *victimhood racism* is defined as "a competitive victimhood consciousness that seeks to secure moral superiority in intergroup relations based on racial identity, by emphasizing that the harms inflicted upon the ingroup are greater or more unjust than those experienced by their adversarial group." Kim's analysis of the discourses of BLM in South Korea shows that the internalized racial identity has formed through the collective memories of the experiences of harm suffered within the ingroup, even though the majority of the ingroup members (South Korean internet users) did not experience the victimization that their imagined ingroup members (Korean Americans in 1992) had to undergo.

REFERENCES

Abelmann, Nancy, and John Lie. 1995. *Blue Dreams: Korean Americans and the Los Angeles Riots*. Cambridge, MA: Harvard University Press.

A Devoted Yogi [pseud.] (@ADevotedYogi). 2019. "History clearly shows us that criminals prefer unarmed victims and easy targets especially when rioting and looting during civil unrest!" *X*, December 17. https://twitter.com/ADevotedYogi/status/1206854302079373312.

Being Libertarian [pseud.] (@beinlibertarian). 2019. "In 1992, Korean-American immigrants in LA were defending their property from being destroyed, and looted by rioting thugs, after the Police, & Government abandoned them, following the Rodney King Verdict." *X*, April 5. https://twitter.com/beinlibertarian/status/1113944309512929281.

Cho, Sumi K. 1993. "Korean Americans vs. African Americans: Conflict and Construction." In *Reading Rodney King/Reading Urban Uprising*, edited by Robert Gooding-Williams, 196–211. London: Routledge.

Daniel [pseud.] (@BigDanielEnergy). 2019. "'Self-defense with a gun isn't a real thing.' It is very much a real thing, thank you very much." *X*, April 10. https://twitter.com/BigDanielEnergy/status/1115876757989658626.

Im Chi-hyŏn (Lim, Jie-Hyun). 2021. *Hŭisaengjaŭisik minjokchuŭi: kot'ongŭl kyŏngjaeng hanŭn chigujŏk kiŏk chŏnjaeng* [Victimhood nationalism: The global war of memory in competitions over pain]. Seoul: Humanist.

Kahuna, Captain [pseud.] (@Captain_Kahuna). 2018. "After the savaging of Reginald Denny, what I remember most clearly: #RoofKoreans ..." *X*, May 1. https://twitter.com/Captain_Kahuna/status/991138069616062464.

Ken Willey [pseud.] (@kenwilley). 2020. "#RoofKoreans taught us that during times of civil unrest you can't depend on the government." *X*, March 17. https://twitter.com/kenwilley /status/1239693880926375936.

Kim, Han Sang. 2023. "P'ihaejaŭisik injongjuŭi: 2020nyŏn yŏrŭm ŭi tu nollan ŭl chungsim ŭro" [Victimhood racism: The two controversies in the summer of 2020 in South Korea]. *Munhwa wa sahoe* [Korean journal of cultural sociology] 31, no. 2: 81–145.

KLAB. 2019. "Ne siganmane 'pudae' mandŭrŏ pŏrin LA yebigun hyŏngnimdŭrŭi tchamba" [Our skillful reserve forces dudes in LA who established a "unit" in only four hours]. YouTube, November 12. https://www.youtube.com/watch?v=J7CSsmo5gjo.

Lah, Kyung. 2017. "The LA Riots Were a Rude Awakening for Korean-Americans." *CNN*, April 29. https://edition.cnn.com/2017/04/28/us/la-riots-korean-americans/index.html.

Lee, Jae-lim. 2020. "Okyere Deletes Instagram Account after Two Controversies." *Korea Joong-Ang Daily*, August 26. https://koreajoongangdaily.joins.com/2020/08/26/entertainment /television/Sam-Okyere-Instagram-deleted-Once-you-go-Black-you-never-go-back /20200826101600728.html.

Lee, Jin-kyung. 2010. *Service Economies: Militarism, Sex Work, and Migrant Labor in South Korea*. Minneapolis: University of Minnesota Press.

Lindsay, Daniel, and T. J. Martin, dirs. 2017. "LA 92." https://www.youtube.com/watch ?v=uaotkHlHJwo.

MBC. 2020. "1992nyŏn LA p'oktong tangsi oksange ollagan kyomindŭl . . . i siguge 'rup'ŭk'orian' sohwani pulp'yŏnhan kkadalgŭn?" [Korean Americans who went up to the rooftop during the 1992 LA riots: Why is it uncomfortable to bring back "roof Koreans" at this time?]. YouTube, June 4. https://www.youtube.com/watch?v=UYNpOGVLrhI.

Moon, Seungsook. 2005. *Militarized Modernity and Gendered Citizenship in South Korea*. Durham, NC: Duke University Press.

Noor, Masi, Johanna Ray Vollhardt, Silvia Mari, and Arie Nadler. 2017. "The Social Psychology of Collective Victimhood." *European Journal of Social Psychology* 47: 121–34.

Oesŏni [pseud.]. 2020. "Miguk sahoe ŭi hŭgin ŭn han'gugin egen kahaeja yŏssŭmnida.jpg" [To Koreans, black people in the American society have been assailants.jpg]. Clien.net, August 7. https://www.clien.net/service/board/park/15249816.

Palumbo-Liu, David. 1994. "Los Angeles, Asians, and Perverse Ventriloquisms: On the Functions of Asian America in the Recent American Imaginary." *Public Culture* 6, no. 2: 365–81.

Palumbo-Liu, David. 1999. *Asian/American: Historical Crossings of a Racial Frontier*. Stanford, CA: Stanford University Press.

Park, Kyeyoung. 1996. "Use and Abuse of Race and Culture: Black-Korean Tension in America." *American Anthropologist* 98, no. 3: 492–99.

Rosie's Mylar Turkey Shoot [pseud.] (@DarnelSugarfoo). 2020. "The mayor of Los Angeles wants to keep the city locked down for 'at least 2 months.' Things will get interesting. [laughs in rooftop Korean]." *X*, March 27. https://twitter.com/DarnelSugarfoo/status /1243389290572156928.

Sailer, Steve (@Steve_Sailer). 2018. "Atlantic: 'Where Have All the Black-Owned Businesses Gone?' Mentions redlining not #RoofKoreans on 25th anniversary https://./.unz.com/isteve /where-have-all-the-Black-owned-businesses-gone." *X*, May 2. https://twitter.com/Steve _Sailer/status/859172313853435904.

YUKO KAWAI

Studying Race and Racism in South Korean and Japanese Contexts

ABSTRACT This commentary introduces cases in Japan similar to those depicted in the five contributions to this forum and discusses the necessity of attending to the local concept of race to study race and racism in South Korea and Japan. The five articles evoke two cases that occurred in Japan. Like South Korea, Japan is well known for its strong and persistent myth of homogeneity despite the presence of diverse ethnic/racial (or racialized) minority groups: the Indigenous Ainu, Okinawans (or Ryūkyūans) who ran an independent kingdom across many small islands before Japan colonized it in the late nineteenth century, Koreans who migrated to Japan against the backdrop of Japan's colonization of the Korean Peninsula, return migrants from Brazil and Peru, increasing numbers of migrants from China and other Asian countries, "mixed-blood" persons, and many others. The myth of South Korea or Japan as a monoethnic/racial nation has played a significant role in racial problems in both countries. Intersecting race with gender, nation, class, science, military, and memory, the forum contributors raise many other important issues. However, this commentary focuses on the local concept of race, which is tied to the myth of monoethnic/racial nationhood and the author's research interests.

KEYWORDS imperialism, Japan, mixed race, race and racism, South Korea

JAPAN'S TWO CASES

The first case is the "mixed-bloods problem" in the 1950s. In 1945 Japan was defeated in World War II and placed under the occupation of the General Headquarters of the Supreme Commander for the Allied Powers, led by the United States, until 1952. During this period approximately one million American soldiers in total were stationed in Japan (Dower 1999: 206), with over 450,000 in the country at the peak (Aoki 2011: 37). Some of them fathered children with Japanese women, and most of these children were born from prostitution, concubinage, and/or rape (Kamita 2018: 31). One estimation is that less than 10 percent of American fathers married Japanese women and took care of their children (Kano 2007: 221). During the occupation of Japan, Allied headquarters had suppressed news reports on mixed-blood children. However, Japanese media started to give them huge media coverage after the occupation ended in 1952. Although Japanese media spread the misinformation that their number was approximately 150,000–200,000, later a governmental survey found that the actual number was around 5,000 (Kano 2007: 224).

Inga Kim Diederich's article in this issue's forum, addressing mixed-blood Koreans, describes state-involved eugenicist interrogation of mixed-blood Korean bodies. In the 1950s state-backed Japanese scientists also performed a large-scale study in which they scrutinized white and Black mixed-blood Japanese bodies, collecting biological and phenotypical data (e.g., blood, fingerprint, skin and eye color, hair color and texture), as well as data on their personality and intelligence (Sakano 2009: 199). The dominant view of mixed-blood Japanese children, particularly those with one Black parent, was as "misfits" who would disrupt the "racial purity" of the Japanese and the social homogeneity of Japanese society (Kano 2007; Sakano 2009: 200). Like Korean media, which represented mixed-blood children as symbolizing Korean women's immorality, vice, or indulgence, Japanese media depicted the Japanese counterparts negatively as promiscuous, shameful, or betrayers of the nation (Kano 2007: 228–32).

People problematized in the "mixed-bloods problem" were those who were born between a foreign man and a Japanese woman (Shimoji 2018: 75–88). Before Japan's Nationality Act was revised in 1985, citizenship was passed down through the male line: children of a Japanese man and his foreign wife acquired Japanese nationality at birth, whereas children of a Japanese woman and her foreign husband did not. Mixed-blood children with Japanese fathers were officially categorized as Japanese and were neither counted as part of the mixed-blood population nor subjected to eugenicist scrutiny. Sunhye Kim's article on IVF (in vitro fertilization) in this forum mentions different evaluations of donated eggs and sperms: donated eggs from non-Korean Asian women are preferable to sperm donated by non-Korean Asian men. The difference is tied to the former Korean citizenship laws, which automatically granted Korean nationality to children born between a Korean man and his foreign spouse, but not to those born between a Korean woman and her foreign spouse. The two examples of South Korea and Japan demonstrate the intersection of race, gender, and nation, illuminating the patriarchal ideology of the father determining the race/ethnicity/nationality of the child.

The Japanese government implemented two measures to make mixed-blood persons invisible in Japan, which contributed to establishing Japan's myth of monoethnic/racial nationhood. One measure was sending children raised in orphanages to the United States to be adopted. By the mid-1950s, approximately twenty-five hundred were sent as "refugees" to the United States, since the US Immigration Act prohibited immigration from Asia at that time (Minamikawa 2015: 150). Another was assimilating those who stayed in Japan simply as Japanese, by endorsing "the principle of nondiscrimination and equality," meaning that mixed-blood children were to be treated the same as other Japanese children (Shimoji 2018: 88–120).

This principle overlaps with the "don't investigate, don't document" policy discussed in Ga Young Chung and Hee Jung Choi's contribution on "multicultural soldiers." After conducting a population survey on mixed-blood children a few times in the 1950s, the Japanese government stopped, while eugenicist scientific studies continued until the 1970s (Sakano 2009: 201–3). In addition, Japan's census questionnaires after World War II have included only one question about respondents' nationality and none about their ethnic/racial background. Japan's Nationality Act did not and still does not permit adults to hold multiple citizenships. Therefore, mixed-blood persons and ethnic/racial minorities, such as the Ainu, Okinawans, and Koreans and Chinese with Japanese citizenship, have been all recorded simply as Japanese. Just as South Korea's policy obscured the marginalization of South Korean multicultural soldiers, Japan's principle also hid similar practices against mixed-blood persons and other ethnic/racial minorities. Consequently, racism becomes "somebody else's problem." Han Sang Kim's article in this forum introduces online comments such as "Are we in the US here?" and "Are you American?" to accuse people who criticized high school students using blackface and to defend the students' action. Such comments reflect the attitude that racism is not a South Korean problem but an American problem. Likewise, racism in Japan has been generally seen as a foreign problem (e.g., Kawai 2015).

The second case occurred in Otaru, a port city of Hokkaido, the northernmost island of Japan (Arudou 2018: 55–63). In 1999 a white American man and other foreign nationals were barred from entering a public bath, which had put up the "Japanese only" sign written in Japanese, English, and Russian.[1] Similar signs appeared in Otaru public baths in the 1990s when Russian sailors started to visit frequently, and the facilities received complaints from Japanese customers that they were not following Japanese public bath rules and causing hygiene problems (Arudou 2003: 34, 97). The American man changed his citizenship to Japanese and visited the public bath again as a naturalized Japanese citizen in 2000, but he was still denied entry. He and two foreign nationals sued the public bath and the city of Otaru in 2001, and the court found the bathhouse guilty of racial discrimination.

Sohoon Yi's contribution to this forum discusses the 2011 incident of a marriage migrant woman from Uzbekistan who was refused entry to a public sauna. The sauna put up a "no foreigners" sign because of Korean customers' fear that they might "catch AIDS," which is akin to the case of the "Japanese only" sign posted due to Japanese customers' complaint of foreigners causing hygiene problems. Depicting a group as spreaders of disease is an often-used racist rhetoric. For example, in the late nineteenth and early twentieth centuries, Jews were "viewed in biological terms as a race that carried tainted and diseased blood in its veins, a course of dangerous 'bacilli,' of venereal disease and vague but horrifying germs, that threatened to infect European society" (McMaster 2001: 92).

PLURALIZING RACE AND RACISM

The perception that race and racism are Western (i.e., American and European) matters has been prevalent both inside and outside of academia. Race, which European and later American intellectuals started to conceptualize in the eighteenth century, is undoubtedly a Western product (e.g., Hannaford 1996: 6; Rattansi 2007: 23). The Western concept of race and race theories were accepted as scientific knowledge and spread around the world. Yet, they were appropriated in non-Western contexts, which led to producing the local concept of race and different racisms (see Kawai 2015, 2020). Nevertheless, race and racism in Asian contexts have been studied insufficiently, or if done, they are often classified as something else, such as discrimination, xenophobia, ethnocentrism, or nationalism. Even today, both academically and popularly, race still most commonly refers to Black, Brown, red, white, and yellow, and racism is largely viewed as a white problem.

When race denotes these dominant color categories, it does not seem appropriate to call racism those discriminatory practices that involve one group of yellow people against another, such as those by Japanese against Koreans or by Koreans against Vietnamese. However, race comprises not just categories but also a concept or an abstracted thought. Étienne Balibar (1991: 100) claims that "the symbolic kernel of the idea of race . . . is the schema of genealogy, that is, quite simply the idea that the filiation of individuals transmits from generation to generation a substance both biological and spiritual and thereby inscribes them in a temporal community known as 'kinship.'" If race is understood as this core idea, any "ethnic" or "national" group can become a race—a group of "family members" passing down physical and cultural traits through generations.

However, racialization does not occur in the same way. For example, in the American notion of the "one-drop rule," people were designated as Black if they had a single Black ancestor, while the existence of a single white ancestor did not qualify a person as white. Western knowledge, culture, and institutions have often been seen as "universal," "norms," or "global standards" without its particularity being fully acknowledged. Likewise, racialization in the West tends to be directed more intensely at nonwhite peoples, assigning particularity to the nonwhite others while universalizing the white self. As Richard Dyer (1997) succinctly phrases, "Other people are raced, we [whites] are just people" (1), or "whites are not of a certain race, they're just the human race" (3).

In contrast, the Koreans and the Japanese, who have been racialized under the Western gaze (and the Japanese gaze for the Koreans, discussed later), cannot be "just people" or "just the human race." Thus, their racialization begins with racializing themselves, which is more central than racializing others. This explains why what Sohoon Yi calls "double racialization" occurs and why some racial others, such as Korean biracial populations, are not seen as a reproducible group and thus do not seem to be fully racialized based on the "schema of genealogy."

Moreover, racialization practiced by white peoples is not monolithic. In the context of Britain's or France's overseas imperialism, in which they colonized nonwhite peoples outside of Europe, the British or the French would be "just people" while racializing Black, Brown, red, and yellow others (Arendt 1966). On the other hand, in Germany's continental imperialism, derived from the "frustrated ambition of countries which did not get [or retain] their share" in the Western colonization of Africa and Asia in the late nineteenth century, they subjected other white peoples to its rule (Arendt 1966: 227). In this case, the Germans could not be "just people" and instead needed to stress their particularity by engaging in self-racialization, because differences between the Germans and other white peoples, including the Jews, were less physically distinct than those between the Germans and other races.

Japan engaged in an imperialism similar to Germany's, subjugating other yellow peoples under its rule, which necessitated the production of an additional concept of race (Kawai 2015, 2020). The Western concept of race, which was translated into Japanese as *jinshu* (人種), was imported along with Western race theories as scientific knowledge in the nineteenth century. However, the Japanese were lumped in with other peoples in Asia as yellow, Mongoloid, Oriental, or Asian—an "inferior" race—and were placed below the white race in the Western racial hierarchy. Japanese intellectuals created the local concept of race, *minzoku* (民族), to differentiate the Japanese from other yellow peoples such as the Koreans and the Chinese and make Japan's own racial hierarchy in which the Japanese were able to become a "superior" race. The term *minzoku* started to appear in the Japanese language between the late 1880s and the early 1890s and came into popular use in the 1900s (Yasuda 1992: 66). During this period, Japan established itself as an imperial nation-state, fighting the First Sino-Japanese War (1894–95) and the Russo-Japanese War (1904–5) and thereby acquiring colonies in Asia.

Minzoku drew influence from the German concept of *Volk* (e.g., Kawata 1999: 457–58; 2009: 138; Morris-Suzuki 1998: 87; Yoon 1994: 42–44), which embraced the core idea of race—the "schema of genealogy." Differentiating the Germans from other peoples in Europe, such as the French and the Jews (e.g., Hutton 2005: 7–8), *Volk* defined the German nation as a linguistic cultural group and yet racialized them by treating their culture and language as "biological" traits passed down from German ancestors and viewing the German people as "plants" rooted in the homeland (Hutton 2005: 18–20). Similarly, the concept of *minzoku* portrayed the Japanese nation as a racialized cultural group by essentializing Japanese language and culture and imagining the Japanese as "children" of the emperor and thus having "blood ties" with one another. After World War II, the Japanese avoided the word *minzoku* in self-reference due to its close association with Japan's prewar imperialism. Today, the Japanese rarely call themselves *Nihon* or *Yamato* (Japan) *minzoku*, referring to themselves simply as *Nihon* (Japan) *jin* (human). However, the idea of *minzoku* has remained in the postwar meaning of the Japanese, which manifests in the influential myth of Japan as a monoethnic/racial or, in Japanese, *tan'itsu minzoku* (a single *minzoku*, 単一民族) nation, a popular term to describe Japan despite the name of the *minzoku* being unspecified (see Kawai 2015, 2020).

Although more studies are needed, *minzoku*'s influence on the Korean concept of race cannot be completely dismissed. The word 民族 was adopted into the Chinese, Korean, and Vietnamese languages soon after the word was created in Japan (Kawata 2009: 136). Against the backdrop of Japan's colonization of the Korean Peninsula, modern Korean identity has been unavoidably entangled with the Japanese counterpart (see contributions by Diederich and by Yi in this forum). When the Japanese imagined themselves as a *minzoku*, or "a group tied in blood" (*kettō dantai*) (Hozumi 1910: 1), and subjugated the Koreans as colonial subjects, the Koreans would also become a *minchok* (the Korean pronunciation of 民族) to defy subjugation under Japan's colonial rule.

In addition, the term *mixed blood* or 混血, which is pronounced as *honhyŏl* in Korean and as *konketsu* in Japanese, is inseparable from the concept of *minzoku*. *Konketsu* came into popular use in the Japanese language in the 1900s (Okamura 2013: 28) when the word *minzoku* was popularized. This is not a coincidence, because *mixed bloods* premises and reifies people who are "pure bloods" or 純血 (pronounced as *sunhyŏl* in Korean and *junketsu* in Japanese) or, more specifically, the Japanese *minzoku*. In Japan, the word *konketsu* ceased to be used publicly in the early 2000s, after Japanese advocacy groups disputed the term as discriminatory because it contrasted with *junketsu*, or "pure blood," which assumed a "superior" position

(Okamura 2016: 42). However, mixed-blood Japanese continue to be differentiated from pure-blood Japanese by using the word *hafu* ("half" in English), which was popularized in the 1970s and is currently the most popularly used term for mixed-blood Japanese (see, e.g., Imoto and Horiguchi 2016).

To further advance race and racism studies and intervene in racial problems in Asian contexts, it is necessary to examine how the dominant Western and local concepts (or, more precisely, categories) of race are deployed in each problem. Seemingly contradictory cases discussed in this forum can be better understood by attending to the selective use of the two concepts. For example, while "multicultural soldiers" included mixed bloods born between one Korean parent and one non-Korean Asian parent (see Chung and Choi, this forum), Asian-Korean mixed bloods were not subjected to eugenicist surveys, whose main targets were children of a white or Black parent and a Korean parent (see Diederich, this forum). In the former, Asian mixed-blood soldiers are assigned to the "them" (non-Korean) based on the local concept of race, whereas in the latter, Asian mixed-blood children are included as part of the "us" (Korean) based on the Western concept of race.

For another example, on the one hand, Korean couples who underwent IVF welcomed donor eggs from Taiwanese women (see S. Kim, this forum), and Korean men in rural areas looking for marriage partners chose Chinese and Vietnamese women because of their physical and cultural similarities to Koreans (see Yi, this forum). On the other hand, mixed-blood or "multicultural" children born between Korean and non-Korean Asian parents were discriminated against because they were not "pure-blood" Koreans (Yi, this forum). With IVF, non-Korean Asians are viewed as part of the "us" (Korean), employing the dominant Western concept of race, whereas Asian mixed-blood Korean children are excluded from the "us," employing the local concept.

Attending to the local concept of race will be helpful to acknowledge racism as "our" problem. Korean online users employed the memory of the 1992 Los Angeles riots to trivialize the Black Lives Matter (BLM) movement and justify students using blackface in South Korea (see H. S. Kim, this forum). In this case, they grasp race and racism only with reference to the Western concept of race, in which Koreans in South Korea are a racial minority group or victims of racism. Yet, the local concept of race shows that they, the racial majority group in South Korea, can be instigators of racism. As Sohoon Yi and Han Sang Kim point out in the editors' introduction to this forum, Western racial problems, those in the United States in particular, tend to draw more attention in general and regulate what is counted as race or racism. Undoubtedly racial problems in South Korea and Japan share more similarities than those in the United States, and yet as a former colonizer, Japan has different problems from those in South Korea. We need to discern racial problems more contextually and engage in more dialogues among scholars who study issues concerning race and racism in Asian and other contexts that have received less attention.

YUKO KAWAI is professor of communication in the Department of Intercultural Communication at Rikkyo University in Tokyo, Japan.

NOTE

1. The sign read "Gaikokujin no kata no nyūjyō wo okotowari itashimasu" (We refuse entry to foreigners) in Japanese and "Japanese only" in English. The literal meaning of the Russian sentence is not certain.

REFERENCES

Aoki, Shin. 2011. "Nihon hondo ni okeru beigun kichi no bunpu to hensen" 日本「本土」における米軍基地の分布と変遷 [A historical review of the distribution and evolution of US military bases in mainland Japan]. *Dōjidaishi kenkyū* 同時代史研究 4: 36–52.

Arendt, Hannah. 1966. *The Origins of Totalitarianism*. London: Harcourt.

Arudou, Debito 有道出人. 2003. *Japanīzu onrī* ジャパニーズ・オンリー [Japanese only]. Tokyo: Akashi shoten.

Arudou, Debito. 2018. *Embedded Racism: Japan's Visible Minorities and Racial Discrimination*. Lanham, MD: Lexington Books.

Balibar, Étienne. 1991. "The Nation Form: History and Ideology." In *Race, Nation, Class: Ambiguous Identities*, by Étienne Balibar and Immanuel Wallerstein, 86–106. London: Verso.

Dower, John W. 1999. *Embracing Defeat: Japan in the Wake of World War II*. New York: Norton.

Dyer, Richard. 1997. *White: Essays on Race and Culture*. New York: Routledge.

Kamita, Seiji 上田誠二. 2018. *'Konketsuji' no sengoshi*「混血児」の戦後史 [The postwar history of Japanese "mixed-bloods"]. Tokyo: Seikyūsha.

Kano, Mikiyo 加納実紀代. 2007. "'Konketsuji' mondai to tan'itsu minzoku shinwa no seisei"「混血児」問題と単一民族神話の生成 [The "mixed-bloods" problem and the formation of the myth of monoethnic/racial nationhood]. In *Senryō to sei* 占領と性 (Occupation and sex), edited by Keisen jyogakuen daigaku heiwa bunka kenkyujo, 213–60. Tokyo: Impakuto shuppankai.

Kawai, Yuko. 2015. "Deracialised Race, Obscured Racism: Japaneseness, Western and Japanese Concepts of Race, and Modalities of Racism." *Japanese Studies* 35, no. 1: 23–47.

Kawai, Yuko. 2020. *A Transnational Critique of Japaneseness: Cultural Nationalism, Racism, and Multiculturalism in Japan*. Lanham, MD: Lexington Books.

Kawata, Junzo 川田順造. 1999. "Minzoku gainen ni tsuite no memo"「民族」概念についてのメモ [On the concept of *minzoku*]. *Minzokugaku kenkyū* 民族学研究 63: 451–61.

Kawata, Junzo 川田順造. 2009. "Minzoku." In *Bunka jinruigaku jiten* 文化人類学事典 [Encyclopedia of cultural anthropology], edited by Nihon bunka jinrui gakkai, 136–41. Tokyo: Maruzen.

Hannaford, Ivan. 1996. *Race: The History of an Idea in the West*. Baltimore, MD: Johns Hopkins University Press.

Hozumi, Yatsuka 穂積八束. 1910. *Kokumin kyōiku: Aikokushin* 国民教育:愛国心 [National education: Patriotism]. Tokyo: Yūhikaku. https://dl.ndl.go.jp/info:ndljp/pid/754600.

Hutton, Christopher M. 2005. *Race and the Third Reich*. Cambridge: Polity.

Imoto, Yuki, and Sachiko Horiguchi. 2016. "Historicizing Mixed-Race Representations in Japan." In *Multiculturalism in East Asia: A Transnational Exploration of Japan, South Korea, and Taiwan*, edited by Koichi Iwabuchi, Hyun Mee Kim, and Hsiao-Chuan Hsia, 163–82. London: Rowman and Littlefield.

McMaster, Neil. 2001. *Racism in Europe*. New York: Palgrave.

Minamikawa, Fuminori 南川文里. 2015. "Posuto senryōki ni okeru nichibei kan no imin to sono kanri" ポスト占領期における日米間の移民とその管理 [US-Japan migration and control in the post-occupation era]. *Ritsumeikan kokusai kenkyū* 立命館国際研究 28, no. 1: 145–61.

Morris-Suzuki, Tessa. 1998. *Re-inventing Japan: Time, Space, Nation*. New York: Sharpe.

Okamura, Hyoue 岡村兵衛. 2013. "'Konketsu' wo meguru gensetsu"「混血」をめぐる言説 [Discourses on "mixed blood"]. *Kokusai bunkagaku* 国際文化学 26: 23–47.

Okamura, Hyoue 岡村兵衛. 2016. "'Hafu' wo meguru gensetsu" 「ハーフ」をめぐる言説 [Discourses on "hafu"]. In *Jinshu shinwa wo kaitaisuru 3* 人種神話を解体する3 [Dismantling the race myth, vol. 3], edited by Kohei Kawashima and Yasuko Takezawa, 37–67. Tokyo: Tokyo daigaku shuppankai.

Rattansi, Ali. 2007. *Racism: A Very Short Introduction*. Oxford: Oxford University Press

Sakano, Toru 坂野徹. 2009. "Konketsu to tekiō nōryoku" 混血と適応能力 [Mixed blood and adaptability]. In *Jinshu no hyōshō to shakaiteki riaritii* 人種の表象と社会的リアリティ [Racial representations and social realities], edited by Yasuko Takezawa, 188–215. Tokyo: Iwanami shoten.

Shimoji, Lawrence Yoshitaka 下地ローレンス吉孝. 2018. *'Konketsu' to 'nihonjin'* 「混血」と「日本人」 ["Mixed bloods" and "the Japanese"]. Tokyo: Seidosha.

Yasuda, Hiroshi 安田浩. 1992. "Kindai Nihon ni okeru minzoku kannen no keisei" 近代日本における『民族』観念の形成 [Construction of the concept of *minzoku* in modern Japan]. *Shisō to gendai* 思想と現代 31: 61–72.

Yoon, Keun Cha 尹健次. 1994. *Minzoku gensō no satetsu* 民族幻想の蹉跌 [The failure of the illusion of *minzoku*]. Tokyo: Iwanami shoten.

BOOK REVIEWS

CHINA & INNER ASIA

Animals in Chinese Religion and Science

In the Land of Tigers and Snakes: Living with Animals in Medieval Chinese Religion. By Huaiyu Chen. New York: Columbia University Press, 2023. xi, 271 pp. ISBN: 9780231202619.

Animals and Plants in Chinese Religions and Science. By Huaiyu Chen. London: Anthem, 2023. vii, 205 pp. ISBN: 9781839985010.

Human contact with other animals helped to shape Chinese religious practice from at least the beginnings of China's "medieval" age. It seems likely, for example, that the practice, appearing in the early centuries CE—the first glimmerings of that age—of placing protective objects in tombs to ward their occupants from the dreaded spiritual contagion called *zhu* 注, or "miasma," was in part a reaction to the terrible spread of animal-borne diseases characteristic of the age, caused, again in part, by the expansion of the Eastern Han empire into new animal habitats.[1] The "battle for habitats"[2] that resulted from this imperial expansion is also visible in texts from slightly later periods, where the need for religious and medical practitioners to arm themselves against animals dangerous to them on forays into their habitats became a central feature in the development of ritual talismans, seals, and other objects key to Chinese religious practice.[3] Indeed, though demons and ghosts are often blamed for the ills of humans, examining these materials, it can often seem that it was the history of human immersion in the worlds of their fellow animals that inspired the needs for many of the elements that came to dominate Chinese religion through the centuries. A study, rooted in environmental history, of actual human interspecies contact and its deep and wide-ranging influences on the history of Chinese religion would thus greatly improve our understanding. Huaiyu Chen's 2023 book *In the Land of Tigers and Snakes: Living with Animals in Medieval Chinese Religion*, though it does survey some forms of physical encounter between humans and other animals and is set against its background—chapter 2, for example, gives a helpful overview of hunting practices—instead focuses squarely on the human side, on elements in the human *imagination* of animals in this age of unprecedented growth in habitat incursion, on what Chen describes as the ways that "medieval people redefined animals and themselves, based on their literary, cultural, and life experiences with animals" (8).

In doing this, *In the Land of Tigers and Snakes* makes valuable contributions to our understanding of the character and workings of Chinese Buddhist, Ruist, and Daoist writings. It does so largely in terms native to those discourses rather than terms central to contemporary environmental or Anthropocene criticism. So, for example, in chapter 1's study of animals in the elite priest Daoxuan's writings, the picture of "animals" excludes humans. As Chen says, "Use of the word 'animals' in this study refers only to nonhuman animals" (16). He has, of course, clear reasons for doing this. This was, after all, Daoxuan's own distinction—for, according to traditional Buddhist understandings, the human and the animal constituted different orders of beings entirely, each shaped within separate trajectories of rebirth in the Buddhist cosmos. But in analytically separating humans and other animals in this way—and in effect taking the path of writing a basically Buddhist or traditional Chinese study of Buddhist and traditional Chinese thought—the book loses opportunities both to enter easier conversation with the contemporary fields of animal studies and environmental criticism and, more to the point, to offer readers a thoroughgoing critical analysis of Daoxuan's positions, and those of Buddhism as a whole, from a vantage point located outside them. As a study of Chinese Buddhist thought in the traditional "buddhological" mode, however, and especially of the ways that its Indic inheritance had to be reshaped within its new intellectual and biotic communities, the chapter is expert. Chen, starting with his first book, *The Revival of Buddhist Monasticism in Medieval China*, has become one of our best interpreters of Daoxuan's methods as a thinker and reader. This book extends that project by showing how animal imagery helped this Tang Buddhist bring the vast and originally alien Buddhist tradition into legibility.

The following chapters are just as illuminating. Chapter 2 examines animal imagery in an impressive range of sources, from imperial histories to tomb inscriptions, showing how their careful reading reveals, among other things, deep shifts in the human world of governmental power. Chapter 3 focuses in large part on hagiographical tropes of Buddhist monks taming, or living in harmony with tigers, mainly as ways to make clear the monks profound spiritual mastery. It contains, as well, a helpful comparison of similar imagery in European Christian accounts of figures such as Saint Anthony and Saint Francis. Chapter 4 turns mainly to Daoist texts, where tigers—especially in the contrastive pair of tamed versus wild/violent—were, in ways parallel to the ways they were used by Buddhists, figures employed to illuminate the transformative powers of the Daoist master. Chapter 5 presents tales of Buddhists and snakes, delving (among other things) into the ways their very real dangers to people were at times twisted together in Buddhist writings with strains of misogyny ever present in the human cultures that produced them. The final chapter returns to a study of a single author's work, centering here on the lay Buddhist Wei Gao's (745–805) epitaph for a parrot. Like the other essays in the book, it uses Wei's parrot imagery to explore elements in the nature of the political and religious history of its age. Like the other chapters, too, it displays the depth of Chen's sinological learning, his skills in using the full range of textual materials available to him, from transmitted literature to excavated media like manuscripts and epigraphy (visual images appear as sources in the book as well, though they are never given the same close analysis as the texts). The reader, finishing this book, will have gained a wealth of new insights into the religious writings of medieval China.

Yet—and this is perhaps a personal complaint—the book shows little interest in actual environmental or interspecies history, opting instead always for discussions of the symbolic or discursive animal over the real one. Again, the book is a skillful and helpful discussion of discourses of animals across Chinese religious traditions. But I think—given the exciting recent growth in both environmental history, including that of China, and of transspecies approaches in the "humanities"—that readers can reasonably expect a study like this to embrace methods beyond the anthropocentric philology that has characterized religious studies for so long. Of the increase in tiger attacks on humans in the period, which had such a dramatic impact on the religious imagination in China, Chen mentions only in passing, in an endnote (197n5), that these were due in large part to mass deforestation and other forms of habitat destruction (indeed, neither "deforestation" nor "habitat" is to be found in the index). Surely, there is more there to structure a study of humans "living with animals." Oddly, the final pages of the epilogue, on contemporary concerns, which take a very different approach to thinking about animals than that found elsewhere in the book, would seem to agree. The "land of tigers and snakes" the book is concerned with is rich and fruitful symbolic terrain, but much less the living biomes shared by both human and nonhuman animals in medieval China.

Chen's second book, *Animals and Plants in Chinese Religions and Science*, is, in this respect, often more satisfying. This is especially true of its first three chapters, two on plants and one on a "cult of the pig" and its relationship with divination. The chapters on plants succeed in these terms in large part because traditional Chinese writings on plants, owing in good part to their centrality in medicine, were so much more extensive and detailed than those on animals. The first chapter, "Plant Science and Technology in Medieval China," provides a detailed survey of the plant-based material culture of the period. It gives a brief but wide-ranging and often vivid picture of the natures, uses, and origins of the timbers, papers, textiles, aromatics, spices, foods, drinks, ornamentals, and other plant-based things that helped power the metabolism of medieval Chinese societies. It gives special attention to trees and the products made from them: cooking and eating utensils, oils, buildings and ships, carts and sedan chairs, printing blocks, and so on. Helpfully here, Chen does place the primary sources he relies on within their historical context of mass deforestation and dramatic habitat change driven by the need for such materials. In doing this, the chapter makes clear that the age's dramatic growth in studies of plants was a feature of these human projects and not, for the most part, of a desire to understand the nonhuman world for itself. The discussion provides the kind of background that would have been helpful in *In the Land of Tigers and Snakes*—and, indeed, first raises a question I found myself asking again and again in my reading of this second book: Why are these two books and not one larger and more encompassing, deeper, and more synthetic study? The question arose most sharply in chapter 2, "Ordering Plants in the Buddhist World: A Medieval Botanical Taxonomy," which returns to Daoxuan and makes many of the same points about his view of the natural world made in the first chapter of the first book: his approach to plants, as it was to animals, for example, shows how he synthesized Indic pictures within Chinese culture and within a northeast Asian bioregion. Indeed, mirroring Chen's revelations about Daoxuan's treatment of animals, specifically a northern Chinese bioregion: southern plants such as mangoes, so important in India and Indic writings, were absent from Daoxuan's revision of the received picture. Again, one of the great contributions of both books is to show the depths to which, and the fine levels of detail at which, Indic cosmologies were remade by Chinese Buddhists. The two chapters, one from each book, on Daoxuan's classifications would have made a truly helpful and fully coherent second chapter in a larger book.

The remaining substantive chapters of the book return to the study of animal imagery. The third chapter, "Animal Divination and Climate: An Environmental Perspective on the Cult of the Pig," is, for me, the high point of both books. Perhaps because it was originally written for a journal of environmental criticism—and nearly all the chapters of this book were first written for journals or edited volumes—it engages environmental history at a deeper level than do other chapters. In doing so it succeeds in good part in achieving its aims: "[documenting] the processes by which these deities developed [by providing] a fresh perspective on the ecological and environmental context in which the pig's behavior was understood, depicted, and interpreted" (59). We see how careful observation of pigs' behavioral affinities for wet environments within a climate characterized by seasonal monsoons contributed to the development of a form of divination intended to predict rainfall and flood. Chen shows decisively here productive interrelations between human practice, animal behavior, and climate. The three chapters that follow, however—"Zoomancy in Medieval China," "The Changing Images of Zodiac Animals in Medieval Chinese Buddhist Literature," and "The Were-tigers in Medieval China and Its [*sic*] Asian Contexts"—do not continue this method but return to philological approaches. Like others in both books, they present helpful pictures of how close examinations of animal imagery in Chinese religious thought clarify continuities and changes within its various traditions. The final chapter, "The Animal Turn in Asian Studies and the Asian Turn in the [*sic*] Animal Studies," is a collection of Chen's reviews of recent books in Asian animal studies strung together with little attempt at editing them into a coherent whole. In fact, it must be said that the book would have been greatly improved by a firmer editorial hand. The chapters are distinctly uneven in their copyediting, with those that first appeared in academic journals showing fewer grammatical errors than those that first appeared in other sorts of venues or those that seem to have been written for this book.

These two books have much to offer, and I hope that they inspire a real and lasting turn in the study of Chinese religions toward their fulsome contextualization within environmental history and criticism. Toward this end, in the conclusions to certain chapters, Chen provides brief but welcome comments about the ethics of scholarship here in the "Anthropocene." May other scholars, and Chen himself, carry this forward in future work.

PAUL COPP
University of Chicago
DOI: 10.1215/00219118-11591209

Notes

1. On this expansion into new habitats, see, for example, Robert B. Marks, *China: An Environmental History* (Lanham, MD: Rowman and Littlefield, 2017), 108–9.

2. Mark Elvin, *The Retreat of the Elephants: An Environmental History of China* (New Haven, CT: Yale University Press, 2006), 54.

3. See, for example, the "Dengshe" 登涉 [Climbing mountains and fording streams] chapter of Ge Hong's 葛洪 (ca. 280–ca. 343) *Baopuzi* 抱朴子 [The master who embraces the unhewn].

Fantastic Fauna from China to Crimea: Image-Making in Eurasian Nomadic Societies, 700 BCE–500 CE. By Petya Andreeva. Edinburgh: Edinburgh University Press, 2024. xvi, 316 pp. ISBN: 9781399528528.

In this new volume, Petya Andreeva provides a comprehensive examination of the visual imagery of Iron Age pastoralist societies across northern Eurasia. Generously illustrated with 106 figures, the book engages with a wide range of interdisciplinary sources and provides a thorough review of previous interpretations of zoomorphic imagery traditionally termed "animal-style" art. While the theoretical coverage is inclusive, the approach is firmly rooted within an art history approach. The book consists of six thematically structured chapters that examine image making from roughly 700 BCE to 500 CE. As the author states at the outset, one of the key aims of the volume is to "decipher and understand the underlying principles of image-making along the Eurasian steppe network and trace its distant echoes in China and other parts of Central Eurasia" (6–7). Rather than focusing on the origins and geographical transmission of "animal-style" art, the volume reframes it as a process of zoomorphic image making that was entangled within a broader visual rhetoric of "super-elites" within Iron Age pastoralist communities.

Chapter 1 frames the conceptual and methodological focus of the volume and briefly introduces the specific themes explored in the subsequent chapters. The author draws intently on foundational works by Ernst Gombrich, Erving Goffman, Wilhelm Worringer, and Alois Riegl.[1] She also emphasizes the need to move beyond simplistic culture historical associations and ethnonyms (Scythians, Saka, Sarmatians, etc.) first generated by early Greek, Persian, and Chinese writers. Instead, she focuses on broader networks of communication, interaction, and collective memory that facilitated the creation, use, and spatial diffusion of "animal-style" art. This provides an important perspective for examining image making as a more dynamic component of social identity formation, cultural interaction, and political alliance building.

Chapter 2 introduces the concept of "image-making" (19) and offers a wide-ranging exploration of zoomorphic imagery associated with objects such as metal plaques, belt buckles, and other personal adornments. These artifacts, recovered from archaeological sites across northern Eurasia, are frequently encountered within museum displays representing this region and period. The discussion largely centers on objects dating from the seventh to third centuries BCE and, rather than emphasizing specific object categories or archaeological contexts, the intent is to examine the "specific sets or rhetorical tropes instead of traditional divisions based on tomb clusters or sets of objects" (37). This detachment from archaeological context provides an opportunity for the author to be more free ranging in her treatment of zoomorphic configurations and to juxtapose these interpretations over a vast temporal and spatial zone stretching from Eastern Europe to China. This is a refreshing approach and provides a rare opportunity to escape the rather conventional bounds of typological and chronological artifact ordering.

Chapter 3 examines "image-transfer" (19) with a detailed analysis of Pazyryk materials recovered from well-preserved tombs in the Altai Mountains. The chapter also reviews late Bronze Age and early Iron Age stone monuments and deer stone from the Transbaikal region and Mongolia as early forms of "animal-style" imagery. Due to permafrost conditions, an extraordinary variety of organic materials have been recovered from Pazyryk sites, including textiles, wood and leather, and human and horse remains. This provides an exceptional opportunity to examine tomb construction and mortuary display and the zoomorphic representations on material culture that typically do not survive the ravages of time and deterioration. The author offers an engaging discussion of these materials through an exploration of the role that visual imagery played in the reification of the social power of the deceased through the process of collective memorialization activities. The author also examines evidence of the horses sacrificed by the Pazyryk and their "animal-style" adorned accoutrements. However, given the well-preserved nature of the Pazyryk materials, a more nuanced discussion of the zoomorphic imagery found in the tattoos on preserved Pazyryk human remains would have been valuable. Such body marking and modification have been shown to reflect life biographies, social identity, and apotropaic practices and may offer important insights into the transfer and incorporation of zoomorphic meaning and intentionality.

Chapter 4 moves firmly to the eastern Eurasian steppe to focus on "animal-style" imagery use during the emergence of the Xiongnu confederation. The principal aims of the chapter are to examine how Xiongnu elites chose to incorporate or ignore earlier forms of animal imagery and how steppe-influenced zoomorphic styles ultimately diffused into early imperial China and even further south into Northern Korea. This discussion productively engages with the role of not only conventional forms of zoomorphic imagery but the creation of new styles combining elements of the local and the exotic as a response to broader systems of interaction, metal production and trade, and new visual vocabularies being utilized by sociopolitical elites.

Chapter 5 critically examines the conventional perception that "animal-style" imagery underwent a rapid decline by the end of the Iron Age. Focusing on the Xianbei and Türks of eastern and central Eurasia, and Finno-Ugric populations in Western Siberia and the Ural Mountains region, the author raises important questions about the longevity of "animal-style" imagery into the late first millennium CE and early medieval period. This important discussion raises numerous questions about the legacy of zoomorphic representation and highlights the need for more nuanced research and comparative discussion of these cultural contexts.

In chapter 6, the author draws together many of the key conceptualizations and theoretical frameworks explored in the earlier chapters. At the core of this is an emphasis on how zoomorphic visual tropes functioned within the political systems utilized by steppe elites and how such display (in life and death) was interpreted by others (i.e., an "audience"). The author's conceptualization of the "audience" here is significant, as it reflects how such imagery was perceived and transmitted within and between cultural contexts, whether directly to associated community members, broader regional alliances, or pan-Eurasian networks of trade and exchange.

Overall, this is an important and timely volume that offers a new perspective on the ways in which animal imagery formed a powerful "visual language" among Iron Age populations inhabiting the northern Eurasian region and thus played a crucial role in social identity, collective memory, and political networking. While wide-ranging geographically and interdisciplinary in its coverage of scholarship, the author's own perspective is predominantly art historical and at times somewhat indifferent to other disciplinary perspectives (e.g., archaeological contextual analysis). However, this does not discount its important contribution, and the volume will appeal especially to regional specialists, advanced students, and scholars from other regions looking for comparative treatments of zoomorphic imagery.

BRYAN K. HANKS
University of Pittsburgh
DOI: 10.1215/00219118-11591219

Note

1. Ernst Gombrich, *The Sense of Order: A Study in the Psychology of Decorative Art* (Oxford: Phaidon, 1979); Erving Goffman, *Frame Analysis: An Essay on the Organization of Experience* (Cambridge, MA: Harvard University Press, 1974); Wilhelm Worringer, *Abstraction and Empathy* (London: Victoria Miro Gallery, 1989); Alois Riegl, *Stilfragen: Grundlegungen zur Geschichte und Ornamentik* (Mittenwald: Mäander-Kunstverl, 1985).

The Sounds of Mandarin: Learning to Speak a National Language in China and Taiwan, 1913–1960. By Janet Y. Chen. New York: Columbia University Press, 2023. xii, 424 pp. ISBN: 9780231209038.

Janet Chen's *The Sounds of Mandarin: Learning to Speak a National Language in China and Taiwan, 1913–1960* is one of the most deeply researched and comprehensive surveys of the social history of the standard national language across the Taiwan Strait. Necessarily plural, the sounds of Mandarin, *guoyu*, and *putonghua*—all used in the book with adequate conceptual distinctions—defined and defied a national language in formation. These sounds, regulated in textbooks and dictionaries, enunciated by intellectual elites and common people, turned classrooms, phonographs, films, and radio airwaves into busy soundscapes that told a story beyond linear linguistic nationalism.

The book charts "both the making and unmaking of a national language" (295) in five chronologically ordered chapters. Chapter 1 begins with the Conference to Unify Pronunciation in 1913 as the first salvo to forge a standard modern Chinese national language; the conference ended up introducing "dueling sounds and contending tones" of two national languages, presumably teachable with one National Alphabet (*zhuyin zimu*) and recorded in two sets of phonographs. Chapter 2 chronicles the fraught implementation of the national language between 1928 and 1937 as a crucial component of state building during the golden decade of the Republic of China (ROC). Although the new national language based on the "Beijing pronunciation" has risen from its dueling match with the old national language to be the reigning standard, it was persistently challenged in the classroom, over the airwaves, and on the silver screen. The search for the standard Mandarin continues into chapter 3, when the national language went into exile during the War of Resistance against the Japanese, showcasing how national language pedagogy both fueled wartime mobilization (138) and paled in comparison to the "staying power of local speech" (120). Chapter 4 takes the national language across the Taiwan Strait with the ROC's retrocession and presents a troubled triangle formed by the local tongues of Taiwan, the colonial language of Japanese, and the nascent *guoyu*, casting a long shadow over the linguistic engineering project to forge "allegiances to the nation through language" (19). Chapter 5 takes the national language back to the mainland for a social history of the *putonghua*, both as a common language for and a political project of a new China, contrasting the "bombastic" state mandate of a unified linguistic model with the "mercurial" realities of the common speech. The epilogue concludes with the different trajectories traveled by *guoyu* and *putonghua* in the 1980s and 1990s, showcasing once and again how the plurality of the sounds of Mandarin should be heard as testimonials against linguistic unity and for historical complexity. Treating standard speech as a process and in its plural form offers a useful reminder that linguistic engineering and political identification are just as collective as they are individual. The collective call to standard speech and the individual practices—whether successful or not—are the necessary two sides of the same coin of linguistic nationalism.

In addition to the central argument of the book that the making of the modern Chinese national language is just as important as its unmaking, the book makes two important contributions. First, it supplements the usual intellectual history of the Chinese national language—unavoidably tinged by elitism to varying degrees—with a ground-up social history of how ordinary people respond—or not—to the making of the standard speech. It lends us an ear to how people learned and "talked back" and allows Chen's analysis to telescope between "national horizons, regional factors, and individual concerns" (16). With a wealth of details, the state's stern rhetoric to standardize speech is consistently contrasted with the polyphony and cacophony created by the "fluid and messy" (69) and at times playful answers to the call of unification. My personal favorites are the various gamification and entertainment experiments— the game of "telephone," cross-talk performances (255), and a proposal of *zhuyin* "mahjong" (130)—all grassroots attempts to make the national language enjoyable and learnable. The lofty endgame of linguistic unity is undermined by the chaotic and uneven efforts of standardization on the ground, which are almost always tied to the persistence of dialects (*fangyan*). If the correct-sounding national language seems a moving target throughout the book, dialects were mainstays that were used—though not without controversy—as linguistic clutches to teach *guoyu* (71–72). Dialects proved to be more popular on the silver screen despite censorship of dialect films in the 1930s (103–10), flourished in the wartime capital Chongqing (144–45), and even led to a particular "dialect comparative method" (174) championed by *guoyu* advocates in postwar Taiwan.

Relatedly, the book's other major contribution is its inclusion and treatment of the Taiwan story, whose plurality of sounds include two national languages—Chinese and Japanese—and various local speech forms such as Minnanese, Hakka, and many Austronesian languages. Not only a convincing account of how the GMD eventually failed in its *guoyu* policy with political repercussions that shook the core of linguistic nationalism, Chen highlights an important but largely overlooked and sidelined *guoyu* pedagogy that espoused a more inclusive and less antagonistic approach to the national language. This method proposed to learn *guoyu* from Minnanese, seeking to create "a sibling relationship between the local vernacular and the national newcomer" (171). A continuity from the earlier effort using dialects to teach Mandarin, this initiative advocated by the key figure of linguist Wei Jiangong was a strategic attempt to set the GMD's national language apart from the Japanese national language, emphasizing that if the Japanese *kokugo* was learned as a foreign language, the Chinese *guoyu* should be approached as a familial undertaking. Here Chen gives the most elaborate definition of *guoyu* in the book, from its Manchu origin to the Japanese rendition to the ROC's own history of linguistic standardization (171). The Taiwan chapter is a prominent instantiation of the limits of the linguistic nationalist narrative and the importance of going beyond it. The limits of linguistic nationalism are borne out, first, in the competition between Japanese and Chinese and, second, in the dialect comparative method, both its moderate success and eventual failure. The dialect comparative method was conditioned by and in turn supported a theory of common origin shared by dialects—variations of Minnanese and Hakka—and *guoyu*, thus suggesting affinity and solidarity among people's mother tongues and the national language of the fatherland. Supplanted by initiatives to learn *guoyu* directly and eventually banning Minnanese for the sake of *guoyu*, modern Chinese linguistic nationalism created its own enemy in Taiwan's linguistic nativism, unwittingly legitimizing such movements as "Give Me Back My Mother Tongue" (288–94).

Chen's reflection on the phonocentric limits of linguistic nationalism necessarily takes her into the realm of writing, though perhaps against her own design. Chen states that "in general, the scholarship has privileged writing over speech" and professes that the book "takes speech as the starting point" of her investigation (2), while the goal of the book "is to disaggregate Mandarin into historically specific moments of linguistic change" (4). Setting out to go "beyond the script" (7) means circumventing issues related to writing (script reform and character literacy among others), giving the impression that modern Chinese linguistic nationalism either had little to do with the question of script and writing or could be treated as such. Granted that the period covered by the book, 1913–60, is indeed a period that saw the rise of the modern Chinese national language, which meant that the concern over scripts and writing did theretofore overshadow that of language and speech, the flip side of modern phonocentrism also meant that the "privilege" enjoyed by the Chinese script was called into question. The struggle over the correct sound of the national language is thus fatefully coupled with the search for the correct script. This coupling between sounds and scripts is historical, theoretical, and inevitable for the book, yet it is largely flattened out as a quest for standard speech. One example is its treatment of the National Alphabet. Chen is meticulous in tracking the history of this syllabary writing system, from the ambitious *zhuyin zimu* to the auxiliary *zhuyin fuhao*, from its initial thirty-nine symbols to forty symbols along with five tones (25, 76), and from its national appeal to dialect versions (115, 174), including an account of vacillating positions on its necessity for *guoyu* education citing the prime example of Wu Zhihui (149, 160, 320n167). Thanks to Chen's thorough coverage, we understand that the National Alphabet was designed to teach standard pronunciation with the capacity to spell regional dialects as testified by Chao Yuen Ren's "Union Table of Phonetic Notation" (111–12); we also appreciate the tension between the National Alphabet, alphabets used by ethnic languages such as Uyghur and Tibetan, as well as *Gwoyeu Romatzyh* and Sin Wenz—all mentioned briefly in the book—vying to be the most fitting writing system for phoneticization. So why was the National Alphabet chosen as the ROC's official phoneticization scheme in the first place? The question could hardly be contained within the considerations of standard speech. The analytical choice of speech over writing falls short of explaining the centrality of the National Alphabet in GMD's *guoyu* pedagogy, not to mention the invention of a plethora of phoneticization schemes for a script that the book chooses not to engage with. Without accounting for the reversed privilege of speech over writing, one risks missing the inherent limits of linguistic nationalism that overdetermines the unmaking of a national language.

In short, in lending us an ear for the sounds of Mandarin enunciated by real people of different social strata and reproduced by various media technologies, Chen offers a magisterial and absorbing account of the surprising making and unmaking of the modern Chinese national language. *The Sounds of Mandarin* is a must-read for anyone interested in linguistic nationalism and its overcoming.

YUROU ZHONG
University of Toronto
DOI: 10.1215/00219118-11591229

The Cold War in the Himalayas: Multinational Perspectives on the Sino-Indian Border Conflict, 1950–70. By Reed Chervin. Amsterdam: Amsterdam University Press, 2024. 293 pp. ISBN: 9789048559350.

Some years ago a Cold War historian, bemused by some of his colleagues' seemingly unending drive to visit ever more countries and archives, began asking them whether Djibouti might yield anything, too. The risk was to see the search for new primary sources, essential to history as a discipline, turn into a scenery-chewing quest of archival accumulation for its own sake—and with it, to harm the environment and scholars without the logistical, financial, and institutional resources.[1]

Sadly, *The Cold War in the Himalayas* exemplifies that "archival fetishism." To recover the international ramifications of the war that pitted China against India over swaths of the Himalayas in 1962, Reed Chervin has combed thirty-two collections in Australia, Canada, China, India, Myanmar, New Zealand, Russia, Taiwan, the United Kingdom, and the United States—to mention only institutional repositories. Such determination is welcome. Despite a wealth of works on the conflict,[2] more can be done to restore its significance for twentieth-century international history. The work Chervin has done in sourcing these documents constitutes a highly valuable step toward this. Indeed, scholars owe him a significant debt for obtaining the declassification of documents from the JFK Presidential Library and the US and Australian national archives.

These finds do yield worthy insights, most importantly by fleshing out Taipei's complex posture vis-à-vis the conflict, but also by illuminating New Zealander, Australian, and Canadian perspectives on the war. Chervin argues, for instance, that supporting India helped Canberra strengthen relations with Delhi. Smaller points or archival finds are also worth pondering. Chapter 1 reveals a relative diversity of opinions about the war (and who was to blame for it) in the PRC and the United States at the time, while chapter 2 suggests that military defeat offered Indian opponents of nonalignment a chance to express their foreign policy preferences. I also found the claim that Britain, rather than confronting China or directly supporting Tibetan resistance after 1959, promoted development aid elsewhere in South and Southeast Asia, interesting; likewise for source material on China's attitude toward Sikkim, Bhutan, and Nepal.

Yet *The Cold War in the Himalayas* does too little with its archival haul to build on these insights. Covering the two decades between the PRC's annexation of Tibet in 1950–51 and 1970, the book seeks to offer "multinational perspectives" on the collapse in relations between the two Asian giants. Unfortunately, Chervin treats these perspectives in a largely self-contained fashion: chapter 2, typically, thus discusses Washington's response to Delhi's requests for help, then Britain's, then Australia's, then New Zealand's, and so on. Shorn of an overall framing, this siloed approach offers a mechanical take on 1962 that struggles to be more than the sum of its archival parts.

For the two belligerents, these thematic and analytical siloes are especially problematic. China and India hold diametrically opposed—and equally weak—historical discourses about the legitimacy and antiquity of their presence in the Himalayas. Their official accounts of the war similarly clash. Chervin puts them side by side, neither analyzing them against one another nor probing their veracity. The result is a parcellated and limited view of the conflict's underpinnings. Among other actors, Britain and the United States, and secondarily Taiwan, occupy the lion's share of the discussion. The USSR, Australia, New Zealand, and Canada get the rest, while Afro-Asian nations—notably the Ceylon-led group who tried to mediate—are entirely left out of the picture despite having as much if not more of a stake than the former White Dominions. It is hard to accept that this book oriented toward Western countries represents a truly multinational perspective on 1962.

Indeed, its rich evidence on Western perspectives is not sufficiently confronted with its Indian, PRC, and Taiwanese sources. The latter two illuminate lesser-known Chinese takes on 1962. Yet Chervin does not do enough to integrate, interpret, and contextualize them. To give but a few examples, it is not clear whether Britain minded or dismissed the PRC's strategic threat to India in the early 1950s; Chervin talks of Whitehall's "anxiety" about Himalayan geopolitics, but there is little sign of this in the evidence supplied prior to 1959 (186)—the year the deterioration in Sino-Indian relations became clear for all to see. Elsewhere, the assertion that the Foreign Office "needed to hide a British map when Chinese dignitaries visited since it corroborated their border claims" (83) is hasty: British maps did not corroborate China's claims but rather Beijing's criticisms of India's claims—a crucial nuance.

Nor does Chervin sufficiently engage with the historiography, weakening his arguments' contours and strength. Robert McMahon's and Paul McGarr's important contributions regarding Anglo-American perspectives on the war do not get the attention they deserve;[3] likewise for studies of independent India's complex relations with the Commonwealth[4] or of China's assistance to northeastern India's armed movements.[5] These historiographical shallows have consequences. To give one example, Chervin claims that "frontier military neglect by India reversed with the onset of the 1962 war" (217) and that "New Delhi used tactics beyond the military kind in its border conflict with China"—namely, "frontier development and administration as well as state visits" (163)—when the Himalayas' militarization predated 1962 (but came too late to avoid defeat) and development preceded it.[6]

This leads to problematic framing. The complex history of Sino-Indian relations and Himalayan geopolitics is flattened out, sometimes beyond recognition. Thus, Chervin asserts that "Due to India and Burma's belonging to the British Empire . . . , the two enjoyed close relations for centuries" (145). Nor is there discussion of the Hindi Chini Bhai Bhai era. China and India's claims and activities in the Himalayas pre-1950 are dispatched in cursory fashion, bypassing a nuanced scholarship on China and India's connections with Tibet and their state-building competition in the Himalayas.[7] As for the 1963–70 period, Chervin claims that China "sought to lead a coalition of Afro-Asian countries against the Soviet Union and the United States," but "Beijing's capacity to do so decreased after 1965 because its diplomatic structure collapsed during the Cultural Revolution" (202) without further elaboration. The Great Game and the Cold War are presented as key framing devices but taken for granted.

The structure reinforces this problematic framing. Chervin begins with a blow-by-blow military account of the war (which seemingly breaks out of nowhere), followed by other countries' perspectives, then turns back to discuss the roots of the conflict in the 1950s before pivoting to the postwar period. It is not clear what such chronological back-and-forth achieves, save for a headache for the reader.

In the end, rather than a novel argument, this book reads more like a chronicle. We are told that "the 1962 war affected many countries beyond India and China. Power blocs became a defining feature during and immediately after the war, and countries as far flung as New Zealand held stake in it. These states lent allies moral and/or material support and at the same time used the war to bolster existing policies toward the two combatants. Governments around the world interpreted and responded to the conflict in assorted ways" (112). None of this should be news to anyone interested in Sino-Indian relations and their diplomatic impact. Nor is the kind of truly pluricentric account an important conflict like the 1962 war demands impossible to achieve—a recent account of the Soviet invasion of Afghanistan shows as much.[8] Chervin has given us a diplomatic history of the most traditional kind, but without the thorough source analysis, historical specificity, and historiographical heft this demands. The romance of the archive can be taken too far.

BÉRÉNICE GUYOT-RÉCHARD
King's College, London
DOI: 10.1215/00219118-11591239

Notes

1. Benjamin R. Young, "Wealth, Access, and Archival Fetishism in the New Cold War History," *History News Network*, June 23, 2019, https://historynewsnetwork.org/article/172318.

2. For example, Alastair Lamb, *The China-India Border: The Origins of the Disputed Boundaries* (Oxford: Oxford University Press, 1964); John W. Garver, *Protracted Contest: Sino-Indian Rivalry in the Twentieth Century* (Oxford: Oxford University Press, 2001); Srinath Raghavan, "A Bad Knock: The War with China, 1962," in *A Military History of India and South Asia: From the East India Company to the Nuclear Era*, ed. Daniel Marston and Chandar Sundaram (Westport, CT: Prager Security International, 2007), 157–74; Manjari Chatterjee Miller, "Re-collecting Empire: 'Victimhood' and the 1962 Sino-Indian War," *Asian Security* 5, no. 3 (2009): 216–41.

3. Paul M. McGarr, *The Cold War in South Asia: Britain, the United States and the Indian Subcontinent, 1945–1965* (Cambridge: Cambridge University Press, 2013); Robert J. McMahon, *The Cold War on the Periphery: The United States, India, and Pakistan* (New York: Columbia University Press, 1994); Robert J. McMahon, "U.S. Policy toward South Asia and Tibet during the Early Cold War," *Journal of Cold War Studies* 8, no. 3 (2006): 131–44.

4. David Walker, "General Cariappa Encounters 'White Australia': Australia, India, and the Commonwealth in the 1950s," *Journal of Imperial and Commonwealth History* 34, no. 3 (2006): 389–406; Lorna Lloyd, "An Acutely Embarrassing Affair: Whitehall and the Indian-South African Dispute at the United Nations (1946)," *Journal of Imperial and Commonwealth History* 46, no. 5 (2018): 909–34; Paul M. McGarr, "'A Serious Menace to Security': British Intelligence, V. K. Krishna Menon, and the Indian High Commission in London, 1947–52," *Journal of Imperial and Commonwealth History* 38, no. 3 (2010): 441–69; Harshan Kumarasingham, "The 'Tropical Dominions': The Appeal of Dominion Status in the Decolonisation of India, Pakistan, and Ceylon," *Transactions of the Royal Historical Society* 23 (2013): 223–45; Alexander E. Davies and Vineet Thakur, "'An Act of Faith' or a New 'Brown Empire'? The Dismissal of India's International Anti-racism, 1945–1961," *Commonwealth and Comparative Politics* 56, no. 1 (2017): 22–39.

5. Subir Bhaumik, "The External Linkages in Insurgency in India's Northeast," in *Insurgency in North-East India*, ed. P. Phakem (New Delhi: Omeons, 1997), 89–100.

6. Bérénice Guyot-Réchard, *Shadow States: India, China and the Himalayas, 1910–1962* (Cambridge: Cambridge University Press, 2017).

7. For instance, Melvyn C. Goldstein, *A History of Modern Tibet, 1913–1951: The Demise of the Lamaist State* (Berkeley: University of California Press, 1989); Elliot Sperling, "Tibet and China: The Interpretation of History since 1950," *China Perspectives*, no. 79 (2009): 25–37; Hsiao-Ting Lin, "Boundary, Sovereignty, and Imagination: Reconsidering the Frontier Disputes between British India and Republican China, 1914–47," *Journal of Imperial and Commonwealth History* 32, no. 3 (2004): 25–47; Xiuyu Wang, *China's Last Imperial Frontier: Late Qing Expansion in Sichuan's Tibetan Borderlands* (Lanham, MD: Lexington Books, 2011); Swargajyoti Gohain, "Selective Access; or, How States Make Remoteness," *Social Anthropology* 27, no. 2 (2019): 204–20; Benno Weiner, *The Chinese Revolution on the Tibetan Frontier* (Ithaca, NY: Cornell University Press, 2020); Guyot-Réchard, *Shadow States*.

8. Elisabeth Leake, *Afghan Crucible: The Soviet Invasion and the Making of Modern Afghanistan* (Oxford: Oxford University Press, 2022).

After Eunuchs: Science, Medicine, and the Transformation of Sex in Modern China.
By Howard Chiang. New York: Columbia University Press, 2018. xvii, 391 pp.
ISBN: 9780231185783.

Eunuchs wielded immense power at pivotal moments in Chinese history. Yet in the twentieth century, they symbolized weakness, an embodiment of China's national loss and injury on the global stage. Castrated men no longer held political, social, or cultural capital in a modernizing China. Howard Chiang investigates the conditions that led to this change and more in *After Eunuchs: Science, Medicine, and the Transformation of Sex in Modern China*. This is an engaging and enterprising work about the rise of sexology in Republican China. Over the course of five chapters organized chronologically from the waning years of the Qing dynasty to Cold War–era Taiwan, Chiang explores the impact of this new sex regime on the surgical body. He masterfully unravels the intellectual processes by which webs of scientific and medical knowledge linked eunuchs and transgender people within a realm of bodily experience of sex, sexuality, and gender.

He argues that the concept of sex (*xing*) arose only in the twentieth century when it became a topic of empirical study—which is to say, ostensibly publicly knowable, diagnosable, and recordable truth. Chiang investigates "its three epistemological coordinates—as the object of observation, the subject of desire, and a malleable essence of the human body" (178). Challenging previous scholarship that anchors China's sexual revolution in the 1970s, Chiang pinpoints the Republican period as a meaningful moment in China for the global coproduction of contested notions of sexual knowledge based on an increasingly shared set of modern scientific beliefs about what constitutes truth. In doing so, Chiang unsettles familiar discussions about Chinese nationhood and race to instead focus on the topic of nationhood and sex in which sexology became a chief element of Chinese modernity.

The chief contribution of *After Eunuchs* is Chiang's concept of "epistemic modernity." Much more than a history of castration or sexuality, Chiang provides a new framework for understanding knowledge production in modern China. Introducing historical epistemology as part of his Foucauldian approach, epistemic modernity allows Chiang to unpack, as he states, "a historical moment during which a new science of sexuality became epistemologically rooted in Chinese culture" (132). Through this process, as Chiang states succinctly in chapter 3, "sexology in Republican China was indeed a new system of knowledge in which, literally, new subjects were made" (131). Epistemic modernity interrupts assumptions about a passive China simply internalizing Western modernity and instead allows readers to see the creativity and ingenuity with which Chinese thinkers grappled with scientific concepts and transformed them, serving as active agents in a global conversation about and invention of sex.

Chapter 1 investigates the ways unprecedented visual and textual public exposure of the castrated body in the twentieth century ushered in eunuchism's demise. This conclusion is the result of Chiang's interrogation of the archive of castration, in which he constantly questions the reliability and intent of photographs taken of eunuchs' bodies, lithographs in the press, and accounts of castration from Western observers. Chiang challenges the legacy of May Fourth rhetoric that defined eunuchism as emasculation and impotence; rather, Chiang argues that up until the twentieth century, castration "was a source of masculine identity and a mechanism of its social reproduction" revealing the agency of eunuchs within their lived experience of castration (18). Continuing to explore the visuality of sex, chapter 2 delves into the relationship of Western biomedicine, specifically the techniques of anatomy, morphology, and genetics, with the growing field of Chinese sexology. In what many will likely find to be the most methodologically thought-provoking chapter of the book, chapter 3 discusses the second epistemic coordinate of sex: desire. Exploring the ideas of some of China's most prominent sexologists, Chiang underscores Chinese contributions to the sexual sciences while also revealing the disciplinary power of this new regime of sex in its privileging of the category of heterosexuality as the "natural" sexual preference. Same-sex desire was not just evaluated as a social problem during this modernizing period of Chinese history, as other scholars have suggested. Sex scientists engaging with Western psychiatry produced "homosexuality" as a discursive category of experience that recognized the existence of gay identity.

Bodily malleability, the final piece of Chiang's paradigm of sex epistemology, is taken up in chapter 4 through a discussion of sex change. Chinese scientists increasingly viewed biological sex as something that was not fixed but in fact a pliable component of the human body. To quote Chiang directly, "[Chinese sexologists] no longer drew on the limited language of anatomy to talk about two different but equal sexes; rather, they started to think of men and women as two versions of a universal human body" (178). Yet this did not fuel more fluid and liberal views of sex, sexuality, and gender in the ways one might expect. Theories of "universal bisexuality" led to portrayals of eunuchs as "feminized males," eroding any semblance of their former masculinity (194). It is at this point that Chiang comes full circle in his analysis, bridging the gap between eunuchs in chapter 1 and transgender persons at the site of surgical intervention. Chiang's impressive study culminates in chapter 5 with a discussion about the consequences of Republican sexology on the lives of transgender people in postwar Taiwan. He highlights the role of geopolitics in fomenting popular and scientific interest in sex transformation. Chiang focuses on how the "first" transgender person in Taiwan, Xie Jianshun, became a "cultural icon," embraced as a symbol of national pride rather than merely anxiety through the ability of doctors to enact human bodily transformation on Taiwanese soil.

The strength of the book lies in its subversion of the familiar. Chiang challenges readers to confront their preconceptions about the meaning of sex, sexuality, and gender in a modernizing world. Traversing an array of evidence, including medical and scientific journals, popular presses, fiction, tabloids, and visual sources, *After Eunuchs* demonstrates how concepts or categories such as "sex" and "homosexuality" are socially constructed, historically contingent, and politically invested— without losing sight of the way that they impacted the real people whose lives collided with the output of the ever-evolving global laboratory of modernity.

STEPHANIE PAINTER
University of Chicago
DOI: 10.1215/00219118-11591249

A History of Uyghur Buddhism. By Johan Elverskog. New York: Columbia University Press, 2024. xiv, 278 pp. ISBN: 9780231215251.

Apart from a small group of specialists, few people know that the historic Uyghurs were anything other than Muslims in northwest China. Johan Elverskog's eloquent and highly accessible book provides an important and timely corrective to that view. His study answers several questions that connect topics usually treated separately; how and why the medieval Uyghurs converted to Buddhism, what role the Uyghur Buddhist kingdom in the Tarim Basin played in central Asia and in wider East-West relations over time, and how and why those Uyghurs eventually converted to Islam. He reminds readers that the medieval Uyghurs who established new states in eastern central Asia and Gansu in the mid-ninth century played important roles in wider Asian history but are mostly either overlooked or not well understood. Elverskog's exhaustively sourced history not only retrieves their story for readers, it also reminds us of the importance of Buddhism to Asian history as the first "pan-Asian faith" (4). His history will also satisfy readers who think of the Uyghurs as Muslims because he ends by examining the eventual conversion of the Uyghur Buddhists to Islam. This story provides a convenient case study for Elverskog to return to the topic of historic interactions between Buddhism and Islam, the subject of some of his earlier work.

Elverskog sustains several arguments through the book's chapters, organized chronologically and focused on political and economic aspects of Uyghur Buddhism. Chapter 1 provides readers with a satisfying account of conversion to Buddhism by the first generation of diaspora Uyghur elites who settled in the Tarim Basin and Gansu after they were evicted from their steppe empire in the mid-ninth century. Readers familiar with the scholarship on the medieval Uyghurs will be especially glad for Elverskog's coherent narrative because the sources have been written in several languages, much of it philological in nature, and are sometimes difficult to track down. The second chapter focuses on the central role that Tanguts and Tibetans played in stimulating Uyghurs to convert to Buddhism. Elverskog's main argument in these first chapters is that the Uyghur aristocracy, not the ruling clan, converted to Buddhism. This is an important argument and goes against traditional assumptions that conversion was tied to the Uyghur court. It also ties into Elverskog's argument that the conversion was part of a larger trend that occurred across most of Asia in the eleventh century.

Chapter 3 focuses exclusively on the economics of the West Uyghur kingdom in the Tarim Basin in the eleventh and twelfth centuries, by which time the Ganzhou Uyghur state ceased to exist. It is no surprise to learn that those Uyghurs became the main intermediaries of trade between Liao in north China, Song, Tibet, and Qarakhanid central Asia. Perhaps more surprising, at least for readers not familiar with the economics of religious institutions, will be Elverskog's convincing argument that the Uyghur elites in the Tarim Basin converted to Buddhism precisely because it legitimized their production and accumulation of wealth, which they invested in their Buddhist institutions to support the propagation of the Dharma. The Tarim Basin Uyghurs were perhaps uniquely positioned to act as commercial agents in the monetized world of commerce, continuing a trend that they doubtless learned from Sogdians.

Elverskog then describes the Buddhism of the Tarim Basin Uyghurs in the tenth through thirteenth centuries in chapter 4, titled "Uyghur Buddhisms." The title embeds his argument that several schools of Buddhism thrived in the Uyghur kingdom, at least until the Mongols showed up in the early 1200s. The wide range of textual and visual sources that Elverskog draws on in this chapter is striking and illustrates his deep familiarity with the scholarship on the historic Uyghurs. This is also the most complex topic of the book, and readers will be very happy for Elverskog's clear narrative that is surprisingly jargon free. Most important, Elverskog opposes the traditional view that the history of Uyghur Buddhism was a smooth, one-way evolution from Tocharian Nikaya giving way to Chinese Mahayana, which was displaced by Tibetan Tantrism in the Mongol period. Instead of assuming sharp divisions between Buddhist schools, lingering "Protestant presuppositions" (94), he draws on evidence from a range of different textual and visual sources to convincingly show that the Tarim Basin Uyghurs were remarkably flexible in their adoption and use of Buddhist schools precisely because their religion was not managed or mandated by the state. That changed once the Uyghurs were subsumed into the emerging Mongol Empire.

Some readers may be surprised that the last chapter discusses Uyghur conversion to Islam, but it fits with Elverskog's argument that it happened because the West Uyghur kingdom had lost its political independence when they became Mongol subjects; "it was within this larger historical context [the Mongol Empire] that Uyghur Buddhists came to engage with Central Asian Muslims, which ultimately led to the Uyghurs abandoning the Dharma and becoming Muslims" (135). Elverskog identifies the Qarakhitay state as the source of tensions between Buddhists and Muslims in the West Uyghur kingdom—in his words, "the first time in Islamic history that Muslims were under the rule of a non-Muslim state" (136). The Uyghurs submitted voluntarily to Chinggis in 1209, ensuring their favorable treatment in the rapidly growing empire. Unfortunately, the Uyghurs were also dragged into the Mongol civil wars after 1260, which culminated in the division of the Chagatai Khanate and their long process of conversion to Islam. Elverskog provides important evidence showing that relations between Buddhists and Muslims were not altogether hostile. Even more important and less well known is the fact that Uyghur Buddhists continued to thrive for over a century after their ruler's conversion! In fact, it was not until the 1449 Tumu crisis that Uyghur Buddhists were driven out of their homeland. The last official visit of Uyghur Buddhists to the Ming court came in 1473, to request asylum for some two hundred monks.

This book is the result of Elverskog's long interest in the historic Uyghurs, Buddhism, the interactions of Buddhism and Islam along the historic silk roads, and the Mongol Empire. It certainly delivers on the promise made by the book's title, to provide a history of the Buddhist Uyghurs. It also provides much more, exploring a wide range of themes and topics across several disciplines, all pivoting around the story of the Uyghurs. The book is also noteworthy because the narrative is jargon free and easily accessible to readers of all levels due to Elverskog's lively and animated writing style, amply illustrated and backed up with endnotes that will be of interest to specialists. It is good to have an updated history of the medieval Uyghurs, a people who were uniquely able to connect steppe and sown, eastern and western Asia, and Buddhism and Islam.

MICHAEL C. BROSE
Indiana University Bloomington
DOI: 10.1215/00219118-11591259

Structures of Governance in Song Dynasty China, 960–1279 CE. By Charles Hartman. Cambridge: Cambridge University Press, 2023. xiv, 452 pp. ISBN: 9781009235648.

With the publication in 2021 of *The Making of Song Dynasty History: Sources and Narratives, 960–1279 CE* (Cambridge University Press) and two years later *Structures of Governance in Song Dynasty China, 960–1279 CE*, Charles Hartman has established himself as one of the most productive and accomplished historians of premodern China. The 2021 book is a thorough investigation of the four most important works of official Song historiography. The 2023 book, under review here, introduces the idea of a technocratic-Confucian continuum as a key to understanding how the Song was governed. Hartman's work thus challenges the long-established view of the Song as an age of Confucian rule and Song political history as centered on a series of struggles between different factions of literati.

Part 1 of the book, "Dual Faces of the Song State" (chapters 1 through 5), introduces four basic bipolar elements that shaped the "contours of Northern Song political culture" (115), two on the theoretical level (gentlemen versus petty men and virtue versus talent), and two on the practical level (outer versus inner governance and collective versus unilateral decision-making). Part 2, "The Technocratic and Confucian Models of Governance" (chapters 6 through 8), traces the origins and interaction of the two modalities in the Northern Song. In part 3, "Interactions" (chapters 9 throughout 11), Hartman uses the continuum paradigm for a close examination of a twenty-year period (1162–82) in Southern Song history, a key period in both the history of *daoxue* and the compilation of Song official histories. Combining a sophisticated theoretical framework, meticulous analysis of key sources, and impressive familiarity with Song history and historiography, Hartman's book is historical scholarship at its best.

A major goal and contribution of this book is its analysis of the "full range of Song political culture" (139). Hartman argues that not all civil servants with *jinshi* degrees were committed Confucian officials. Those intent on governing along Confucian principles consisted of no more than a few hundred individuals occupying senior government positions. At the other end of the spectrum were tens of thousands of lesser, non-literati actors who were charged with a wide array of military, inner palace, and other routine administrative responsibilities, their primary goal dynastic strength and stability. They are the technocrats. The Confucian and technocratic practitioners differed in their ideological and philosophical orientations, political values, and career patterns. They also diverged in their views of the purpose and structure of government, the ideal configuration of political spaces, and even preferred channels of communication and decision-making processes, hence the different labels for the two visions of governance. Throughout the book, Hartman stresses that "a purely Confucian or a purely technocratic governance are theoretical abstractions." Song political culture is best understood as a "dynamic arena" in which leaders achieved the "maximum benefit for their coalition or policy goal" by adjusting their strategies and mobilizing their resources (133).

Hartman demonstrates the utility of his paradigm by skillfully delineating the competition and interaction, both in theory and practice, of the technocratic and Confucian approaches. The result is a new version of Song political history. Inheriting the political system of the late Tang and Period of Five Dynasties, the Song found-ers were strong advocates of the technocratic model. "The goal of governance was to strengthen the dynasty and ensure the prosperity of its leaders" (185). This trend culminated in "Great Peace governance" under Zhenzong (225). In the next several decades, the Qingli and following generations of Confucian officials contested both the theoretical foundations and administrative practice of the technocratic vision, promoting the concept of Confucian "shared governance" and institutions that sym-bolized and helped realize Confucian political principles. This era of Confucian resur-gence "furnished the initial ideological grounding for Wang Anshi's New Policies in the late 1060s" (225). Emperor Shenzong's reign nonetheless witnessed a return of the center of administrative authority from the outer to inner court, paving the way for the flourishing of the technocratic state under Emperor Huizong.

In addition to showcasing the interaction and transitions between the techno-cratic and Confucian visions, Hartman's discussion reveals deep structural tensions between the inner and outer court systems throughout the dynasty. Especially illu-minating in this context is his elaboration of the Song monarchy as including not only male emperors but also eunuchs and women, who played crucial roles in the functioning of the inner palace and, as operatives of the technocratic state, in rou-tine governmental administration. Female secretaries, for example, handled a large variety of official documents, frequently communicating with the emperor on offi-cial matters and helping him draft his inner directives. As private agents of the mon-archy, eunuchs served not only as messengers and couriers within the inner and between inner and outer courts, but they were also deeply involved in the manage-ment of financial, military, and other state affairs.

Through the lens of the monarchy as a "multifaceted, corporate institution" (386) and "nexus of the technocratic state" (183), we are reacquainted with the Song emperors, female regents, and other empresses. To explain their success in balanc-ing the technocratic and Confucian tendencies, Hartman introduces the careers and talents of many important technocratic operatives, such as the "dynasty's best financial officer," Chen Shu (964–1004), and the versatile eunuch Dong Zhongyong (1104–1165). The discourse and policy proposals of the committed Confucians, such as Fan Zhongyan (989–1052), Ouyang Xiu (1007–1072), and Sima Guang (1019–1086), receive a close reading, leading to the conclusion that Song governance was never "a unified Confucian project" (11). Their "outsized political power" aside, Hartman shows, these top civil servants were in constant competition with their non-Confucian counterparts throughout the dynasty.

Hartman's book is a must-read for scholars interested in imperial China, offering important insights that will surely inspire new research topics for years to come. For example, in what ways did the personal relationship between emperors and their chief councillors shape the interaction of the technocratic and Confu-cian visions as well as actual administrative practice? Did the networks of Con-fucian and technocratic officials overlap? If most civil servants with *jinshi* degrees lacked a "personal commitment to Confucian principles that was deep enough to influence their thinking and behavior in the conduct of their bureaucratic careers" (230), do we need to rethink the Song educational and examination systems? Applying Hartman's interpretive model to these and other questions promises a new and more nuanced understanding of the governance of imperial China as well as its institutional history and political culture.

CONG ELLEN ZHANG
University of Virginia
DOI: 10.1215/00219118-11591269

Betting on the Civil Service Examinations: The Lottery in Late Qing China.
By En Li. Cambridge, MA: Harvard University Asia Center, 2023. xxiii, 348 pp.
ISBN: 9780674293779.

En Li's *Betting on the Civil Service Examinations* is a timely intervention in an area that has received almost no attention in English. It studies the formalization of the lottery game known as *weixing* (romanized as *Wai Seng* in earlier sources) in the second half of the nineteenth century in Guangdong Province. *Weixing* was a game where bettors predicted the surnames of those who passed the civil service examination system. It was one of many games of lottery that were common at the time. The book argues that this game "created a new community" (7–12) by linking people together in a popular pastime, forging a kind of civil society not only within Guangdong but also with the overseas Chinese community. Li also contends that the game provided a new and significant source of revenue for Guangdong Province at a time of desperation and was an example of how innovation and flexibility during this period was instrumental in shoring up otherwise shaky finances.

Although the author did not expressly demarcate them as such, the book can be divided into two parts. The first part, consisting of the first three chapters, is on the broader historical background of gambling in Chinese history (chapter 1), the sociocultural context of various lotteries in the late Qing (chapter 2), and the specific rules and mechanics of the focus of the book, the *weixing* lottery (chapter 3). These three chapters serve to give readers a broad overview of the context in which *weixing* existed and to describe in detail how the game was played. The next three chapters forming the second part discuss the historical background of the formalization of government regulations governing *weixing* in Guangdong Province (chapter 4), the crisis of confidence endured in 1885 with accusations of cheating and game fixing (chapter 5), and a biographical sketch of Zhang Zhidong and a few others whose careers and lives were intimately intertwined with the lottery (chapter 6). In the final chapter, Li turns her attention to the gambling activities of overseas Chinese community mainly in Southeast Asia and the United States and the implications of such a worldwide adoption of a type of lottery game (chapter 7).

The book does achieve the objective of demonstrating how the lottery was a useful tool of public finance. Using primarily materials from Zhang Zhidong, who was the governor-general of Liangguang when *weixing* became fully licensed in 1884, as well as a collection of materials from the archives, Li tells the story of the difficulties of officially licensing a gambling game based on the examination results and the moral implications it entails. Despite a crisis of confidence due to a case of examination rigging in 1885, fiscal pressures prevailed, and licensing continued until the abrupt abolishment of the examinations in 1905. In the intervening years, the revenue from *weixing* lottery was instrumental in building a financial cushion for Guangdong Province and helped it fund military and other expenses in neighboring provinces. However, as with many reform-minded policies of the late Qing, the later implementation of the licensing scheme was also beset with short-termism on the part of officials who undermined its attraction to game organizers.

The impact of the lottery on civil society is more implicit in Li's study. Since little of the physical evidence about *weixing* has survived, it seems we do not have many sources from which to draw firm conclusions about the makeup and motivations of the player base. The material culture left behind is chiefly documented in George Thompson Hare's 1895 report published in Singapore titled *The Wai Seng Lottery*, on which Li relies heavily for both details of the lottery's operation and reproductions of the game's materials. What we do know about the bettors are morsels of information and anecdotes of various types. As with other topics of similar moral ambiguity, it is perhaps asking too much to hope for firsthand accounts of participants. Literati who were also avid gamblers were not likely to wax lyrical on the lottery, and the average bettor was not in a capacity to write a treatise on the game. Thus Li draws much of her evidence from secondary accounts by foreign observers looking in at a Chinese system of gambling, such as Hare's work, William Farwell's *The Chinese: At Home and Abroad*, and Stewart Culin's *The Gambling Games of the Chinese in America*. This is not to say that their accounts are unreliable, but the lack of firsthand accounts does weaken any argument that can be made about the social ties and linkages that a lottery might or might not have created. Just because many people bought the same lottery does not automatically make them coparticipants in a greater civil society. Likewise, the suggestion that *weixing* was somehow a meritocratic competition where skilled bettors would win (15, 112–13) would be stronger if we have a number of cases where bettors did consistently win in the game. As it is, however, the evidence seems to suggest that, as in all games of chance, the house always wins given how lucrative it was for the organizers despite paying large sums to the provincial government for the privilege of running these lotteries.

Given the difficulty of researching this subject, this book is a wonderful addition to the study of late Qing institutions that cross the boundaries of state and society. Graduate students studying the late Qing and early Republic would do well to absorb the materials in this book, and scholars of Chinese popular culture and overseas community will find the accounts and details found here an important addition to the literature.

LAWRENCE ZHANG
Hong Kong University of Science and Technology
DOI: 10.1215/00219118-11591279

Sentiment, Reason, and Law: Policing in the Republic of China on Taiwan.
By Jeffrey T. Martin. Ithaca, NY: Cornell University Press, 2019. 186 pp.
ISBN: 9781501740053.

Jeffrey Martin's *Sentiment, Reason, and Law* is a hidden gem. Perhaps it is parochial to say "hidden" simply because one came across it belatedly. It is possible that in the circles in which it moves—police studies, Taiwan anthropology, political theory—it already is a word-of-mouth classic. But while this reviewer is over-the-top excited about the book, there may be some justification for its not receiving the wider attention that it richly deserves. I will return to this point at the end of the review.

As a literary scholar with an abiding interest in comparative political-legal culture, I am immediately intrigued by the author's bracketing of the nearly universal equation of policing with law enforcement. Indeed, what are police for if not defending law and order against antisocial, criminal elements—with force if necessary? Martin's ethnography of policing in Taiwan, the distillation of multiple years of fieldwork as an embedded anthropologist at street-level police substations (*paichusuo*), is full of revelations for those of us whose understanding of policing is almost entirely informed by media and fictional representations derived from liberal Western milieus. In brief, policing in contemporary Taiwan is political, administrative, and pastoral. The average Taiwanese policeman is less a crime fighter than a paper-pusher, a fixer, and a (drinking) buddy who might also issue you a ticket.

This offbeat image of the cop arrived in post–martial law Taiwan from a century of colonial and autocratic rule. At the end of the nineteenth century, the Japanese colonial regime introduced the *hoko* grid (adapted from the imperial Chinese *baojia* system) and the capillary institution of neighborhood *paichusuo* in charge of each and every resident in its jurisdiction by means of the population registry (*hukou*). The registry-based policing model proved highly effective during Japan's fascist mobilization during World War II. The Nationalists or KMT consolidated this model by accentuating its political and surveillance functions. Under both regimes, the police were ancillary to the military, serving primarily as an intelligence apparatus with the overriding goal of securitizing the state against a putatively hostile, noncooperative population.

By the time Martin began his fieldwork in the late 1990s, Taiwan was already a fledgling democracy. The rule of law has become a political reality and the police have been professionalized and relieved of much of their ideological mission (no more "hoodlum registry"!). However, the *paichusuo* with its reams of population registry and intimate local knowledge has remained a fixture of the urbanscape and a nerve center of local society. Beyond the two dozen or so patrolmen attached to a typical substation, all manner of people frequent its tea-serving reception area or its backroom—to bring a plaint, to settle a dispute, to repay a favor, to cultivate patronage, or simply to pass time and "enjoy the spectacle of other people's problems" (in the case of a lonesome retiree; 21). The vast majority of the "problems" that land in the laps of the *paichusuo* police are the problems of living cheek by jowl in a bustling, teeming metropolis: traffic accidents, unlicensed food stalls, illegally built structures, and the perennial vices of prostitution and gambling.

The patrolmen do patrol the streets, though it is not nearly as central to their work as Martin initially thought. The anecdotes he tells have a general arc: two cops on duty respond to a call (or repeated complaints) by showing up at the scene, exchange pleasantries with the target of complaint and may even sit down for a couple of bowls of noodles (gratis), exhort the former to work out a deal with the complainant, and give instructions on how to put on an appearance of compliance for their camera. And for their trouble they are not above taking "red envelopes" (*hongbao*; cash bribe-cum-donation). This unprincipled mode of papering over wrinkles can easily strike an observer as at best bureaucratic incompetence and at worst the antithesis of rule of law. Moreover, all that schmoozing and carousing with the constituencies of their beat (*qinqu*)—"in back rooms of local businesses, in the back-alley clubhouses of borough chiefs and corner bosses, or in the private rooms of local restaurants and karaoke bars" (77)—reek of corruption. Yet according to the policemen themselves, this kind of socializing is "the beating heart of their job" (77).

The Taiwanese policeman, argues Martin, cannot afford to adhere to the letter of the law or act on public reason alone. Instead, he must at all times attend to *qing*—the dense web of affective bonds, trust, loyalty, informal economy, and solidarity. "Over the *longue durée* history of modern policing in Taiwan, [*qing*] has come to stand as the ritual center of an independent 'jurisdiction,' or authoring discourse, which speaks for local community against central power" (8). Policing for all intents and purposes boils down to balancing the claims of *qing* and the demands of *fa*/law, and *li*/reason is where the police hope all parties are willing to dwell long enough to reach a resolution. Martin's most illuminating insight is a rather counterintuitive one: policing in Taiwan is not about imposing a rational order from above but about getting enough people in the community to tolerate a degree of discord and localized lawbreaking for the sake of the experiment in living together that is democracy. Policemen are thus administrative curators more than law enforcers, repairmen more than surgeons, adjunct players more than quarterbacks.

The real heroes in Martin's account are the local political and business elites, *difang renshi*, who enjoy a special status as "friends of the station" and who expend their political and social capital in the backroom of the substation to "speak *qing*" (*shuoqing*). The prominent role played by these "sentiment brokers" casts a shadow on the ideal of democracy since not everyone has a seat at the table in the shadowy, smoke-filled backroom "parliament." Justice yields to the complications of *qing*-based ritual order, with its hierarchies, exclusions, and dialogism. And yet this "jurisdictional pluralism" is precisely the source of strength of Taiwanese democracy. Martin illustrates this central thesis through a comparison of the Sunflower movement in Taiwan and the Umbrella movement in Hong Kong, both taking place in 2014 with divergent outcomes, which he argues can be attributed to the relative autonomy (Hong Kong) or entanglement (Taiwan) of the police vis-à-vis the political processes. Weak police, in other words, served Taiwan's democracy well.

The Taiwan–Hong Kong comparison appears in the final chapter, which contemplates the larger ramifications of a policing model with illiberal roots. The book was written shortly before the fateful spring of 2020 when the murder of George Floyd sparked nationwide calls to defund the police in the United States. The author makes it clear where he stands with regard to the American military-style policing in which armed-to-the-teeth police squads descend upon "crime-ridden" neighborhoods like an occupying force and in which police discretion is synonymous with racial profiling and abuse. The red-envelope style of corruption seems eminently preferable to law and order by shootouts.

Reading this book, slender though it may be, has put many things into focus for me. What puzzles me, however, is the author's studious avoidance of making the PRC a point of comparison, despite the many family resemblances, such as the virtue-centric notion of legitimate authority and how the *hukou* system configures state-society relations in paternalistic terms. On the questions of *guanxi*, corruption, and communities of complicity, the author could have engaged more substantively with the works of Mayfair Yang, John Osburg, Hans Steinmüller, Andrew Kipnis, and Yunxiang Yan (the latter two are cited, albeit not for their insights on the PRC specifically). On policing and politics, not to bring up Michael Dutton is a sorely missed opportunity. To be sure, the *paichusuo* on the mainland has evolved into a very different beast (down to the perverse ritual of coercive tea-drinking), but there is enough commonality to warrant a survey of the secondary scholarship. At the very least, a Taiwan-PRC comparison might reveal a fuller picture of the perils and promises of *qing*-oriented policing.

Sentiment, Reason, and Law has many gemlike qualities, not least the elegant ease with which it shifts between ethnographic narratives, institutional analyses, and theoretical expositions—all in a precise, well-chiseled language with not a word too many. But like all brilliant works, it is not free of shortfalls and blind spots. In addition to the missing comparison mentioned above, I would have liked to see the author reflect on the gender politics of doing participant observation in an evidently all-male institution that casually partakes of sexploitation in the course of exercising its pastoral powers.

HAIYAN LEE
Stanford University
DOI: 10.1215/00219118-11591289

Saying All That Can Be Said: The Art of Describing Sex in Jin Ping Mei. By Keith McMahon. Cambridge, MA: Harvard University Asia Center, 2023. xiv, 287 pp. ISBN: 9780674291355.

Keith McMahon's most recent book proposes a new framework for understanding the significance of explicit sexual content in the Ming novel *Jin Ping Mei*. He argues that the novel's explicitly sexual passages, many of which are still excised from modern editions of the novel, serve a crucial aesthetic function, and that they are fundamental to the novel's project of "exposing all the affairs in the world" (2). All readers of *Jin Ping Mei*, McMahon suggests, should grapple with its sexual descriptions, because they emblematize the defiance of social norms and the power of creativity, "taking sex as a vehicle for reading the world" (259).

What does it mean to "take sex as a vehicle for reading the world"? McMahon's argument relies on two overlapping interpretive strategies: first, he takes a granular approach to classifying the novel's explicit descriptions, analyzing particular passages and words. He cites liberally from the text, including translations of almost all its explicit descriptions. Second, he offers a broad comparative analysis with other premodern Chinese texts, including erotic manuals that had been in circulation for millennia, pornographic fictional works in classical and vernacular Chinese from the late imperial period, and novels that were influenced by *Jin Ping Mei*'s descriptions.

Chapters 3, 4, and 5 are devoted to developing a taxonomy of *Jin Ping Mei*'s rhetoric as operating in the "high erotic" and "graphic" modes. He treats the former in general terms in chapter 3, and in the more specific context of battle as a metaphor for sexual encounters in chapter 4. Chapter 5 describes the range of nonallusive, graphic description in *Jin Ping Mei*. Across these chapters, McMahon reiterates that all descriptions of sex in the novel are "linguistically performative rather than realistically descriptive" (68) and that even those descriptions that seem most naturalistic should be read as formulaic. These chapters aim to identify how the register of a particular sexual description contributes to the overall narrative. For example, he observes that the high erotic mode is never used in Ximen Qing's affairs with servants but that it is used in an exaggerated way in descriptions of courtesans, thereby enhancing "the brothel's theatricality" (94). Chapter 6 proposes a typology for the various female sex partners of Ximen Qing, reducing them to literary types; McMahon might have considered, instead, how their distinctiveness contributes to their agency.

Chapters 2, 7, and 8 compare the treatment of sex in *Jin Ping Mei* with other sexually explicit texts from premodern China. Chapter 2 offers a composite introduction to the instructional manuals known as "arts of the bedchamber" (*fangzhong shu*), important in this context for the way that tradition "addresses the problem of excess by creating an entire discourse about non-excessive sex" (64). Despite their divergences in both vocabulary and style, McMahon identifies four instructive commonalities between those manuals and *Jin Ping Mei*: an emphasis on women's formidability, the description of sex as a battle, the idea of one man engaging with multiple women, and an openness in describing sex. Chapter 7 compares *Jin Ping Mei* with other explicit Ming and Qing fiction, concluding that other pornographic works from this period are relatively more focused on "entertainment, shock, and titillation" (203). *Jin Ping Mei*'s "greater length and linguistic complexity," McMahon argues, put it "in a separate category of sexually explicit literature of the late Ming" (204). This comparative approach allows McMahon to identify what *Jin Ping Mei does not* say about sex—for example, it does not depict Ximen Qing sleeping with all his wives at once or write about one named sexual position after another "without adding more elements of tension and thematic significance" (211). That distinction tells us something about *Jin Ping Mei*'s politics, which never depicts Ximen Qing's polygamous household as a "pornographic utopia" (217); instead, it insistently depicts women as active negotiators with their own interests. Chapter 8 considers *Jin Ping Mei*'s influence, discussing a pair of "outlandish" (241) eighteenth-century novels that are "blatantly and obsessively pornographic yet make it seems as if the pornography takes place somewhere else" (241–42) as well as the more moderate *Shenlou zhi* (*Mirage*, 1804), which contains what McMahon describes as "a form of hedonistic polygamy" (242) intended to correct the excesses of *Jin Ping Mei*. Taken together, these chapters offer a comprehensive and convincing assessment of the significance of the sex in *Jin Ping Mei* in the context of late imperial Chinese culture.

Saying All That Can Be Said is an excellent introduction to how to think cross-culturally and transhistorically about the question of literary pornography. In chapter 1, McMahon makes a case for calling *Jin Ping Mei* "pornographic" rather than "erotic," because it features "obsessive repetition" (13) of explicit descriptions of sexual acts that "violate social norms" (12), because it relates to "social and political criticism" (15), and because it functions as "a vehicle of provocation" (17). These final two qualities get at what lends pornography its social power, even across centuries and through translation. Ultimately, however, *Saying All That Can Be Said* misses the opportunity to clarify the implications of its argument as pertains to the politics—and gender politics—of *Jin Ping Mei*'s pornography, and how those politics have changed from the Ming moment of the novel's creation to its present global existence in many editions and translations. McMahon engages early on with Naifei Ding's feminist critique of *Jin Ping Mei* as a "deeply misogynist" text that offers pleasure without consequences to presumed male readers (quoted on p. 6) from the Ming to the present. McMahon suggests that "it is unwieldy to contain [the dissolute voice] entirely under the umbrella of misogyny or dominant male perspective" (7), and he borrows Ding's terms "leaks and letups" to suggest that the novel's "shifting perspective" (9) subverts easy summary of its sexual politics. The chapters frequently highlight differences in the way that sex is described between particular characters, most of them female, but nowhere are the implications developed in a substantial way.

Saying All That Can Be Said showcases McMahon's erudition and considerable expertise across a wide array of Ming-Qing fiction. Attentive to minute textual details and broadly conversant with related texts, this is a balanced study that offers new perspectives to specialists while remaining accessible to pornography scholars of other cultural contexts.

S. E. KILE
University of Michigan
DOI: 10.1215/00219118-11591299

The Chinese Computer: A Global History of the Information Age. By Thomas Mullaney. Cambridge, MA: MIT Press, 2024. x, 359 pp. ISBN: 9780262047517.

To train a language model, the first step is transforming a language into a format that computers can understand. It involves extracting stems of words and tokenizing a large corpus. The resulting training data is nothing natural, despite how Natural Language Processing makes it sound. What makes a language computable is this transformative process called input. Input is the hidden subject of Thomas Mullaney's recent book *The Chinese Computer*. It highlights the importance of Chinese language input for computation. The book opens with anecdotes that make one marvel at the speed with which Chinese people type Chinese texts in China. But what does typing have to do with computing? Is this book just a sequel to Mullaney's previous chart-topping book on typing, *The Chinese Typewriter*? The answer is not so simple: typing a Chinese character, like transforming a language for machine learning, requires turning words into a tableau of computable data—that is, encoding. A typist of Chinese must master that encoding.

In China, typists "operate entirely in code *all the time*" (7). What happens if the entire nation focuses on so much coding that people no longer hold a pen to write on paper? "They are forgetting how to write Chinese" is the intrigue that frames *The Chinese Computer*. This is a gripping scene (almost science fiction–like) because it depicts a language less "written" than "typed." The amnesia of writing has to do with Chinese input methods, tools that encode Chinese characters for computer processing. Unlike typing Latin languages, Chinese input reveals the "mediation unseen in mainstream Anglophone computing" (9). This insight (an "axiom of Chinese computing," as Mullaney calls it) shows why Chinese is crucial in the global information age.

The chapters tell the histories of inventors and typists, some of whom believed that entire populations could learn to write Chinese through coding. For a coder, the same task has multiple solutions. Chapters 1 to 6 showcase various coding solutions (i.e., input methods), from the 1940s to the 1990s, from hardware to software, and from stroke-based spelling to phoneticized retrieval. The successes and failures of these methods depend on their business contexts and political climates.

Chapter 1 focuses on a device developed in the 1940s. A typist needs to memorize the exact four-digit code for each character. Any mistake in the code would produce the wrong word. The success of this device in the United States relied on the demonstration of a single typist: an average Chinese immigrant woman, Lois Lew. She was beautiful, "very sexy looking" (57), but unlike the educated white women typically associated with office work. The combination of her beauty and her status as an immigrant without much education did the trick: if she could master the device, Chung-Chin Kao's typewriter, others could, too. Her demonstration convinced people that Kao's typewriter was a good investment for the US military.

Chapter 2, moving into the 1950s, frames Chinese computers as a Cold War strategy for the United States to demonstrate supremacy of "free-world" technologies (63). The message—"capitalism would bestow upon China the gift of computing" (63)—came from the Pentagon. A computational system for Chinese would help Cold War propagandists "flood the world with Chinese texts at rates never seen" (63). Efficiency of typing, a key theme that connects all the chapters in the book, was a major concern of the person who invented this system. It was called "Sinotype" by MIT professor Samuel Hawks Caldwell. For Caldwell, "spelling" a Chinese character means to "input the 'address' of that character from memory" (66). Caldwell's Sinotype is a retrieval system: it locates the address of a word. The chapter details the military funding, the small successes, and the eventual obsolescence of Sinotype.

Chapter 3 shifts to the 1970s, when alternative hardware (not the QWERTY keyboard we use today) was invented in Taiwan, Shanghai, and Cambridge. The 1970s were important for Chinese computing. Despite the Cultural Revolution, China was "more advanced in mainframe computing" (that is, not minicomputing) "than most outsiders realized" (100). But hardware did not usher China into the computational age. Software did. Chapter 4 details the parallel history of software and minicomputing. Old hardware like the QWERTY keyboard returned with new software. Programming became key because many systems could be run on the same device and global computer manufacturers (such as IBM) could enter China's market through software innovations. Chapter 5 details China's importation of computers in the 1980s and the "modding and "hacking" that helped Chinese engineers "find inroads into an exclusionary global information order" (157).

Chapter 6 finally arrives at the 1990s. By then, there had been many attempts to phoneticize Chinese using the Latin alphabet, which would make Chinese compatible with the QWERTY keyboard. But that trend did not pick up until this late stage, when predictive texts were invented. Word associations help predict the likely sequence after a given input. Phoneticized Chinese took advantage of associative meaning and achieved simpler coding for faster retrieval. This invention brings us to back to the central concept mentioned in the introduction: orthography, "writing as composing" (28), ceding to hypography, "writing as retrieving." Retrieval is how Chinese typists aced all competitions and entered the "hypographic age" (20).

The Chinese Computer is an engaging read. It details political histories and the inner workings of technologies, all written in compelling narratives threaded with personal stories. The book connects the many inventions of Chinese input by the efficiency principle: how to achieve the fastest input. Here, a user is presumed to be a typist: not a writer, not a copyeditor, but someone who needs to type a document fast. The efficiency principle leaves one question open: If the user is a copyeditor or a writer (like myself), not so focused on how fast she can retrieve a sequence of words, how would her experience in this hypographic age differ?

XUENAN CAO
Chinese University of Hong Kong
DOI: 10.1215/00219118-11591309

Lotus Blossoms and Purple Clouds: Monastic Buddhism in Post-Mao China.
By Brian J. Nichols. Honolulu: University of Hawai'i Press, 2022. xiv, 274 pp.
ISBN: 9780824889005.

Two central questions animate Brian J. Nichols's thought-provoking analysis of the Kaiyuan Monastery in Quanzhou, Fujian: the fate of Buddhist monasticism in Communist China and, by extension, the changing role of Buddhism in a country controlled by a secular, atheist state. Among a growing number of books on Buddhism in post-Mao China, Nichols's study stands out as among the most historically informed. Expertly weaving together textual sources such as Ming and Republican-era temple gazetteers with months of firsthand ethnographic observation, Nichols complicates sharp dichotomies between pre-Communist and post-Maoist Buddhism, observing perceptively the many similarities between the present-day monastery and its earlier versions in terms of cycles of decline and revival; its need for the patronage of authorities; and its multiple functions, both religious and nonreligious. At the same time, Nichols is sensitive to the particular challenges that monasteries like Kaiyuan face in the Communist era: this, Nichols argues, comes less from the commodification of Buddhism than the related but separate process of "museumification": the deliberate efforts of the Communist state to construct Buddhist temples as features of China's heritage rather than sites of living religion (193–95).

Lotus Blossoms is divided into three parts exploring the history, contemporary religious life, and material culture of the Kaiyuan Monastery. In the historical section, chapter 1 explores the history of the temple from its Tang founding through the Cultural Revolution. The lotus blossoms and purple clouds in the book's title refer to auspicious miracles in its early history—namely, the blossoming of lotus flowers from mulberry trees that was said to have inspired its initial construction and a providential "purple cloud" (*ziyun* 紫云) that was said to have passed over the temple as its main hall was first built (20–21). The temple reached its apogee during the Song when it became a prominent Chan temple, and it later again rose to prominence in the late Ming, early Qing, and Republican periods. During the Cultural Revolution, it was spared destruction because it housed important cultural treasures. In chapter 2, Nichols explores the temple's history since the death of Mao. Through interviews with key players, he recounts how the temple, led by its entrepreneurial abbot Daoyuan, eventually raised enough funds to buy back much of its original land.

In the second part, Nichols explores the contemporary religious life of the Kaiyuan Monastery, particularly that of its monastics, in greater detail. Chapter 3 provides rich detail on the temple's daily, monthly, and annual ritual events. In chapter 4, Nichols profiles monks of different ranks within the temple, describing their varying reasons for joining the sangha, their everyday practices, and their long-term life goals, both religious and secular. The third part of the book focuses on the temple's material culture. Chapter 5 details the different ways in which temple space is experienced by its residents and visitors: as sacred space, as a repository of China's cultural heritage, and as a recreational space. Chapter 6 focuses on the legends and myths that surround the temple's history. Just as the temple's physical space is experienced in different ways by those that enter its space, so, too, do myths and legends work both in secular terms, as "branding" that establishes the temple's unique cultural character for tourists and officials, and "sanctification," as testament to the temple's sacred character for believing practitioners and worshippers.

Chapter 7 introduces the two main players (as well as the two major modes) that dominate Buddhist temple culture in the post-Mao period: that of the "curator," who seeks to restore temples as monuments to the cultural heritage of China's past, and the "revivalist," who aims to restore them as active religious sites. Putting his research at Kaiyuan in conversation with his broader observations of other prominent temples across the country, Nichols shows how some temples have been completely "museumified," their halls dedicated not to worship but to the display of cultural treasures to tourists by paid employees. Others have no cultural treasures to speak of and function solely as spaces for intensive monastic cultivation. Kaiyuan falls in the middle of these two extremes, being a site of cultural treasures to be admired by tourists but also one of active religious practice. In this chapter, Nichols shows how the talent and determination of the temple's abbot has enabled Kaiyuan to win a battle of control against state-controlled bureaucratic entities that aimed to showcase the temple's cultural heritage for tourists rather than allowing it to be controlled by monastics for mostly religious purposes.

The strength of *Lotus Blossoms* lies in its combination of detailed ethnographic fieldwork, historical research, and comparison with other present-day Buddhist temples in China. I particularly appreciate how Nichols's insights into Kaiyuan's history complicate the easy distinctions one sometimes hears from both practitioners and scholars between the rigorous cultivation of monastics from the past and the perceived superficiality and overcommercialization found in present-day Chinese Buddhist monasteries. Nichols's distinction between the "curators" and "revivalists," along with his observations about the very different ways in which varying groups use contemporary temple space, sheds much light on the dynamics of Buddhist revival in post-Mao China, but I wonder if it is not a little too tidy in parts. As we hear neither from tourism officials nor visiting tourists themselves, Nichols's book leaves me wondering to what extent "curatorial" forces are really committed to an agenda of cultural preservation at the expense of religious revival. Are the tourists who come to the temple really just interested in observing its cultural heritage at the expense of its religious dimensions? Moreover, given the abbot Daoyuan's concern with building up the physical space of the temple, how different was his vision of temple development from that of "secular" state agencies committed to reviving the temple as an important reminder of China's cultural heritage? Was his struggle with tourism officials one of two distinct visions for the temple—one religious and one secular—as Nichols portrays it, or merely a personal tussle for control over its resources?

Richly described and beautifully written, *Lotus Blossoms and Purple Clouds* is required reading for students of modern Buddhism, state, and society in post-Mao China, and other scholars interested in the relationship between Buddhism and social change. Given its strong readability, it is also appropriate for introductory undergraduate courses on Buddhism and Asian religion as an example of the challenges and opportunities facing present-day Buddhist communities.

GARETH FISHER
Syracuse University
DOI: 10.1215/00219118-11591319

Uyghur Women Activists in the Diaspora: Restorying a Genocide. By Susan Palmer, Dilmurat Mahmut, and Abdulmuqtedir Udun. New York: Bloomsbury, 2024. vii, 164 pp. ISBN: 9781350418349.

Uyghur Women Activists in the Diaspora: Restorying a Genocide, by Susan Palmer, Dilmurat Mahmut, and Abdulmuqtedir Udun, offers a poignant collection of narratives. Based at McGill University, the authors have collaborated on this research project, which, like many other academic ventures, began with a different but parallel thread of inquiry. While conducting field research with Uyghur families connected to a Uyghur language school in Canada, they found many commonalities across their subjects' experiences both within their homeland and during their transition abroad. However, not all were comfortable with having their personal details shared for fear that their families would be impacted back home. Therefore, Palmer, Mahmut, and Udun turned to conversations with more established Uyghur figures to represent the role that "restorying" has to offer historically marginalized communities.

Part 2, the main body of the volume, centers on the narratives of ten Uyghur women who have taken on the heavy burden of being the "voice" of a community that is being forcibly silenced. As reiterated by several women who do not self-identify as activists (a nuance that I wish was reflected in the titling of the book), their work is a necessary and natural response to witnessing ongoing violence and genocide against their people. Their discomfort, primarily stemming from experiences as young adults in China—whether discrimination in the workplace, racism from university classmates, or retaliation for behaviors perceived as a threat to the status quo—became too much to bear. Many came to the West as students and professionals eager for a new start but found themselves using their relative positions of freedom to bring awareness to the atrocities continuing back home. Others came as survivors of China's reeducation apparatus, bringing with them stories of violence that have been instrumental in moving hearts and minds to respond to threats of genocide. Collectively, their stories remind readers that the post-2016 campaign of mass incarceration in the region is an intensification of efforts to enforce political compliance through censorship, interrogation, and arbitrary disappearances that have been ongoing for decades.

The authors use oral history—specifically, "restorying"—as the methodological framework of their research. They write that "restorying is the process of reconstructing new meanings from old, 'official' narratives." It has "been applied by psychiatrists in therapeutic settings and by sociologist in the research field," as well as in reconciliation initiatives (113). Narrating one's story can be an act of exerting agency, particularly for populations whose voices have been marginalized or misconstrued in some way, an experience acutely relevant to the Uyghur community. The value of these stories does not lie in their representation of a static "truth" since storytelling relies on the fragilities and subjectivities of personal memory. Instead, they offer a "window into the mind" of the narrators,[1] gesturing toward broader impacts of social, cultural, and historical realities (9). As Uyghur stories have been widely targeted by propaganda and misinformation campaigns initiated by the Chinese state and its sympathizers, this book offers a humanizing look at the broader trajectory of these women's lives, showing that the current atrocities are nothing new.

There are remarkable similarities that span across these women's experiences, offering testimony to the patterns of discrimination and marginalization experienced by Uyghurs under China's rule. Zubayra Shamseden, Rushan Abbas, and Rahima Mahmut, all prominent leaders in Uyghur human rights work, specifically discuss their involvement with prodemocracy movements in China while at university during the late 1980s, some finding emerging allyship with Han student activists and sympathetic professors. However, there was still discrimination from those who saw their difference as a threat to the status quo. After graduating from top universities, their Han peers easily found work in an opening Chinese economy. However, these women returned to their hometowns to be rejected time and again for being Uyghur. This was an early, and impactful, experience of being explicitly discriminated against and denied equal opportunity in their own homeland.

These experiences are an example of what the authors describe as "turning points" in the women's lives, key moments that pushed their limits of tolerance. For several women, a turning point was the aftermath of the Ghulja incident in 1997, when several thousand primarily Uyghur men were detained and hundreds killed by Chinese security forces. Among the dead were several of Zulbayra Shamseden's relatives, while her brother was sentenced to life in prison (32, 35). Dilnur Reyhan, Rahima Mahmut, and Raziya Mahmut all expressed the distressing residual impacts left on their communities. Other turning points toward political engagement were informed by their exposure to China's reeducation apparatus well before the current campaign of mass incarceration. Rushan Abbas's childhood was acutely impacted, as both her parents would disappear for weeks at a time (38). Raziya

Mahmut's father was exiled to a remote village for over ten years, her mother eventually joining him (74).

Alongside the stories of women who emigrated several decades ago, the authors include the narratives of Zumret Dawut and Mihrigul Tursun, both recent refugees who have become key witnesses to the atrocities committed against detainees in China's prisons and reeducation camps. Having been targeted for allegations of having established connections abroad, they share much darker details of the violence they experienced during their incarceration in China. In a twist of fate, it was these very family connections to foreign citizens that helped them obtain passports and permission to temporarily leave the country. Once out, they had no hesitation in contacting journalists and advocacy groups, all in the hope of bringing evidence to the global community.

This collection of narratives provides particular insight into the gendered impact of Chinese colonial violence. Women, particularly Muslim women, often bear the burden of being perceived as symbols of culture. Under a colonial apparatus that seeks to erase cultural and religious identity, women's bodies are held under scrutiny as an indication of compliance. Arzu Gul discusses how she was required to perform Uyghur dance in the streets to "create a fake happy mood of Uyghurs" for visiting tourists (66), a phenomenon that continues today with China's "Xinjiang is a nice place" campaign. As Arzu Gul observes, Orientalist depictions of beautiful and compliant Uyghur women were used to encourage Han men to migrate to the region for work and marriage (64). Zumrat Dawut and Mihrigul Tursun speak about sexual harassment from Han "relatives" (96, 105), a government program where Han men are sent to live in Uyghur homes, as well as the systemic sexual violence and forced sterilization that occurs in the camps.

The authors lay out their analysis and additional topical context in part 3, which I felt could have been benefited from a more direct discussion of the Uyghur organizations that many of these women have come to work for, particularly in building bridges between Western academic discourse and camp survivor testimonies. Additionally, for a book that focuses on the stories of women, I would have liked to see more explicit dialogue with decolonial and Muslim feminist discourse. This would have added context and depth to discussions on gender and culture in Uyghur society that risk appearing reductive at times. However, these are minor concerns as the authors have managed to cover a wide breadth of material, giving a much-needed platform for Uyghur women in positions of leadership to tell their stories. While they have positioned their work to a general Western audience with a moderate or superficial understanding of the Uyghur crisis, readers who are more familiar with the situation will still find worth in the intimate details of these women's lives, making it a valuable source for scholars, journalists, and policymakers alike.

SONYA IMIN
Université Libre de Bruxelles
DOI: 10.1215/00219118-11591329

Note

1. Martin Cortazzi, *Narrative Analysis* (London: Falmer, 1993), 2.

Singer of the Land of Snows: Shabkar, Buddhism, and Tibetan National Identity.
By Rachel H. Pang. Charlottesville: University of Virginia Press, 2024. xiii, 222 pp.
ISBN: 9780813950655.

Rachel Pang's *Singer of the Land of Snows* is an in-depth investigation into the writings of Shabkar Tsokdruk Rangdrol (1781–1851), a nineteenth-century Tibetan Buddhist scholar from Eastern Tibet. Pang argues that in Shabkar's lifetime "Tibet" already was conceived of as a plateau-wide collective identity. This intervention is particularly timely at a period when the Chinese government maneuvers to replace the very name of Tibet with "Xizang" in Western languages. Employing Anthony Smith's "ethno-symbolist model of nationhood" (11), Pang explores Shabkar's conceptualization of Tibetan national identity through elements such as literature, cartography, myths, and religion. Moving beyond the state-centric view of nations that emerged in eighteenth-century Europe, the book posits that Shabkar articulated a conception of Tibetan collective identity—a Buddhist imagined community—that drew on myths of ethnic election, the mapping and visualization of Tibet as a predestined Buddhist landscape, vernacularization of his autobiography, and Buddhist ideals and practices. Together, these elements serve as a "coalescing force" (4) for the imagined Buddhist polity Shabkar envisioned.

Highlighting the significance of being what Smith calls "a named and self-defined human community" connected by shared myths, memories, symbols, and values (9), the first chapter analyzes Shabkar's use of the terms *Tibet* (*bod*) and *Tibetans* (*bod pa*) and various metaphoric equivalents such as "people of the land of snows" (*gangs can pa*). It demonstrates that Shabkar's understanding of Tibet unequivocally included his homeland of northeastern Tibet (Amdo) and that he identified himself as "the singer of the land of snow," emulating the eleventh-century poet-saint Milarepa (17–19, 57). Tibet in the early modern period (fourteenth to eighteenth centuries) experienced increased transregional travel and exploration, but the nineteenth century especially saw a concomitant development of travel literature in a variety of genres that facilitated what Sanjay Subrahmanyam calls a "geographical redefinition" of one's inhabited world.[1] As Pang presents in chapter 2, Shabkar's autobiography (*rang rnam*) stands as one such fascinating example that combines the genre of Buddhist life-writing (*rnam thar*) with a variety of geographical literary genres like pilgrimage guides (*gnas yig*), praises of place (*gnas stod*), and gazetteers (*dkar chag*). Providing useful context to simultaneous developments occurring in other parts of Tibet, Pang argues that Shabkar's pilgrimages and writings on sacred Buddhist geographies allowed him to conceive a narrative map of a Buddhist nation extended across the expanse of the Tibetan plateau (58–59). Despite the absence of a political agenda or nationalistic sentiments, this narrative mapping of sacred sites enabled Shabkar to envision an ethnoscape of Tibet imbued with collective historical and cultural memories, articulating the territorial basis for Tibet as an imagined Buddhist polity.

A powerful literary style and technique employed by Shabkar is what Pang calls the vernacularization of his writings (64). This involved extensive references and efforts to sustain literary connections and continuity with popular and folkloric Tibetan oral traditions. Shabkar drew on a repertoire of folk songs, traditional Tibetan opera, and various forms of traditional orality that sustained embryonic national consciousness conducive to his imagined Buddhist community (77–79). Deftly illustrating how the mythic narratives associated with both Avalokiteśvara and Padmasambhava were continually deployed throughout history by Tibetan scholars, including the fifth Dalai Lama, Pang contends that Shabkar skillfully revived and adapted these myths of ethnic origin and election to envision Tibet as a Buddhist polity under the protection of Avalokiteśvara incarnated in the form of the Dalai Lamas (89–104). Aware of the need to avoid imposing intentionality and acknowledging the lack of clear evidence, Pang refrains from assuming that Shabkar was motivated by political or nationalistic aims. Instead, Pang underscores Shabkar's focus on religious and spiritual goals. Nevertheless, Pang asserts that Shabkar's efforts reinforced the concept of a Tibetan people with a distinctive destiny (94) and served as an antecedent to the emergence of Tibetan nationalism and nationalist movements in the twentieth century.

The last chapter culminates in an investigation of Shabkar's imagined Buddhist community focusing on specific Buddhist values and practices that intricately connect Tibetan identity to Buddhism. Drawing on political scientists Jon Fox and Cynthia Miller-Idriss's notion of "everyday nationhood," which emphasizes routine activities like talking, consuming, and engaging in religious practices within an imagined religious community (115), Pang illustrates how Shabkar's seemingly ordinary practices and ideals—such as vegetarianism, pilgrimage, and nonsectarianism—contributed to his vision of Tibet as an imagined Buddhist nation. Pang maintains that for Shabkar Buddhism did not serve as an instrumental tool but rather played a fundamental "ordering role" in unifying Tibet (115). In Shabkar's worldview, Buddhism was the only framework and value system that organized and shaped Tibetan society and identity.

Pang's examination of Shabkar's nonsectarianism overlooks the broader political environment and tensions stemming from conflicts between the Central Tibetan state in Lhasa and Eastern Tibetan polities like that of Golok Khangsar or Nyarong in the nineteenth century. Shabkar's close connections with political figures, including his root teacher Ngawang Dargye (Chogyal Ngakyi Wangpo, 1736–1807), a ruler of the Khoshot Mongols in Amdo, and Tsemonling Ngawang Tsultrim (1721–1791), the regent of Tibet, underscore his engagement with worldly affairs. While Shabkar played a pivotal role in revitalizing nonsectarianism in Amdo, confining his nonsectarian stance solely to soteriology ignores the intertwined nature of religion and politics, potentially reinforcing a dichotomy between these realms. This is not to imply that nonsectarianism fostered quasi-nationalist desires, given that intrasectarian conflicts and competition among incarnational institutions (*bla brang*) were as widespread as intersectarian issues. Rather, it notes that the nonsectarian movement in Eastern Tibet during the nineteenth century was far more complex and multifaceted than mere ecumenism. A broader discussion of the political climate within which the nonsectarian movement arose could be productive in historicizing how nonsectarianism might be connected to, and contributed to, the idea of Tibetan national identity.

An evident question raised by Shabkar's monolithic conception of Tibet as an "imagined Buddhist community" is the place of Bonpos within this vision. While Padmasambhava's significant role in transmitting Buddhism and pacifying Tibet's Indigenous deities is celebrated, there exists a counternarrative of resistance from Bonpos and practitioners of pre-Buddhist Tibetan religious practices and rituals. In essence, how does Shabkar's nonsectarianism accommodate non-Buddhist Tibetans, or are Bonpos relegated to the status of "uncivilized" border populations akin to the Monpas? One potential area for further investigation seems to be Shabkar's assertion of himself being an incarnation of Drenpa Namkha (88), an important religious figure in both Tibetan Buddhism and Bon from the eighth century.

Furthermore, Pang's discussion in the epilogue of concepts like early modernity and countermodernity appears misplaced. If integrated earlier, thereby weaving these broader concepts into the discussion of cultural nationalism, they might have provided valuable insight and context while enhancing their heuristic value. For example, the framework of the early modern—which emphasizes the expansion of one's world through travel and writing that connected regions across vast territories—aptly situates Shabkar and his contemporaries, such as Jamgön Kongtrül (1813–1899), within their historical milieu amid the expanding geographic and cultural dimensions of their imagined national community.

Finally, when considering the supposed "effect" of Shabkar's conceptualization of Tibetan identity and imagined Buddhist community, it remains challenging to discern clear causal connections or to determine the specific contributions of his autobiography and other writings. While Shabkar was indeed popular and his works were printed in several places, available sources offer limited information about their circulation or their direct impact on shaping Tibetan identity and national consciousness during his time or afterward. Therefore, assessing the exact influence of Shabkar's works remains speculative. There are also a number of typos, spelling errors, and transliteration inconsistencies that have slipped past editorial scrutiny.

Aside from these minor issues, *Singer of the Land of Snows* stands out as an important work of conceptual history. Pang moves beyond the conventional Westphalian conception of nation and nationalism by emphasizing myths, symbols, and historical memories that unified Tibetans into a cohesive nationhood a century before its annexation by the People's Republic of China. Pang's monograph fills a significant gap in historical research and scholarship on the relatively understudied nineteenth-century Tibet. It is highly recommended for both general readers and specialists alike, including in seminars on modern Tibetan history, the intersection of religion and politics, and cultural nationalism.

PALDEN GYAL
Columbia University
DOI: 10.1215/00219118-11591339

Note

1. Sanjay Subrahmanyam, "'Connected Histories' Notes toward a Reconfiguration of Early Modern Eurasia," *Modern Asian Studies* 31, no. 3 (1997): 735–62.

Common Ground: Tibetan Buddhist Expansion and Qing China's Inner Asia. By Lan Wu. New York: Columbia University Press, 2022. xvi, 248 pp. ISBN: 9780231206174.

Scholars have debated the nature of the Qing empire for decades. Whereas some historians argue that the Qing was a sinicized regime, pioneers in the United States of an academic trend known as New Qing History, influenced by long-standing scholarship of Europe and Japan, have shown that the Qing significantly differed from previous "Chinese" dynasties.[1] Inspired by this scholarship, in recent years a number of books on Qing and Inner Asian history have been published, forming a new trend sometimes called New Qing History 2.0.[2] Compared with the earlier scholarship, which mainly focused on the perspectives of the Manchu elites and the Qing court in Beijing, the younger generation of New Qing historians intends to pass beyond the dichotomous "sinicized/Manchunized" debate by paying attention to diverse ethnic groups living on the Qing Inner Asian frontiers, including Mongols, Tibetans, and Uyghurs. Moreover, within Inner Asian history, "religion" is increasingly being considered a substantial area of study indispensable for understanding the complicated nature of the Qing formation. That is to say, studies of Buddhism and Islam provide scholars new scopes to interpret the interactions between Inner Asian peoples and the Qing empire, allowing studies focused on Qing empire-building and the Tibetan Buddhist reincarnation system analytical space to move beyond the dichotomous stereotype of "politics versus religion."[3] In this context, the publication of Lan Wu's *Common Ground: Tibetan Buddhist Expansion and Qing China's Inner Asia* offers readers insightful observations on the making of both Qing China and Inner Asia from the perspective of Mongol and Tibetan Buddhists.

Delving into the intricate and multifaceted relationship between the Qing court in Beijing and the Geluk government in Lhasa before and after the eighteenth century, the author explores ways the Qing empire and Mongol-Tibetan Buddhists encountered, interacted, and compromised with one another. Wu argues that over time the Qing state and the Geluk regime gradually formed "common ground" and developed strategies for mutual growth and governance. The author conceptualizes the idea of "Buddhist Inner Asia," which refers to a multiethnic and cross-cultural space that emerged within the Qing empire. This space was not a static or neatly defined administrative unit but a dynamic and fluid area shaped by religious and political interactions. This concept challenges conventional historiography that often isolates regions into distinct, bordered entities, and instead emphasizes the interconnectedness and mobility of people, ideas, and practices across Inner Asia. As such, *Common Ground* destabilizes traditional notions of fixed borders and highlights the movement and interaction of Buddhist knowledge and practices, helping to capture the transregional flow of power and influence and illustrating ways Tibetan Buddhism extended its reach eastward while the Qing empire simultaneously incorporated these religious dynamics into its strategies of governance.

It is widely known that Tibetan Buddhism played a significant role in the Qing empire. Previous scholars share different interpretations of the relationship between the Qing and Tibetan Buddhism. Based on the Proclamation on Lamas (Ch. Lama shuo) by the Qianlong emperor in 1792, a group of scholars have proposed an instrumentalist view suggesting that the Qing rulers worshipped Tibetan Buddhism only to appease the Mongols for the concerns of governance. In contrast, following the Tibetan Buddhist discourse of the patron-priest relationship (T. *mchod yon*), others dogmatically claim that Tibet was not subject to the Qing empire by insisting that the Dalai Lamas served as mentors rather than as subordinates of the Manchu emperors. These two contradictory explanations of instrumentalism and dogmatism share a binary premise that sets politics and religion in opposition. More recently, scholars in Inner Asian studies have shown that Mongol-Tibetan Buddhism played a significant role in the making of China before and after the collapse of the Qing empire. That is to say, state-building and religious identity have profoundly interacted with each other and could not be fully understood separately.[4] Wu adeptly shows that finding common ground was a fragile and contested process, requiring constant negotiation and concession. This mutual dependency was a recurring process throughout the Qing-Tibetan relationship, underscoring the delicate balance maintained between Beijing and Lhasa. In doing so, Qing rulers did not impose a monolithic administrative system but engaged in a variety of governing practices responsive to shifting geopolitical landscapes. This adaptability is exemplified in the Qing's support and regulation of Tibetan Buddhist practices, such as the institution of *trülkus* (reincarnated lamas) and the establishment and patronage of monasteries.

Moreover, *Common Ground* successfully shows the agency of Inner Asian peoples in the construction of Qing Buddhist Inner Asia by illustrating Buddhist networks that moved between Beijing, Inner Mongolia, Amdo, and Lhasa. The book's detailed exploration of religious infrastructures, including monasteries and *trülkus*, highlights their crucial role in shaping the political and religious landscape of Inner Asia. These institutions were not merely passive recipients of Qing patronage but active agents in the negotiation of power. Monasteries, as fixed structures, provided stability to otherwise fluid Buddhist Inner Asia, while the mobile *trülkus* and other Buddhist practitioners facilitated the spread and exchange of religious knowledge. In turn, the book addresses the broader implications of empire building by reflecting on the metropole-periphery discourse. Instead of viewing Inner Asia as a periphery of the Qing empire, the author contends that the incorporation of Tibetan Buddhist practices into the Qing's imperial framework was not solely a top-down process but involved significant agency on the part of Tibetan Buddhists. This perspective challenges the traditional view of the Qing empire as a hegemonic power imposing its will on subjugated regions, and instead presents a more nuanced picture of mutual influence and adaptation.

In brief, *Common Ground* is an essential read for scholars of Qing history, Inner Asian studies, and religious studies. Offering a fresh and compelling account of how the Qing empire and Tibetan Buddhism jointly shaped each other's identities, the book stands as a testament to the importance of transregional perspectives and the need to rethink traditional historical narratives of the Qing-Tibetan relationship in light of new evidence and approaches.

LING-WEI KUNG
Academia Sinica
DOI: 10.1215/00219118-11591349

Notes

1. See Joanna Waley-Cohen, "The New Qing History," *Radical History Review*, no. 88 (2004): 193–206.

2. These include Matthew W. Mosca, *From Frontier Policy to Foreign Policy: The Question of India and the Transformation of Geopolitics in Qing China* (Stanford, CA: Stanford University Press, 2013); Jonathan Schlesinger, *A World Trimmed with Fur: Wild Things, Pristine Places, and the Natural Fringes of Qing Rule* (Stanford, CA: Stanford University Press, 2017);

Eric Schluessel, *Land of Strangers: The Civilizing Project in Qing Central Asia* (New York: Columbia University Press, 2020).

3. See Peter Schwieger, *The Dalai Lama and the Emperor of China: A Political History of the Tibetan Institution of Reincarnation* (New York: Columbia University Press, 2015); Max Oidtmann, *Forging the Golden Urn: The Qing Empire and the Politics of Reincarnation in Tibet* (New York: Columbia University Press, 2018); Brenton Sullivan, *Building a Religious Empire: Tibetan Buddhism, Bureaucracy, and the Rise of the Gelukpa* (Philadelphia: University of Pennsylvania Press, 2021).

4. See Gray Tuttle, *Tibetan Buddhists in the Making of Modern China* (New York: Columbia University Press, 2005); Johan Elverskog, *Our Great Qing: The Mongols, Buddhism, and the State in Late Imperial China* (Honolulu: University of Hawai'i Press, 2006); Matthew King, *Ocean of Milk, Ocean of Blood: A Mongolian Monk in the Ruins of the Qing Empire* (New York: Columbia University Press, 2019).

Wuhan: How the COVID-19 Outbreak in China Spiraled out of Control. By Dali L. Yang. New York: Oxford University Press, 2024. xviii, 392 pp. ISBN: 9780197756263.

Following the 2003 SARS crisis, China developed a national disease reporting network, providing a mechanism for local hospitals to notify authorities at multiple levels of government about infectious disease cases. Yet in December 2019, the director of the Chinese Centers for Disease Control and Prevention found out about mysterious SARS-like pneumonia cases in Wuhan not through the centralized reporting system but belatedly through social media. In *Wuhan*, Dali L. Yang provides a riveting ethnography of decision-making that unveils the causes of this and many other critical failures and missteps, all of which culminated in a global pandemic that has claimed millions of lives.

Yang utilizes a wealth of Chinese media and social media sources, many of which he preserved in real time, as well as in-depth interviews with individuals who were on the frontlines of the COVID-19 disaster. In doing so, he demonstrates how pathologies within China's political system led to the suppression of information by local and central government authorities, and allowed entrenched cognitive biases to go unchallenged. In chapters 1 and 2, Yang draws on theoretical insights about organizational culture and fragmented authoritarianism to describe the political structure within which key decision-makers involved in public health policy operate. This disjointed political structure allows for local discretion and the flexible implementation of central directives, but it severely penalizes officials for failing to maintain social stability. As Yang argues, fragmented authoritarianism and the heavy emphasis on social stability often work against the imperative to respond adequately to public health emergencies and, in the case of COVID-19, repeatedly led officials to squander opportunities to control the spread of the deadly virus.

In the body of his monograph, Yang shines a spotlight on the string of official missteps, taken in December 2019 and January 2020, that the Chinese government has worked so hard to conceal. Chapter 3 provides an account of attempts, made as early as mid-December, by clinicians and commercial laboratories to alert Wuhan authorities to unusual pneumonia cases linked to the now infamous Huanan Seafood Market. Their reporting efforts gained the attention of both municipal and provincial health officials, who authorized a joint investigation but failed to report the situation to their national-level counterparts. Moreover, the joint investigation yielded a case definition that excluded instances of infection that did not involve direct exposure to the seafood market. This led health authorities to severely downplay the possibility of human-to-human transmission, even though clinicians were already observing the occurrence of multiple cases without any connection to the market. As detailed in chapters 4 and 7, even following the involvement of national health authorities, this case definition remained in place. In fact, national health authorities, operating with strong cognitive priors and under the faulty assumptions made by the case definition, recommended that local leaders focus their attention on shutting down the seafood market. The closure of the market, along with a crackdown against "rumormongers," gave officials and the broader public "a false sense of security that the source of the virus had been closed and thus addressed" (93).

Yang is at his best when discussing the political motivations that guided local and national authorities. Chapters 5 to 7 provide a fascinating account of the drivers and implications of official efforts to suppress information about the virus. For example, Yang notes that provincial and municipal authorities—particularly Ma Guoqiang, the ambitious Wuhan party secretary who was regarded as a "rising star" (96)—were under pressure to finish the calendar year with an impeccable health record. This was viewed as key to ensuring that Wuhan achieved national recognition for its ecological achievements. Under these circumstances, Yang muses, "would you be tempted to conceal the outbreak and contain it with the resources at your disposal?" (99). Local authorities also had the backing of the central propaganda apparatus, which was guided by the imperative to maintain social stability and paternalistically prioritized the need to prevent public panic.

Central and local efforts to prevent the sharing of crucial information about the spreading virus, including by punishing whistleblowers like Dr. Li Wenliang, not only kept the public in the dark but also prevented China's health authorities from receiving accurate information about the virus's infectivity in a timely manner. In chapters 8 and 9, Yang notes how the start of two major political meetings in January (known as the "two sessions") provided local authorities with an added incentive to continue their information suppression campaign. This campaign persisted even as local hospitals were becoming overburdened by a surge of pneumonia cases, the vast majority of which involved patients who had no exposure to the seafood market. Local officials also actively kept visiting national health authorities from finding out about health-care worker infections, a telltale sign of human-to-human transmission, confining their "closely chaperoned" (183) visits to handpicked hospitals.

Local and national authorities stubbornly continued to suppress information and downplay the infectivity of the coronavirus, even as cases emerged in provinces beyond Hubei and abroad. Chapters 10 and 11 provide an account of national health authorities' increased intervention as they came to the realization that they had a public health emergency on their hands. Even so, as local authorities across China were urged to "prioritize epidemic prevention and control" (198), they were still told to avoid raising public alarm. It was not until January 20, as millions were set to travel for the Chinese New Year holiday, that the government informed the public that the novel coronavirus was indeed transmissible from human to human. And yet local authorities proceeded in hosting a gala and announced that they would distribute free passes to local tourist attractions. Amid mounting concerns that the World Health Organization would declare the coronavirus a public health emergency on the eve of the holiday, which would surely be a "major humiliation" (230), Xi Jinping gave the order for a lockdown of Wuhan. Chapters 12 to 14 highlight the Chinese government's admirable ability to marshal resources to aid Wuhan, including the dispatching of medical teams from across the country, the rapid construction of two new hospitals, and the mobilization of grassroots actors. However, these chapters also reveal the initial disarray and widespread skepticism, predictable products of the government's hasty implementation of the lockdown and abrupt about-face regarding the need to inform the public.

This incredibly lucid, detailed monograph provides a valuable analysis of how the suppression of information at multiple layers of government enabled the spread of COVID-19. While *Wuhan* will be of most interest to public health and disaster management specialists, as well as students of authoritarian politics, I would hope that it attracts a far broader readership that includes anyone interested in understanding the political mishandling responsible for the deadly coronavirus pandemic. Some readers may wish that the author had more squarely placed blame for the pandemic on the shoulders of Xi Jinping, rather than on China's fragmented political structure and individual cognitive biases. However, a careful reading of Yang's ethnography reveals a far more complex story and demonstrates how Xi's pursuit of personal power and emphasis on ideological cohesion have only exacerbated preexisting pathologies that make China particularly susceptible to public health emergency failures.

KACIE MIURA
University of San Diego
DOI: 10.1215/00219118-11591359

The Labor of Reinvention: Entrepreneurship in the New Chinese Digital Economy. By Lin Zhang. New York: Columbia University Press, 2023. 281 pp. ISBN: 9780231551298.

Lin Zhang's timely book *The Labor of Reinvention* adds to the growing body of critical studies on tech labor in the Majority World. Zhang's analysis weaves political economy with extensive multisited ethnography conducted over the past decade, positioning and historicizing entrepreneurialism in the blurring interstices between workplace and family, worker and owner, urban and rural, state and market, resistance and consent.

By spotlighting what she terms "actually existing experiences of life" (x), Zhang provides crucial insights into the dynamic and contradictory relationships among variously situated workers in the emerging IT realm. Moving from elite and marginal tech entrepreneurs in Zhongguancun, the then poster child of tech innovation in Beijing, to rural women weavers in Shandong and Jiangsu, model sites for Alibaba's rural initiatives, Zhang skillfully portrays the tactics through which aspiring workers navigate the new digital landscape, as well as the processes by which these players are unwillingly dragged into the new economy. Using Anna Tsing's notion of "friction," Zhang documents surprising and uneasy encounters between multiple stakeholders along the tech supply chain.

Readers will delve into the often overlooked but self-reinforcing hierarchies among entrepreneurs. Elite practitioners, who constitute a small fraction of male overseas returnees with tech proficiency, government connections, and alumni networks, claim the largest share of the benefits. Their strong identification with state-championed technonationalism overshadows the majority of grassroots entrepreneurs whose projects never receive funding or the assumed benefits awarded to elite players. Meanwhile, previous electronic vendors in Zhongguancun (ZGC), who came from humble backgrounds, were driven out of business amid the government's sponsored tech park upgrades, resulting in vacant office spaces. Perhaps the most revealing episode occurred when Zhang returned to her fieldwork in 2019 and discovered that most grassroots respondents were stuck in precarious gig work, with some deeply in debt.

One of the crucial interventions of this book is the reimagining and recentering of the contradictory rural conditions amid digital capitalism, which defies the metronormativity of platform studies while also adding a critical lens to feminist value chain analyses. In the second part of the book, the platformization of rural e-commerce is coupled with the revitalization and solidification of village-based familial divisions of labor between entrepreneurs and stay-at-home women weavers. As a proactive policy maneuver to tackle rural China's crisis of reproduction and rural residents' reactive responses to the shrinking overseas market since the 2008 financial crisis, the platformization of handicraft practices presents multiple contradictions. It creates new opportunities for self-employment but also inflames interpersonal conflict in e-villages due to widespread copycat practices encouraged by platforms. Its promises enriched a new cohort of rural e-commerce elites who quickly capitalized on alliances with existing village elites while marginalizing older women weavers whose already meager income was further devalued. Even within the countryside, urban-to-rural migrants have higher odds of success than their rural born counterparts. The intricate case of rural e-commerce contributes to critical AI studies' efforts to excavate various data industries' extraction of raw materials and labor power from rural geography. Meanwhile, its findings align well with other platformized sectors in China, such as the garment industry's family workshops in Guangzhou's urban villages.

The book also complicates the urban/rural, production/reproduction binary by adding a third transnational case of *daigou* laborers, who primarily engage in reselling Western luxury goods to the rising Chinese middle class. This case unveils the unique labor of these feminized diasporic players, who operate in a legal gray zone without Chinese state support on one side while conforming to a long racialized tradition of Asian immigrant women performing home-based subcontracting work on the other. Although constrained by the strengthening biopower of state-driven patriarchy, heteronormative gendered subjectivities are strategically mobilized to navigate competing marketized imaginations of what constitutes neoliberal femininity in post-2008 China. For *daigou* workers, reworking women's work in this context constitutes a creative maneuver to carve out an alternative career path beyond the typical entrepreneurial tech-bro clubs and the strong waves of housewifization.

In addition to its rich ethnographic tones that weave the three cases together, the book is also deeply historical. It uncovers interconnected antecedents—ranging from China's investor state to Silicon Valley venture capitalism—that together contribute to remodeling entrepreneurial subjects in China's tech pockets. The rise and decline of ZGC, for instance, reflect China's reform era anxieties and aspirations to curb US hegemony, as well as the rhythm of the global financial regime that has fundamentally structured global labor hierarchies. The investor state is also funneled through "decentralized power at local levels" (29), which largely determines local entrepreneurial models. ZGC's decline partly results from its failed bid to attract more foreign direct investment in competition with tech hubs in the South. In another example, the book chronicles the development and reorganization of handicraft labor in Shandong Province throughout the twentieth century. The reinvention of handicrafts into private business in the new century and later on platformized labor partly hinges upon previous supply chain infrastructure that extends well beyond Asia.

Although the book discusses the role of the US state in laying the groundwork for financialization, Zhang could have been even more ambitious in arguing the centrality of state and local political elites in organizing and mapping the potentiality of entrepreneurial labor in seemingly incongruent contexts from advanced capitalism to postsocialism, as illustrated by recent works such as Malcolm Harris's *Palo Alto* and Erin McElroy's *Silicon Valley Imperialism*.

Overall, the book serves as an engaging historical testimony of the creative ways various entrepreneurial subjects live in post-2008 China, moving past the often meso-level portraits of tech labor and platformization. It is a rare scholarly work that recenters Chinese labor in the fast-moving reterritorialization of global digital capitalism while never losing sight of the historical contingencies that continue to produce stratified digital labor. This makes it highly relevant for both Asian studies scholars and researchers of digital capitalism in general.

MENGYANG ZHAO
University of California, Santa Cruz
DOI: 10.1215/00219118-11591369

NORTHEAST ASIA

Homesick Blues: Politics, Protest, and Musical Storytelling in Modern Japan.
By Scott W. Aalgaard. x, 256 pp. Honolulu: University of Hawai'i Press, 2023.
ISBN: 9780824895587.

Protest music is not a new phenomenon in Japan. Yet research in English on protest music in Japan, however defined, is scarce, with a smattering of material on pre–World War II *enka*, post-handover Okinawa, and the Japanese antinuclear movement. Politics certainly appear in other writings on Japanese music, but typically in a limited role and as the setting for analysis rather than an integral element of it. The study of music in Japan needs greater engagement with politics. Scott W. Aalgaard's *Homesick Blues: Politics, Politics, Protest, and Musical Storytelling in Modern Japan* is thus a welcome addition to the existing research.

Aalgaard organizes *Homesick Blues* into five "tracks" bookended with "liner notes" and an "overture," using terminology from sound recordings rather than that from traditional print publications as a way of "remixing storytelling with musical practice," both to provide a model of how this remixing can help understand the many ways in which people engage with music and to demonstrate storytelling as a research method. Each track begins with a different arrival trope putting the ethnographer (and the reader) into the scene. Tracks move from there through a range of voices and sources in an effort to present the polyphony of discourse swirling around a primary theme.

The first track sets the stage with the story of the early postwar relationship between Japan and the US military, focusing on the reception of singers Peggy Hayama and Eri Chiemi by the *Stars and Stripes* reviewer Al Ricketts. Much of the discourse here focuses on assertions of authenticity or, in the case of Ricketts's perception of Japanese jazz, inauthenticity, underscoring the paternalistic attitude of the US authorities. Track 2 fast-forwards to the Kansai "folk boom" of the late 1960s, bringing special attention to singer-songwriter Takada Wataru; track 3 moves sideways to another Kansai folk legend, Takada's protégé Kagawa Ryo. Both of these tracks follow the rise of American-style folk music in Japan and its sibling protest music, arguing for a complex relation between the two both in Japan and between Japan and the United States. Track 4 shifts the attention quite sharply to amateur musicians and an annual karaoke contest that features *enka*, noting through media and interviews that, contrary to the reading by Yano linking *enka* to national identity,[1] contest participants did not see themselves expressing Japanese identity. Rather, they linked the music to their own personal life stories. Finally, track 5 brings us close to the present day, giving a look at the fandom surrounding protest music and the importance the fans place on being able to craft their own stories about the music and its role in their lives, thus making a strong connection with the *enka* singers in the previous chapter.

As indicated above, in general I find *Homesick Blues* to be a valuable contribution to the study of protest music in general, and in Japan in particular. I do have two misgivings about the book, however. First, the author could have brought greater historical depth to the study. The US-Japanese musical story began long before the period covered in *Homesick Blues* with a musical exchange featuring blackface minstrelsy, then continued with parlor songs, ballroom dances, and military band music; surely there are roots there left unexplored. Similarly, the history of *enka* in the Meiji and Taishō periods is precisely one of protest music, but Aalgaard's discussion of this in the track on the karaoke contest is cursory at best, drawing solely on two old and somewhat problematic articles that are essentially summaries of deeper Japanese research. I also expected to see greater engagement with the work on the Japanese antinuclear movement by Manabe, which has strong parallels to Aalgaard's work.[2] Finally, there is no mention in the book of the music of Okinawan protest against both US military occupation and mainland Japanese cultural and political hegemony, particularly *uchinaa pop* and *kumiodori*,[3] which influenced Japanese popular music beginning in the 1980s, much of it protest music. Given repeated references to the US-Japan Status of Forces Agreement as an important stimulus for protest music, the invisibility of Okinawans themselves is disappointing.

My second concern relates to presentation. Aalgaard's writing is too often challenging to parse, with parenthetical comments hedging and, in some cases, contradicting the primary thesis of the sentence itself. Frequent qualification and requalification of premises and concepts dilute the force of otherwise cogent arguments, rendering the text unnecessarily opaque.

My criticisms notwithstanding, I still commend Aalgaard for what is clearly long-term engagement with the topic and for producing a book that holds great value for scholars interested in Japanese music and the musical politics of protest music. His experiences with the karaoke contest and his interviews with fans are also very helpful additions to the literature on Japanese music, the culture of amateur performance, and fandom.

RICHARD C. MILLER
University of Nevada, Las Vegas
DOI: 10.1215/00219118-11591379

Notes

1. Christine Yano, *Tears for the Nation: Nostalgia and the Nation in Japanese Popular Song* (Cambridge, MA: Harvard University Asia Center, 2002).

2. Noriko Manabe, *The Revolution Will Not Be Televised: Protest Music after Fukushima* (Oxford: Oxford University Press, 2016).

3. James E. Roberson, "Uchinaa Pop: Place and Identity in Contemporary Okinawan Music," *Critical Asian Studies* 33, no. 2 (2001): 211–42; Ruth Forsythe, "Identity Politics in Okinawan Kumiodori: 'Mekarushi and Hana no Maboroshi' (Vision of Flowers)," *Asian Theatre Journal* 34, no. 2 (2017): 322–46.

Impossible Speech: The Politics of Representation in Contemporary Korean Literature and Film. By Christopher P. Hanscom. New York: Columbia University Press, 2024. viii, 225 pp. ISBN: 9780231208499.

In *Impossible Speech*, Christopher P. Hanscom delves into a question that, to my mind, has been the most critically dealt with in the history of modern Korean literature— namely, What is the relationship between art and politics? In modern Korea, the imperative of literary practice as an emancipatory force became especially relevant in times of sustained resistance against hegemonic forces. The task of exposing social reality and giving voice to those oppressed by the structures of colonial domination and, subsequently, of totalitarian governmentality spawned major terms of debate among writers and critics throughout the twentieth century, including the question of which literary aesthetic can best address the anticolonial and antiauthoritarian imperatives. But what happens when the politics of resistance in the past come to bear on how we understand the present? What does it mean for a work of art—be it textual or visual—to expose social reality and *represent* a political subject matter? And, most importantly, what does it mean for a work of art to be political? *Impossible Speech* addresses precisely these questions in the context of contemporary Korean fiction and film by tackling the fine line between representation of politics and politics of representation.

The site of Hanscom's analysis is speech. Building on Jacques Rancière's critique of the "'verisimilar tale of social necessity'" in realist literature as a totalizing aesthetic in which only some people are recognized as capable of meaningful speech, Hanscom challenges the conventional definitions of political art that derive their significance by depicting subject matter already perceived as "political" by existing standards (7). Such artwork "[takes] on the status of a document, subjected to a logic of proof and read on the basis of evidentiary standards" (153). Hanscom contends that the conventional narrative modes of political art—trauma, confession, and salvation—often end up silencing the very subjects of representation despite the intentions to foster empathy and "break the silence" by foreclosing the possibility for speech in excess of what is recognized as intelligible by normative consensus (7). Accordingly, Hanscom conceptualizes politics as a "speech situation"—that is, "as the very decision on what may be said, seen, or heard in a given situation, an adjustment in the configuration of sensibility linked to a configuration of subjects" (152).

Impossible Speech centers on four figures, each related to recent key sociopolitical phenomena: the rise of migrant labor in South Korea during the 2000s and 2010s; the massacre and uprising in Kwangju in 1980; the erosion of social infrastructure in North Korea in the 1990s; and the neoliberal reforms in South Korea following the International Monetary Fund (IMF) intervention that brought about greater social and economic instability. Rather than focusing on the representative role played by the literary and filmic texts under discussion, each chapter locates the four figures in textual moments that both reflect and expand the "normative limits of common sense and speech," (10) thereby making possible what has been impossible. Chapter 1 examines the figure of the foreign migrant laborer in recent fictional works of Kim Insuk, Kim Chaeyŏng, and Kang Yŏngsuk. Diagnosing the emergence of the dispossessed migrant laborer as a return of the *minjung*-oriented discourse of the authoritarian era, Hanscom argues that the attempt to forge a transnational affective community among the dispossessed relies on a fantasy of supralingual communication that leaves intact the fantasy of nation-bounded monolingualism and ultimately silences the political subject (the migrant laborer, that is). Chapter 2 critiques the twin tropes of victimhood and heroism that have hitherto shaped how Kwangju has been memorialized and appropriated for national history along political lines. Against such attempts to shape the history of Kwangju "into a common sense of the [national] community," Hanscom offers a reading of Han Kang's *A Boy Is Coming* (*Sonyŏn i onda*, 2014) as a work of art that resists the compulsion of total visibility in testimony and instead foregrounds a different perception of trauma as that which demands repeated attempts at interpretation (45). The pressure of veracity and conformity to preconfigured identities in political art continues in chapter 3 through Hanscom's analysis of the figure of North Korean escapee in Adam Johnson's *The Orphan Master's Son* (2012). Analyzing the novel's play on the forms of biography and confession to debunk the very idea of a stable, fully knowable identity, Hanscom draws attention to the uncanny semblance between human rights and totalitarian discourses in their respective attempts to frame the parameters of possible speech of North Korean escapees according to established identificatory criteria. Chapter 4 explores the possibility for new relationalities in the postnational, globalized space of contemporary South Korea among the socially isolated subjects in the films *Castaway on the Moon* (*Kimssi p'yoryugi*, 2009) and *I'm a Cyborg, but That's OK* (*Ssaibogŭjiman kwaench'ana*, 2006). The two films initially appear to follow the soteriological arcs produced by the generic conventions of a robinsonade and romantic comedy, respectively. However, the failed urban dweller's spatial transgression of national territory in *Castaway* and the mentally ill's fantastic transgression of one's own body in *Cyborg* ultimately produce a liberatory potential that offers alternative ways of belonging "beyond the limits of the acceptable" (137).

Impossible Speech offers theoretically rich and innovative groundwork for a new way to conceive a liberatory politics of art beyond such familiar narrative modes of trauma, (auto)biography, and confession in which only some are designated capable of meaningful speech. In the context of twenty-first-century South Korea where democracy after democratization has become a question rather than a given, Hanscom's book is both timely and radical in its attempt to challenge the very ways in which we represent and contest marginality through art. Particularly useful is the book's critical analysis of the impulse toward verisimilitude in literature and public discourse that works in tandem with the privileging of the nation, which often operates on exclusionary principle. For these reasons, the book is highly recommended for all students and scholars of Korean literature and cultural studies, as well as scholars interested in the relationship between aesthetics and politics.

SUSAN HWANG
University of California, Santa Barbara
DOI: 10.1215/00219118-11591389

Theorizing Post-disaster Literature in Japan: Revisiting the Literary and Cultural Landscape after the Triple Disasters. By Saeko Kimura, translated by Rachel DiNitto and Doug Slaymaker. Lanham, MD: Lexington Books, 2022. xlix, 160 pp. ISBN: 9781793605368.

This translation of Saeko Kimura's 2018 book *Sonogo no shinsaigo bungakuron* is a welcome addition to the growing scholarship on Japanese cultural production following the "triple disasters" of earthquake, tsunami, and nuclear catastrophe caused by the March 11, 2011, tectonic shift off the coast of northeastern Japan (hereafter referred to as 3/11). Kimura is one of the foremost scholars of this body of work in Japan, and Rachel DiNitto and Doug Slaymaker have done a great service by making this volume available in English.

As is apparent in the word "revisiting" in the title, this is Kimura's second book on the subject, the first being *Shinsaigo bungakuron: Atarashii Nihon bungaku no tame ni* (*Theorizing Post-disaster Literature: Toward a New Japanese Literature*) from 2013.[1] The translation reviewed here provides Kimura's most recent theorizations of "post-disaster" literature. It also includes a "preface to the English translation" taken, in part, from an essay Kimura wrote for the journal *Subaru* in 2021 that updates her analysis to draw a connection to the COVID pandemic and address recently published works. Whereas Kimura's first book was about the production of postdisaster literature from 2011 to 2013, this book centers on reception, on interpreting texts through the disaster. "It is reading and analyzing *as* postdisaster literature that provides the more important axis for our reading" (xlv).

Postdisaster literature is something Kimura defines broadly. She writes, "I have come to call it postdisaster literature, but the works I take up are much broader than fiction. Film, theater, [and] fine arts all came within my purview" (143). The scope also extends beyond Japan to exhibitions and performances in Europe as well, because, as she writes, "'Fukushima' refers to an issue that needs to be discussed at a global scale" (xxvi). Although most texts she discusses depict disaster, Kimura does not limit herself to material that explicitly addresses natural disaster. This broad interpretation helps her see texts about World War II as part of her scope, including pre-3/11 works that provide additional insight when read through the lens of 3/11. Kimura writes that "memories of the disasters, not forgotten, become part of the reading" afterward (xxxvii).

Chapter 1 centers on postdisaster literature and minorities. In the first half of the chapter, Kimura reads postdisaster fiction through a queer and feminist lens. In the second half of the chapter, she analyzes the final novels of the author Tsushima Yūko, who explored the intersection between the disasters and the visible anti-immigrant sentiment of the time in her novel *Hangenki wo iwatte* (*Commemorating the Half-Life*).

In chapter 2, Kimura explores radiation and "the problem of 'Fukushima.'" She questions arbitrary borders, such as those between victim and nonvictim. Kimura argues that the impossibility of knowing the boundaries between safe and dangerous causes an anxiety that she labels "unfathomable" (*etai no shirenai*) and "abstract" (*bakuzen*) (29). This anxiety is often revisited in the chapters that follow.

Chapter 3 connects the disaster to wartime experience, especially that of the *hibakusha*, or atomic bomb victims. Kimura explores how individuals are affected by larger political choices that surround them. This chapter contains a masterful rereading of Alain Resnais's 1959 film *Hiroshima, mon amour* to explore questions of memory and forgetting tied to war and atrocity along with the perilous consequences of unchecked use of nuclear power, illustrating Kimura's innovative analysis of pre-3/11 texts through the postdisaster lens.

In chapter 4, Kimura examines new works about the war that appeared after 3/11. Here Kimura raises a concern that carries throughout the rest of the book—namely, the way that traumatic pasts like the war, the bombings of Hiroshima and Nagasaki, and the 3/11 disasters haunt the present. In so doing, she draws on Derrida's "hauntology," a concept that is further developed in chapter 5. Kimura notes that, in many cases of postdisaster literature, including those written about the disaster and those written about the war, the dead tell their own stories. One example of this phenomenon is Itō Seikō's *Sōzō rajio* (*Imagination Radio*), narrated by a DJ from beyond, discussed extensively in Kimura's first book. This chapter further explicates the hauntology of traumatic literature with reference to Noh theater. She carries this analysis not only to works of literature but also to ghost stories that appeared in Tōhoku after the disasters. Kimura sees these works as showing the importance of remaining in a state of "hauntological melancholy" to listen to the voices of the dead (103).

Chapter 6 returns to the anxiety surrounding radiation after 3/11 and includes an analysis of the film *Shin-Godzilla*, which Kimura reads as showcasing the famous monster as "the very embodiment of postdisaster anxiety" haunting Japan (116). Kimura sees this anxiety as central to the current state of Japan in the lingering aftermath of 3/11, a topic that is further explored in the final chapter, "Radiation and Precarious Life." Here, Kimura reads works such as Kirino Natsuo's *Barakka* and Fukuda Kōji's film *Sayonara* through Judith Butler and Giorgio Agamben. Kimura shows how postdisaster literature thinks through the many social issues of what Anne Alison has called *Precarious Japan*.[2]

Kimura's ambitious and inclusive scope enables her to draw particularly insightful connections across eras and geography. Her reading of postdisaster literature both through Noh drama and Derrida combines a theoretical perspicacity with a knowledge of Japanese arts befitting her status as an important scholar of classical Japanese literature. Kimura's postdisaster scholarship is essential for anyone studying the arts after 3/11, and this translation is highly recommended for scholars of Japan, Japanese literature, and disaster studies. Along with studies such as DiNitto's excellent monograph *Fukushima Fiction: The Literary Landscape of Japan's Triple Disasters* and the collection *Fukushima and the Arts: Negotiating Nuclear Disaster*, which includes an essay by Kimura, *Theorizing Post-disaster Literature in Japan* should be included in any collection of Japanese postdisaster culture.[3]

ALEX BATES
Dickinson College
DOI: 10.1215/00219118-11591399

Notes

1. Kimura Saeko, *Shinsaigo bungakuron: Atarashii Nihon bungaku no tame ni* [Theorizing post-disaster literature: Toward a new Japanese literature] (Tokyo: Seidosha, 2013).

2. Anne Allison, *Precarious Japan* (Durham, NC: Duke University Press, 2013).

3. Rachel DiNitto, *Fukushima Fiction: The Literary Landscape of Japan's Triple Disaster* (Honolulu: University of Hawai'i Press, 2019); Barbara Geilhorn and Kristina Iwata-Weickgenannt, eds., *Fukushima and the Arts: Negotiating Nuclear Disaster* (New York: Routledge, 2017).

Moral Authoritarianism: Neighborhood Associations in the Three Koreas, 1931–1972. By Shinyoung Kwon. Honolulu: University of Hawai'i Press, 2023. xiii, 372 pp. ISBN: 9780824896232.

Moral Authoritarianism is an ambitious book that traces the history of neighborhood associations over four decades, from the 1930s to the 1960s, across three distinct states—colonial Korea, South Korea, and North Korea. While there are some scholarly works on the neighborhood associations within each of these states, this study stands out as the first comprehensive examination of these associations across all three states through the analytic concept of moral authoritarianism.

The book's overarching argument is that these associations shared similar features despite distinct ideological differences—Patriotic Neighborhood Associations (*aegukpan*) in colonial Korea, Citizens' Neighborhood Associations (*kungminban*) in capitalist South Korea, and People's Neighborhood Associations (*inminban*) in socialist North Korea. During what the author labels "the war decades" (2), all three authoritarian states on the Korean peninsula utilized these neighborhood associations to penetrate local society for the total mobilization of human and natural resources through various functions such as information gathering, economic regulations, and public space management. This emphasis on convergence is not entirely new. As the author mentions, historians of modern Korean history have pointed out essential features that persisted from colonial Korea into the authoritarian regimes of postcolonial Korea (3–5). Building on previous scholarship, this book uniquely explores the concept of "moral authoritarianism" as a core feature shared by all three states. This concept describes how all three authoritarian regimes utilized community-based morality for mobilization, drawing voluntary participation rather than relying exclusively on direct bureaucratic enforcement. The author analyzes how all the states reframed political policies as moral imperatives to obey the morality of the local community and furthermore to enlighten Korean society. This blurring of the line between state policy and morality enabled the states to demand people participate in mobilization projects such as consumption regulations, suggesting that the measures were an enlightening task to rationalize the everyday life of Koreans rather than state policies for war mobilization.

Moral Authoritarianism primarily focuses on the political history of the states, using state sources to analyze the thoughts and decisions of high-ranking officials, including governors-general, Syngman Rhee and Kim Il Sung, regarding neighborhood associations. To be sure, assessing whether the states' intentions were realized with the moral support of the populace presents a different challenge. Acknowledging the difficulty in assessing the effectiveness of state policies and understanding "how the people felt" (265), the author also examines local society's reactions to state-led mobilization. This involves using various sources to shift the focus from state policy to the experiences of local communities. For instance, chapter 5 examines an elite intellectual's diary to provide a detailed eyewitness account of how his neighbors interacted with the associations in Seoul under North Korean seizure during the Korean War. Similarly, chapter 9 utilizes a North Korean official newspaper, *Minju chosŏn*, to offer a window into the everyday life of ordinary people under socialist economic development in the 1960s.

In examining state-society interactions, *Moral Authoritarianism* concludes that neighborhood associations ultimately contributed to the creation of the two extremely authoritarian constitutional systems in both postcolonial Koreas in 1972. Beyond this history of state consolidations, however, the book also documents numerous examples of neighborhood associations not working as planned, as people did not always follow the states' goals for voluntary participation. For instance, the Patriotic Neighborhood Associations in wartime colonial Korea used ration stamps to increase attendance rates, which implies that many people responded only to material incentives rather than to moral imperatives (90). Quite a number of urban residents in South Korea reported false census information, frustrating the state's efforts to handle the so-called ghost population (107–15). Despite the moral emphasis on a socialist way of life, no one cleaned dirt piles in a new apartment complex in North Korea, sometimes causing quarrels between residents in what the official discourse claimed as the Great Red Family (240).

Moral Authoritarianism pays particular attention to gendered tensions, highlighting the essential role of gender in the functioning of neighborhood associations. All three states aimed to impose a patriarchal family structure and morality, with figures such as Japanese emperors, Syngman Rhee, and Kim Il Sung at the apex. However, the author demonstrates, this aim also encountered significant challenges. Chapter 3 on wartime mobilization of women effectively illustrates tensions between men and women over the leadership of the Patriotic Neighborhood Associations. The colonial state wanted to give males the head roles. But as domestic work like the rationalization of kitchen work and air defense became synonymous with women's work, men became reluctant to participate in wartime mobilization campaigns. Instead, women took leadership roles, hoping for empowerment in a newly opened space for their agency. While the examples in colonial Korea mainly involve a small number of elite women in urban areas, such gendered tensions could broaden the scope of politics in war mobilization, which might otherwise be simplified as conflicts between the state and the general populace.

Moral Authoritarianism is a welcome addition to recent Korean historiography, offering a more nuanced understanding of state-society relations during periods of mass mobilization. Readers interested in detailed trajectories of the changes in state apparatuses and discourses will particularly find valuable sources and analyses in this work. Those interested in negotiations between the state and local people will also find valuable sources and insights.

SUNHO KO
York University
DOI: 10.1215/00219118-11591409

Shooting for Change: Korean Photography after the War. By Jung Joon Lee. Durham, NC: Duke University Press, 2024. xx, 279 pp. ISBN: 9781478025993.

Why do we often compel encounters with photography to yield knowledge about a place? How has South Korea, a nation-state but also a geopolitical imaginary, contributed to this habit of mind and of disciplinarity, especially within Asian studies? And what emancipatory role can photography play in helping us "unlearn" this habit? If we bring to photographs and their study an expectation to learn more about their country of origin, its people, and their culture and history, Lee's book interrogates these assumptions without completely refusing our wish to know more about Korea and Korean photography. It does this by rejecting the call to account for the "Koreanness" of Korean photography while serving as a query on the evolving interplay between knowing and becoming—what Lee calls "onto-epistemology"—of Korean photography. How we produce knowledge about and theoretically frame photography contributes to this onto-epistemology; "shooting for change" refers to Lee's praxis of scholarship as much as the photographers and the photographs she analyzes.

The book is also about the living legacy of militarism. It elaborates on three critical concepts to investigate militarism's relationship with the history of photography within the nationalizing frame, all of which rely on a sustained reflection on temporality. The first is the multitemporal event, which upends the conventional thinking of photography as capturing a moment as it "really" was; Lee shows how the supposed afterlives of the image are part of the unfolding durations enabled by the act of photography, which constitutes an event in its own right. Per Walter Benjamin's notion of the dialectical image, the past is not entirely past; it remains available for appropriation and redemption, albeit partially. The second is the multisensorial encounter, which conceptualizes photography as a broadly affective rather than a narrowly visual medium. (Here Lee engages with prominent scholars of decolonial Black thought, such as Tina Campt and Fred Moten.) Third, photography is seen as a medium of plural performativity, rather than a procedure of spectacle making and objectification.

Lee divides the book into three thematic (rather than strictly chronological) parts, which invite rhizomatic reading across the six chapters. The first, organized around the notion of "catachrony," from Lisa Yoneyama, examines how "remembering wrong things at a wrong moment" can engender an *"unlearning* that critically unsettles the way we believe we know our history" (19). Chapter 1 explores how photography can both help solidify and undo the tripartite relationship between family, *minjok* (the ethnonation), and the militaristic nation-state by focusing on the war orphan, the figure par excellence for emphasizing the nation's victimhood and the permanent urgency of maintaining economic development and transnational militarism, no matter the cost. Chapter 2 shows how the genre of portraiture performatively produces an idealized patriarchal and monoethnic family, then expands to discuss how contemporary Korean women artists "problematize the contradictions within the rhetoric of family in the midst of racist, misogynist, and ableist campaigns" (57).

The second traces photography's pride of place in South Korea's august history of protest. Chapter 3 discusses iconic photographs from the April Revolution of 1960 and the 1987 June Uprising, while emphasizing their still unfolding duration and their refusal of fixity; Lee elaborates on Benjamin's use of a photography's "contingency" as a kind of opening that gives the photograph the capacity to connect with future events, while retroactively transforming the "original" meaning of the earlier event. Chapter 4 formulates the potent concept of "the photo public," showing how the candlelight protests of 2008 and the public's mobilization against President Park Geun-hye in 2017 mark a kind of paradigm shift in the political ontology of the protest image, from the aesthetics of martyrdom that privilege singular iconicity to the plurality of photographic performance by which one's political subjectivity is made visible and actuated.

The final part visits spaces that are emblematic of the US-ROK's military alliance: the borderlands of the DMZ and camptowns. Chapter 5 shows how such spaces reverberate as a kind of "theater of repetition" in which the victim-savior dynamic, albeit with variations, continues to dominate the memory of the Korean War. The turn to "the sonic and somatic fields of sensing" shows how enterprises like *Real DMZ Project* can produce and reproduce memories of the DMZ even while providing "a critique of the current methods of doing so" (142). Chapter 6 explores how camptowns have long served as sites of national abjection and sexual scandal, particularly through the portrayal of the bodies of Black male GIs. But more recent multimedia works such as *Narrow Sorrow* also offer "ways in which the viewer can interrogate and resist [their] ethno-nationalist symbolization" (168). Both chapters emphasize suspending the visuality of partition, exclusion, and exception so that the affect of the multisensorial can give way to "the *enactable* possibility of the multitemporal" by helping viewers imagine forms of futurity beyond militarism (144).

While eschewing the survey form, Lee does not shirk the task of introducing crucial events in Korea's photo history to unfamiliar readers. She manages to convey the tenor of South Korea's *grands récits* of development and democratization without allowing readers to fall under their spell. Particularly emblematic of Lee's modus operandi is how she yokes together a discussion of Yi Kwangsu's 1929 family portrait with an analysis of contemporary multiculturalism and Zainichi identity. Some treatment of Yi, a legendary and notorious figure, is practically de rigueur in cultural histories of colonial Korea, but Lee dispels the monoethnic and heteronormative aura formed around the photograph with an evocatively queer reading, thereby opening new horizons of possibility for radical genealogies of photography as they might pertain to problems of genre, gender, and the nation.

Lee's work is part of a growing constellation of recent Korea-related monographs devoted to the problem of historical memory. (Of special relevance is Namhee Lee's *Memory Construction and the Politics of Time in Neoliberal South Korea*, which also draws from Benjamin's ideas on temporality.)[1] Some may feel that the insistence on unlearning and unseeing minimizes the salutary force of photography's visuality and that even more attention might have been given to past moments where photographic encounters frustrated the intended "lessons" in the first place. Still, the book's interdisciplinarity courageously confronts the legitimately pressing methodological convolutions of the day with grace and rigor by pulling together photo studies, media studies, postcolonial theory, diaspora studies, and critical Asian studies. The impact of Lee's onto-epistemological project should be felt powerfully even by scholars of Asia whose primary objects of study may not include photography.

JAE WON EDWARD CHUNG
Rutgers University
DOI: 10.1215/00219118-11591419

Note

1. Another comparable volume, recently reviewed alongside Lee's monograph in the *Journal of Asian Studies*, is Jie-Hyun Lim, *Global Easts: Remembering, Imagining, Mobilizing* (New York: Columbia University Press, 2022).

The Immersive Enclosure: Virtual Reality in Japan. By Paul Roquet. New York: Columbia University Press, 2022. 254 pp. ISBN: 9780231205344.

This is the first book on VR (virtual reality) in Japan and an immensely valuable scholarly account of VR as a form of enclosure. Given the continuing hype and reality around VR, it is a welcome and important addition to the study of that technology and to the history and cultural politics of its technological update in Japan. Its analysis of VR and the new media environment of Japan during the period under consideration—roughly the 1980s to the present—is important and insightful, key as well to pluralizing accounts of technological development that tend to center the United States by default. The book is also eminently readable and teachable. Roquet has a knack for clear prose, engrossing narrative, and conceptual innovation.

In *The Immersive Enclosure*, Roquet extends his previous work on ambient control in new directions, primarily by paying close attention to how VR shapes perception.[1] He "sets out a historical and theoretical framework for understanding the cultural politics of immersive perceptual control" (16). As Roquet argues throughout the book, VR operates via perceptual enclosure and control: user activities in a VR environment are perceptually contained (within the headset and virtual world), mined for their data (as new frontiers of surveillance capitalism), and fitted into normative models of labor and leisure. Alongside the promotional language around VR as promising new worlds to explore, Roquet finds new techniques of power and control (4). Indeed, one of the delights of the book is its attention to a variety of different enclosures—from experimental ones in the development of the technology, to fictional spaces, to virtual workplaces.

Chapter 1 is a history of sound and listening technologies—in headphone technologies and uses—that were crucial to the development of VR. A refreshing counterpoint to typically ocular-centric accounts of VR, it tracks the "arrival of *detachable ambience*" (21) and "personal listening enclosures" (20) that are foundational for VR in Japan in particular, later impacting VR in the United States subsequently. The Walkman figures large here. Sony's product allowed for the popularization of the very idea of enclosed spaces as culturally sanctioned. In Roquet's words, "What has yet to be recognized is how the Walkman normalized the practice of strapping stereo recordings directly to the head" (40)—a significant shift in cultural practice, indeed. The history concludes with the development of "head-tracked audio" or virtual spatial audio, a prerequisite for VR technologies insofar as it allows the user to feel that they can move inside a virtual space.

Chapter 2 argues that the contemporary concept of VR comes via two lineages: first, a US military lineage that includes flight simulators and heads up displays; and second, a Japanese lineage that grew out of telecommunications and home electronics (as well as the "popularity of fantasy narratives and RPGs" [112]). In Japan, companies like Sega and Nintendo were, alongside university researchers, some of the first to release VR-like tools (61–63), keeping the dream alive during the "so-called VR winter" (65). Roquet soberly tracks this history of cycles of hype, noting how "the first VR boom played a critical role in shaping both the research and the reception of later VR in Japan" (70).

Chapter 3 moves from technological play to work, focusing our attention on the changing labor practices that VR enables. As convenience stores are increasingly operated by telepresent workers located in other countries controlling robots to restock store shelves (93), VR presents itself as a salve for a Japan's demographic crisis. As Roquet notes, "This ability to reshape the space of work stands to be one of the most socially significant aspects of virtual reality going forward" (82). What Roquet calls "telepresence enclosure" (83) enables a hardening of national borders, bringing the national back into focus in a manner quite distinct from the fluid US-Japan transits of the last chapter. Telework promises workers without the inconvenience of foreigners (99). VR brings not only the organization of personal perception but also the policing of racialized bodies in space.

Chapter 4 analyzes fictional representations of VR in Japanese manga, anime, and video games. In doing so, Roquet tracks a key turning point from earlier fictional representations to the *isekai* ("other world") genre, of which *Sword Art Online* is a key early instance in which players get stuck—enclosed—in the game, unable to remove their headsets until they complete the game or die trying. In these *isekai* works Roquet detects a colonial impulse present in VR discourse as well (127). The portal fantasy inherent to *isekai* marks the world into which the user enters as ahistorical and fantastical—despite being shot through by forms of oppression (racism, sexism, colonialism).

Chapter 5 extends this point to emphasize the sexism across both Japanese and American VR gaming. What inflects Japanese VR is otaku culture and its particular aestheticization, and sexualization, of 2-D images. Against the celebration of otaku sexuality, Roquet shows that VR collapses the distinctions between real and virtual that support the defense of otaku sexualities.[2] Here VR is most clearly a "masculine enclosure" (166), leading one to wonder at the gendering and racialization of the VR enclosures earlier in the book. This again allows the reader to see that there are a plurality of enclosures and modes of enclosure, rather than a single immersive enclosure.

If there was something that I wished this book delved into further, it is the close relationship between tech platforms and perceptual enclosures, since the 2016 rebirth of VR coincides with the consolidation of the platform era. Likewise, extending the quite fascinating account of VR-for-work in chapter 3 could have made the book a better interlocutor for tech labor studies scholars, including those who work on "virtual migration," given that VR-mediated telework presents itself as a powerful technology for managing racialized border regimes amid labor shortages.[3] Finally, more clearly explaining the plurality of enclosures from the outset would better prepare the reader for the travel across the multiple timescales and sites of VR enclosure that the book presents.

These quibbles aside, this book deftly guides the reader through the varieties of VR enclosures, Japanese and otherwise. Mixing archival work with narrative analysis of fiction offers a lively methodological toolkit for others to use. The attention to the heterogeneous sites of VR enclosures offers a richness to this book that will impress. This makes the book a significant contribution to recent work on platform studies, digital media, labor studies, and transpacific technological exchange in Japan. It is sure to become an essential entry into Japanese media studies and cultural analysis and is well worth teaching and learning from.

MARC STEINBERG
Concordia University, Montreal
DOI: 10.1215/00219118-11591429

Notes

1. Paul Roquet, *Ambient Media: Japanese Atmospheres of Self* (Minneapolis: University of Minnesota Press, 2016).

2. Patrick W. Galbraith, *Otaku and the Struggle for Imagination in Japan* (Durham, NC: Duke University Press, 2019).

3. Aneesh Aneesh, *Virtual Migration: The Programming of Globalization* (Durham, NC: Duke University Press, 2006).

SOUTH ASIA

Traders and Tinkers: Bazaars in the Global Economy. By Maitrayee Deka. Stanford, CA: Stanford University Press, 2023. xiv, 230 pp. ISBN: 9781503636002.

This wonderful study is an examination of street vendors in India's bazaars, where much of the subcontinent's market activity takes place. On the one hand, it is a particularly rich empirical study of three Delhi marketplaces in which tradespeople on the street specialize in selling electronic games and providing technical services to customers. Rather than cater to the rich, who more typically habituate shopping malls and can afford the newest goods in standardized form, traders in these markets sell used items, sometimes illegally, to the "popular classes" and continuously "tinker" with the products to make them work for their customers. The author bases her study on extensive ethnographic research, having observed vendors in day-to-day interactions over a decade, gaining their confidence and acquiring insight into closely guarded commercial and cultural practices. On the other hand, the book offers an ambitious theoretical discussion of the role of bazaars in South Asia, one that is steeped in a wide array of secondary work. As a whole, the book conveys a picture of bazaar tradespeople not as residual figures operating in narrow interstices of an expanding global economy but as significant dynamic and innovative actors who nevertheless must constantly cope with positions of economic and legal precarity.

Traders and Tinkers constitutes one of the closest and most illuminating studies of Indian marketplace activity. Deka devotes one chapter to the physical manifestations of bazaars, discussing such issues as the presence of waste in the streets, the public sociality of traders and consumers, the existence of crowds composed of buyers and of other people simply engaged in "timepassing," and the use of displays to publicize available goods. Bazaars are places characterized by chaotic and unregulated space, ones where non-elite consumers move comfortably in ways they cannot in the shopping centers habituated by the rich. A particularly valuable section of the book is committed to bargaining and the setting of prices in the bazaars, in which the author unearths the highly situational social logics by which street vendors shrewdly arrive at prices in bargaining contexts. Because most customers are persons with modest economic backgrounds unwilling to spend large sums on market goods, traders must usually accept low profit margins. Storytelling is part of the traders' repertoire in persuading consumers to buy goods. Another chapter explores bazaar "ethics"—for instance, the context-specific reasoning vendors use to justify their profit-taking. Vendors make constant allusions to a flexible set of values lodged in Hinduism to understand their practices in the bazaar. A moral system based on "frugality, aversion to greed, and emphasis on honesty" (145) partially allows traders to cope with the precarity of their market position.

A major contribution of the book is Deka's understanding of street vendors as "tinkers"—that is, as persons who constantly participate in addressing technical problems with the products they sell; this capability is crucial to their ability to develop and maintain their customership. In this way, the book is thus a highly novel contribution to the study of everyday technology in Indian society. Street vendors lack the prestige and the market power of technology institute graduates, and yet they provide technical services not for large enterprises but for consumers of modest background. They possess practical knowledge of their products and access to social networks that allow them to engage continuously in *jugaad*, or "frugal innovation." The final chapter of the book depicts the considerable resilience of the street vendors in facing the advent of e-commerce after 2010. This development initially threatened the survival of bazaar operators by providing cheap products (including video games) directly to consumers. Deka discovers in recent follow-up research that bazaar actors had learned to adapt to these challenges, without overcoming their place of precarity, by providing more personalized services that e-platforms could not duplicate and sometimes by cleverly participating online themselves. Through observing the street vendors' interactions with e-commerce over the last decade or so, Deka vividly documents the value of *jugaad* in coping with large-scale change.

Deka's work effectively counters a historical logic—reflected in work on Europe, China, and the Middle East—that depict bazaar economies as precapitalist forms that are superseded with the advent of large-scale capitalist structures. Such explanations, she suggests, simply do not account for the vitality of face-to-face commerce in modern South Asia and the dynamic relationships between different levels of the economy. The book might have provided an alternative history that would outline how the street vending economy in electronic products emerged in the first place, perhaps by using oral histories. To some extent, the book implicitly relies on an overly sharp opposition between the bazaar economy and the practices of "capitalism." Deka argues that practices in the bazaar show that the actors there are "not in their day-to-day life strictly capitalist" (7) and that they even present a "subversive" "alternative to capitalism" (176). The book, she suggests, "presents how bazaars operate quite differently from the neoclassical idea of *homo economicus* and, in some cases, its opposite idea of reciprocity and redistribution" (8).

Such an opposition may underestimate the role of profit to petty dealers and at the same time may presume that large-scale capitalists operate in a purely rational universe free from the sociality of markets and without their own internal ethical conceptions. Indeed, I would suggest that the richness of the ethnographic method so richly championed in this study might be used to undermine any simple of understanding of a purely rational *homo economicus* operating even at the highest levels of the Indian economy. These concerns, however, are not Deka's major preoccupations and raising them by no means calls into question the central accomplishments of this book, which, rather than focusing on large-scale economic structures, brings to life the actions and values of everyday market actors. This book is a major contribution to understanding India's informal economy and should be an invaluable resource for anyone seeking to appreciate how bazaars on the subcontinent actually work.

DOUGLAS E. HAYNES
Dartmouth College
DOI: 10.1215/00219118-11591439

The King and the People: Sovereignty and Popular Politics in Mughal India.
By Abhishek Kaicker. New York: Oxford University Press, 2020. 376 pp.
ISBN: 9780190070670.

Abhishek Kaicker's new book sheds a bright light on a segment of Indian society that is severely neglected in the historiography of the Mughal Empire—the urban proletariat. Curiously, the author does not refer to this class as "subalterns," notwithstanding the efforts of the renowned Subaltern Studies Collective to give voice and agency to India's non-elite classes. But, of course, most of those studies focused on India's colonial or postcolonial periods. By examining the century or so preceding the advent of British rule in India, Kaicker's book pushes the horizon of this historiographical tradition considerably deeper in time.

What *The King and the People* convincingly does is to trace the slow and steady political awakening of the commoners of Shahjahanabad—today's "Old Delhi." Although emperor Shah Jahan had established this splendid capital in 1648, Kaicker opens his study with the book's chronological endpoint: the invasion and sacking of the city in 1739 by the Iranian warlord Nadir Shah. Here he describes how a politically conscious urban underclass rose in violent opposition to the foreign invader, even when much of the nobility was secretly colluding with him. Unlike events in Paris fifty years later, Delhi's commoners supported their king and the ideology of sacred kingship that he embodied. The book therefore does not argue for a growing radicalization of the city's proletariat in the manner of a teleologically driven Marxist analysis. Rather, it explores the growing political self-awareness, and agency, of an urban class that in some contexts supported the emperor and in others challenged him.

By beginning his narrative with its endpoint, the study takes the form of a long flashback, starting with the accession of emperor 'Alamgir in 1658, when we catch the first glimpse of an urban underclass, and progressing into the first half of the eighteenth century, when that class's self-awareness and activism gather momentum. Kaicker focuses on notable moments when the voice of Delhi's urban folk could be heard. Two of these occurred in the years 1712 and 1719, when for the first time in history Mughal emperors were assassinated, thereby removing what in traditional imperial ideology had been the linchpin connecting heaven and earth. Other events also stirred Delhi's underclass to political action. In 1711, when the people felt that the traditional tie between them and the king had been altered in the Friday sermon in Delhi's great congregational mosque, they violently interrupted the sermon. In 1714 an urban riot broke out when an enraged mob looted the marketplace in response to what it saw as the failure of the state's agents to provide justice. The book closes with a fascinating analysis of Delhi's last major uprising before Nadir Shah's invasion—the little-known shoemakers' riot of 1729, a story Kaicker tells with flair and analytical power.

The author's analysis of these uprisings also underscores the book's main theme—namely, the totally transformed relationship between the king and the people that had taken place by the 1730s, setting the stage for Nadir Shah's invasion of 1739 and beyond. The shoemakers' riot was a major turning point in that process. Whereas formerly the emperor had majestically heard commoners plead for justice in the Hall of Public Audience, by the time that riot had run its course, even the lowliest elements of Delhi's populace were not only demanding justice but even challenging the king's right to rule. Whether the people were rising up to support the king, as happened in 1739, or to challenge the king as they did a decade earlier, Delhi's urban classes had altogether ceased being passive bystanders in a grand pageant of stately power and authority, in the manner of Clifford Geertz's "theater state." They had become political actors in their own right.

The book thus brilliantly explores two interrelated themes—the emergence of Delhi's commoners as political actors and the changing nature of Mughal sovereignty. Here Kaicker challenges conventional scholarship on South Asian history, which tends to characterize Mughal sovereignty in static, essentialist terms ("absolute monarchy," "millennial kingship," "Oriental despotism," etc.). The book examines not only the various attempts to recast the nature of sovereign authority—by emperors 'Alamgir, Bahadur Shah, and Farrukh Siyar, the nobility, and the urban public—but also the ways that the king and the people related to each other. It is not that sovereignty had devolved completely from the king to the people (as in the French Revolution) but rather that by the mid-eighteenth century the Mughals' "social contract" had been repeatedly transformed in response to popular agitations.

Also striking is this book's rich data base. Conventional studies of Mughal history betray a markedly elite-centric perspective since most historians of this period rely so heavily on Persian court chronicles that focus mainly on courtly affairs and imperial politics. Efforts to examine layers of society below the empire's elite classes are further hampered by a lack of anything like Istanbul's vast archive of the Ottomans' revenue and judicial machinery. On the other hand, Kaicker is able to write convincingly about Delhi's common folk (with asides to those in Lahore, Ahmedabad, and other Mughal cities) because of his wide methodological net, which gathers up a range of contemporary materials: memoirs, essays, biographical compendia, miniature art, contemporary poetry. Above all, he has unearthed troves of unpublished and underused Persian records in the form of *akhbarat*, or news reports, preserved in local libraries or other repositories scattered across South Asia and Europe. Often written anonymously, these records were never intended to be literary monuments that, recorded for posterity, would cast a glowing halo over the emperor. Rather, they were straightforward, descriptive accounts of daily affairs across the realm. By imaginatively making use of such materials, Kaicker has found a collective, popular voice undetected by previous historians. The book will become a classic in Mughal history and historiography.

RICHARD M. EATON
University of Arizona
DOI: 10.1215/00219118-11591449

A Fragile Inheritance: Radical Stakes in Contemporary Indian Art. By Saloni Mathur. Durham, NC: Duke University Press, 2020. xiii, 235 pp. ISBN: 9781478001867.

Saloni Mathur's *A Fragile Inheritance: Radical Stakes in Contemporary Indian Art* is an eloquent, compelling, and theoretically sophisticated study of the achievements of Geeta Kapur (b. 1943) and Vivan Sundaram (1943–2023), a critic and an artist, respectively, based in New Delhi and married to each other since 1985, who joined hands in various projects, including the Kasauli Art Centre, an experimental space for making and thinking established in 1976, a group exhibition of painting *Place for People* (1980) held in New Delhi and Bombay, the interdisciplinary *Journal of Arts and Ideas* established in 1982, and the Safdar Hashmi Memorial Trust, a collective of secular artists and activists established in 1989 following the murder of playwright, director, and actor Safdar Hashmi (1954–1989). Despite these joint ventures and lifelong allegiances to the Left, especially the Communist Party of India (Marxist), Kapur's and Sundaram's careers are rarely, if ever, analyzed together. At the time of the book's publication, they were energetically producing new artworks, writing, exhibitions, and programs, some of which were sponsored by the Sher-Gil Sundaram Arts Foundation, a nonprofit organization Sundaram and his sister Navina Sundaram (1945–2022) established in 2016. Sundaram died in March 2023 soon after his photography-based project *Six Stations of a Life Pursued* (2022) debuted at the Sharjah Biennial in February 2023.

Focusing on Kapur's and Sundaram's "late styles" in Edward Said's sense, Mathur does not provide a comprehensive account of their practice over five decades. Rather, she examines *relay* and *retake*, words and ideas that recur in Kapur's writing and Sundaram's art and that signal shared commitments to repetition, revision, and refusal of closure or finitude. Across four chapters, three of which are dedicated to Sundaram and one to Kapur, *A Fragile Inheritance* addresses Kapur's and Sundaram's engagements with the careers of artists such as Amrita Sher-Gil (1913–1941), Sundaram's maternal aunt, and Bhupen Khakhar (1934–2003), a friend; the imbrications of oil, war, art, and ruin in Sundaram's paintings *Works in Engine Oil and Charcoal* (1991) and the politics of museums, monuments, and memory in his site-specific installation *History Project* (1998) at the Victoria Memorial Hall and Museum in Kolkata; and themes of death, absence, oppositionality, and indeterminacy in a series of five exhibitions called *Aesthetic Bind* (2013–14) that Kapur curated at the Chemould Prescott Road Gallery in Mumbai. Citing thinkers from Frantz Fanon, Stuart Hall, Gayatri Spivak, Dipesh Chakrabarty, and David Scott to Theodor Adorno, Michel Foucault, Chantal Mouffe, Susan Sontag, and Raymond Williams, Mathur elaborates on agonism, partisanship, affiliation, and generation as aesthetic and political terms that are significant for Kapur and Sundaram, the art world in India, and contemporary cultural practice. In so doing, she links discussions of critique, postcoloniality, secularity, and citizenship in anthropology, history, political science, film studies, and literary studies to those in art history.

This interdisciplinary humanistic approach, along with a call for renewing postcolonial studies, is timely and welcome given contemporary debates on decolonizing art history. Mathur shows how a long history of struggles around visual art and representation in the Global South might inform disciplines, professions, and institutions in the Global North by acknowledging critics and artists who are little known there and whose contributions to theory and practice have been immense. Alert to "an increasing preoccupation with the rise of a globalized art world," she writes against "the suspect category of 'global contemporary art,' a broad, typically ahistorical, banner under which the great difficulties of entire societies, their particularities and paradoxical trajectories, are too often superficially treated or wholly subsumed" (xi). By contrast to those detached and distant methods, Mathur writes with deep, intimate knowledge of Kapur's and Sundaram's work and describes herself as implicated—or "partisan," as Kapur might put it—in the art world she narrates, evident in the exhibition of Sundaram's art *Making Strange: Gagawaka + Postmortem* (2015), which Mathur curated with fellow art historian Miwon Kwon at the Fowler Museum at UCLA. Through such projects, Mathur reflects on her position as scholar and presents her career as unfolding in dialogue with that of the subjects of her book.

Although close attention to a singular pair is original and illuminating, this microhistorical perspective excludes a consideration of cultural production outside New Delhi and connections between that city and other art centers, especially Bombay (Mumbai), Baroda (Vadodara), Santiniketan, and Madras (Chennai). It does not offer an analysis of structures—institutions, organizations, and associations—that were crucial to the making of Kapur's and Sundaram's careers and the art world in India such as Group 1890, the National Gallery of Modern Art, the Lalit Kala Akademi (National Academy of Art), the Triennale-India, Bharat Bhavan, and the Radical Painters and Sculptors Association. Nor does it provide a social-historical account of Kapur's and Sundaram's relationships to their predecessors and peers, including the critics Mulk Raj Anand, Richard Bartholomew, and J. Swaminathan and the artists Nalini Malani Sudhir Patwardhan and Gulammohammed Sheikh. For Mathur, the rewards of studying an "exemplary practice," which cuts across divisions between Global South and North and carves out space for difference and dissent, far outweigh these limitations. Her book reveals art to be an intellectual and ethical project, the work of creativity and conscience, and an urgent and unfinished task in the postcolony. With the rise of religious and ethnic nationalisms, authoritarianism, censorship, and other threats to democracy in India and around the world, such an art has indeed proven to be a fragile, and precious, inheritance.

SONAL KHULLAR
University of Pennsylvania
DOI: 10.1215/00219118-11591459

SOUTHEAST ASIA

Fixing the Image: Ultrasound and the Visuality of Care in Phnom Penh. By Jenna Grant. Seattle: University of Washington Press, 2022. xii, 242 pp. ISBN: 9780295750606.

During my fieldwork, maternity clinics in Thailand displayed advertisements featuring golden fetal images for "4-D" ultrasound. Why gold? I wondered. A fetus in the womb has wrinkled and almost translucent skin, covered in vernix, nothing like the attractive golden smooth surface in the ultrasound images. Such images evoke the *kuman thong* (Thai กุมารทอง), or sanctified golden (boy) child, a tutelary deity believed to bring luck and fortune. Although the term refers to amulets formerly made from dried stillborn and unborn fetuses covered in gold leaf; representations of *kuman thong* remain ubiquitous as plastic figures visible on many shrines. In

Fixing the Image, Jenna Grant takes up this question of the multiplicity of knowledges entailed in ultrasound in Cambodia. Her work skillfully parses how ultrasound is an instrument of knowledge production, the images created entail differing functions and efficacies: for medical diagnosis; for enacting kin; for demonstration of care; to symbolize Cambodian postcolonial modernity; all within a Buddhist cultural repertoire of healing through "skilled seeing." She examines how the relationship between humans and technologies in Cambodia is not a project of disruption, unsettling prior notions of health and the body, but is a relationship of continuities, of interventions designed to stabilize symptoms and uncertainties and to secure fate through the predictability of a machine. The aim in the book is to understand the stability and instability of images and their claims to truth about the inner body and their referents and aesthetics. Ultrasounds *fix* images, Grant argues, even if only temporarily, and are technological compulsions.

Stories punctuate this highly readable text: vignettes of seemingly banal encounters are skillfully unpacked to reveal the complex local affects entangled with this technology. Chapter 1 begins by situating ultrasound technology within the public health history of Cambodia, through the association of advanced medical technologies with white colonizers, to the destruction under the Khmer Rouge and later association with national reconstruction in the Socialist era through to the dramatic influx of consumerist modernity in the authoritarian capitalism of the present. In chapter 2, using a concept of "post-political care" (referring to there being no alternative to capitalism) Grant argues that following the end of Socialist medicine, diagnostic imaging services had a role in the expansion and popularity of private practice. The rapid expansion of free market ultrasound became a means of entrepreneurial speculation due to the low capital expenditure and labor costs and the popularity of a valued tangible product for patients.

In her ethnography in chapter 3, Grant presents a significant reconceptualization of care by examining the notions and practices of care inside and outside an imaging ward, arguing that ultrasound amplifies forms of care that are respectful and neglectful, in ways that are patterned along social hierarchies. She argues the concept of care in Cambodia is understood as practice with respectful attention involving a concentration upon technical practice rather than mental states or feelings, posing an alternate concept of care to that used widely in feminist science and technology studies. Overcare involves the excessive use of technologies merely to extract money, and this happens in both the public and private sectors. Undercare involves the withdrawal or failure to provide care, usually directed at the poor who are unable to pay sufficient "appreciation" (under-the-table payments to ensure care). She also relates how race and gendered bias are built into technologies through a discussion of the conundrum of standardized fetal measurement tables and the need to calibrate ultrasounds to correctly scan "small" Cambodian babies.

In chapter 4, Grant examines local epistemologies of knowledge that rely upon vision. In Cambodia, authoritative knowledge to see inside the body is not the exclusive domain of biomedicine; rather, it is skill shared by monks and local healers who have their particular modes of vision inside the body through dreams, prayers, charms, and ancestors that can reveal the relations of a person's body to other realms, their karmic path, children-to-be, or spirits. She describes how patients and monks place ultrasound within a hierarchy of therapeutic or harmful agents rather than in opposition to biomedicine. Ancestors and amulets are understood to potentially interfere with the vision of doctors and ultrasound images, disrupting biomedical claims of technological verisimilitude and the objective transparent body.

Chapter 5 delves in greater detail into the affective and aesthetic practices related to the images produced—the clarity, color, and beauty of an ultrasound image and its reception by viewers. For radiologists and obstetricians, color can obscure information and is only used for specific reasons (to convey information about blood flows, for example). Yet radiologists regularly produce color scans for patients to take home. As Grant notes, across Indochina, complex cultural and political histories of color inform its use and reception. She reminds us that in Cambodia ultrasound images are interventions and portraits may invoke a certain fate. For example, within Buddhist understandings, what a pregnant woman does and sees can influence her fetus; hence, seeing a beautiful image of her fetus can intimately influence the fetus. This explains the disturbance when a black-and-white scan seems to reflect the fetus as influenced by the mother's relationship with her pet cat.

Fixing the Image advances the interpretation and translation of the multiplicity of visual practices in medicine and healing. It explores the long histories of thought and practice shaping biomedical technologies as they intertwine with understandings of life uncertainties. It demonstrates the bidirectionality of knowledge production and transfers. This is a perceptive, transdisciplinary book recommended for academic readers across Asian studies, anthropology, STS, and visual studies. Despite the sophisticated engagement with STS theories, this work remains accessible and highly recommended as a model study of the local entanglements of a global technology.

ANDREA WHITTAKER
Monash University
DOI: 10.1215/00219118-11591469

Experiments in Skin: Race and Beauty in the Shadows of Vietnam. By Nguyen Tu Thuy Linh. Durham, NC: Duke University Press, 2021. viii, 230 pp.
ISBN: 9781478010661.

This book offers a reading of the Vietnam War, its effects, and its ongoing legacy as seen through the "superficial," the surface of the body. Thuy Linh aims to show how "military, medical, and commercial interests in our body's surface have given shape to the desires for beauty and the hierarchies of race, under changing geopolitical, economic, and ecological conditions" (21).

The book draws together a large number of sources (US military archives, scientific archives, interviews and observation at Calyx spa in Ho Chi Minh City, scholarly accounts, photographs, books, etc.) to reveal changes that developed in the aftermath of the war, in the "shadows of Vietnam."[1] Apparently unconnected phenomena—paddy foot, American soldiers' severe acne, Vietnamese women's faces—are considered together to "illuminate what would otherwise not be visible" (21).

The introduction focuses on the mysteries of the visible (1). Skin reveals that which is hidden: the intersecting histories of science in the service of militarism, biomedicine, race, and aesthetics, colonialism and capitalism, the visible and the invisible. Skin acts as a metaphor for distinction, for separateness, for a border between the self and the world (6).[2] It is material and metaphorical: "In its colour, texture, accumulated marks and blemishes, it remembers something of our class, labour/leisure activities, even . . . our most intimate psychic relation to our bodies."[3]

In chapter 1, Thuy Linh shows how, in the context of the transition from a planned economy to a socialist market economy and the new opportunities for consumption this opened up, Calyx represented renovation (Đổi Mới) and personified hopes for postwar modernization (26). Using Calyx as a prism, she examines how the war and economic development redefined beauty as strength and vitality—in short, as life—and how Vietnamese women responded, in and on their bodies, to a "politics of uncertainty" (15). Skin bears the marks of time, of war, worries, and wounds. In a world that is unpredictable, a contemporary world haunted by the ravages of Agent Orange, where feelings of dispossession can be overwhelming, working on the body represents a means of regaining control, of charting a project for self-improvement, a project that is one's own and for oneself.

Chapters 2, 3, and 4 delve into the plethora of US military research programs in dermatology and their main players: Holmesburg Prison, which, from 1951 to 1974, was among the largest scientific laboratories in the history of medicine, where Albert Kligman conducted experiments on inmates on behalf of the US Army and the chemicals industry; Marion Sulzberger and the Military Dermatology Research Program launched in 1964; and many others. Thuy Linh discusses the processes whereby the violence visited upon the bodies of prisoners, soldiers, and Vietnamese civilians in medical experiments was legitimized and rationalized as a means of attaining biomedical knowledge. Through a "science of conquest," violence was used in the name of biomedical knowledge, and risk-taking was presented as a price that had to be paid to ensure better overall security.

Race science contributed to a racial capitalist division of labor through the hiring of Blacks in the chemicals industry and the army on the basis of the claim that Blacks are less sensitive to pain and irritation than are whites. "Race" appears as the production of differentiated vulnerabilities while also as glossing over difference by applying to racialized people a narrative of their invulnerability.[4]

The question of how white skin could be made resilient became a major military preoccupation, with hopes pinned on a "white corporeal armature" (65). In addition to protective clothing for soldiers' bodies and to the forging of these bodies through regulated exercise, diet, and hygiene, an "armor of skin" had to be built (79). Sulzberger's dream of ultimate security was one of a soldier who is protected even when naked, the self-protective "idiophylatic soldier" (see the image on p. 84). If up until then scientists worked to mitigate the effects of conditions of humidity and tropical heat and the diseases these promote, now they also had a new challenge to grapple with, that of chemical warfare. The author shows (chap. 4) how, in the quest for a white soldier's body that was robust and refashioned for a new kind of war, military, academic, and commercial interests converged, leading to the emergence of dermatology in the United States. Tretinoin (Retin-A), developed by Kligman as a treatment for severe acne in soldiers, also reduced wrinkles, fueling a flourishing antiaging market in Vietnam and elsewhere; as Kligman declared, "We were swimming in cash" (73).

Starting at chapter 5, the reader meets the women at Calyx. They come to Calyx to fix imperfections and improve their bodies. Assessments circulate in terms of what is beautiful (đẹp) and what is not (không đẹp) (137). Fears (of a weak and deteriorating body, contaminated by dioxins) (143) exist alongside fantasies (of a flawless appearance). At Calyx beauty is defined as strength and vitality, as something that can protect women against that which may weaken them. The author aptly refers to Michel de Certeau (151), who shows how humans invent everyday life through the arts of making do, subtle ruse, and strategies of resistance by which codes and objects are distorted and spaces and practices reappropriated.[5] Through an array of creative practices, the women at Calyx show that they are not passive and compliant but rather are trying to make the best of the social order and the undercurrent of violence, and that they strive to build their lives.

This work takes the reader from the war to what came after, from destruction to care, from vulnerability to safety, from the consumption of dermatological and cosmetic products to the repair and beautification of the skin. It takes us from soldiers' feet to women's faces, brought together in the archives but linked even more closely by the historical relations that have shaped our experiences of race, beauty, and war.

CATHERINE SCORNET
Aix Marseille University-Institut de Recherches pour le Développement
(The French National Research Institute for Sustainable Development)
DOI: 10.1215/00219118-11591479

Notes

1. Janet Hoskins and Viet Thanh Nguygen, eds., *Transpacific Studies: Framing an Emergent Field* (Honolulu: University of Hawai'i Press, 2014).

2. Claudia Benthien, *Skin: On the Cultural Border between Self and the World* (New York: Colombia University Press, 2002), 1, 62.

3. Jay Prosser, "Skin Memories," in *Thinking through the Skin*, ed. Sara Ahmed and Jackie Stacey (London: Routledge, 2001), 52.

4. See the conclusions reached by the US Army Medical Department, published in *Skin Diseases in Vietnam, 1965–72*, the first and only compendium of skin diseases among the people of Vietnam, in which is presented evidence of racial difference (with white skin seen as a condition of vulnerability); Alfred M. Allen, *Internal Medicine in Vietnam*, vol. 1, *Skin Diseases in Vietnam, 1965–72* (Washington, DC: Medical History Division, Center of Military History, United States Army, 1977).

5. Michel de Certeau, *The Practice of Everyday Life* (Berkeley: University of California Press, 1984).

TRANSNATIONAL AND COMPARATIVE

Shadow Empires: An Alternative Imperial History. By Thomas J. Barfield. Princeton, NJ: Princeton University Press, 2023. 384 pp. ISBN: 9780691181639.

Thomas Barfield is an anthropologist who has written a number of important works about Afghanistan dating back to the early 1980s and is perhaps best known for *The Perilous Frontier*, published in 1989, which focused on the relationship between the Xiongnu Empire and Han China during the second century BC. This work raised a few eyebrows at the time because it was composed by a scholar unable to read any of the main primary source languages, but at the same time the book was recognized as providing a fresh anthropological overview that was not overly bogged down (as often happens) by the microscopic foci of the real specialists.

The book under review here bravely wades into similar territory but takes it very much further, since it attempts a taxonomy of all world empires in a survey so broad no one could possibly claim competence (linguistic or otherwise) of all the cultures and territories involved. The result is a tableau full of imagination (and a little hubris) based on his many years of research into comparative empires that traces back to a presentation (also on the Xiongnu) during a prestigious Wenner-Gren Foundation conference on comparative empires held in 1997.

According to Barfield's own account, the discussions at that conference led him to propose a new model that attempted to divide empires into two basic types, primary and secondary, the latter coming into being not of their own accord but through interactions with the primary ones. These secondary empires, the real center of his analysis, were referred to as shadow empires, and the result was a thirty-page discussion, still mainly on China and the Xiongnu, appearing as the first chapter of the conference volume, *Empires: Perspectives from Archaeology and History*, published in 2001. Now more than twenty years later, we are being offered the full version of this essential insight, covering seven chapters and more than three hundred pages, and classifying some two dozen empires into what are now called endogenous and exogenous (shadow) empires, the latter being further subdivided into five different types: maritime, mirror (steppe), peripheral (including vulture and vanquisher), nostalgic, and vacuum.

While this may seem a bit hard to follow, the polemical importance of the subject is clear: first, that there were many different kinds of empire that cannot be reduced to those that only fit the Western or rather the Roman model, which of course is the source for the word empire itself; and second, that the so-called shadow empires have remained largely understudied when compared to "classic" endogenous ones like Persia, China, and Rome. There is also much to be gained from sometimes surprising comparisons between cases that are not normally thought of together or perceived to have much in common. But in the end, a question remains: How much more does the three-hundred-page version teach us compared to the more modest suggestiveness of the original theory as presented in the conference volume? On the one hand, it certainly does teach us more, owing to the breadth of the analysis and the patient planning of such a detailed taxonomy. But on the other hand, specialists will inevitably feel that their own subject(s) of expertise have been rather simplistically summarized with long block quotations from just one or two authors (and absolutely nothing is cited in a language other than English).

Inevitably, too, the distinctions between these cases may seem overly rigid or difficult to pigeonhole as a single type. For instance, Barfield characterizes both Portugal and Spain as shadow empires, which was certainly true, but he sees Portugal as purely maritime and Spain as land based. How far can this point be sustained, however, considering that Portugal had territories such as Brazil in addition to its global string of seaports, while Spain had considerable maritime strengths in maritime trade in addition to its massive tracts of land? And what about empires that changed over time, perhaps bleeding over into other categories than in the original taxonomy?

Such objections do not really detract from Barfield's main point, which is that one must distinguish between two basic types of empire in this "alternative imperial history." It allows the reader to make new connections and consider other less familiar examples, and although the book may be a bit too broad for my own personal tastes it is also provocative and stimulating and compels one to consider different ways in which such a large percentage of humanity was at one time or another subject to the rule of outsiders.

MICHAEL KEEVAK
National Taiwan University
DOI: 10.1215/00219118-11591489

Southeast Asia in China: Historical Entanglements and Contemporary Engagements. By Ying-kit Chan and Chang-Yau Hoon. Lanham, MD: Lexington Books, 2023. 167 pp. ISBN: 9781793612144.

Southeast Asia in China is an important interdisciplinary work that contributes to multiple academic fields. These include China studies, Southeast Asian studies, Chinese migration studies, history, and international relations. The book is less of a traditional monograph and more of a compilation of six articles revolving around a common theme—namely, Southeast Asia–China relations in historical and contemporary contexts, since Southeast Asia has been "part of 'China's south'" (x–xi). The authors dedicate their book to Wang Gungwu, the doyen of Chinese migration studies, as he "has inspired generations of scholars in the study of China and Southeast Asia" (dedication page). Despite Wang's long and distinguished academic career, during which he has won multiple accolades and published countless books and articles, research related to ethnic Chinese migration, China's centuries-old relationship with Southeast Asia, and even maritime China has remained on the periphery of the English-language American historical scholarship on China. As for Chinese migration studies, the field has tended to focus on destination countries in locations such as Southeast Asia. More recent publications such as this book are contributing to a gradual (and long overdue) shift away from the domestic emphasis in the English-language historiography on modern China while also connecting the Chinese mainland with ethnic Chinese communities beyond China's shores. Thus, the book is a noteworthy interdisciplinary and transnational "collaboration between a China historian and a Southeast Asian specialist" (xi). It features two main parts that collectively argue that while Southeast Asia "has historically assumed a peripheral position when juxtaposed against the giant Middle Kingdom" and "has been commonly identified as being peripheral to China's rise," nevertheless "individual Southeast Asian countries possess and exercise their agency" to the extent of influencing "the power struggle between China and the United States in the Asia-Pacific region" today (x–xi).

The first section on "historical entanglements" comprises chapters 1–3. Chapter 1 focuses on the Nanyang Chinese from Malaysia and Singapore who volunteered as truck drivers and mechanics along the Burma Road during World War II to resupply Kuomintang China and aiding the war effort against Japan. These volunteers negotiated identities, and their story reveals "inconvenient truths and irresolvable dilemmas about citizenship, memory, and nationhood" (19) since they "were regarded as neither 'Chinese' nor 'Southeast Asians'" (xii). Chapter 2 explores the topic of national identity through examining ethnicity and frontier studies in southwestern China during 1932–45 in relation to Pan-Thai nationalism, suggesting that wartime Chinese intellectuals "debunk[ed] myths about Thai origins" (39) by "suppressing any overt display of ethnic identity by the Tai" and treating them as "unquestionably 'Chinese' citizens to be educated and developed" (xii). Chapter 3 is based on the autobiographies of Singapore's first ambassadors to Thailand from 1965 to 1990 and biographies about them. It applies Philip Kuhn's idea of "the 'migrant's corridor,'"[1] concluding that important ethnic Chinese businessmen who served as Singapore's ambassadors to Thailand "maintained cultural and commercial ties to both their ancestral homeland [China] and other members of the [Chinese] diaspora in places such as Thailand" (48).

As for the second part of the book on "contemporary engagements," it consists of chapters 4–6. Chapter 4 discusses Southeast Asian studies in China from the Qing era till today. Despite the overall state of the field being "subpar" (54) due to state censorship, it has nonetheless succeeded in becoming "a niche discipline" (67), with some universities and research institutes specializing in it, and has influenced governmental policymaking. The chapter also uses, as a case study, Thai studies from the late nineteenth century to the present day. Chapter 5 analyzes China's use of soft power since the 1990s through the example of increased demand for Mandarin in Indonesia since 1998. It argues that "diasporic Indonesian student organizations" in China (99) have successfully utilized cultural events in peer-to-peer (P2P) exchanges "to bridge the knowledge gap between the two countries and influence China's public perception to Indonesia by offering counter-narratives to negative media representation" (103). Chapter 6's topic is Southeast Asian capital in China since 1978, with case studies revolving around Myanmar, Singapore, Indonesia, Malaysia, and Thailand due to the activities of ethnic Chinese communities there. It examines the relationship between the Chinese state and what the authors call "the Chinese diaspora" (105), discussing how "ethnic Chinese conglomerates . . . respond to the dynamic geopolitical contexts of China and Southeast Asia" (xiv).

Overall, *Southeast Asia in China* makes a significant scholarly contribution to several academic fields. However, the authors could have considered knitting the six articles together in a tighter manner through the use of a proper introduction instead of the preface that the book contains. For example, while they briefly state that the term "Nanyang" is "often translated as 'Southeast Asia'" but that "it is more accurate to regard Nanyang as 'China's south'" (xii), they could have provided further elaboration in an introduction, especially since the Chinese-language track of Southeast Asian studies is descended from the field of Nanyang studies that was established at Jinan University in China. More importantly, the authors emphasize the historical agency of Southeast Asians (including ethnic Chinese in the region), yet they do not seem to reject the China-centric concept of "Chinese diaspora" and its associated terms (such as *diasporic* when used to describe ethnic Chinese migration).

In fact, they do not mention Shelly Chan's argument about the Chinese mainland being "diaspora's homeland" even though they implicitly agree with her Sino-centric perspective.[2] Nor do they engage with Madeline Hsu's critique of the mainland-centrism in Chan's book.[3] Similarly, Tu Weiming's notion of "periphery as center" is cited uncritically (xi) without mention of Ien Ang's valid reservations about the concept.[4] These flaws notwithstanding, *Southeast Asia in China* is undoubtedly a very welcome, stimulating, and important addition to fields such as China studies, Southeast Asian studies, Chinese migration studies, history, and international relations.

LEANDER SEAH
Stetson University
DOI: 10.1215/00219118-11591499

Notes

1. Philip A. Kuhn, *Chinese among Others: Emigration in Modern Times* (Lanham, MD: Rowman and Littlefield, 2008).

2. Shelly Chan, *Diaspora's Homeland: Modern China in the Age of Global Migration* (Durham, NC: Duke University Press, 2018).

3. Madeline Hsu, "Decoupling Peripheries from the Center: The Dangers of Diaspora in Chinese Migration Studies," *Diaspora* 20, no. 2 (2011): 204–15.

4. Ien Ang, *On Not Speaking Chinese: Living between Asia and the West* (London: Routledge, 2001).

Pacific Literature as World Literature. Edited by Hsinya Huang and Chia-hua Lin. New York: Bloomsbury Academic, 2023. 228 pp. ISBN: 9781501389320.

Pacific Literature as World Literature, edited by Hsinya Huang and Chia-hua Lin, is a welcome and much-needed contribution to transpacific studies in how it converges transpacific methodologies and Indigenous Pacific studies. Transpacific studies has developed over the past twenty years, offering insight into the struggles over hegemony over the Pacific, between the United States, Japan, China, and other industrialized hegemonic nations. However, as various scholars have pointed out, one glaring omission in studies of the "Pacific pivot" is the ocean from which the field derives its name.[1] Indeed, despite repeated calls to center the Pacific Islands, only a handful of works in transpacific studies have done so.[2] As Huang and Lin themselves point out, this omission "bypass[es] the important work of Indigenous Pacific in dismantling various forms of colonialism" (6).

The present volume engages the Pacific as both object of study and methodology, enriching the transpacific framework by centering the cultural productions of those inhabiting what Epeli Hau'ofa famously reconceived of as a "sea of islands." This will be a helpful resource to students and teachers of transpacific and Indigenous Pacific studies, as well as world literature and literary studies; in the college classroom, it will generatively round out other foundational texts in transpacific studies.[3]

Huang, Lin, and the contributors' intervention lies in their "re-worlding" Western hegemonic conceptualizations of the Pacific with "alternative ways of knowing, sensing, and thinking" grounded in the Indigenous Pacific (3). As part of this re-worlding, the editors make a compelling case for Pacific literature as world literature, or *Weltliteratur*, a field that, in the nineteenth century, was conceived by writers such as Johann Wolfgang von Goethe as a project of literary nationalism. Scholars in the twenty-first century expanded definitions of world literature,[4] which is reflected in the current volume's theoretical orientation. Establishing, by way of Damrosch, that world literature encompasses any literary text that circulates beyond its original culture, Huang and Lin reframe Pacific literatures as world literature while moving beyond categories of the nation-state or even regionalism. They argue that in a field that has otherwise overlooked their contributions, centering Indigenous Pacific writers reveals a decolonial genealogy shaped by "fluid oceanic imaginaries as a means of resistance to colonial hegemonic oppression and demarcation" (8). Chapters such as Craig Santos Perez's reading of *Mariquita, a Tragedy of Guam* by CHamoru writer Chris Perez Howard, and Perez's own poetry as analyzed by Anna Erzsebet Szucs, well demonstrate these points and their assertion that the Pacific as both object of study and methodology can teach us lessons in "planetary co-belongings" based on mutuality, care, and relationality (8).

The collection includes an introduction and twelve chapters, plus a foreword by the Tao Aborigine writer Syaman Rapongan, whose thoughtful meditation on the "different planets" of colonial versus Indigenous epistemology sets the tone for the theme of planetarity that runs throughout the text. Part 1, "Colonialism: The Pacific Ocean," examines the discursive and material colonial legacies in the Pacific. In "The Wilkes Expedition (1838–1842)," John R. Eperjesi examines the overlooked significance of the Wilkes Expedition in expanding the US empire of bases and the function of hydrography and natural history in representing oceanic space for their potential military value. In a similar vein, Chia-li Kao's "Mountains of Taiwan, Japanese Colonization" examines how the legacy of Japanese colonialism shapes the aesthetics of natural history writing in Taiwan. As with Eperjesi, Craig Santos Perez in "Decolonization and Demilitarization" interrogates the militarization of the Pacific and specifically of Guåhan (Guam), where CHamoru literature contests the violence of US militarism and advocates for decolonization and demilitarization. A brilliant contribution in this section comes from the late Paul Lyons, to whom the volume is dedicated. In "Epeli Hau'ofa's Pronouns," Lyon examines the writings of the Tongan scholar whose conception of Oceania as a "sea of islands" have undeniably shaped the legacies of decolonial ethics in Oceania. Lyon suggests that Hau'ofa's "pronominal poetics" in the collective possessive pronoun affirm the values and lives of Oceanians while inviting affective connections with other non-Oceanians to envision a "planetary 'our'" that is inclusive and relational (39, 45).

Part 2, "Indigenous Resistance to Colonialism," centers Indigenous Pacific literatures. Anna Erzsebet Szuc's chapter, "Decolonizing Guam with Poetry," analyzes Craig Santos Perez's activist poetry and the everyday objects (water, *sakman* [canoe], stones, maps) whose "mission" is to decolonize Guåhan by reconnecting Chamorros to their land, culture, and histories. In "Remapping Mānoa Valley in Hawaiian Literature," Chia-hua Lin turns to Hawaiian literary maps and Kanaka Maoli practices of resurgence to illuminate the deep cultural and spiritual significance of place in Hawaiian language and culture that is missing from Western maps. "Planetary

Boundaries, Planetary Imaginaries" by Hsinya Huang analyzes the poetry of Mar-shallese poet and activist Kathy Jetñil-Kijiner, whose Indigenous Pacific ecopoetics of "homing in" show the "lifeworld" of (is)land ecologies contaminated by nuclear histories. According to Huang, this centering of Pacific lifeworlds offers a frame-work to move beyond planetary boundaries of division and bordering and reach toward planetary imaginaries shaped by an ethos of mutuality, care, reciprocity, and relationality. The significance of Indigenous ecological thought continues in Hitoshi Oshima's "The Ecological Vision of the Ainu," which examines the divine songs of the Ainu that express their ecological vision of animals and made objects as part of the sacred and divine in Nature.

Part 3, "Ocean Ecology," rounds out the collection and emphasizes the central-ity of the Pacific. In a dizzying survey of Pacific literary and cultural productions spanning Brandy Nālani McDougall, Craig Santos Perez, and Epeli Hau'ofa, to Mos Def and Jack Kerouac—Rob Wilson's "Becoming Oceania" argues for a decenter-ing of Pacific Rim discourse and articulating instead an oceanic ecopoetics that envisions the ocean as a bioregion of cobelonging, care, and mutuality. Kathryn Yalan Chang's insightful account in "Island Imaginations, Bioregionalism" shows how grassroots environmental activism to protect the Da-chen wetlands culmi-nated in a successful campaign to block development by petrochemical companies. Her analysis of *Wetlands, Petrochemicals, and Imagining an Island*, edited by Sheng Wu and Mingyi Wu, as an exemplar of the environmental humanities, offers a com-pelling case study of how an environmental imagination can enhance the work of environmental justice. Iris Ralph's "Decolonizing Oceanic Realms" examines oce-anic imaginaries in the works of Australian writers Ray Lawlor and Tim Winton, whose respective works on the colonial practices of blackbirding and whaling illus-trate how settlers can support decolonization by "taking responsibility for the acts of one's colonial forebears" (184). Joni Adamson's "Whale as Cosmos" returns full circle to the work of re-worlding by examining how notions of "cosmos" in Niki Caro's film *Whale Rider* (2002), about Maori Indigenous whaling communities, and Linda Hogan's novel *People of the Whale* (2008), about First Nations communities in the northern Pacific, disrupt notions of the "ecological Indian" by modeling new modalities of multispecies ethnography.

If there is one critique to be made, it is the lack of engagement with the Black Pacific and the Indigenous islanders who inhabit Melanesia.[5] To be sure, an exhaus-tive account of Oceania, including Anglophone, Francophone, and Indigenous lan-guage literatures would be a near-herculean task, and its omission here speaks to a more general issue within transpacific studies than any oversight by the editors. If anything, the collection shows there is not a singular Pacific, as Alice Te Punga Somerville has cogently argued. Drawing on decolonial genealogies that emphasize relationality not only between Indigenous communities in the Pacific but with mul-tispecies communities, the contributors to this volume show the Pacific is multitu-dinous, relational, and "intimately bound up with the health and thus the well-being and future flourishing of the planet" (15).

In conclusion, *Pacific Literature as World Literature* fruitfully expands the field of transpacific studies through thick readings of Taiwan, America Sāmoa, Guåhan, Hawai'i, the Marshall Islands, the Indigenous Ainu lands of Hokkaido, Australia, and the Pacific Northwest. By centering Oceania's writers, essayists, poets, and film-makers, the collection paints a fluid picture of multiple oceanic histories and ecological imaginaries that re-world the Pacific.

NOZOMI NAKAGANEKU SAITO
Amherst College
DOI: 10.1215/00219118-11591509

Notes

1. See, for example, Paul Lyons and Ty P. Kāwika Tengan, "Introduction: Pacific Currents," *American Quarterly* 67, no. 3 (2015): 545–74; Gary Okihiro, "Afterword: Toward a Black Pacific," in *AfroAsian Encounters: Culture, History, Politics*, ed. Heike Raphael-Hernandez and Shannon Steen (New York: NYU Press, 2006), 313–30; Nitasha Tamar Sharma, *Hawai'i Is My Haven: Race and Indigeneity in the Black Pacific* (Durham, NC: Duke University Press, 2021); Teresia Teaiwa, *Sweat and Salt Water: Selected Works*, ed. Katerina Teaiwa, April K. Henderson, and Terence Wesley-Smith (Honolulu: University of Hawai'i Press, 2021).

2. See *Empire and Environment: Ecological Ruin in the Transpacific*, ed. Jeffrey Santa Ana, Heidi Amin-Hong, Rina Garcia Chua, and Zhou Xiaojing (Ann Arbor: University of Michigan Press, 2022); Erin Suzuki, *Ocean Passages: Navigating Pacific Islander and Asian American Literatures* (Philadelphia: Temple University Press, 2021)

3. See Setsu Shigematsu and Keith L. Camacho, eds., *Militarized Currents: Toward a Decolonized Future in Asia and the Pacific* (Minneapolis: University of Minnesota Press, 2010); Viet Thanh Nguyen and Janet Hoskins, eds., *Transpacific Studies: Framing an Emerging Field* (Honolulu: University of Hawai'i Press, 2014).

4. See Emily Apter, *Against World Literature: On the Politics of Untranslatability* (New York: Verso Books, 2013); David Damrosch, *What Is World Literature?* (Princeton, NJ: Princeton University Press, 2003); Wai Chee Dimock, "Literature for the Planet," *PMLA* 116, no. 1 (2001): 173–88.

5. See, for example, Joy Enomoto, "Black Is the Color of Solidarity: Art as Resistance in Melanesia," *Postmodern Culture* 31, nos. 1–2 (2020–21), https://dx.doi.org/10.1353/pmc.2020 .0027; Robbie Shilliam, *The Black Pacific: Anti-colonial Struggles and Oceanic Connections* (London: Bloomsbury Academic, 2015); Quito Swan, *Pasifika Black: Oceania, Anti-colonialism, and the African World* (New York: New York University Press, 2022). For this brief list, I am only including those works in Black Pacific studies that focus on Oceania.

Boats in a Storm: Law, Migration, and Decolonization in South and Southeast Asia, 1942–1962. By Kalyani Ramnath. Stanford, CA: Stanford University Press, 2023. 272 pp. ISBN: 9781503636095.

Kalyani Ramnath's *Boats in a Storm: Law, Migration, and Decolonization in South and Southeast Asia, 1942–1962* is a stunningly researched and beautifully written tale of decolonization in South and Southeast Asia. The Second World War disrupted Indian Ocean networks of capital and human mobility, and by the late 1940s postcolonial governments were trying to reorder these to suit sovereign territorial concerns. Newly independent Ceylon, Burma, and Malaya defined citizens by residence and ethnicity, but the transnational lives of Tamil and Malyali labor migrants, merchants, and financiers raised questions about whether they were potential citizens or, as was more often the case, to be made alien. The metaphor of the boats sailing on the Indian Ocean, with the ebbs and flows of migration mimicking tides, is an apt description of mobility in this region. This book is the postcolonial counterpart to colonial histories—like Renisa Mawani's—of the transnationalism of law, of imperial control, and of individual resistance and manipulation of law.[1] In using the records of everyday legal interactions to build this story, the fluidity of the ocean also becomes an analogy for competing and overlapping jurisdictions that both new states and migrants navigated.

In each chapter, Ramnath makes a strong case for a focus on temporality— How long had a person or a firm or an individual been in a particular place, and so what nationality, permit, or citizenship could they claim? Could states use that time away to pose limits on these claims? In considering citizenship and nationality as an everchanging, everyday experience in this age of state building, Ramnath also finds what historians of forced migration have been trying so hard to locate—"the refugee voice."[2]

Ramnath begins in 1942, with the Japanese advance across Southeast Asia spurring flight for all those with the means and opportunity to flee to British-ruled India. In doing so, she firmly sets her book as the successor to twentieth-century histories of the region, notably by Sunil Amrith, that understand that transnationalisms of migrant lives in the Indian Ocean could not be easily reconciled with decolonized citizenship.[3] Indian migrants' flight had implications for citizenship, capital, and travel, with new governments imposing limitations on them based on this decision. The story is bookended by a final chapter on 1962, perhaps best known for the decisive exodus of Indian capital from Burma.

The second chapter tells the story of economies ravaged by the Second World War, with governments trying to assert order over Chettiars, who had long controlled key capital in Malaya and Burma even as they retained ties to India. In imposing new restrictions on remittances and in the many acts of legislation around debts incurred in or paid in "banana money," states were creating new and competing jurisdictions representative of their sovereignty. In turn, Chettiars were considering family business structures, deputed agency, and even the extent of their networks to retain business, cut their losses, or to move on. In the third chapter, the changed postwar economic landscape and the need for reconstruction—whether in India or in Burma or Malaya—raised the question of which country could lay claim to Chettiar capital through tax residence.

While the first few chapters focus on those who controlled capital, in the fourth chapter, Ramnath's story points to class and documentation through the "problem" of Tamils in Ceylon. In "Application Forms," individual migrants met the postcolonial state's wholehearted embrace of far too much documentation, further complicated by the assumptions and interpretations of intermediaries. What in legislation seemed like fair documentation of residence and nationality unfolded as a subjective process. With both recent histories of passports in the region and in histories of force migration tracing government and elite efforts to control and categorize, here Ramnath tells us how individuals tried to make themselves legible to one or the other state.[4]

Families are made key in this story, with migrant loyalties and belonging traced through both monetary bequests and wills as well as the simple geographic and temporal proximity of family to a migrant's stated homeland. This chapter also challenged the universality of liberal principles that saw only the patriarchal nuclear family as the appropriate means of ascribing nationality.

The penultimate chapter explains how unwanted labor migrants who could not fit ethnonationalist ideas of state belonging found themselves deported or removed on grounds of dissent—usually as "communists" threating the postcolonial state's stability.

Rather than restricting herself to immigration archives, Ramnath has searched for legal documents where "personal and familial histories provide glimpses of lives that cannot be captured in the statistical tables of emigration and return" (7). While citizenship was indubitably heavily negotiated between migrants and state, Ramnath is able to illustrate exactly how her actors experienced the disruptions and displacements of war and of new-state formation in their enjoyment of citizenship after British subjecthood. To do so, she looks beyond documents solely pertaining to citizenship and immigration, scouring local court records and regional collections like those of Madras and Travancore. As she points out, migrants encountered the law in many ways, whether in the form of travel documents, restrictions on money, or, later, in taxation and bequests and even in trade union activity (6–11). In these documents, Ramnath finds not only the anxieties of the state but also the voices and stories of journeying, of family ties, of business concerns and capital, of hopes, and of separation. As multiple territorial sovereignties came to govern their lives, "Indian"' migrants to Ceylon, Malaya, and Burma engaged with the law to understand and claim their rights and statuses in these competing jurisdictions. What Rohit De's *A People's Constitution* did for subaltern and marginalized voices through his social history of the making of the Indian constitution, Ramnath accomplishes for diasporas and transnational lives in the mid-twentieth century.[6]

While the "refugee" may not be a category that formally applied to many of Ramnath's actors, here lies another key contribution, decentering categories created by the West. In looking at mobility intertwined with dispossession without getting caught up in terminology, she pivots to the "View from the South" in understanding postcolonial South and Southeast Asia on its own terms.[7] Ramnath opens up new perspectives in our global understanding of legal categories, understanding national belonging as a spectrum from full citizen's rights to statelessness, punctuated by visas and temporary permits.[8]

And finally, Ramnath reminds us that, besides the borders laid down by Radcliffe, the connected former British Indian Ocean World was Partitioned as well. While Punjabi and Bengali refugees and borderlands have been fertile grounds for studying the construction of nationality within South Asia,[9] Ramnath writes about recovering nationality and belonging out of the remnants of British subject-citizenship *across* its Asian empire.

This book is a scholarly triumph, reforging the connection between South and Southeast Asia that territorial sovereignty tries to make us forget. It is also full of heartbreak, individual choices, resilience, and interminable waiting, never letting the reader forget that migration is a story of humanity above all else.

RIA KAPOOR
Queen Mary University of London
DOI: 10.1215/00219118-11591519

Notes

1. Renisa Mawani, *Across Oceans of Law: The Komagata Maru and Jurisdiction in the Time of Empire* (Durham, NC: Duke University Press, 2018).

2. Peter Gatrell, Anindita Ghoshal, Katarzyna Nowak, and Alex Dowdall, "Reckoning with Refugeedom: Refugee Voices in Modern History," *Social History* 46, no. 1 (2021): 70–95.

3. Sunil Amrith, "Reconstructing the 'Plural Society': Asian Migration between Empire and Nation, 1940–1948," *Past and Present* 210, suppl. 6 (2011): 237–57.

4. Radhika Singha, "The Great War and a 'Proper' Passport for the Colony: Border-Crossing in British India, c. 1882–1922," *Indian Economic and Social History Review* 50, no. 3 (2013): 289–315; Kalathmika Natarajan, "The Privilege of the Indian Passport (1947–1967): Caste, Class, and the Afterlives of Indenture in Indian Diplomacy," *Modern Asian Studies* 57, no. 2 (2023): 321–50.

6. Rohit De, *A People's Constitution: The Everyday Life of Law in the Indian Republic* (Princeton, NJ: Princeton University Press, 2018).

7. B. S. Chimni, "The Geopolitics of Refugee Studies: A View from the South," *Journal of Refugee Studies* 11, no. 4 (1998): 350–74.

8. For an example of a legal category, see this history of European and North American political and legal thought on statelessness: Mira Siegelberg, *Statelessness: A Modern History* (Cambridge, MA: Harvard University Press, 2020).

9. This is an extensive historiography, but see, for example, Vazira Zamindar, *The Long Partition and the Making of Modern South Asia* (New York: Columbia University Press, 2007); Joya Chatterji, "South Asian Histories of Citizenship, 1946–1970," *Historical Journal* 55, no. 4 (2012): 1049–71; Sarah Ansari and William Gould, *Boundaries of Belonging: Localities, Citizenship, and Rights in India and Pakistan* (Cambridge: Cambridge University Press, 2020); Uditi Sen, *Citizen Refugee: Forging the Indian Nation after Partition* (Cambridge: Cambridge University Press, 2018).

A Soviet Sultanate: Islam in Socialist Uzbekistan, 1943–1991. By Paolo Sartori. Vienna: Austrian Academy of Sciences Press, 2024. xvii, 354 pp. ISBN: 9783700194309.

A characteristic of Paolo Sartori's wide-ranging scholarship is its critical assessment of a diversity of sources, almost all newly discovered by the author and hitherto untapped, in the service of pathbreaking arguments. These traits are on vivid display in *A Soviet Sultanate*, the first social history of Soviet Islam. This field-changing book argues that "Islam outlived Sovietization and its violent secularist policies through a process which may be termed as resilience, recomposition, and reinforcement" (xv). The significance of this seemingly succinct claim cannot be overstated, for it invites historians to reconceptualize Soviet central Asia as a religious space. Sartori uncovers a rich world of Islamic belief, ritual, and communal life hiding in plain sight within the tapestry of Soviet Uzbek sources related to religion, from ethnography, to oral histories, to the classified documentation of antireligious bureaucrats. He paints a landscape of a religious world engaging with, adapting to, and taking advantage of the constraints and opportunities of Soviet life.

Sartori writes: "When we begin to hypothesize that such a thing as Soviet Islam existed and represented a distinctive lived reality emerging from a unique convergence of circumstances, then our next task must be to fill in the vast gaps in our knowledge with all the texture, details, and nuance of lived life" (139). This is just what the book does, in five chapters devoted to different aspects of the experience of Muslimness (Uzbek *musulmonchilik*), "an emic notion which encapsulates the embodiment of intellectual traditions, beliefs, and reflections on being Muslim as a religious and moral subject" (6) in Soviet Uzbekistan in the decades following World War II. All break new ground in the historiographies of modern central Asia and religion in the USSR.

The first two chapters are interrelated. While chapter 1 ("Sufis into Villains") charts the joint demonization of Sufis by the officially tolerated central Asian muftiate (SADUM) and the Communist Party, chapter 2 ("Soviet Muslim Authority Contested") uncovers and engages with a new genre of source material. The term *patta* refers to letters, usually complaints, sent to SADUM by mail from Uzbek Muslims. These *pattas* contain a host of questions and queries from ordinary Muslims, frequently challenging the muftiate's puritanical pronouncements. Sartori reproduces letters from as late as the perestroika years dealing with Wahhabism, making the chapter one of the first scholarly works to substantively treat this topic (133). Sartori's analysis of the *pattas* confirms the muftiate's engagement with a wide swathe of Soviet Uzbek society, while positioning SADUM as both an object of criticism and source of scholarly and symbolic authority.

The next two chapters build on each other by immersing readers into realms of religious life far beyond the aegis of the muftiate. Chapter 3 ("Shrines' Spacetime") argues that "although at school [Muslims] were taught an impoverished, distorted account of the Islamic history of their region, Uzbeks were still able to access the past through the surviving architectural presence of Islam" (145). This presence acquired meaning through the interpretive framework of Sufism. Sartori relies both on the fieldnotes of ethnographer Gleb Snesarev (1910–1989) and a shrine catalog stored in the Khorezm State Historical Museum composed by Bobojon Safarov (1891–1983), "a local Muslim scholar" who "repurposed himself to work in various jobs, including as the cashier of the Pahlavan Mahmud shrine complex," one of the most important shrines in Khorezm (157). Sartori shows how this unique source—written by hand in 1961, at the height of Khrushchev's antireligious campaign—charts the sacred geography of Soviet Khorezm by preserving and disseminating oral traditions concerning local saints, such as Najm al-Din Kubra (1145–1221) and Sulton Bobo Uvaysi (d. 657?). These narratives "encapsulate approaches to communal religiosity that are alternative to, if not ultimately subversive of, the religious episteme sponsored by the Soviet state." They acquired such power through physical grounding in sacred shrines, "public spaces in which forms of communal organization were sublimated into practices of saintly commemoration" (203). Sartori finds little evidence that the ideological arsenal of Soviet atheism disrupted these spaces and narratives; sacred "spacetime" furnished an important counterweight to the hostility toward religion Muslims might encounter in other spheres of their lives.

Chapter 4 ("Living with the Spirit") takes some inspiration from Snesarev's inquiry into "places where people congregated for religious purposes other than formal worship" (242). Sorcery and exorcism, the stuff of the spirit world, constitute the subject of this fascinating chapter, brimming with eye-catching anecdotes of healing and treatment that Sartori brings to life with appropriate color and panache. Through the fieldnotes of the ethnographer Vladimir Basilov (1937–1998) we meet the exorcist Momokhol, who cleansed people of demons from her home in the village of Shurob, near Afghanistan, for a good chunk of the late Socialist period. These practices and others pertaining to spirits and demons described in the chapter contributed to "a highly meaningful discourse on Islamic sacredness" that was "constitutive of Uzbeks' Muslimness in the Soviet period" (262). Sartori conceptualizes this sacredness in terms of recomposition, a concept borrowed from Charles Taylor. Practitioners communicating with spirits, and Muslims (and, in at least one case, a Russian ethnographer) consulting them, did not so much resist the multipronged forces of Soviet modernization as adapt, reinforce, and recompose themselves in response to those forces.

The final chapter ("Bureaucratic Anxiety about Muslimness") mostly addresses the ossified groupthink characterizing reports by atheistic bureaucrats in late Soviet Qaraqalpaqstan, who could offer no explanation for religion's endurance. This chapter lends *A Soviet Sultanate* an elegant dissonance, sounded by the contrast between the dynamism of religious life described throughout much of the book, and the singular unoriginality of atheistic bureaucratese. Sartori's lack of sympathy for the authors of this bureaucratic correspondence stems, no doubt, from their exceptionally unimaginative framing of the figures and practices they recount. Yet a more critical engagement with this very obfuscation might have permitted the author to position the sources' formulaicity with more deliberation. As Sartori himself admits, "to dismiss them as the work of bureaucrats detached from reality may be misleading" (285).

Sartori has little patience for "the obtuseness of the dominant frameworks for analyzing manifestations of Muslimness in the USSR" (138), and thus devotes mercifully passing attention to tackling the schemas of "underground," "traditional," and "nationalized" Islam ("Islam as national custom"), relics of Soviet social science and antireligious propaganda that continue to reign supreme in some sectors of central Asian studies. It will be a fine day when scholars of Soviet Islam no longer feel obliged to reference them at all. When that moment arrives, we will, in no small part, have this book and its author to thank, for creating new conceptual possibilities in the study of Islam, for opening new vistas of exploration, and for offering a new way of thinking about religion in the USSR.

EREN TASAR
University of North Carolina at Chapel Hill
DOI: 10.1215/00219118-11591529

Russian Orientalism in a Global Context: Hybridity, Encounter, and Representation, 1740–1940. Edited by Maria Taroutina and Allison Leigh. Manchester: Manchester University Press, 2023. 277 pp. ISBN: 9781526166234.

This collection of essays considers Orientalism in Russian art history from several angles: if art historians might consider Russian art to be Oriental; how Russian artists exoticized eastern Others both within and outside the Russian Empire and Soviet Union; and how Soviet Russian artists adapted Asian styles to express spiritual or political ideas. This is a rich but difficult field of inquiry for art historians because the Oriental in Russia is both "other" and "us" on several levels. The multivalent uses of Orientalism in, about, and by Russians undermines the coherence of categorizing art into "Western" versus "Eastern" or "global." The volume illustrates its arguments, using well-produced color plates and black-and-white images in every essay.

The essay of most direct interest, specifically for readers of the journal, looks at art as a tool in relations with China. In the mid-eighteenth century, porcelain chinoiserie was fashionable across Europe, assuming that they were products of a fabled, and safely distant, land. But Russia and Qing China were competing with each other in terms of spheres of influence in Eurasia. For Russians, Chinese designs were the products of a technologically superior rival. The Russian court had not fully cracked the secret of porcelain, but its ability to produce its own ceramic and chinoiserie decor served to show Chinese diplomats that Russia both desired friendly relations and claimed mastery. Ambiguity and Russia's liminal status across the European/Asian divide are important themes in all the essays, shown here by close examination of porcelain figurines depicting Chinese designs, and transforming Chinese shell cups into Russian snuff boxes.

Later artists used Chinese Buddhist and Iranian tropes, both to depict an exotic Other and to highlight Russia's long intertwining with Iranian and Turkic cultures. Early twentieth-century avant-garde painter Kazimir Malevich studied the large collections of Asian artifacts and realist paintings of Asian sites in St. Petersburg and Moscow which, Maria Taroutina argues, influenced his art as much as French modernism did. Meanwhile, Russians were acutely aware than many Europeans regarded them as "Asiatic" as well. Some embraced this by using Iranian or generic Asian imagery in illustrations to highlight real connections, such as the origins of the Russian tale "Ruslan and Liudmila" in the ancient Iranian epic the *Shahnameh*. The painter Vasilii Vereshchagin valorized Russian imperialism and accused British imperialists of being barbarians. In the 1880s Vereshchagin executed a grisly painting of the British blowing mutinous Sepoys from cannons and had the temerity to exhibit it in London. He also made many paintings of the Russian conquest of central Asia which, while condemning war in general, showed that brutal central Asians needed Russia's civilizing hand. He then turned around and displayed himself as a Russo-Tatar exotic while on tour in America.

Russian culture straddles the categories of "Europe," "Asia," and "Middle East," which makes it an excellent ground for reconsidering the meanings of these categories. This volume's opening essay by Allison Leigh examines the history of art history and the futile attempts to create a stable conception of Russian art as Western or non-Western. Her argument goes to the foundations of a discipline that classifies art based on geography and culture. If Russian art is categorized as Western, it disappears from historical surveys as a minor offshoot of European tradition. If it is exoticized it becomes worthy of study, but only as an interesting appendix to the normative narrative. Leigh hopes that the study of Russian art can help eliminate the distortions of rigid categorization.

The Soviet Union tried to unite its many nationalities under a proletarian identity by the paradoxical route of creating nations that would eventually dissolve themselves in the working masses. Mollie Arbuthnot discusses how Soviet Uzbek propaganda posters used Orientalism to clothe strange political ideas in familiar art forms, similar to the way that Russian artists appropriated Eastern Orthodox iconography for Communist propaganda. Posters drew on Tatar didactic prints called *shamail* and on the Perso-Turkic tradition of manuscript illumination to frame exhortations to liberate women or mundane instructions to village executive committees. Some Russian avant-garde thinkers hoped to create a synthesis of Islamic abstract and European figurative painting, but the state doctrine of socialist realism buried all such experimentation. Arbuthnot points out the irony that few ordinary Turkestanis would ever have seen an illuminated manuscript. The Soviet attempt to convey Communist ideas through central Asian art was actually another act of Orientalist stereotyping.

This is a thought-provoking anthology, but it fits uncomfortably with scholarly debates started since Putin's 2022 invasion of Ukraine. Another bad Western habit of categorization has been to subsume the many peoples of the Russian Empire and USSR under the label "Russian." Further, scholars are trained to view Russians as the defining norm for everyone else. How would this collection be different if the editors had approached Orientalism through the works of Uzbek, Armenian, and Yakut artists in addition to Russians? Two of the important "Russian" artists who are considered here, Malevich and Ilya Repin, were born in Ukraine (Malevich, in particular, comes from a Polish family), while others were of Baltic German background. Imperial Russification policies affected how these artists saw themselves and led us to consider them Russian without question. While we are reconfiguring the categories we use to understand the world, this is another area that needs attention.

SHOSHANA KELLER
Hamilton College
DOI: 10.1215/00219118-11591539

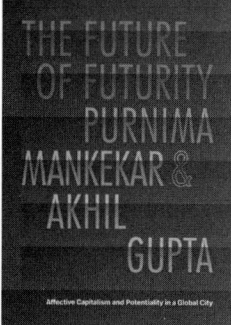

Keep up to date on new scholarship

Issue alerts are a great way to stay current on all the cutting-edge scholarship from your favorite Duke University Press journals. This free service delivers tables of contents directly to your inbox, informing you of the latest groundbreaking work as soon as it is published.

To sign up for issue alerts:

1. Visit **dukeu.press/register** and register for an account. You do not need to provide a customer number.

2. After registering, visit **dukeu.press/alerts**.

3. Go to "Latest Issue Alerts" and click on "Add Alerts."

4. Select as many publications as you would like from the pop-up window and click "Add Alerts."

read.dukeupress.edu/journals